All books are due back to the Lending Library by the last day of finals.

Failure to do so will result in a minimum fee of $25, or the used resale price of the book on Amazon.

Questions? Email: sustainability@conncoll.edu

Book

The Lending Library runs off the generous book donations of students like YOU!

 Connecticut College Office of Sustanablity

PASTORAL CAPITALISM

URBAN AND INDUSTRIAL ENVIRONMENTS

Series editor: Robert Gottlieb, Henry R. Luce Professor of Urban and Environmental Policy, Occidental College

For a list of books in the series, see the back of the book.

PASTORAL CAPITALISM

A History of Suburban Corporate Landscapes

LOUISE A. MOZINGO

THE MIT PRESS   CAMBRIDGE, MASSACHUSETTS   LONDON, ENGLAND

For information about special quantity discounts, please email special_sales@mitpress.mit.edu

This book was set in Adobe Garamond and Futura by the MIT Press. Printed and bound in Canada.

Library of Congress Cataloging-in-Publication Data

Mozingo, Louise A.
Pastoral capitalism : a history of suburban corporate landscapes / Louise A. Mozingo.
    p.   cm. — (Urban and industrial environments)
Includes bibliographical references and index.
ISBN 978-0-262-01543-1 (hardcover : alk. paper) 1. Industrial location—United States—Case studies. 2. Corporations—Headquarters—United States. 3. Land use, Rural—United States.   I. Title.

HD58.M69   2011
338.70973'091733—dc22

2010038852

10   9   8   7   6   5   4   3   2   1

For Anna Martellani Mozingo

CONTENTS

ACKNOWLEDGMENTS

I owe thanks to many. My professional and institutional home, the Department of Landscape Architecture and Environmental Planning at the University of California, Berkeley, has allowed me to engage with good colleagues and challenging students. Their many provocations have helped me think more clearly about the landscape of metropolitan regions, both past and future. A Committee on Research Junior Faculty Grant of the University of California, Berkeley funded initial site visits, and a Harvard University Dumbarton Oaks Fellowship for Studies in Landscape Architecture and a Humanities Research Fellowship of the University of California, Berkeley provided time to produce initial research and articles on the subject of suburban corporate landscapes. A Townsend Initiative Grant from the Doreen B. Townsend Center for the Humanities at Berkeley allowed me to begin a book, and two of my department's endowment funds supported its publication: the Beatrix Jones Farrand Faculty Research Fund and the Geraldine Knight Scott History Fund. My colleague, mentor, and friend Randy Hester connected me to Clay Morgan at the MIT Press, a most careful and patient editor. In addition, it was my pleasure to work with senior editor Sandra H. Minkkinen and designer Molly Ballou Seamans who tended to the book's production with utmost attention and intelligence.

I owe a heap of thanks to the many archivists and librarians in public, private, nonprofit, and corporate institutions who zealously guard the evidence of history from turning to dust and then share it willingly. For this project, these institutions ranged from the Library of Congress to the New Providence Historical Society staffed entirely by volunteers. Their archivists and librarians are too numerous to mention individually, but rest assured I am amazed at their fortitude, dedication, and passion.

I would not have been able to be at the stage of writing acknowledgments without the steadfast efforts of graduate student research assistants: Ian Moore, who in the days before digital archives copied enough journal articles to fill four bank boxes; Elizabeth Burns and Alyssa Machle, who started the process of scanning photos and producing crisp drawings of site plans; and Laura Tepper, who finished it off and was the world's best permissions tracker—no retired cartoonist ensconced in Cape Cod safe from her assiduous efforts—and who, best of all, was cheerful through it all, in marked contrast to the author with whom she worked.

Without a doubt, any good parts in what follows are the result of colleagues who have extended themselves to me as both critics and friends. I have had the great good fortune in the past decade to be part of the Berkeley Americanist Group, an interdisciplinary band of faculty who read each other's work and offer counsel on how to make it better. Thanks to Margaretta Lovell, Kathy Moran, Richard Hutson, Carolyn Porter, Chris Rosen, Don McQuade, and Paul Groth for reading really bad chapter drafts and, in return, offering me wit, smarts, and good ideas. Paul Groth has a special place in that constellation—he is the whole reason I ventured into the arena of academic life in the first place and found a place to stay. I am so very grateful to Richard Walker who was my "counterpart scholar" during my semester at the Townsend Center and later, very generously, read the entire draft, shaping it in immeasurably good ways.

My late father, Roulé C. Mozingo, was a person of intent curiosity about the world, and this book reflects the legacy of interested observation that he passed on to me. I have been sustained in inestimable ways by my siblings, the ones I was born to—Mary, Donald, Robert, and George—and the ones I have acquired—Dona, Rolly, Lelia, and Steve (in order of acquisition). With enormous affection they have tolerated the many foibles of their younger sister, especially when I got cranky about my work. Finally, this book is dedicated to my mother, Anna Martellani Mozingo, with great admiration, profound gratitude, and much love.

1

POSTWAR CORPORATIONS, CITIES, AND THE PASTORAL LANDSCAPE

When I was a twenty-something landscape architect, I interviewed at the offices of Peter Walker, a landscape architecture firm of national standing and well known for what the stalwart legatees of Frederick Law Olmsted's public-minded profession referred to, and not always approvingly, as "corporate projects." One of the firm's principals conducted the interview and at a certain point showed me around the office to look at models and drawings of current projects. Displayed on the surface of several tables pushed together was a huge model of a suburban office project in Texas. When I expressed astonishment at the sweep of oak-studded meadows, juxtaposed bosques of trees, long allées traversing topography, and snaking willow-lined canals extending over a property larger than Central Park, the principal turned to me and said, "Well, you know, *this* is the American Versailles."

The comment was professional puffery, to be sure, but this not-quite-offhand remark stuck with me. It raised a number of questions that I could later attend to as I became an academic in landscape architecture. Who would attempt a "Versailles" of offices on the Texas prairie, and, more important, why did they want to go to the trouble and expense to do so? The Texas project turned out to be by no means unique. I found corporate headquarters on hundreds of sylvan acres in the Midwest, "research parks" in the suburbs of Boston, and "campuses" of technology corporations outside Seattle. All supposedly ventures of capitalists in the thick of thinking about profit margins and returns on investment, their buildings do have an obvious bottom-line logic—they can be occupied and rented—but the landscape expanses can only be looked at. They seemingly do not square, at least not in a straightforward financial sort of way.

The existing scholarship on the suburbs, while substantial, is not very illuminating about these places; suburban corporate workplaces have been passed over for robust consideration.[1] Yet developments like these exist in the suburbs of every American metropolitan area, large and small, and, increasingly, at the edges of cities across the globe. Their ubiquity and extent in the urban periphery merit focused investigation.[2] Beyond that, they warrant attention because of the institutions they house. For the past half-century, the corporations that inhabited these suburban places have controlled large sectors of the national and international economy. How these dominant entities configure their workplaces matters: commanding considerable power from a particular kind of place inevitably links the characteristics of that place to the expression and exercise of power. Manuel Castells and Peter Hall, in *Technopoles of the World: The Making of Twenty-First Century Industrial Complexes*, note in their opening paragraphs that the "image of a new economy . . . consists of the series of low, discrete buildings, usually displaying a certain air of quiet good taste, and set amidst impeccable landscaping in that standard real-estate cliché, a campus-like atmosphere. Scenes like these are now legion on the periphery of virtually every dynamic urban area of the world."[3] Castells and Hall go on to discuss in illuminating detail the role of capital, governments, education, corporations, developers, infrastructure, technology, and social structures in the thriving economy of "technopoles" around the world. They do not ask, much less answer, why the "impeccable landscaping" of the "campus-like atmosphere" is a given.

The new landscape of corporate work—what I call *pastoral capitalism*—is an American invention of the post–World War II period. Business management workplaces were the last of the center city land uses to emerge in the suburbs after housing, manufacturing, and retail commerce. They did so during a particular moment in postwar America when corporations reconceived their management structures, the private and public governance of cities acceded to the forces of accelerated decentralization, and pastoral landscape taste triumphed as an American ideal. Each of these circumstances had to come together to create pastoral capitalism as a new component—and new force—in American urbanism.

The Apex of the American Corporation

By the late 1940s, the management of American corporations looked forward to an era of remarkable growth. The United States was the only intact advanced industrial economy in the world, and after almost two decades of economic depression and war, an expansive, even heady economic optimism buoyed the leaders of American business—an expectancy that would prove to be entirely justified. The confident economic scenario matched an absolute political surety engendered by the recent military victory and the hegemonic struggle of the Cold War.

Inside corporations, *managerial capitalism*, a new form of organization, had institutionalized a transparent, rationalized administrative hierarchy. Leading corporations had been carrying out this corporate restructuring since the 1920s, and it became generalized by the 1940s. Rather than conferring positions based on ownership or nepotism, corporations awarded management authority to a meritocracy of salaried, professional managers. This professionalization of corporate managers became necessary as the scope of corporations expanded nationally and then internationally establishing or acquiring geographically distant branches and diversified ventures. Corporations organized the many divisions, locations, and functions of their enterprises through an executive system that relied on and rewarded expertise and initiative. Under the auspices of this management system, American corporations came to dominate global capitalism.

The new managerial hierarchy consisted of three tiers of managers: lower management, which was immediately responsible for production, sales, and purchasing; middle management, which coordinated the activities of lower management and provided operational resources through finance, sales, production, purchasing, traffic, and research departments; and top management, which coordinated the activities of middle managers, allocated overall corporate resources, and initiated competitive strategies (figure 1.1) Each level of management carried on its activities in different facilities: lower management in factories, sales, and purchasing offices; middle management in departmental and divisional offices; and top management in corporate headquarters. The hierarchy enabled corporations to direct dispersed and diverse enterprises by distributing management across the corporate landscape while establishing a clear chain of command and accountability.[4]

1.1

The hierarchy of managerial capitalism. The distributed management structure created a coherent system to organize specialized management functions, diverse corporate enterprises, and geographically distant corporate elements. (Based on Alfred Chandler, *Scale and Scope: The Dynamics of Industrial Capitalism* [Cambridge, MA: Belknap Press of Harvard University Press, 1990]. p. 16)

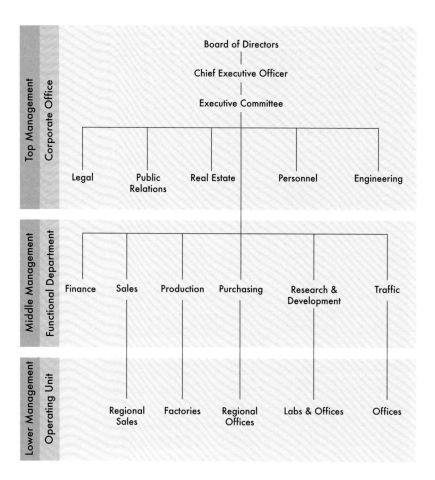

Leading American corporations that perfected managerial capitalism had also reshaped industrial production and distribution. New suburban factory complexes of unprecedented scale contained mass manufacturing systems using advanced machinery, electric power, new materials, and highly orchestrated industrial processes with carefully engineered divisions of labor. Railroads and trucks fed the factories with huge quantities of raw materials and distributed millions of finished goods.[5] Corporate management coordinated these massive and complex activities and dramatically increased the cost-effectiveness and scale of production. By the late 1940s, American firms controlled 60 percent of the world's industrial production and dominated global markets.[6]

Thus, by the 1940s, American corporations appeared to have reached an apotheosis of the modern capitalist enterprise. They were peerlessly poised for postwar expansion: masters of the means of production, bearers of the best systems of business management, and flush with war profits.[7] The leaders of American corporations had access to heads of state, commanded the resources of financial markets, and helped mold national and international policy. American managerial capitalism became the model for aspiring industrial capitalists throughout the world.

To make the most of the growth opportunities of the postwar years required adoption and extension of the management hierarchy. In a highly competitive labor market, corporations needed to attract qualified personnel and keep them working efficiently as management expanded in scale. As corporations had reinvented production facilities in the suburbs in the first half of the twentieth century to accommodate a new scale of manufacturing, so too would they reinvent management facilities in the suburbs in the second half to accommodate the new "scale and scope" of management. Notably, the men who made the pioneering decisions to move the professionalized and specialized management hierarchy to the suburbs instituted managerial capitalism in their corporations and were themselves exemplary of it: they were expert, strategic, and noted for their initiative. Frank Baldwin Jewett of AT&T Bell Laboratories was one of the first scientists with a doctoral degree to work for a corporation. Alfred Sloan of General Motors is widely recognized as one of the executives who invented managerial capitalism. Charles Mortimer of General Foods and Frazer B. Wilde of Connecticut General Life Insurance Company had risen through the ranks from sales offices (figure 1.2).

1.2
Connecticut General Life Insurance Chief Executive Officer Frazar B. Wilde and Connecticut Governor Abraham Ribicoff at the corporation's new suburban headquarters in Bloomfield, Connecticut, outside Hartford . Wilde is showing a model of the building; the large landscape expanse of the actual site is visible in the window beyond (see also figure 1.6). The occasion was a conference on the future of city planning that Wilde convened as part of the inauguration of the corporation's new offices. The photo was part of a five-page 1957 article in *Life* magazine about the conference and the new headquarters. (Nina Leen/ Time & Life Pictures/Getty Images)

William Hewitt of Deere & Company was a graduate of the University of California business school and studied for a Master of Business Administration, a new academic credential developed in the wake of the managerial revolution. As highly successful chieftains in key economic sectors—electronics, processed foods, defense technology, automobile production, insurance, and agricultural machinery—these men considered management as essential to corporate success as rationalized production systems. Moreover, their influence extended beyond their own companies and other big businesses followed suit.

Adoption of the new managerial system was a necessary precursor to the physical redistribution of the labor force of corporate management to the suburbs. Indeed, a big advantage of this rationalized hierarchy was the concentration of business decisions over geographically and technologically vast enterprises in large headquarters, while at the same time separating and decentralizing regional and divisional offices, most notably research. Corporate offices located in the expanding suburban zones of postwar American cities were a parallel manifestation, in geographic form, of decentralization, specialization, and concentration.

The American City at Midcentury

As the corporation was growing ever more powerful at midcentury, the American city was also undergoing a period of fundamental change. While urban decentralization in the form of middle- and upper-middle-class residential suburbs, suburban industries, and working-class suburbs had been extending metropolitan zones since the nineteenth century, the dense and diverse city center remained the energetic and magnetic hub of American cultural and economic life before the 1950s.[8] The postwar milieu tipped the balance toward the rapid decentralization of urban cores and their concentrations of commerce, industry, and residential neighborhoods. It precipitously accelerated the restructuring of the American city into the lower-density, dispersed, multifocal, auto-dependent metropolitan pattern that characterizes it early in the twenty-first century. The accelerated restructuring encompassed both a new scale, as vast city additions dwarfed the old centers, and a new scope, as enterprises previously resistant to edgeward movement joined the energetic rush to the urban periphery.[9]

At midcentury the land uses of the American city were spilling out over an enormous geographic territory, sorted by defined activity, and merged into building types of two to three stories (figure 1.3). As a number of scholars have

recently emphasized, the iconic suburbs of white, middle-class, nuclear families were a well-known part of this story but by no means all of it.[10] Added to prewar suburban expansion, the rapid restructuring of postwar metropolitan areas formed a complexity of patches, spokes, and swaths of separated, specialized, and low-density land uses in the peripheral zones around older city centers, including industry, retail centers, ethnic enclaves, and working-class neighborhoods.[11]

This rapid decentralization created the conditions that were conducive to the invention of specialized suburban management facilities by large corporations. To many privileged Americans of the 1950s and 1960s, the center city appeared to be in a state of inexorable decline. The proliferating automobile inundated the center city's gridded nineteenth-century street pattern, and "congestion" seemed intractable and highly detrimental to economic activity. Increasing numbers of people of color walked the streets.[12] Vacancies and abandoned properties were on the rise as tenants relocated to the suburbs and owners could find no replacements. New construction in the city center required homage to an ensconced and

1.3

The Southern State Parkway, Long Island, New York, 1951. Postwar highway development spurred rapid decentralization of center cities and opened large tracts of agricultural land for development. Although residential suburbanization is the best understood part of this decentralization, highways enabled corporate offices to move to the periphery as well. (UCLA Department of Geography, Benjamin and Gladys Thomas Air Photo Archives, The Spence and Fairchild Collections) layered system of political patronage. Even then, wedging in new skyscrapers that could accommodate large corporate staffs in a single building proved difficult in blocks divided into multiple parcels of land and built out with varied buildings, including many used for industry.[13] To redress these perceived shortcomings, the urban renewal process acquired property, removed tenants, destroyed buildings, and reparceled land in order to insert freeways, offer large lots for corporate offices, supply parking, and confine the poor to mass public housing. In the process, it took apart what remained of the vitality of the old urban core and added to the inventory of open urban lots and dysfunctional neighborhoods.[14] The center city was noisy, diverse, crowded, unpredictable, inflexible, expensive, old, and messy— a dubious state of affairs for postwar capitalists bent on expansion.

In contrast, the suburbs seemed to warrant a sense of forward-looking optimism. At the city's edge, an effective alliance of well-financed real estate investors, large property owners, local governments, federal loan guarantors, and utopian planners opened property for speedy development. Building along fed-eral- and state-funded road systems that brought these large tracts of land into the economy of metropolitan regions, this alliance conceived of low-density, auto-accessed landscapes of highly specified uses with plenty of parking, and wrote these forms into stringent zoning and building regulations. Once built, these suburban expansion zones were deliberately resistant to change, with the end of producing both social stasis and secure real estate values.[15] The suburbs as a whole may have been diverse, but the process of building their component parts created insidious racial and class divisions.[16] While the separation of dif-ferent classes and races of home dwellers is the best understood part of this spatial process, all kinds of workers were categorically set apart in discrete land-scapes as well—corporate executives from factory labor, retail clerks from typists, electronics researchers from accountants. Hence the suburbs were predictable, spacious, segregated, specialized, quiet, new, and easily traversed—a much more promising state of affairs to corporations bent on expansion.

In the suburbs, people and functions that were once stacked, mixed to-gether, and in proximity to each other in the center city resided in separate build-ings in separate suburban zones. The process was not complete in the 1950s, but it was continuing and predominant.[17] Between the detached suburban buildings lay parking lots, ever wider roadways, and, in good measure, green space—vaguely "natural" in appearance and trimming even the most utilitarian of land uses. And while the restructuring of activities and transport made sense in the efficiency calculus of capitalism, the inclusion of green space reflected a more ineffable yet deeply ingrained value—the ideal of the pastoral in the American landscape.

The American Pastoral Ideal

The pastoral landscape ideal has broad Western origins, but its immediate antecedents in American culture lay in the aesthetic theories of eighteenth-century
Britain. During this period, landowners executed estate designs not of the obvious contrivance of geometry and axes, as had prevailed among elites since the
Roman era, but rather as a reproduction of a various, sinuous, and undulating
nature—what Raymond Williams calls "pleasing prospects." To this idealization
of nature, the philosophical and political discussion of the period attached notions of morality, goodness, and social order.[18]

Versions of nature became the subject of aesthetic debate that by the end
of the eighteenth century had resolved into a three-part landscape classification. The "beautiful" displayed gently rolling expanses of grass interspersed with
copses of trees, inducing a soothing tranquility. The "picturesque" presented the
juxtaposition of rock outcrops, pitched slopes, shrub masses, and contrasts of
light and shadow from dense tree groves, creating a sense of curiosity and stimu-
lation. The "sublime" could not be made, only found in the awesome, even terri-
fying, drama of mountains, waterfalls, cliff faces, river gorges, and roiling ocean.

By the mid-nineteenth century the popular literature of the American
landscape gardener Andrew Jackson Downing introduced these versions of ideal nature and their implications to American audiences. His widely read books
and journals promoted the picturesque as a landscape ideal and, in particular,
as an ideal landscape for Americans to live in. Downing was America's early
and influential advocate of the suburbs. While he accepted the growth of cities
and their commerce, he also understood them as demoralizing and requiring
the antidote of retreat, preferably in a residence outside the city. Picturesque
nature bolstered the spirit and restored moral order. For those constrained to
remain in the city itself, Downing proposed large-scale public parks.[19]

Downing did not stand alone in his views; they resonated with the re-
current skepticism about the enterprising exertions of urban life that harkened
back to Thomas Jefferson and found new force in the mid-nineteenth century
with Ralph Waldo Emerson and Henry David Thoreau.[20] As elites began their
withdrawal into picturesque suburbs like Llewellyn Park, New Jersey, a coalition of urban reformers, self-styled philanthropists, real estate interests, and
political bosses determinedly brought a version of Downing's landscape and the
American pastoral ideal to the masses in the form of the urban park. Due to his
untimely death, Downing never saw the advent of Central Park in New York
City. Instead, Frederick Law Olmsted took over Downing's cause and became

the first superintendent of Central Park and, later, its codesigner with Calvert Vaux, Downing's former partner.

Olmsted explicitly described the park's design intent as "pastoral" on the whole, limiting "picturesque" zones to areas where the existing terrain was so craggy with granitic outcrops that smoothing out was impossible. Olmsted eschewed the heightened contrasts of the picturesque as agitating to the already stressed urban dweller.[21] Versed in Downing, an admirer of Emerson, and nostalgic for the Connecticut countryside of his childhood, Olmsted employed the term *pastoral* instead of the beautiful or picturesque to evoke a familiar, tranquil, and cultivated nature as a counterpoint to the city. Olmsted's pastoral wove together the precepts of eighteenth-century landscape theory and Jeffersonian agrarianism.[22]

Even more than Downing, Olmsted regarded the landscape as an instrument of social order. Gently undulating grass, serpentine lakes, sinuous pathways, and leafy woodland groves provided urban dwellers a much-sought-after alternative to the dense industrial city, presumably with salutary moral as well as physical effects. Not intended as a zone of active use, the pastoral public park presented composed scenery for passive viewing. The purpose of this engagement Olmsted described with typical zeal: "No one who has closely observed the conduct of people who visit Central Park can doubt it exercises a distinctly harmonizing and refining influence upon the most unfortunate and lawless of the city—an influence favorable to courtesy, self-control, and temperance."[23] Urban dwellers proved much more resistant to "harmonizing" than Olmsted expected, and in the face of American pluralism, public parks became more diverse in their activities and accommodations.[24] Nevertheless, as reiterations of Central Park appeared in cities large and small across the United States by the beginning of the twentieth century, the enveloping pastoral aesthetic of the public park prevailed and carried with it the equation of pastoral scenery and ameliorative social influence.

Public parks reinforced the pastoral as an ideal aesthetic to the striving classes of industrializing cities. Like Riverside outside Chicago, the application of this ideal to residential districts on the city periphery by Olmsted and his followers created polite pastoral suburbs typified by open-lot houses, coordinated infrastructure, limited building heights, and expansive, fenceless front yards presenting a continuous streetside landscape (figure 1.4). These pastoral suburbs proved immensely appealing to upwardly mobile Americans and lucrative to investors. The ongoing advocacy of zealous housing reformers and marketing efforts of speculative real estate developers enthroned leafy residential suburbs as

the right and proper environment for a family. Government policy, tax subventions, zoning, and mortgage regulations subsidized and sustained the proliferation of pastoral suburbs.[25]

By the mid-twentieth century the trenchant correlation of greenness with goodness held sway in American culture.[26] The introduction of corporate landscapes into the pastoral suburbs usefully subsumed the capitalist enterprise into the pastoral suburb's implied moral order. After all, the broad public viewed the new phalanx of giant corporations as suspect, even threatening. As the business historian Alfred Chandler put it, the majority of Americans found the "concentrated economic power such enterprises wielded violated basic democratic values."[27] Their acceptance as part of the pastoral landscape embodied Leo Marx's assertion that the American pastoral ideal mediated "the moral ambiguity, the intertwining of constructive and destructive consequences, which are generated by technological progress" and thus quelled skepticism in the moment, if not beyond.[28] In this sense, the appropriation of the pastoral landscape by American business became a useful trope for corporate capitalism.

1.4
Riverside, Illinois, a typical nineteenth-century pastoral suburb outside Chicago. Designed by Olmsted and Vaux, it is a quintessential example of a suburban ideal that was widely promoted in the late nineteenth and twentieth centuries. (Landscape Architecture Collection, Environmental Design Visual Resources Center, University of California, Berkeley)

The Pastoral Corporation

The postwar structure of corporations, the decentralization of American cities, and the dominance of pastoral taste convened to mold a discrete set of three suburban forms comprising pastoral capitalism: the corporate campus, the corporate estate, and the office park.[29] For both functional and emblematic reasons, these three interrelated landscape types materialized in the suburbs to serve a particular stratum of the corporate hierarchy. Each has a distinct layout of buildings, parking, driveways, and pastoral surround. Therefore, this book's landscape history of pastoral capitalism is situated at the site plan scale, between the fine scale of gardens and architecture and the large scale of planning and suburbs. Site plans—that is, the arrangement of buildings, parking lots, driveways, roads, infrastructure, and green spaces of a particular property and its location within the larger suburban fabric—are key to understanding how pastoral capitalism served big business and affected metropolitan form. Because of the way site plans configure a development's density, expected use, means and extent of access, and relation to the public realm, they have a profound effect on the environmental costs, long-term adaptability, and social milieu of built environments. The detail designs of both the green spaces and buildings of suburban corporate workplaces do matter, but they cannot be seen without the frame of their consequential site plans.

The *corporate campus* first appeared in the 1940s and contained office and laboratory facilities focused around a central green quadrangle, surrounded by parking and an enclosing driveway (figure 1.5). Modeled on the American university campus, it provided facilities for a singular division of middle management: corporate research. The corporate campus initiated the shift of white-collar work into pastoral suburban settings. Corporations such as Bell Labs, General Electric, and General Motors built corporate campuses to move their research divisions out of baldly industrial surroundings, valorize the industrial scientist, and validate the use of science for profit. The corporate campus gave rise to the *corporate estate* of the early 1950s, which consisted of an imposing building complex arrived at by a coursing entry drive through a scenically designed landscape of 200 acres or more (figure 1.6). Built for top executives and their staffs, corporate estates provided companies such as General Foods, Connecticut General Life Insurance Company, and Deere & Company a prestigious suburban alternative to the urban skyscraper. Corporations used the corporate estates' image as a public relations tool in communicating with employees, local residents, stockholders, competitors, and bankers.

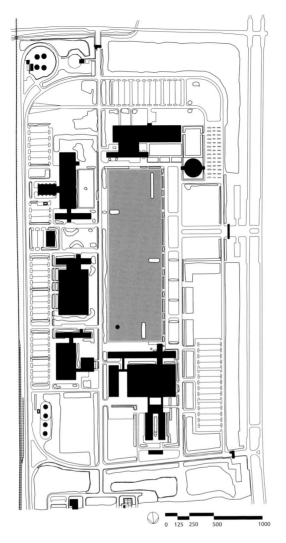

1.5
Site plan of the 1956 General Motors Technical Center in Warren, Michigan, an early and influential corporate campus. The essential site plan components of the corporate campus are the central open space surrounded by laboratory buildings circumscribed by peripheral parking and driveways. Corporations built corporate campuses to house middle management research and development divisions made up of prized corporate scientists and engineers.

0   125   250   500   1000

Speculative developers devised the *office park* by the late 1950s to provide a lower-cost, flexible alternative to the corporate campus and estate. The office park scheme provided lots for office buildings, each encircled by a pool of parking within a matrix of landscape edges, medians, and verges that provided suburban consistency (figure 1.7). Occupied by multiple businesses, office parks housed lower-level regional corporate management, corporate back office functions, start-up companies, and corporate service providers. By the later twentieth century, the flexibility of the office park proved particularly useful to restructured corporations, which could easily expand and contract personnel and offices. By the 1980s, office parks emerged as the landscape of international

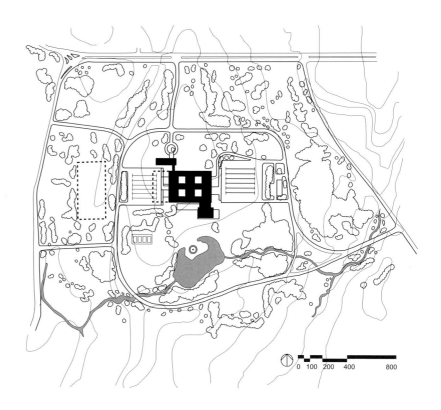

1.6

Site plan of the Connecticut General Life Insurance Company headquarters that opened in 1956 (see figure 1.2). A suburban office for top executives, it typifies the corporate estate. An approach drive culminates at the central building complex, and two blocks of parking flank the building, providing parking for hundreds of employees. Two hundred and eighty acres of carefully composed pastoral scenery envelop both the structure and parking, to be viewed from both the interior of the office structure and the outside, as a bucolic frame for the corporate facility. By the 1960s the corporation had expanded the buildings (the dashed line to the left of the building) and added a parking garage (rectangle also to the left).

managerial capitalism and became integral parts of peripheral development around the globe.

Corporations adopted corporate campuses, corporate estates, and office parks through a recognizable process of innovation and diffusion. A handful of companies devised the basic form, function, and image of each type of suburban corporate landscape. The circumstances of these original projects reflected both generalized trends and motivations particular to the individual corporate entity. The function and philosophy of these companies and, notably, the dispositions and preferences of their risk-taking leaders came together to create the new landscape forms. These corporate leaders had histories of successful innovation and credibility among fellow executives, boards of directors, and stockholders that carried the projects past any hesitation. Notably, pastoral capitalism started with well-established corporations in the Northeast, Midwest, and Southeast regions, the hearth of Olmsted's pastoral aesthetic, and only later spread to California and the rest of the West.

Partly in defense of unproven models, corporate early adopters generated publicity for their projects through extensive public relations efforts: opening

1.7
A typical office park found at the periphery of most American metropolitan areas: Cornell Oaks Corporate Center, Beaverton, Oregon, outside Portland, first developed in the 1990s. Individual buildings and surrounding parking lots are encircled by narrow pastoral landscape verges; interior "parkways" provide circulation. As is characteristic with most other office parks, an adjacent highway provides easy access for users and visibility to passing motorists.

0 200 400 800

ceremonies, political endorsements, press releases, brochures, and photo opportunities. The mass media were more than obliging; these projects were shiny and new, impressively large, and housed the nation's capitalist elite. The sites' stylistic flourishes made good visuals: crisp yet weighty structures framed by green. The media attention particularly extended to specialized literature such as real estate reports, technical journals, business magazines, and design periodicals, which spread the word on the new corporate project types (figure 1.8). This was especially opportune if the new facility coincided with a noticeable ascendancy of the corporation or marked the advent of a new growth industry.

The influence of the early projects resonated through several channels. These widely publicized developments came to be understood as a model for forward-looking corporations, an attractive package for developers, and an appealing setting to potential employees. Since corporate boards were commonly interlocking, that is, members served several corporations, board members spread the word on the new building types and encouraged suburban moves. The initial corporate projects established new ordinances and zoning practices in suburban

At Bell Labs, Industrial Research Looks Like Bright College Years

Ivy is crawling up the brick walls of the huge Murray Hill (N. J.) research plant of Bell Telephone Laboratories, Inc. (above). And the ivy is perfectly at home; the whole 230-acre layout near Summit feels more like a university than an industrial workshop.

Inside, the visitor can easily get lost in the long corridors. But the staff, or faculty—largely made up of faintly tweedy looking people—obviously knows precisely where it is going, though it goes there in no hurry at all. The feeling of a college is strong, a college with its youthful students deleted, though some of the instructors are very young.

You hear no chains of command clanking in the corridors. The staff looks purposeful, and each man's purpose, you feel, is to a surprising extent his own.

Murray Hill, in a rural setting, comes easily by its university ambiance. But the Bell Labs have other centers, in other urban spots, and these, too, preserve the scholarly feeling. It's present even in headquarters, in downtown New York.

• **Relaxation**—The atmosphere is a little startling to some scientists and researchers from other industrial laboratories. All this freedom, this almost relaxed freedom, seems a little odd in the family of Mother Bell whose bustling communications empire is the largest noncommercial company in the world. Bell Labs itself is a giant in the research field, with an annual budget around $100-million, fed in partly by American Telephone & Telegraph Co. and partly by its manufacturing arm, Western Electric Co. The feeding sus-

tains a staff of some 3,000 professional people, backed by 6,000 technicians and others.

Rival researchers have long since learned that the air of leisure connotes no sluggishness of productivity. Technical inventions, and improvements, flow steadily from the labs. And as revolutionary developments—transistors for example—appear, other companies tend to ask a little wistfully just how you set up an organization that can produce so much with so little sweating and panting. They also wonder, often, just how so many scientists—notoriously uncontrollable—can be kept working in such fruitful harmony without visible controls.

• **Selection**—The answers, of course, aren't simple. Partly, the freedom is illusory. The lab has firm plans, and

knows precisely what it wants. Organization can function smoothly without being obtrusive. A more important factor in the relaxed atmosphere is the background of the labs. Over the years, personnel has been meticulously selected, and precisely trained. Men chosen to fit a mold will fall into the desired pattern without any pressure from the mold itself.

Essentially, what Bell Labs has achieved is a pervasive harmony—of programs, of methods, and of people. But it would be a great mistake to think that this harmony is preserved without constant planning and training.

• **Pattern**—Dr. Mervin J. Kelly (cover), president of Bell Labs, weighs with a careful hand the whatness or how-muchness of the different types of research. The even balance between pure

research and developmental work is maintained with hairline care. It is within this nicely measured framework that the individual scientist is given freedom that is rare in industrial work.

Over-all, the labs' functions are split into three compartments, though there are no tight divisions to prevent the interplay of talents.

Research and development is the haven of the pure scientists. Their work can wander anywhere in the areas of physics, chemistry, and mathematics, provided there is some possibility of contributing to the advancement of electronic communications.

Systems engineering is peopled largely with electrical and mechanical engineers. Over-simplified, their function is to help translate the theoretical findings of the pure scientists into im-

proving the service of the Bell Telephone empire and lowering its costs.

Specific design and development is made up of engineers who build the laboratory models of new equipment, iron out the wrinkles, and finally help to design the pre-production models of telephones and other equipment. This group works more closely than the others with the engineers from Western Electric, to whom will fall the final job of turning out the working products.

• **The People**—With so much depending on the cooperation of these three groups, Bell Labs is exceedingly careful in picking people who will get along together. Working for labs is made a lifework, as much as possible. Recruitment is exacting. Bell wants to have its men grow up with the job, rather than be hired from outside.

New employees are run through the company's Communication Development Training Program—a three-year study course combined with practical experience in the various specialized labs.

Hiring at a steady pace each year, and sturdily refusing to expand just to meet the calls of a single new project, Bell Labs has achieved an astonishing age balance in its staff, with no preponderance of graybeards or of dewy youth. Actually, the age distribution year by year is almost constant in the whole range from 25 to 65.

• **Age Groups**—Young and old, the professional staff is remarkably homogeneous. To a degree it even looks alike. Shirtsleeves, rather than lab jackets or coats or what have you, are almost a uniform in working hours.

Mother Bell picks her scientists to fit

The lab is the key . . .   . . . but reading rooms . . .   . . . classes for trainees . . .   . . . lounges for relaxing . . .   . . . and sound room all help.

1.8

A *BusinessWeek* article from 1954 acclaiming the AT&T Bell Laboratories' corporate campus near Summit, New Jersey, as a tool of competitiveness and productivity. Popular and specialized journals spread the word among corporations and the public about the effectiveness and prestige of pastoral capitalist landscapes. (Reprinted from the February 6, 1954, issue of Bloomberg *BusinessWeek* by special permission, copyright © 1954 by Bloomberg L.P.)

jurisdictions, which eased permissions for other new projects of the same type. As suburban power brokers, large developers, and local governments became equipped to handle these new development types and stifled opposition, they encouraged and even sought out new corporate ventures. The early projects also established a stable of knowledgeable designers who went on to promote these types of projects with other corporations. Design literature disseminated the building types among professionals who were consulting with clients considering new workplaces. In turn, corporations that made the decision to suburbanize had the added assurance of design and engineering firms already experienced, or at least familiar, with suburban management facilities.

The following chapters describe how pioneering projects established the essential landscape patterns of the corporate campus, corporate estate, and office park and how, from those few early projects, other corporations followed suit in great numbers. These landscape types became embedded in the expectations of the corporate class and could at a glance embody both the reality and prospect of capitalist power. Hence, the development forms have remained remarkably consistent for the past six decades. By the end of the twentieth century, the suburbs, not the central business district, contained the majority of office space in the United States.[30] This was a new and potent force in the process of suburban expansion.

Nevertheless, the evolution of pastoral capitalism as a significant component of decentralization has been obscured as the corporate campus, corporate estate, and office park became conventional and omnipresent in metropolitan peripheries. In part, this is because the precise way that this book defines corporate campus, corporate estate, and office park does not reflect the much more free-wheeling use of these terms in the language of developers, journalists, office workers, corporate executives, designers, and scholars. As explained in detail in chapter 5, the Microsoft Corporate Campus is actually a series of office park lots accreted over time by Bill Gates's corporation. Corporate estates are never referred to as "estates" by corporations but are a classification of a certain type of suburban corporate headquarters, which the owners might call a campus. Depending on developer preferences or marketing strategies to attract prospective tenants, an office park could be labeled a research park, industrial park, executive park, business park, corporate park, science park, or technology park. While these colloquial variations in terminology will no doubt continue, one of the purposes of this book is to add clarity and accuracy to our views of the suburban corporate landscape and contribute to an informed discussion about decentralization, suburbs, and the future of urbanism.

As a first cut through the terrain of pastoral capitalism, no doubt this book contains glaring lapses in the next chapters that I hope others will rectify in the future. I welcome the revisions; I am writing this book in order to understand the presumed and actual advantages of metropolitan forms as they have been promoted, built, and reproduced over the past century because I think they need to change. If during the next century business as usual continues in the way we build and inhabit cities, the consequences will be dire for many and palpable by all. But unlike so many, if not most, in pursuit of change in the metropolitan order, I think that understanding metropolitan history is essential in this transformation. You cannot change, at least constructively, what you do not know.

2

THE CORPORATION IN THE SUBURBS

"A development that bespeaks orderliness, spaciousness, and well-being"

As postwar American corporations considered their futures in an expanding economic era, their facilities were a fundamental part of the business equation. Until the 1940s, corporate management offices had existed in two places. First, management resided in central business districts to be close to bankers and insurance companies, often in tall office buildings. In a few of those cases, corporations built downtown skyscrapers for themselves, but notably, the buildings were usually not entirely occupied by the corporate staffs but also rented to other tenants—a handy combination of public relations and income-generating investment.[1] Second, corporate management resided in manufacturing works, to be close to production. Less well known and less acknowledged in the history of business buildings, factory offices nonetheless constituted a substantive sector of management locations. By the postwar era, in both central business districts and factory sites, large corporate offices were often in various and separate buildings and poorly integrated with one another.

Many corporate management staffs remained in or relocated to established central business districts during the decades after World War II, building new downtown buildings or occupying speculative ones. Some built new, consolidated management headquarters near center city factory sites, such as the Johnson Wax headquarters in Racine, Wisconsin, designed by Frank Lloyd Wright. Nonetheless a significant set of companies chose the suburbs for new, consolidated management offices. While ideas about business, cities, and American landscapes framed pastoral capitalism (as discussed in chapter 1), another set of more specific contexts impelled the formation of corporate campuses, corporate estates, and office parks. Corporations had to decide to eschew the city center, which had the advantage of synergistic connectedness to other businesses, palpability of power brokers' pulse, and the impressive modernity of skyscrapers. A range of actual and perceptual drawbacks of the city center trumped its once well-established advantages. In opting out of the central business district, corporations still had to address the status aspirations of the corporate management employees, while satisfying the goals of efficiency and productivity that their shareholders and corporate boards demanded.

To do so, corporations revisited ideas from production facilities in the first decades of the twentieth century that used the landscape surround as a strategic corporate tool to control labor and manipulate public opinion. As corporations promoted the advantages of the urban edge, they also had to find a suitable place within it. Unlike the central business district with established corporate offices, this was unknown territory for large management buildings. Corporations had to respond to the equivocation of their new neighbors since locals perceived large business buildings as incongruous with conventional residential suburbs. In the process, they had to invent the form of the suburban management facility, a new building type of significant size, occupying large tracts of property, and shaped by issues of public relations and corporate identity. For the inherently conservative corporate enterprise, the impetus to work through all these obstacles had to be considerable.

These contextual forces resolved around a distinct pastoral conception of the suburban management workplace. Unlike central city buildings occupying entire lots, properties were ample, and the buildings within them were set back from surrounding roads. In varying proportions, the setback contained parking, driveways, underground utility infrastructure, and an obvious, ample, verdant landscape of trees, shrubs, and lawn. The specific forms of the corporate campus, the corporate estate, and the office park that emerged from the imperatives of managerial capitalism share a consistently pastoral sheen that materialized from common circumstances.

Leaving the City Center

As the economic geographer Richard Walker has astutely discerned, a "basic pattern of escapism from capitalist reality" underlay the creation of American suburbs with the "Arcadian look."[2] Like many suburban dwellers before them (and many executives were themselves suburban home owners), corporate managers were propelled to the pastoral urban periphery by a distaste for the sensory and social realities of industrial production, the noise and congestion of dense urban cores, and class and ethnic conflicts. An exceptional concern of the postwar era, civil defense, added to these motives and incited the first wave of what came to be known as the corporate exodus.

Although the corporate exodus is commonly characterized as an abandonment of the central business district, the first corporations that built suburban workplaces exclusively for management relocated their personnel from factories. In the first decades of the twentieth century, industrial landscapes, once celebrated as emblems of progress and economic prowess, became symbols of manual labor and the working class (figure 2.1).[3] The public health movement of the Progressive Era also identified factories as noxious, unhealthy environments.[4] By the mid-twentieth century, corporations wanted to distance their

management echelons from what they considered to be the unsavory social and physical situation of the manufacturing plants they controlled.

Thus, the initial sector of the corporate hierarchy to migrate to the suburbs was not the top echelon but rather middle management research divisions. Although scientists were ascendant in the managerial capitalist hierarchy, they worked at factory sites, a legacy of earlier industrial workshops attached to production facilities (discussed in detail in chapter 3). Companies such as AT&T, General Electric, and General Motors wanted to move their estimable scientists and research units out of industrial situations. But the tight conditions of the prestigious central business district could not accommodate the technologically complicated laboratories. The suburban spaciousness of the corporate campus both resolved infrastructural demands and created a prestigious ambience for the facilities.

Since many top-ranked executives of leading industrial companies worked in manufacturing plants as well, the objection to industrial settings also influenced their removal to pastoral situations. When Deere & Company president William Hewitt assumed the leadership in 1955 of the 118-year-old firm, his initial and most transformative action was to remove himself and his executives from the company's sprawling factories along the Mississippi in central Moline, Illinois (figure 2.2). Because the executive leadership had always resided at the industrial site, the decision created much internal controversy. But Hewitt believed that this was an essential part of creating the dominant global corporation that Deere & Company became within a decade.[5]

While the downtown was the celebrated location of corporate business, in the decade after the World War II, it was also jam-packed. Few new office buildings had appeared during the Great Depression, and wartime materials restrictions severely limited construction. With postwar economic growth in full gear, businesses stretched the limits of scarce office space. The size of corporate staffs doubled between 1942 and 1952, and each employee required more room than their prewar counterparts. In addition, businesses demanded flexible office configurations in which partitions could be easily moved and employees added and shifted around.[6] As early as 1945, *Architectural Record* reported on competition in the central business districts: "Office buildings are crowded, top quality space is at a premium, and room for expansion is all but impossible to find. . . . In such a situation tenants are forced to look ahead, and many are called upon to establish new quarters."[7]

General Foods illustrates the combined impact of expanding headquarters staff and postwar spatial constraints in central business districts. In 1921, the corporation occupied leased office space in a single Manhattan office building. By 1945, multiple floors in three different buildings housed 1,300 corporate employees, an inefficient arrangement by any business reckoning. In 1946 General Foods, unable to find sufficient space in Manhattan, scouted locations as far away as the Midwest, but the Fortune 500 company determined that it needed to remain close to its New York bankers. By 1949 they found Manhattan saddled with significant "discomforts caused by dirt, dust, noise, and the ever increasing problem of traffic congestion" and began to look toward the New York City periphery.[8]

In addition, labor relations played a key role in the decision to seek the suburbs. The late 1940s and early 1950s was an era of assertive unions. *Fortune* reported that corporations considered new suburban management enclaves "in the hope that this will reduce friction . . . between unionized workers and unorganized office personnel."[9] Doubling in numbers in the 1950s, secretaries and receptionists were not unionized, and corporations had an interest in separating them from union strongholds in factory sites and removing them from downtowns, where their concentration made them an easier target for labor organizing.[10]

Particularly for support staffs, the increasing diversity of the center city labor pool alarmed corporate managers. As one executive described in 1952, their quest for employees of "a better type" helped motivate suburban relocations (figure 2.3).[11] By the 1960s, *Fortune* minced no words: "New York is becoming an increasingly Negro and Puerto Rican city. Some companies are reluctant to hire a large proportion of Negro and Puerto Rican help."[12] By 1970, the Equal Employment Opportunity Commission found that the hiring policies of suburban companies were discriminatory, a finding that was upheld in court; the Justice Department considered filing federal discrimination charges against corporations that planned suburban moves.[13] A New York City economic development administrator explained to the *New York Times* in 1971 that the "executive decision maker" lived in a homogeneous "ethnic and class community," while his urban employees came "from communities very different in class and ethnicity." The administrator continued, bluntly, "It's an older generation in charge trying to re-establish a setting that seems to be more comfortable, more the old way."[14]

A circumstance particular to the postwar period also influenced the suburbanization of corporate management: the pervasive context of civil defense. In 1949 President Truman's National Security Resources Board issued *National Security Factors in Industrial Location,* which stated, "There is no known military defense against the atomic bomb itself, except space." The report couched the decentralization of industrial concentrations and central business districts, including "business management," in patriotic, anticommunist Cold War terms.[15]

Corporations and their planning and design consultants responded to the call for dispersal. The architect Eliel Saarinen authored a 1942 master plan for the Detroit metropolitan region; one of the plan's guiding principles was, "In the event of future aerial bombardment, such planning would provide a 'dispersion' factor."[16] Saarinen later worked on the initial planning and design of the General Motors Technical Center, a trendsetting corporate campus outside of Detroit. In a similar vein, the editor's introduction to the December 1950 issue of *Architectural Record,* "City Planning and Civil Defense," enjoined: "Today urban dispersal appears to be the only effective means of minimizing the effects of atomic bombing. . . . We can identify this means of defense with measures for making our cities better places to work and live."[17] Large defense-related manufacturing firms like

SPRING AND GF COME TO WHITE PLAINS, NEW YORK

MAY

GF NEWS

A MONTHLY REPORT FOR ALL GF PEOPLE

2.3
The 1954 cover of *GF News*, a publication distributed to the staff of General Foods, showing four employees at its new headquarters in suburban White Plains, New York. In the 1950s, corporations perceived that well-educated, white, middle-class women, deemed essential for clerical and support staffs, were to be increasingly found in suburbs, not center cities. (Courtesy of Kraft Foods, Inc.)

General Motors and General Electric planned new peripheral facilities, particularly as this dovetailed with their management policies.[18] The Electronics Park, outside of Syracuse, New York, another early corporate campus, was part of a conscious effort on General Electric's part to decentralize management and research from its Manhattan headquarters and vast Schenectady industrial plant (figure 2.1).[19]

Central business districts were considered to be particularly vulnerable to atomic attack. In 1952 *Fortune* reported that downtown executives did not wish to document, much less admit publicly, their considerable fears of nuclear destruction, yet as civil defense activities increased after 1949, interest by New York City corporations in suburban locations increased sharply. Out of twenty-two corporations that consulted with an expert on land acquisitions in suburban Westchester County, each "privately revealed that, among other things, it wanted to avoid target areas."[20] One of the companies was likely General Foods, as the corporation's move was a focus of the *Fortune* article, and its land acquisition corresponds in time with the description. Charles Mortimer, president of General Foods, was certainly in a Cold War mode when he addressed his employees on the opening day of the White Plains headquarters in 1952: "My deepest interest in seeing GF grow and become stronger is *because I want to see this world stay free. . . .* I believe the sound growth of this company of ours is directly connected with *the preservation of world freedom* [emphasis in original]."[21] Long-term employees of the company still remember that the scuttlebutt around General Foods was that the new office was designed to serve as a hospital in the event of a nuclear war (see figure 4.2).[22]

One executive, Howard Russell, general manager of Improved Risk Mutuals, a leading business and industry insurance company, went on record in the *Fortune* article. Alarmed by films of postatomic Nagasaki and protective of

2.4

The gatehouse of the AT&T Bell Laboratories near Summit, New Jersey, in 1942. The complexes might be highly visible from surrounding roadways but corporations carefully controlled access to large, isolated sites. As American corporations engaged in defense-related work during the Cold War era and urban unrest increased in the 1960s, corporations considered these security measures, not possible in downtowns, as ever more important. (Library of Congress, Prints & Photographs Division, Gottscho-Schleisner Collection, LC-G612-T-42011)

the firm's primary asset, its paper archives, he declared: "I wanted to get the files out of the bombing area—and I wanted to get Russell out too!"[23] After occupying temporary quarters in White Plains, New York, the company moved into a purpose-built office building in 1953, complete with "an emergency electric generator . . . and a special bomb-proof shelter in the basement."[24]

In addition to presumed safety from atomic warfare, suburban sites could offer corporate management an extraordinary degree of control over access to their properties. Buildings were distanced from public roads, long approach drives gave ample warning of oncoming vehicles, and guardhouses could vet visitors under the guise of giving friendly directions to the large sites (figure 2.4). For companies such as General Electric, Bell Labs, General Motors, and IBM that were doing extensive research and product development for the Defense Department, only suburbs offered these site layouts. By the 1960s, when it became apparent that the move to the suburbs was the corporate version of "duck and cover," the security mind-set transmuted into concerns for insulation from the urban strife of the 1960s: strikes, riots, antiwar demonstrations, racial conflicts, bombing threats, and bombings.[25] Rather than building obtrusive downtown corporate fortresses, which some companies chose to do, security measures could be tied up in a serene bucolic package.

In leaving the city center, corporate management had to counter internal skepticism about suburban relocations. The pastoral ideal played a critical role in the justification for exiting the downtown. Corporations heralded the verdant pleasures of their new locations as substitutes to urban enticements. General Foods urged employees to view the move to Westchester County as "out of the city . . . and into the trees." Its internal publications repeatedly stressed the company's "park-like setting," while acknowledging that "the move has brought many changes, some immediately welcomed—like a chance to stroll on tree-lined paths at noon—and some that will take a little getting used to—like the distance from the big city."[26]

Lessons from the Factory

As management retreated from the central city, corporations confronted the task of fundamentally reconceptualizing their facilities as suburban emplacements. They had to justify the advantages of suburban locations and formulate a functional alternative to center city buildings. Corporations promoted the suburban pastoral environment as conducive to the function of the corporate enterprise; in this, corporations reiterated the rhetoric of early twentieth-century experiments with the welfare capitalist factory. In devising a new kind of business setting, the design of suburban factories of the 1920s and 1930s provided corporations with a basic formulation of building and site that they then applied to management locations in the postwar era.

In the first two decades of the twentieth century, industries built factories and company towns influenced by welfare capitalism, a strategy devised by industrial corporations to make workers more compliant and resist unionization. The strategy included systematic study of workers performing in the factory environment, promotion among workers and the public of a positive, responsible corporate image through mass media, and the use of employee amenities to quell employee dissatisfaction, including "landscape amenities" such as playfields, allotment gardens, and parks with pavilions and clubhouses (figure 2.5).[27] Although these were certainly the exception and not the rule, these plants set standards lauded by contemporary commentators. George C. Nimmons, an architect who designed a wide range of industrial plants in the Chicago area, authored a 1918–1919 series in *Architectural Record,* "Modern Industrial Plants," that exemplified the emphasis placed on "landscape improvements" in this new factory type.[28] The articles repeatedly advocated the inclusion of landscape areas for both aesthetic and recreational purposes, illustrated with numerous examples (figure 2.6). Among the ten measures Nimmons proposed to address "the excessive turnover of labor," the first two were "convenient and wholesome location for the buildings" and "improved grounds around buildings and landscaped where possible."[29] Nimmons's rhetorical promotion of landscape improvements anticipated the reasons that corporations later used for occupying corporate campuses, corporate estates, and office parks:

> The chief advantages to an industrial plant of attractive buildings and grounds are their advertising value, their important effect in raising the whole character of the community or city in which they are located, the pleasure and satisfaction they give the owner and the strong and valuable influence which at all times exert upon the employees. The last item is now the most important of all, and wherever attractive buildings and improved grounds will aid materially to reduce labor turnover, they will be a good and wise investment for this one reason alone, although their cost is not nearly as great as it is commonly supposed to be.[30]

The presumption behind the inclusion of landscape amenities in the factory was a positive effect on worker satisfaction, pride, productivity, and turnover.

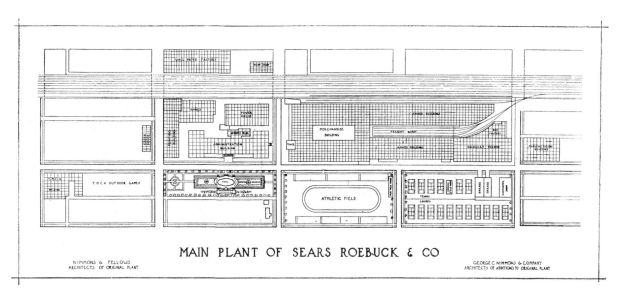

MAIN PLANT OF SEARS ROEBUCK & CO

NIMMONS & FELLOWS
ARCHITECTS OF ORIGINAL PLANT

GEORGE C. NIMMONS & COMPANY
ARCHITECTS OF ADDITIONS TO ORIGINAL PLANT

2.5

Plan of the 1906 Sears Roebuck & Company plant in Chicago designed by George Nimmons. In this kind of welfare capitalist factory landscape amenities such as gardens, playfields, ball courts, and lawn expanses were expected to increase employee morale, productivity, and compliance. (Reprinted with permission from *Architectural Record* © 1919. The McGraw-Hill Companies, www.architecturalrecord.com)

2.6

In welfare capitalist factories, such as the Sears Roebuck & Company plant, features of the pastoral public park became part of the factory site plan. Besides providing space for whatever activities might be organized by management, landscape areas framed the view of the factory from surrounding streets and provided expansive green views from within the factory buildings. (Photo courtesy of Sears Holdings)

Although satisfaction and pride were nebulously assessed, workers' improved reliability and increased work effort were apparently measurable and concrete. The pastoral landscape became an exploitable commodity in labor relations.

Above all, welfare capitalism indicated the extent to which nineteenth-century beliefs in landscape scenery's capacity for mental and social engineering pervaded industrial management. It also demonstrated a level of receptivity among factory workers to the persuasions of the pastoral, though the welfare factory waned as a tool to control labor: blue-collar workers ultimately resisted the inherent paternalism of welfare factories, as they had the company town, and unionization proved to be more beneficial to the lives of industrial employees than any factory amenities. But as postwar corporations redeployed landscape persuasions in their suburban management facilities, they met with a much more receptive target—white-collar workers bearing middle-class values that held the pastoral in particular esteem.

Suburban factories constructed in the two decades prior to World War II provided the essential model for the layout and design of the postwar suburban management facility. After 1920, industrial development took place exclusively in suburban or rural areas because single-story, in-line industrial plants required sizable building footprints.[31] Efficient and cost-effective modular construction and undisguised structural detailing characterized the architecture of production sheds, yet the administration buildings fronting plants were often surrounded by an expanse of lawn and trees.

Through the 1930s and 1940s, the Austin Company and, most especially, Albert Kahn Associates refined the horizontal suburban factory. The Austin Company's designs distinguished administrative offices as "separate entities" and selected "the site commanding the most advantageous view from the major highway approaches and affording adequate space for visitor parking." The firm advocated two-story administrative offices to "effectively mask the irregularities of sawtooth or monitor roofs," the identifying features of a factory.[32] Kahn's firm also faced administrative buildings to adjoining highways and favored site designs to "provide ample area for landscaping, parking and future expansion" (figure 2.7). Similar to later claims for management facilities, they contended that "the physical plant set in landscape surroundings has been made a show place and a calculated element in the public relations program; and even where this is not the aim, community pride is maintained by a plant that is an asset."[33]

Suburban corporate landscapes reiterated the architectural, parking, and landscape dispositions found in the suburban factory. Site plans accommodated low-rise structures, efficiently large floor areas, modular layout, big parking lots, and building expansion. Deep landscape setbacks faced the busiest roadway and presented the corporation's public face to passersby. Like the welfare factory, the landscape was a stratagem to represent the corporation to internal and external audiences. As postwar corporate leaders formulated the working environments of postwar management on the urban periphery, factories of the first half of the twentieth century provided crucial conceptual and physical models to employ the pastoral in the American work environment.

2.7

The low-rise, horizontal suburban factory, with ample room for expansion, preceded the management offices in the urban periphery. Typically an expanse of lawn and trees fronted the two- to three-story administration buildings, as seen here in the Wright Aeronautical Corporation factory, located in Evendale, outside of Cincinati, Ohio designed by Albert Kahn Associates in 1940. (Photo courtesy of Albert Kahn Associates, Inc., www.albertkahn.com)

Midcentury American suburbs were all low density compared to the center city, but they were not evenly pastoral. Although suburban factory schemes influenced the eventual forms of pastoral capitalism, they were located in manufacturing suburbs dominated by industrial plants and working-class housing, both with limited pastoral embellishments.[34] Tellingly, corporate management wanted to locate in a quite separate sector of midcentury suburbs. These were well-established pastoral residential suburbs of large lots, large houses, limited commercial uses, and expansive, unfenced front yards presenting a continuous street-side landscape—spacious, leafy havens of the white upper and upper-middle classes. The AT&T Bell Laboratories located its precedent-setting 1942 laboratory campus near Summit, New Jersey, an early, elegant railroad suburb of New York City (figure 2.8). When General Foods decided to leave Manhattan in 1950, the corporation considered various locations around New York City but determined that their "partly industrial" character "would not suit our needs." This impelled the corporation to scout other locations beyond the metropolitan edge, including Summit; it eventually settled north of New York City in White Plains, Westchester County, where large estates dotted the countryside and prized pastoral scenery was carefully guarded.[35] The developers of the first office park, built outside Birmingham, Alabama, in 1952, chose the residential area of Mountain Brook, described as "a pinnacle of suburban privilege constructed by the city's white elite."[36]

With this choice, corporations confronted an insistent and recurring issue. Until the advent of pastoral capitalism, these classic American pastoral suburbs were pointedly not places of business enterprise, much less industry; indeed, they were partially defined as being devoid of large-scale commerce. As they infringed on bucolic enclaves, corporations had to quell considerable resident resistance to their big employment centers. In an experience that proved prophetic for many subsequent corporate leaders, F. B. Jewett, president of Bell Laboratories, had to convince local politicians that his 1930 campus proposal (not realized until 1942) would fit into the "high" suburban character of Summit.[37] The project type was an unknown, and local residents suspected that the suspiciously industrial project would produce what they deemed unsavory environmental and social conditions. Jewett had to assure both politicians and residents that the few hundred laboratory employees would be primarily scientists and engineers who would be interested in living locally, thereby reassuring his audience that these were people of similar class and means. Jewett and nineteen other top executives and scientists already lived

in the area, and he had to pledge to the worried locals that the new development was not a manufacturing plant. He asserted: "We will develop it with campus-like effect. . . . The buildings will be of artistic design, low, not more than three stories high. All together we expect to make it a show place."[38] Jewett repeatedly stressed that the site was being planned and designed by the Olmsted Brothers, a name that signified a congruous landscape aesthetic to the affluent community, and he prevailed in getting the project approved. (Jewett never mentioned the architects.) Similarly, the presiding mayor of White Plains, who subsequently served as the Westchester County executive into the 1970s, characterized the public hearing to approve the precedent-setting headquarters for General Foods as "the roughest zoning hearing I've ever attended."[39] The General Foods project succeeded because the development dictates imitated the bygone Westchester estates: low-rise build-ing, arcing entry drive, and a pastoral landscape.

Suburban authorities countered ongoing community resistance by using the early projects' restrictions as templates for ensuing zoning, thereby facilitating more corporate investments. By 1932, local ordinances codified Jewett's concept with the first example of research and development zoning in the country. It re-quired ample setbacks, limited building heights to three stories, and restricted uses to "research, design and/or experimentation."[40] Once it was completed in 1942,

2.8
The suburb of Summit, New Jersey, where AT&T built the first corporate campus. This upscale, pastoral suburb was typical of where corporations wanted to locate the facilities for their management echelons. The landscape provisions of pastoral capitalism made corporate workplaces acceptable to residents who had to be convinced that the new developments would not compromise their communities' genteel milieu. (Photo by author.)

Bell Labs quickly spawned a series of other corporate research laboratories in the vicinity.[41] Similarly, General Foods was a "breakthrough" development culminating in Westchester County's "Platinum Mile" along the Cross Westchester Expressway—a string of corporate estates and office parks housing leading American corporations.[42] The development covenants of the 1955 Hobbs Brook Office Park in Waltham, Massachusetts, the second office park in the country, guided zoning ordinances for future development around Boston's Route 128, which became a globally recognized suburban corridor of high-technology companies.[43]

However skeptical the reception of suburban home owners, suburban political and entrepreneurial interests had something to gain from corporate offices beyond whatever profits could be had through the development of specific properties. Rapid expansion of suburban housing was exponentially expanding the need for such community services as police, fire protection, hospitals, public works, and schools. As *BusinessWeek* reported in 1951 after the announcement by General Foods of its intention to build a "garden-type office building" in White Plains, suburban jurisdictions welcomed the new corporate developments for urgent reasons:

> If the trend continues, it will help solve a threatening problem that most of the county's towns now face. Large estates that used to pay the big tax bills are being split up into smaller residential sections. Residential areas don't pay their own way unless average valuations run high.
>
> The answer is business property. But Westchester doesn't want a lot of little business districts or factories. Office buildings look like a heavensent answer. They carry a big share of the tax load, but don't clutter up the countryside. To make sure they do Westchester sets minimum acreage, [and] will allow buildings to cover only a minor part of it.[44]

This kind of "suburban grand compromise" between home owners and power brokers would be repeated all over the country.[45] It was based on a careful leveraging of public funding for suburban expansion through mortgage subsidies and infrastructure financing, especially roadways, attraction of new business enterprises compatible with a suburban aesthetic, and restrictions that ensured race and class segregation. Pastoral capitalist landscapes were a new type of metropolitan form that emerged from this directed set of "capital flows" into the urban periphery.[46]

Corporate enterprises in the genteel suburbs nevertheless challenged local residents as intruding emblems of capitalist modernity, potentially threatening established values and patterns, a tension that was particularly acute in the 1950s across a broad spectrum of cultural manifestations.[47] The pastoral envelope of suburban corporate landscapes ensured environmental conformity that was inevitably linked to the social homogeneity that these communities so carefully defended. The somewhat old-fashioned landscape provisions attached to these modern developments made them palatable in places known for their idealized, and envied, verdant ambience. Concomitantly, the process by which proposals determined local zoning protected corporate investments from incompatible, potentially devaluing future development while facilitating their proliferation among resistant suburban communities. In other words, the pastoral ideal was essential in instrumentalizing the "suburban grand compromise."

The Suburban Corporate Landscape

Even leaving aside local opposition, the placement of the corporate enterprise in residential suburbs was no small task. To accommodate large and growing corporate staffs, corporations had to build their own facilities from scratch and maintain the buildings and landscape. Land prices may have been cheaper per square foot than in the central business district, but corporations needed to buy considerably more property to achieve the desired office layout and pastoral effect. Like earlier industrial production, the initial suburban corporate offices had to draw the majority of their employees out from the center city, which often required giving these employees transport subsidies. In midcentury residential suburbs, transit systems were oriented to move people into the central business district to work, not out to the suburbs, and corporate support services were nonexistent. Local governments were ill equipped to deal with weighty developments, though usually they were more pliable to corporate influence than hard-nosed center city politicians. All of these conditions implied a considerable outlay of time and capital for businesses intent on suburban relocations.

In spite of these drawbacks, corporations determined that the suburban offices merited investment. The first corporations undertaking this shift relied more on conviction than calculation, yet they clearly expected the suburban facilities to profitably heighten and direct employee energies. General Motors mandated that the design of the Technical Center's laboratory windows be such "that the innermost draftsman be aware of the leaves of the trees," and the plethora of public relations materials distributed at its opening promoted the campus design as conducive to engineering innovation.[48] In a speech at the inauguration of the Deere & Company Administrative Center, the chairman and chief executive officer confidently declared that the corporation's new sub-urban headquarters would provide "additional inspiration to all of us to be bold, ingenious and creative, to use our imagination in new ways to keep John Deere out in front as a leader."[49] As *Fortune* recounted in 1952, postwar businesses considering suburban moves simply believed that "everybody can work better and think better in the country" and that top executives, in the words of one vice president, could literally "see the woods for the trees" (figure 2.9).[50] The corporate testimonials evinced the larger cultural belief, shared by corporate managers, in the physical and mental benefits of pastoral landscapes over the city center, even to the point of straining credulity.

Given the central role of these kinds of justifications, corporate leaders, and the designers they hired, had the task of inventing a new type of work-place—a pointedly suburban corporate office that nonetheless incorporated the symbolic and functional purposes of center city locations. The factory, with productive technological muscularity, was the historic backdrop for captains of industry; the central business district, with impressive scale and architecture, was still the imageable realm of capitalist power brokers. In the shift to the suburbs, corporations had to devise different means of distinction and affiliation, and the deployment of the pastoral surround was crucial in this process.

One of the advantages of the dense central city, particularly the business district, was as a nexus of popular and competitive recognition: ready identification in the business landscape. In contrast, the diffuse ubiquity of sylvan settings attenuated corporate visibility. For at least two decades after 1945, corporate developments spread out along the urban periphery lacked conspicuous geographical concentrations that could highlight their presence and importance. To compensate for their geographical obscurity, corporations took advantage of new, prominent viewpoints furnished by parkways and freeways. Of course, expansion of these road systems facilitated suburban building of all kinds by making exurban property easily accessible to automobile traffic.[51] But they also added an essential component to the suburban business environment by creating a novel kind of high-profile site adjacent to well-traveled, limited-access roadways.

In 1945, General Electric located the Electronics Park outside of Syracuse at the intersection of a principal county highway and the New York Thruway, then under construction (figure 2.10). After completion in 1957, *Fortune* used the Electronics Park to demonstrate the Thruway's capacity to show off a struc-ture that "stands out handsomely alongside" and thereby publicize the com-pany that owned it.[52] William Story of Wilcox-Laird, the landscape architects of the Electronics Park, wrote in *Landscape Architecture* of the particular role of

"I'm sorry—Mr. Lee has just stepped away from his desk . . ."

"Turn left at the new research center, go past Palumbo's vegetable stand, and you'll see the executive building . . ."

2.9
Corporate management's move to the urban periphery inspired a series of cartoons by the *New Yorker* regular James Stevenson published in the June 1967 issue of *Fortune*. Stevenson captures the surprise at the intrusion of corporate workplace into the pastoral countryside and the somewhat fanciful expectation that the landscape itself would generate added executive inspiration. (*Fortune* cartoons courtesy of James Stevenson)

"the location, orientation, and treatment with respect to the abutting highway. Here will be our approach; here will be our advertising." Story goes on to recommend 300 to 500 setbacks of "artistic yet skillful" landscape design "for proper circulation, interesting grading, enframement, etc."[53] Similarly, General Foods management dictated that their corporate estate located along the Cross Westchester Parkway (later also part of the New York Thruway) "should in effect 'crown the hill' thus assuring the availability of vistas for all sides."[54] The building projected a prominent image in a county famed for the estates of elite New Yorkers and along one of the most trafficked highways in the metropolitan region (see figure 4.2).[55] The speculative success of the office park, with every feature a hedge against risk, confirmed the promotional advantage of the view from the road.

A 1958 Highway Research Board study revealed that for businesses locating along Boston's Route 128, which included some of the first office parks,

2.10

The General Electric Electronics Park adjacent to the under-construction New York Thruway in the 1950s. New highways provided a new means of projecting a corporation's image to local and distant audiences as thousands of passing motorists saw handsome buildings surrounded by carefully tended pastoral grounds, an image much more akin to a public institution than a profit-making enterprise. (UCLA Department of Geography, Benjamin and Gladys Thomas Air Photo Archives, The Spence and Fairchild Collections)

"aesthetics was a significant consideration . . . expressed as 'a desire to locate in a good looking site, both with respect to buildings and landscaping.'"[56] All office parks directed their most expansive landscape toward the busiest adjacent thoroughfare, most often a highway, since this marketed projects to potential tenants. Sites along parkways and highways broadcast pleasing panoramas of verdant corporate facilities to thousands of passing motorists even as corporations carefully controlled physical access. The highway and the automobile substituted for the downtown street and the pedestrian in making the corporation an evident component of the metropolitan landscape.

The site designs of suburban management facilities removed from the visual field any feature that might be construed as "industrial" by passersby or occupants of the new sites. Infrastructural elements—drainage pipes, utility conduits, climate control systems, and service docks—required underground placement, screening, or disguise. Seemingly decorative lakes managed site runoff from huge parking lots, cooled air-conditioning systems, served as reservoirs to

2.11
The wide expanses of parking
that flanked factories were a sure
sign of an industrial blue-collar
plant. In suburban management
facilities, parking had to be much
more carefully subsumed into
enveloping verdure. (Library of
Congress, Prints & Photographs
Division, Gottscho-Schleisner
Collection, LC-G612-T-55676)

meet fire codes, and supplied water for laboratory experiments.[57] Vast, uninterrupted stretches of parking were typical of suburban factories, and the site plans of suburban management projects minimized the visibility of parking lots to the largest possible extent (figure 2.11). *Architectural Forum* highlighted this issue in its otherwise glowing article on the 1957 Connecticut General Life Insurance Company headquarters outside Hartford: "One evident flaw. . . . The nicely proportioned, precise metal and glass walls of this architecture are embarrassed by the big lots crammed with Detroit's suave bulbous auto bodies."[58] While corporate estates after Connecticut General concealed parking most elegantly and completely, artful grading and strategic planting minimized evidence of the car in all suburban corporate landscapes, at least to some extent. The developer of the first office park characterized this effect as "looking over the tree tops instead of the car tops."[59]

Modernist architecture's shearing of embellishments accentuated the landscape's symbolic and ornamental effects in the suburban corporate workplace. The transparent curtain wall of modernist buildings demanded a suitable exterior panorama, for the entire wall was now window; the only two acceptable views were a dynamic city skyline or verdant pastures (figure 2.12). Furthermore, from a disinterested view, a modernist management building and a factory might look much the same. The need to distinguish between the environments of genteel

2.12

View of the pastoral landscape from inside the Connecticut General Life Insurance Company headquarters in suburban Hartford. As modernist architecture opened wide expanses of glass to the outside view, the composition of the surrounding view became an essential consideration in the design of postwar offices. (Ezra Stoller © Esto)

white-collar management and gritty blue-collar industry necessitated investment in a substantial green surround in a suburban facility.

The familiar aesthetic of the pastoral allowed the reidentification of the corporation as a conformist suburban neighbor. In internal communications, General Foods allied its move to Westchester with the upward mobility of its workers: "For many, the move has meant a whole new kind of life. City apartment dwellers have become suburban property owners—like General Foods."[60] In an era that strictly limited the employment venues of women and valorized domesticity, taking on the trappings of home grounds and parks was useful. Both General Foods and Connecticut General employed unusually high numbers of women, as did the corporate "back office" administrative staffs occupying office parks. Although not applicable to the corporate campus housing scientists and engineers or corporate estates meant to accommodate corporate executives—in both cases, men were the critical labor force—economic studies decisively demonstrate that cheaper, more cooperative female employees were crucial for some suburban businesses.[61]

Corporations that ventured to the suburbs engendered considerable opposition among their leaderships, reluctant welcomes by local communities, many added costs, displacement of employees, and the task of reformulating their workplaces. From the perspective of the contemporary built-out "edge city," these challenges seem inconsequential; they were not. Nor were the prevailing pastoral schemes of the corporate outposts inevitable; they were a strategy to reinforce, facilitate, and justify the decision by corporate leaders to move to the urban periphery. As the landscape architect of the 1948 General Electric Electronics Park described his client's aims, the purpose of the site's trees, lawns, and lakes was "the creation of a development that bespeaks orderliness, spaciousness, and well-being."[62]

The Corporation in the Suburbs

Initial reports from the suburban frontier indicated that corporations had made a good bet on pastoral capitalism. A Bell Labs scientist asserted in an academic journal that the new "quiet country location" optimized scientific research; indeed Bell Labs had no difficulty attracting top researchers to its precedent-setting campus in spite of the dearth of qualified personnel during the postwar period.[63] Central business district headquarters that left for the suburbs testified that employee turnover fell by 50 percent, after making up for losses incurred by the move itself.[64] *Time* described the 1956 Connecticut General Life Insurance Company offices in Bloomfield, Connecticut, as "literally ringed with employee amenities" that "proved to be a powerful lure in a competitive Hartford labor market."[65] Charles Mortimer, the chief executive of General Foods, boasted of low turnover rates thirteen years after the move to White Plains.[66] When Deere & Company occupied the Administrative Center, hiring better-qualified applicants became easier, and want ads with pictures of the site produced decidedly higher response rates.[67] Surveys showed that Deere & Company employees overwhelmingly favored the resplendent site and landscape of the Administrative Center over all other elements of the headquarters. It compensated for the remote office location and cultivated corporate allegiance.[68] Other corporations reported that integrated parking areas boosted employees' effective working hours and amenability to overtime by minimizing out-the-door distractions, eliminating concerns about downtown traffic congestion, and making mass transportation schedules irrelevant.[69] While these indexes were not available until after corporations occupied new facilities, they proved to corporations that suburban settings enabled greater control over their workers, including the suburban women who formed their support staffs. Without doubt the pastoral workplace bolstered the class identity of management workers, reinforced their self-conceptions, and created a more complacent, selective workforce in the process.

In addition to its usefulness as a management strategy, the message of "orderliness, spaciousness, and well-being" conveyed by the pastoral aesthetic served as adroit symbolism for the burgeoning postwar corporation. Even if perceived as

instruments of affluence, corporations exist in a variable but always present ten-sion with a suspicious public. Since the 1920s, they have explicitly addressed this tension through public relations media aimed at internal and external audiences. Corporations allied themselves with the images and, by implication, values of an idealized, if not quite real, America: the edifying civility of bucolic small towns, technological modernity in service to life-enhancing progress, and the nuclear family ensconced in material comfort.[70] Like suburban home owners, corporations understood the capacity of a pastoral surround to communicate identity, status, and right-mindedness, acute concerns to enterprises exercising new power in the twentieth century.

In this context, the corporate appropriation of landscape display fits within a broader picture of "paternal neighborliness and democratic modes" that drove corporate self-representation in the twentieth century.[71] The enthusiastic and continued adoption of pastoral landscapes by corporations is not merely co-incident to broader suburbanization. Richard Walker says of the residential suburb, "Suburbs are not middle class simply because the middle class lives there; the middle class lives there because the suburbs could be made middle class."[72] Similarly, corporations adopted a pastoral landscape not simply because they moved to the suburbs; they moved to the suburbs to replace themselves within a pastoral landscape. This landscape surround fit neatly into the attempted re-contextualization of corporate endeavors to create goodwill across a spectrum of publics. The pastoral landscapes of corporations aptly, and vividly, reiterated in everyday physicality the way corporations wished to be understood—as seamless with traditional American culture (figure 2.13). "Greenery," as the cultural landscape historian J. B. Jackson states, is "a way of communicating with others."[73]

While hawking mythic American themes, this expression of the pastoral landscape also conveyed ascendancy. If the pastoral landscape came to have communal associations, it also held enough vestigial elite associations, sometimes emphasized more overtly, to embody the privileged position of corporations. Like the pastoral landscape of the suburban house, this was an attainable rather than lordly rank, courtesy of the meritocracy of the corporate hierarchy. In evolving from its European origins, American pastoralism, as Leo Marx noted, "took on a new democratic literalism; instead of being a mere fantasy of the privileged and the powerful, in which the ideal place represents a largely nostalgic retreat from social reality, it now was a future-oriented, relatively egalitarian, not infeasible vision of liminal possibility."[74] Most crucial, the corporate campus, corporate estate, and office park were the aspirational landscapes of a triumphant American capitalism and became part of differential spatial consumption that reinforces the experiences, behaviors, and ideologies that form social distinctions in the American city.[75] Thus, pastoral capitalism reflected an integrated set of values that served big business, drove expansive suburbanization, and reinforced elite American values as a whole.

2.13

The renowned photographer W. Eugene Smith, on assignment for *Fortune* magazine in 1957, captured this summary shot of the new Connecticut General Life Insurance Company headquarters. (The photograph ultimately appeared in a 1957 issue of *Architectural Forum*, another Henry Luce publication.) The photograph seems to capture the grand aspiration of postwar American society and capitalism in the family gazing at a lustrous steel corporate structure framed by a verdant, tranquil pastoral landscape. (© Estate of W. Eugene Smith/ Center for Creative Photography, University of Arizona/Black Star)

3

THE CORPORATE CAMPUS

*Where "talented young men
are encouraged to think freely"*

In 1946, Kenneth Meade, director of technical employment for the General Motors Corporation, addressed the American Association for the Advancement of Science: "Our economy is becoming increasingly technical. National defense, public utilities, agriculture and industry have become more and more dependent on scientists and engineers for their survival and their growth to meet the increased demands put on them." Meade went on to emphasize that to be productive, the corporate scientist had to be a management participant. "After all," the scientist, Meade declared," is not recruited as a factory laborer or into a routine job in which he will spend the rest of his life. He is employed because management believes he has the possibilities for development into a management position himself."[1] Meade's declarations manifested that the scientists, engineers, and technical workers in engaged in research for American business had become a breed apart from other corporate employees. Corporate success depended on clever technological innovations to trounce rivals and entice consumers. The researchers who devised these innovations were subject to the direction of top management but nonetheless garnered extraordinary independence and power within corporations because of their much-sought-after and, to the outsider, mysterious expertise. As the *New York Times Magazine* reported in 1956, "The welcome mat is out for eggheads in industry," and research divisions that were deemed "marginal" two decades before now resided at the core of corporate operations.[2] Corporate scientists achieved managerial clout, professional esteem, and public renown.

The corporate campus emerged during the decade after World War II as an instrument to reconceptualize research management, attract scientists from academia, and cloak the corporation in high-minded institutional garb. Composed of specialized laboratories situated within a landscape modeled on the American university, the corporate campus housed the increasingly valuable middle management research divisions in purpose-built facilities at the urban periphery. It concentrated physical, financial, and personnel resources that few universities could muster, and hence accelerated scientific invention and application. The corporate campus produced intertwined, far-reaching effects in business, science, and the structure of American cities.

Four projects contributed to the conception of the corporate campus. The seminal AT&T Bell Telephone Laboratories opened in 1942 in Murray Hill, close to Summit, New Jersey. As *Fortune* declared in 1958, Bell Labs was "the model for research 'campuses' that have sprung up all over the U.S. in the last dozen years."[3] The General Electric Electronics Park in Syracuse, New York, and the Johns-Manville Research Center in Manville, New Jersey, both constructed in 1948, advanced the idea of the corporate campus as a management instrument and refined the fundamental characteristics of the corporate campus site plan. The 1956 General Motors Technical Center in Warren, Michigan, dramatically transfigured the more confined aims of previous research campuses and created an icon of American technological, economic, and corporate supremacy. With the Technical Center, the corporate campus became a symbolic cornerstone of corporate America, as well as a facilitator of profitable research. Other enterprises imitated these influential models, and after 1960, the corporate campus became the normal site of the highest levels of industrial science.

From Machinist to Nobel Laureate, Workshop to Laboratory

Industrial production relies on complex, mechanized processes. As industrialization expanded in the nineteenth century, the organization and design of these mechanized processes became increasingly essential to industrial success and machinists became a specialized type of industrial worker. Early manufacturing focused on goods that previously had been handcrafted, such as textiles, guns, glass, nails, and plows. But soon industrial production created new goods such as steam engines, railroad cars, telegraphs, telephones, and light bulbs. The inventors of these new goods evolved from the machinists of early industrialization and were self-taught, problem-solving tinkerers; their activity normally took place in workshops integrated with production facilities.

But by the end of the nineteenth century (and earlier in Germany), technological innovation was starting to be guided by the application of science. Specialized workers in chemistry, metallurgy, and electricity became integral to industrial production, and their technological talents set them well apart from ordinary factory workers. At the same time, industrial inventors were quite distinct from academically trained scientists who engaged the rigor of the scientific method within university laboratories (not workshops) with the aim of expanding knowledge without regard to practical applicability and unsullied by the profit motive.

As industrial technology became more sophisticated, corporations started employing university-trained workers, referred to as engineers. Higher education in the late nineteenth century began to provide specialized courses of study to meet the demands of the industrial economy: mechanical and electrical engineering, chemical engineering, material science, and applied physics. University degrees increased these corporate employees' distinction from factory labor, though they continued to work in factory settings. This distinction was part of an ongoing, comprehensive division of labor in industrial production, but it also suited corporate owners that this educated cohort of skilled labor identified with management in an era of rising labor unrest.

By the turn of the twentieth century, corporations, particularly in the electric, chemical, and early electronics industries, began to recruit scientists with doctoral degrees to direct advanced scientific inquiry into potential products and processes. Lured from university positions by better salaries, scientists introduced more systematic methods of scientific investigation in industry and set up proper laboratories, instead of workshops, within factory sites. As the number of scientists expanded, industrial research became a recognized part of the corporate endeavor and distinct from the "pure" research of the university. At the same time, scientists existed in at least some tension with the capitalist enterprise. Their advanced education in the academy led them to look beyond management's bottom line, envisioning a larger purpose for industrial research. Trained to pursue knowledge, they couched their work as part of human "progress"—technology applied to the betterment of society and daily life—and deemphasized their role in economic profitability.[4]

The introduction of managerial capitalism in the 1920s established industrial research as a key division, squarely in the middle of the management hierarchy.[5] Though parallel with finance, sales, purchasing, and production departments, the research and development department occupied a more autonomous position: industrial scientists worked in laboratories that were separate from the rest of the corporate offices, they reported directly to top management, and usually they did not manage subordinate field offices. The heads of research and development departments were distinguished engineers and scientists given individual recognition within the corporation, and they were known in the academic science community as well. Like Charles Kettering, chief of research and development at General Motors, who was corporate president Alfred Sloan's most trusted advisor, they often had special access to chief executives.

Along with the consolidation of their role in managerial capitalism, corporate scientists began collecting Nobel Prizes during the interwar years. Besides the prestige, and even fame, that was associated with these awards, they indicated the extent to which the applied research of industry dealt with basic science previously considered the purview of academia. In addition, the research units of corporations such as General Electric, General Motors, and AT&T received contracts from other corporations, the government, and foundations for research itself rather than for specific products. Corporations began to rival universities in the production of scientific knowledge.[6]

As scientists and engineers became distinct and elevated in the corporate hierarchy, they influenced corporate operations as the principal proponents of welfare capitalism. This was an early-twentieth-century management strategy to make industrial labor more controllable and productive, including through the use of pastoral amenities in factory design.[7] Welfare capitalism attempted to recast the corporation from a profit-making business to a public-minded institution, and corporate scientists were deeply involved in its complementary orchestration of image, environment, and industrial culture to manipulate the corporate workforce. In this light, the later corporate campus was a logical outgrowth of scientists' own view of the corporation as an institution, not merely an enterprise.

General Electric exemplified how scientific research played out in industrial facilities in the first decades of the twentieth century. With origins in the workshops of the quintessential inventor, Thomas Edison, GE promoted its group of industrial scientists and engineers as the "House of Magic." Nonetheless, Willis R. Whitney, director of the GE laboratory from 1900 until 1932, had to lobby higher management for purpose-built structures within the corporation's expansive industrial site in Schenectady, New York. He finally succeeded in 1914 and consciously tried to set apart the multistory laboratory from the factory buildings. Whitney chose a site at the beginning of the main street through the works "so that people will see us when they come to work in the morning, and will know we're there to help them." In 1919, he requested that the manager of the factory site clear away the detritus of old machinery in front of his lab even though "it might not reduce cost at all. But as prospective purchasers, physicians, Government officials, etc., often visit us for X-ray help and advice, and to see our facilities, they may be somewhat affected by the care and attention we give our general appearance." By the 1920s a substantial expanse of trees and lawn fronted Whitney's labs and formed an entry to the entire works (figure 3.1).[8]

But laboratories within factory sites had significant drawbacks. Through the first half of the twentieth century, an increasingly complex laboratory infrastructure supported the production of industrial science. Laboratories required distribution

3.1

General Electric's Schenectady works in the 1940s. The GE multistory laboratory buildings are visible just to the right and down of the center of the photograph. The expanse of grass and trees in front of the laboratories was placed there at the insistence of the scientists who wanted to set off their facilities from the rest of the works and favorably impress visitors and potential clients. (Courtesy of the General Electric Archives, Schenectady Museum)

systems for gas, distilled water, power, exhaust, ventilation, and specialized materials. Experimental setups called for large floor areas and the capacity for continuous modification in scale and configuration. Data records had to be filed and easily retrieved and volatile or explosive materials safely deposited and stored. Experimental conditions needed to be controlled to prevent inaccurate results. As the elusive fundamentals of the physical world became the focus of corporate research, industrial science became an increasingly rigorous operation. Old urban factories, crowded, dirty, and noisy, were less and less conducive to experimental rigor. Research facilities competed with production facilities for space. In typical multistory laboratory buildings, floor areas were limited, researchers working on the same project were vertically separated, and distribution of experimental materials was difficult. Before federal and state occupational safety standards, industrial accidents were frequent and toxic contamination common. This had egregious human costs, of course, but also compromised experimental controls.

The exurban factories on large, flexible sites developed in the 1920s seemingly addressed the experimental impediments of the older industrial sites.[9] Site planning constraints eased, and buildings could be separated, stretched out horizontally, and planned for expansion. Plants did not have to be tied to railroad spurs, as trucking made more locations available. The new factory designs efficiently addressed infrastructure needs. They looked better: large, clean, light-filled factory sheds; ample, tidily arranged parking lots and circulation; and laboratory and office buildings given "architectural" treatment, garnished with an expanse of lawn and trees.[10] But while suburban factory laboratories served well enough for many corporations, other leading American companies realized that they would not suffice to advance research at the forefront of modern technology. In the end, these were still industrial works associated with blue-collar labor and insufficiently prestigious for corporate scientists integral to the top ranks of managerial capitalism.

Moreover, harnessing science for the rapidly expanding industrial base of the United States, now the world's largest economy, created unprecedented competition for scientists. By World War II, research and development became not just a means of bringing profitable products to market, but an instrument of modern warfare and an industry in itself. The federal government sponsored an array of scientific research endeavors, establishing government laboratories such as Oak Ridge National Laboratory, a system of university contracts for research, and greatly increased research contracts with corporations. Coupled with low university enrollments during the Great Depression and World War II, this created a marked shortage of scientific personnel in the postwar period. As the Cold War geared up, defense spending hugely expanded, and government laboratories and universities employed an unprecedented number of scientists, amplifying the competitive atmosphere.[11] From 1950 to 1951, government jobs for physicists multiplied by ten, and industrial jobs for physicists increased tenfold between 1950 and 1952; there were "dozens more employers" for every physics Ph.D.[12] Corporations were scrambling for scientists.

The corporate campus was created to entice scientists habituated to the university atmosphere and suspicious of for-profit strictures to join the American corporate endeavor. As research and development expanded, more scientists came to corporations after having spent key formative years in the esteemed university environment. The iconic American university campus encompassed distinct features closely linked to the nineteenth-century American pastoral: distinguished buildings placed in a spacious, designed landscape ideally located in small towns or rural settings.[13] American college life predisposed scientists to associate exciting and exacting intellectual inquiry with pastoral serenity isolated from the city, and as a setting of privilege, the campus was a reliable collective signifier of class and status. Additionally, the aspirations of the postwar generation of scientists conformed to their era; they expected to achieve an elevated level of material comfort and associated the fulfillment of that dream most completely with the suburbs.[14] A pastoral suburban aesthetic that rejected the dense fabric and ethnic diversity of the urban core permeated the cultural ideals of educated and striving Americans.

Besides drawing on multifaceted sources of approbation, the corporate campus became a strategic management tool in another way. After all, corporate research was akin to academic research in certain ways but quite different in other regards. Unlike research in academia that encouraged and rewarded individual achievement, corporate research emphasized cooperative inquiry.[15] With the pressure of profits, laboratory environments had to be conducive to teamwork and the transference of knowledge, instrumental goals congruent with the corporate enterprise. In this context, executives and scientists came to view the corporate campus enthusiastically as a fitting and facilitating arena for their specific kind of work.

A Precedent: Nela Park

The manipulation of image and environment advanced by welfare capitalism in the early twentieth century set the context for a prototype of the corporate campus: Nela Park outside Cleveland, Ohio. An acronym for the National Electric Lamp Association established in 1904, NELA merged General Electric's lesser competitors under a single corporation to ostensibly compete with

GE's dominance in the electric lamp and light bulb industry. In actuality, General Electric secretly owned NELA as a way of monopolizing the industry.[16]

The development of Nela Park was part of a scheme to make the National Electric Lamp Association appear to be a substantial competitor to General Electric and thus avoid federal antitrust prosecution. The appearance of substance took the form of a college quadrangle, with structures surrounding an ample central open space on 40 acres at the city edge, 6 miles from the central business district (figure 3.2). The neo-Georgian buildings housed management, sales offices, and various laboratories. NELA publicity promoted the site as a "University of Industry," emphasizing its established institutional character (figure 3.3).

Almost as soon as NELA occupied the site in 1911, the federal government ascertained General Electric's ruse and sued for antitrust violations.[17] Even

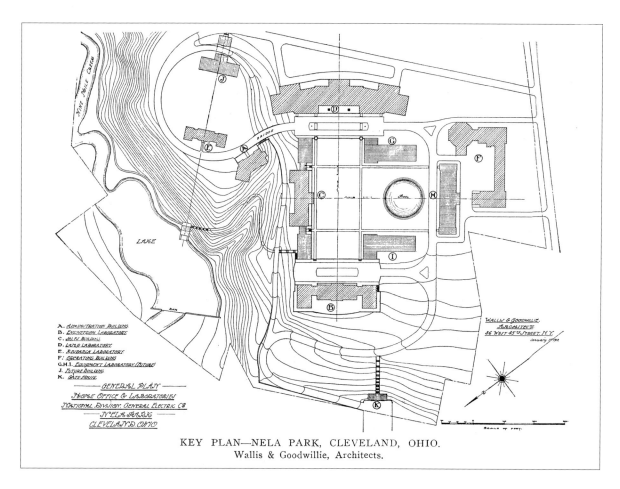

KEY PLAN—NELA PARK, CLEVELAND, OHIO.
Wallis & Goodwillie, Architects.

GENERAL BIRD'S-EYE VIEW OF
NELA PARK, CLEVELAND, OHIO.
WALLIS & GOODWILLIE, ARCHITECTS.

3.3

Perspective of Nela Park from
Architectural Record, 1914.
Nela Park resembled subsequent
corporate campuses in form,
though it never housed General
Electric top research personnel.
The site's noticeably institutional
character, a "University of
Industry," was useful in attempting
to convey the National Electric
Lamp Association as a substantial,
independent contender to
GE's economic dominance.
(Reprinted with permission from
Architectural Record © 1914, The
McGraw-Hill Companies, www.
architecturalrecord.com)

after the discovery of the corporation's illegalities, the famed architectural critic Montgomery Schuyler wrote of Nela Park in *Architectural Record:* "Perhaps the clearest and deepest impression the observant visitor takes away from this scene of co-operative industry is that 'big business' may not only be a very big, but a very beneficent thing."[18] This was a useful dissemblance given General Electric's unlawful monopolization of the electrical industry.

Nela Park differs from the subsequent corporate research campuses in its eclectic architectural style, multiple corporate uses, absence of parking lots, and lack of specialized research infrastructure. It did anticipate the central open space and low-rise buildings of the corporate campus scheme. Nela Park never housed GE's top scientists (they stayed at the main Schenectady works), but when the idea of corporate campuses resurfaced in the 1940s, it served as a touchstone.[19] Nela Park demonstrated the possible rhetorical import of the campus in the American corporate landscape.

AT&T Bell Telephone Laboratories

The first corporate campus, the AT&T Bell Telephone Laboratories, redefined corporate standards for research and development facilities. It did so because of particular intersecting circumstances: the research division of AT&T

needed especially quiet research space in addition to up-to-date laboratory infrastructure; the legitimacy of for-profit science explicitly concerned corporate leadership; many corporate officers, including the president, lived near the site eventually chosen for the campus; though planned for well over a decade, the opening of the campus coincided with a post–Pearl Harbor surge of defense work; and the AT&T scientists attracted to the campus were notably productive and profitable.

Since 1906, the Bell System had conducted research in a south Manhattan loft building at 463 West Street that they shared, until 1916, with manufacturing activities of the Western Electric Company. In 1925 Bell management consolidated other research activities from Manhattan and Boston to create the AT&T Bell Telephone Laboratories. Jointly owned by American Telephone and Telegraph and Western Electric, the new independent research unit took over the whole building, which occupied an entire block.

The first president of Bell Labs was Frank Baldwin Jewett, who had joined AT&T in 1904. One of the first American physics Ph.D.s to eschew academic life and join an industrial research operation, Jewett later testified that his defection elicited the judgment from his science mentors that "I was prostituting my training and my ideals."[20] No doubt his project to resituate AT&T scientists on a corporate campus sought to dignify his choice to pursue science for profit rather than knowledge.

By 1929 the downtown laboratory's tight urban location was interfering with a number of key research activities. Noise, vibrations, and electrical interference made accurate experimental measurement difficult, especially in acoustics, a primary research focus. Work with hazardous chemical fumes and explosive gases in the crammed quarters posed potential safety problems. Buffer areas for safety and isolation from interference required expansive floor areas that were expensive in the central city.[21] Exacerbating this, the labs needed to vacate part of the space by July 1931 because the elevated tracks of the New York Central Railroad would slice 30 feet from the building's east side.[22]

Under these immediate pressures, particularly in terms of acoustical work, the executives of Bell Labs proposed a new facility that would house entire research units, avoid "planes of separation" between parts of a project, facilitate communication, accommodate support staff, and provide "a suitable restaurant." The variously named "field laboratory," "acreage laboratory," or "outside laboratory" needed to be large enough for multiple research units, leave room for expansion, and adapt to experimental exigencies. Additionally, every research department head determinedly did not want "a small portion of his personnel or work isolated in a backwater."[23] The summary memorandum documenting Bell Labs's decision to move forward on the project characterized the new facility as a "general suburban laboratory" of 500 to 1,000 acres. The memo presumed that West Street would continue to house top managers and some limited research activities.[24]

Bell Labs bought 213 acres from nine different owners in Union County, New Jersey, 25 miles from New York City, and appropriated the name of the nearest commuter stop of the Delaware, Lackawanna & Western Railroad: Murray Hill.[25] The nearest town, Summit, was a classic upper-middle-class railroad suburb of large lots, big houses, granite curbstones, absent property line fences, and uniformly white residents. The small settlement adjacent to the laboratory site, the colonial village of New Providence, included old churches, crossroads stores, and flower-growing enterprises. The land accumulated by Bell Labs contained upland woodlands and level farm fields and nurseries. The Watchung Reservation, a permanent open space, bordered the long upland side of the roughly rectangular property, providing protection from encroaching uses. Mountain Avenue, connecting New Providence and Summit, ran along the lowland edge of the property.

The unconsolidated agricultural site was undoubtedly reasonably priced less than a year after the 1929 crash yet near enough to the town of Summit not to be a backwater. Bell estimated that about 40 percent of its employees lived in the vicinity, including nineteen officers and top scientists. Jewett himself lived in Short Hills, just north of Summit.[26] As Bell Labs' president and select top management remained in New York City until 1959, the proximity of the Murray Hill site to their suburban residences certainly facilitated coordination between their activities. It also gave Bell Labs an inside track in dealing with local officials and residents during the approval process.

The architectural firm of Voorhees, Gmelin and Walker was already designing an additional building for the West Street offices on the block north of the Manhattan lab, so Bell expanded its services to include the new site.[27] In July 1930, even before completion of the land acquisition, Bell management contacted the esteemed Olmsted Brothers of Brookline, Massachusetts. At the first meeting with representatives of the Olmsted firm, Bell executives explained that they considered a single large building but preferred a quadrangle of separate buildings—a preference supported by the landscape architects.[28] They subsequently indicated to their consultants that the buildings were to be units 200 by 50 feet, "not over three stories, colonial style," and added to the site as needed. They hoped to begin construction by September 1930.[29]

The prospect of a large employment center, suspiciously and potentially industrial in character, stirred up controversy in the community. On July 29, 1930, the *Newark News* broke the story that AT&T had acquired 200 acres in New Providence "for research purposes which would give employment to several thousand persons."[30] (The *New York Times* picked up the story the following day.) On July 31, Jewett met with local officials at a gathering presided over by the mayor who was "connected with the Bell Laboratories," according to the *Newark News*. Jewett assured the assembled worthies that the lab would employ only 300 to 400 people, "mostly of the scientific and engineering type who will want to live with their families somewhere in the territory between Short Hills and New Providence." Jewett emphatically stated, "It is not a manufacturing concern; it is a laboratory for research and development of things needed to improve telephone and telegraph service. . . . In a sense what we propose is something along the lines of a miniature college or university. . . .The entire property will be landscaped by the Olmsted Brothers of Boston."[31] The local paper assured readers that "Dr. Jewett answered many of the rumors that have been abroad throughout the summer and demonstrated the high type of development and the fact that it will in no way harm the growth of this entire section as a residential community but rather will be of great assistance in keeping this territory on a high plane of a suburban residential community."[32] To further allay fears, the paper published the list of Bell's nineteen officers and scientists who lived in the area, including Jewett.[33]

The local residents' alarm over the proposed laboratories reflected the unprecedented project type. Because large, peripheral, nonresidential developments were baldly industrial up to this time, they had no other point of reference.[34] Resolute on maintaining the social caliber of their neighborhoods, they certainly did not relish either an influx of factory workers or the unsavory environmental results of industry, both obvious in nearby areas of New Jersey. Hence Jewett highlighted the educated stature of Bell Labs employees and underscored the involvement of the Olmsted Brothers, whose name carried the cachet of high-minded environmental taste and implied social values congruous with those of Summit's residents.

The site plan presented by the Olmsted Brothers in the fall of 1930 fulfilled Jewett's characterization of the new laboratories. It placed separate three-story structures around a generous open quadrangle and planned for expansion by adding subsidiary quadrangles in a cruciform pattern. The plan resembled Nela Park and the layouts of many American universities.[35] It nestled the quadrangle in the property's wooded uplands, minimizing visibility from Mountain

Avenue. Assenting to Bell's proposal, two years later the local zoning code designated "laboratories devoted to research, design and/or experimentation" as allowed on the property—the first example of research and development zoning in the nation.[36] However, by October 1932, AT&T's deteriorating business forced deferral of the project.[37]

Bell Labs revived the plans for the Murray Hill Laboratories in 1939. The Olmsted Brothers and the architects returned to the project, the latter under the new name Voorhees, Walker, Foley, and Smith. However, the contractual agreement was different: the Olmsted firm subcontracted to the architects instead of directly with the owner. This arrangement was unprecedented and discomfiting for the landscape architects, but the contractual change reflected a change in the project priorities. By 1939 the laboratories' technological requirements predominated over the Beaux-Arts campus concept. The architects completed the site plan and design of the interconnected lab building and separate acoustic laboratory, and the Olmsted firm undertook the site development, primarily grading and planting (figure 3.4).[38]

0   250 500   1000

3.4
The 1942 site plan of the AT&T Bell Telephone Laboratories, designed by the landscape architects the Olmsted Brothers of Boston and the New York architecture firm of Voorhees, Walker, Foley, and Smith. The large site of over 200 acres amply surrounded the bulky three-story buildings that contained the most up-to-date research infrastructure. The large site also allowed 300-foot landscape setbacks required by the local zoning ordinance, put in place after AT&T proposed the facility in 1930.

The architects organized the building design around an adjustable functional module of a six-foot-wide laboratory. The zoning code restricted the building to three stories, but this dovetailed with the need for short, vertical utility conduits and the elimination of expensive elevators and waiting time for travel between floors. The few elevators transported freight.[39] The buildings, shorn of any Beaux-Arts detailing, displayed a modernist sensibility in their unadorned use of materials, planar simplicity, and functional layout. The main building contained the employees' cafeteria, laboratory bays, and appended office wings, which formed an open-cornered court. The custom brick–faced edifices had copper roofs, and brick head houses crowned each stairwell. Large double-hung sash windows rhythmically punctuated the entire facade on 6-foot centers. Expanses of floor-to-ceiling windows, limestone trim and paving, and facades of

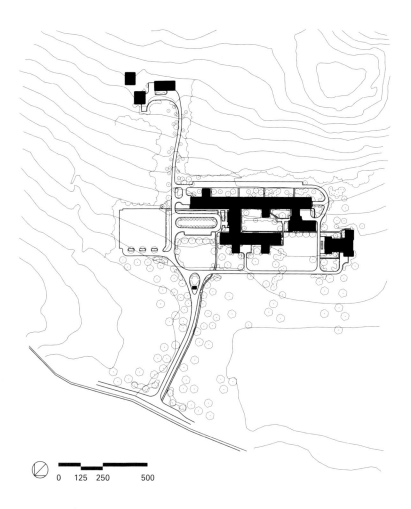

0   125   250   500

Princeton stone (a local schist used extensively at the university) distinguished the reception lobby, cafeteria, and separate acoustics building.[40]

The site included two large parking lots and truck access all around the building (figure 3.5). A fence enclosed the entire building complex, with access limited through a gatehouse (see figure 2.4).[41] Although the entry from Mountain Avenue was approximately the same as in 1930, the complex moved to the more visible front of the site.[42] The building needed numerous retaining walls to incorporate the large structure on the sloping terrain, and the landscape architects also faced them with Princeton stone.[43] Groves of trees followed the entry drive, and allées of flowering trees highlighted the cafeteria and auditorium. Foundation shrubs skirted the common buildings, and scattered clusters of deciduous hardwoods melded with existing trees. The edge of the remaining woodland enclosed the site's upland side. Lawn rolled across the open topography. Throughout the project, utilities ran underground, and curbs of granite block duplicated the style of local neighborhood roads.[44]

The development fulfilled local zoning requirements but produced a less recognizable campus-like effect than the 1930 plan. The architects understood that their "somewhat severe architectural treatment" depended "heavily on the landscape treatment to wed the buildings to the countryside, as well as to tie the architecture together."[45] The landscape architects protested their diminished role throughout the three years of the project; they disagreed with the miserly boxiness of the site conception and the architects' preferences for formal landscape elements. The unfamiliar contractual arrangement and landscape budget cuts to compensate for building cost overruns added to the argument.[46] None of the project's subsequent publications credit the landscape architects' contributions despite emphasizing the unique site development and including copious photographs of the landscape and window views of the grounds (figure 3.6).[47]

As the 906 employees from West Street and other plants took up residence in 1942, Bell Labs's superior functionalism and unique setting attracted publicity, though not initially as a "campus." In 1941 *Newsweek* reported on the research potential of the "streamlined superlaboratory far from the madding throng."[48] The August 1942 issue of *Pencil Points* accorded the complex a detailed thirty-eight-page spread and characterized it as a "functionally designed laboratory unit in rural surroundings . . . a dream . . . project of Dr. F. B. Jewett."[49] The modular lab system was so remarkable that in September 1944, *Life* published a series of photographs illustrating the complex service piping and a before-and-after shot of a research assemblage under the title "Modern Laboratory: A Workroom for Any Experiment Can Be Set Up within 48 Hours."[50]

3.6
The three-story buildings of
Bell Labs set within a classic
Olmstedian pastoral landscape.
Within a few years, Bell Labs
attracted top scientists to work
in its facilities and dominated
industrial research. (Courtesy of
AT&T Archives and History Center)

3.7
A far cry from the industrial sites in which industrial scientists and engineers had typically carried on research, Bell Labs personnel working in the spacious, light-filled rooms looking out onto tended pastoral terrain. (Library of Congress, Prints & Photographs Division, Gottscho-Schleisner Collection, LC-G612-T-42061)

Science journals gave Bell a convenient opportunity to publicize the labs to competitors and potential colleagues. In the *Journal of Applied Physics,* a Bell scientist extolled the surrounding "open country" and underscored the necessity of a "quiet country location" for optimal scientific research (figure 3.7). In the article, illustrated with several photographs, he noted the "broad expanse of lawn studded with newly planted trees and bordered with a thick growth of natural wood" visible from the restaurant and lounge built of "Princeton stone." The article emphasized the experimental utilities of the laboratories and that the "flexible building arrangements at Murray Hill have made it possible to meet quickly all war requirements without the usual time-consuming alterations."[51] Similarly, a laudatory 1945 article in *Science* reported of Bell Labs: "The fields and woods, courtyards and shaded lawns all tend to make it a pleasant place in which to work" and highlighted the gentility of Bell Labs. *Science* was careful to explain that this was no company town, previously the only reason for a corporation to purchase such an extensive tract.[52]

By 1948, Bell Labs produced discoveries that sealed the interlinked reputations of its management, scientists, and site. Its scientists invented the transistor and the bit (the basic mathematical unit of electronic information) and fundamentally revolutionized electronic technology and, arguably, human existence. Though with expansion of the laboratory buildings in 1948, the site became more visually dominated by buildings, and in the postwar years the corporate leadership of Bell Labs emphasized the collegiate atmosphere (figure 3.8). Mervin J. Kelly, future Bell Labs president, addressed fellow scientists in 1950:

> Inspired and productive research in industry requires men of the same high quality as is required for distinguished pure research in our universities. We select our young men from among the most able and promising of the doctorate and post-doctorate of philosophy students of our graduate schools. . . .
>
> They must be given freedoms that are equivalent to those of the research man in the university. This is, indeed, difficult in industry, but we are approaching that ideal. We give much attention to the maintenance of an atmosphere of freedom and an environment stimulating to scholarship and scientific research interest.[53]

In a time of intense competition for scientific personnel, Kelly averred, Bell Labs had "no difficulty in attracting men of this type and quality."[54]

By the time the inventors of the transistor collected their Nobel Prize in 1956, Bell Labs was promoting a full-blown academic concept encompassing both management strategies and premier research facilities (see figure 1.8). A 1954 *Business Week* article, "At Bell Labs, Industrial Research Looks Like Bright College Years," and bannered with an aerial photograph of the facilities, extolled:

> Murray Hill in rural setting, comes easily by its university ambiance. . . .
>
> . . . All this freedom, this almost relaxed freedom, seems a little at odds in the family of Mother Bell whose business communications empire is the largest nonfinancial company in the world. . . .
>
> Rival researchers have long since learned that the air of leisure connotes no sluggishness of productivity. Technical inventions, and improvements flow steadily from the labs. . . . They also wonder just how many scientists—notoriously uncontrollable—can be kept working in such fruitful harmony without visible controls.
>
> . . . Partly the Freedom is illusory. The lab has firm plans and knows precisely what it wants. . . . Over the years men have been meticulously selected and precisely trained. Men chosen to fit the mold will fall into the desired pattern without any pressure from the mold itself.[55]

Bell Labs was strategically positioned for the postwar transformation of high technology research spurred by a booming economy and the Cold War. Its scientists devised myriad technologies that pervade everyday life, contrived defense systems that changed global politics, and competed with only a handful of top universities and national laboratories in the production of basic scientific

research. When *Fortune* lauded the enterprise as "The World's Greatest Industrial Laboratory" in 1958, Bell Labs was a powerhouse of production and, with 4,200 employees, the largest industrial research center in the United States.[56] The next year, Bell Labs's top executive scientists abandoned the vestigial Manhattan offices and moved entirely to Murray Hill.[57]

Bell Labs invented the fundamentals of the corporate campus. At the center of the site was an open green space. The surrounding flexible laboratory spaces with specialized utilities maximized the efficiency and capacity of research units. Truck access and parking conveniently ringed the buildings. Underground utilities distinguished it from industrial works and added to its exclusive air. The large, fenced site provided heightened security necessitated by all-important defense work. Three-story height limits, generous landscape setbacks, and specifically white-collar uses, all codified in zoning ordinances, permitted the incursion of a large corporate employment center into a swank

3.8
At Bell Labs, common areas with large windows that looked out onto the grounds appeared more like student unions than business enterprises and were important in underscoring the "campus" quality of the corporate facility. (Library of Congress, Prints & Photographs Division, Gottscho-Schleisner Collection, LC-G612-T-42356)

suburban residential community. The ample property allowed expansion while maintaining an enveloping verdure. After Bell Labs, no confined urban site could possibly hold an up-to-date laboratory, and other corporate labs followed Bell into this area of New Jersey.[58]

Most important, Bell's campus instituted an industrial research culture that mimicked the university's encompassing environmental prestige and independent intellectual inquiry, supposedly free from corporate constraints. The campus site articulated a research management strategy that *Business Week* described as having "no chains of command clanking in the corridors" and which elided any profit-making intent.[59] It was a useful fiction, but there was no doubt that the new conception was more felicitous than the industrial sites in which the research scientists had formerly labored. Most assuredly, the agility of the site facilities reflected, and probably reinforced, a hoped-for agility of the mind. To the corporate leaders who wished to attract, foster, separate, and elevate the research activities of their scientists, Bell Labs's success quickly proved incontrovertible.

General Electric Electronics Park and Johns-Manville Research Center

While Bell Labs was still firming up as a corporate campus, two corporate projects of the late 1940s explicitly employed the campus moniker to distinguish their corporate research facilities. Though close to manufacturing plants and hence not quite as genteel as Bell Labs, they promulgated the corporate campus scheme, refined its site planning and design parameters, and consolidated the campus as a management instrument. The Electronics Park outside Syracuse, New York, a new division of GE's famed "House of Magic" research labs, was the physical manifestation of GE's postwar dispersed and flexible management strategy. The Johns-Manville Research Center in Bound Brook, New Jersey, evinced the necessity of a new corporate environment for scientists distinct from the factory and the foil of the campus landscape in marking the distinction.[60]

Established in 1900, General Electric Research Laboratories provided research for General Electric, Westinghouse, and, eventually, the Radio Corporation of America (RCA). The GE Labs, like Bell, sought out Ph.D.s (GE recruited from Europe), and their expertise was refining others' basic discoveries and moving them into useful and profitable production.[61] Since its inception, GE research had been located at the company's factory works in Schenectady, New York. The site was typical of vast nineteenth-century industrial sites with huge sheds, smokestacks, and building accretion, all surrounded by railroad tracks. In 1914 the laboratory moved into a specially designed seven-story building within the works, noticeably more polite, and expanded into a comparable building across the street in 1925 (see figure 3.1).[62]

Expansion during and after World War II (General Electric Research Laboratories had participated in the development of the atomic bomb) left GE Labs wedged between the factories and short of space.[63] Even before the war ended, GE had commissioned Voorhees, Walker, Foley, and Smith in 1945 to design a new high-security atomic laboratory outside of Schenectady overlooking the Mohawk River on a former estate known as the Knolls.[64] This was the first time GE had separated any personnel from the research department at the Schenectady factory works. Much smaller than Bell or the subsequent General Electric Electronics Park, the atomic lab was contained in a single building. Like Bell, a profusion of services and moveable interior walls (this time on a 12-foot module) equipped the laboratory. The site plan maintained a handsome old allée of trees, a rectangle of lawn, and the site's rather elegant river prospect.[65]

With the end of hostilities, General Electric planned a large campus for the new Electronics Department formed under the forceful vice president W. R. G. Baker.[66] Convinced of the potential of television and vacuum tube research, Baker conceived of a new facility separate from the crowded Schenectady site.[67] By fall 1945, ground had been broken on what was officially known as the Electronics Park, but dubbed "Baker's folly" by Baker's dubious colleagues.[68] The project combined an expansive research laboratory complex next to new manufacturing facilities. The engineers and architects Giffels and Vallet and the landscape architects Wilcox and Laird planned and designed the Electronics Park, sited on 191 acres of former agricultural land 12 miles northwest of Syracuse. The new complex was located along the New York Central Railroad and at an intersection of a county highway and the alignment of the New York Thruway, an early limited-access throughway.

Advantageously visible from the Thruway's interchange and passing motorists, the campus formed a frontispiece to three factory buildings extending back toward the railroad tracks (figure 3.9). It centered on a large, oval open space with a cafeteria in the middle. A gatehouse controlled access from the county highway, and the looping drive connected all the buildings around the green: reception, administration, laboratories, and the three architectural facades of the factories. The plan distributed parking all around the driveway for management employees and in two large parking bays on either side of the plants for the factory workers. The architecture of the two-story structures and factory

3.9

General Electric Electronics Park outside Syracuse, New York, in the late 1940s. With gracious buildings surrounded by a spacious landscape expanse, the site was a remarkable contrast to General Electric's crowded Schenectady factory works, the previous workplace of the corporation's electronic scientists. (Courtesy of General Electric Archives, Schenectady Museum)

fronts displayed institutional gravity—brick facades highlighted by substantial columns. The campus incorporated programming for outside visitors, and the reception building with a public auditorium essentially operated as a civic building for the local community.[69] The landscape design consisted of gently sloping grass expanses and sparsely planted trees to avoid the extensive underground utilities. A dammed spring and stream formed a lake, that GE claimed was for experimental purposes.[70] Occupying the corner of the site and surrounded by a generous lawn, it was a decorative element strategically placed at the most public view of the site. Not surprisingly, the Electronics Park displayed similarities to Nela Park and, like large public university landscapes, appeared "grand in scale, clearly organized, and open to the outside world."[71]

Even more than Bell Labs, the Electronics Park met the infrastructure challenges of the research center with a flexibility that extended beyond the

laboratory module to the entire site plan. The director of General Electric Research Laboratory stated in 1950, "If there is one thing we know, it is that we do not know what we will be doing ten years from now."[72] By 1951 when the television market boomed, General Electric had tripled the size of the laboratory space and added huge warehouses to the backs of two factories.[73] The nimble scheme easily accommodated complicated infrastructure and large building additions without loss of ambience.

The Electronics Park suited General Electric's postwar implementation of managerial capitalism, decentralizing large, concentrated industrial works, like Schenectady, and central business district offices such as its corporate headquarters in Manhattan. This dovetailed with civil defense decentralization as the answer to cold war vulnerabilities. As Philip D. Reed, chairman of the board of the General Electric Company, stated in 1948, "Our decentralization has been fundamentally economic in nature" yet "automatically offers many of the security advantages which have been advocated by the National Security Resources Board, and in this respect is doubly desirable."[74] Accommodating numerous executives and 600 research employees, the Electronics Park served as one of several new headquarters in this dispersal process. Managers at the Electronics Park controlled plants in thirteen other locations from Illinois to New Jersey.[75]

Although the Electronics Park in some ways was a transitional project that still included manufacturing facilities, General Electric pointedly presented it as a campus, and the contemporary business and design literature consistently used this descriptor.[76] Because dispersal was desirable, the apparent receptivity of the campus fit GE's management tactic to compensate for the diffusion of facilities across several states: a system of visits by personnel from manufacturing to research centers and vice versa, and the designation of lab scientists as full-time liaisons with other corporate divisions. The success of GE's dispersed management and manufacturing hinged on these management interactions, and the campus was a gracious place to host meetings, reinforcing middle management as a distinct class in the corporation.

As a corporate campus, the Electronics Park proved to be a significant corporate asset. It agilely facilitated expansion on site, geographic dispersion, retention of key personnel, and communication across the management hierarchy as well as presenting a favorable facade to a wider public. Similar to Bell Labs, GE grappled with the "psychological problem" of balancing creativity and productivity among its research staff and became convinced that the corporate campus created a context for both ingenuity and profit.[77] As *Business Week* reported in 1955, both AT&T Bell and General Electric attracted and, more important, retained the best

3.10

A view of the GE Electronics Park that appeared in the July 1951 edition of *Architectural Forum*. Note the cluster of men in shirts and ties lying on the lawn slope by the lake—an unimaginable sight before the corporate campus. General Electric expected that the campus context, a new vision of corporate work, would be conducive to creativity and collaboration among its scientists, engineers, and managers.

industrial scientists because "work goes on in a campus-like atmosphere that the brainy youngsters seem to go for" (figure 3.10).[78] In the corporate campus, enterprise and environment apparently coalesced to corporate advantage.

Contemporaneous with the GE Electronics Park, the Johns-Manville Corporation planned and constructed a research center in Bound Brook (now Bridgewater), New Jersey. Not noted for research endeavors but flush with wartime profits, the investment demonstrated the elevated importance of scientists and their inquiries during the postwar era. Although its site design was more modest than either Bell Labs or the Electronics Park, it summarized the identifying components of the corporate campus. More consequentially, the Research Center elaborated the corporate campus as a strategic corporate medium.[79]

Johns-Manville's largest unit was an enormous asbestos manufacturing plant in Manville, New Jersey. Johns-Manville established it in 1912, moving out from New York City in search of cheap, open land with railroad and river access. In 1928 the corporation consolidated its limited research activities at the factory site. Besides the wretchedness associated with unfettered industrial production, Manville displayed the more miserable characteristics of a single-industry town: unpaved roads, substandard housing, spotty public utilities, and poor schools.[80]

Before postwar prosperity and federal grants improved the town of Manville's physical and educational infrastructure, Lewis H. Brown, Johns-Manville's chief executive officer, "recognized the importance of research and engineering in modern business." He planned a research laboratory close to but distinctly removed from the works.[81] The company hired the architects Shreve, Lamb, and Harmon from New York City, well known for its business architecture (including the Empire State Building), and the landscape architects Clark, Rapuano, and Holleran. Brown publicly announced that the project, under construction by September 1945, would be "the largest research facilities in the world devoted to building materials and industrial products development."[82] New Jersey's governor, Alfred Driscoll, dedicated the Research Center on May 24, 1949, but the first building had been up and running by late 1947.[83] *Business Week* reported that the research campus was to "be a star ball carrier in Johns-Manville's drive for the postwar market."[84]

Facing a county arterial, the Research Center sat on 93 acres across the Raritan River from the asbestos works. The complex centered on a long landscaped quadrangle surrounded by laboratory and prototype manufacturing space. (figure 3.11) Similar to Bell Labs, a modular movable system (which Johns-Manville manufactured) formed the lab walls. The administration building, with a cafeteria and outdoor eating facilities, enclosed the front end of the quadrangle and faced the county road. An arcing entry drive led to peripheral parking lots and culminated in an oval turnaround in front of the administration building. Small structures housing mechanical facilities lay outside the parking area.[85]

3.11

The Johns-Manville Research Center, Bound Brook, New Jersey, in 1951. In a classic corporate campus site plan, research buildings surround a central open space with parking and driveways distributed around the periphery, an arrangement of buildings and landscape that continues to be reiterated by corporations. (Courtesy of the Johns-Manville Corporation)

The buildings displayed a similar layout to the Electronics Park: a green quadrangle framed by handsome buildings of gracious proportions surrounded by a spacious pastoral landscape. The simple landscape design retained the few large trees existing on site, clustered groves along the entrance drive and on both long sides of laboratory-prototype manufacturing buildings, framed the principal public facade of the administration building with trees, and covered the rest of the site with lawn. The riparian vegetation along the Raritan River masked the view of Manville and the Johns-Manville plant. From the outset, Johns-Manville expected the site to be completed in stages, and the adaptable campus plan easily accommodated phased construction.

Six years after the opening of the center, Johns-Manville's vice chairman of the board and vice president for research and development, Clifford F. Rassweiler, reported in *Architectural Record* on its success as a corporate research facility. The modular system easily responded to the requisite changes in experimental activities, and the experimental systems built in the prototype manufacturing spaces could move directly into industrial plants. Rassweiler went on to write:

> Before the war ended, it had become apparent that technical personnel of outstanding caliber would be difficult to find and keep in competition with other companies. . . . The site chosen offered good landscaping opportunities and the buildings themselves were designed to be of a character such that the ensemble would resemble a modern college campus. . . .
>
> The company has been amply rewarded for its concern in making the center attractive. In the past two years, turnover of technical personnel has been less than four per cent per year from all causes—an unusually low figure which is a source of pride. Research heads firmly believe that the low turnover is due to making the center attractive to the people the company wanted to have in its research organization. There have been, in addition, public relations and promotional values with both customers and visitors, who see here a buildings materials firm practicing what it preaches.
>
> Also important is the effect the center has on its community. First, employees of both the nearby plant and the center itself are proud of its appearance, and this spirit carries over into the town. Next, the facilities of the center are made available to a wide variety of community groups, who also find the employed personnel invaluable in a surprising number of civic, youth, educational and cultural activities. This of course, redounds to the credit of the company.[86]

Like Bell Labs and General Electric, Johns-Manville consolidated the role of research and development and launched this middle management division through the creation of a corporate campus. The inclusion of prototype manufacturing facilities hastened the adoption of new technology and allowed further retreat of the supervising scientists from industrial sites. This was especially opportune for Johns-Manville because upper management had been aware since the 1930s that asbestos, a primary product material, had mortal health effects.[87] The environment of this early campus shielded corporate scientists, who were working with asbestos as well, from the more toxic conditions of the plant.

As evident from Rassweiler's comments, the campus promoted the corporation as a benevolent entity among local residents, primarily workers in the nearby factory. In lieu of more substantive improvements to labor conditions and worker housing, the campus imparted a civic presence in the local scene in a way no industrial works could. Johns-Manville's campus targeted internal and external audiences for favorable regard through the simple instrument of buildings surrounded by an ample and commodious landscape (figure 3.12).

The completion of Bell Labs, the Electronics Park, and the Research Center set the fundamental plot and ploy of the corporate campus workplace within the managerial capitalist hierarchy. Other similar corporate campuses followed

in the 1950s, but the next key project completed in the postwar era significantly elevated the profile of the corporate campus in the American landscape: the General Motors Technical Center.

The General Motors Technical Center

The General Motors Technical Center transformed the precepts of the corporate campus into an emblem of American business. It changed the aesthetic, scale, and ambition of the corporate campus and, in the process, the scope of corporate building in general. Effusively promoted by General Motors Public Relations, the research facility confirmed to employees, competitors, and the public the corporate mastery of the imperative twentieth-century asset: science. The GM Technical Center signified the commanding stature of the American corporate research, the leverage of modernist design in the American built environment, and the potency of American corporations in the postwar world.

General Motors incorporated in 1908, grouping together a number of smaller automobile makers with the intention that this sustained alliance would prove stable and efficient in the emerging assembly line industrial era. A testing laboratory, set up in 1911, was the first division of the General Motors General Staff, the middle management of GM. Its task was "consulting, advising, fact finding and testing" for GM's manufacturing divisions.[88] The GM middle management corporate staffs that occupied the Technical Center in 1956 were the descendants of this early testing laboratory.

The Technical Center came about because of two GM executives: Charles F. Kettering, director of GM Laboratories, and Alfred P. Sloan, GM's legendary president. Kettering founded the Dayton [Ohio] Engineering Laboratories (Delco) in 1908 and devised an electric self-starter for automobiles. Delco joined GM in 1918, merging with the testing laboratories, and by 1920 Kettering headed the newly formed General Motors Research Corporation, later renamed the GM Laboratories.[89] Until 1925, a factory building in Moraine City, Ohio, housed the Kettering staff, but by 1925 they occupied the annex of the GM headquarters in Detroit, grandly designed by Albert Kahn (figure 3.13).[90] By 1929, the annex was too small, and the laboratories expanded into several floors of a building across the street named the Argonaut Building.[91]

Alfred Sloan, who had become GM president in 1923, carried out over the next two decades a rationalization of corporate management functions that still stands as a model in American business; Sloan effectively invented

managerial capitalism. At the same time that he centralized certain functions such as research and advertising, he decentralized GM's overall organizational framework, allowing relative autonomy to individual manufacturing units of the increasingly diversified corporation.[92] By the 1940s GM wanted to reiterate this decentralized management structure in physically dispersed facilities.[93] Kettering's research success and corporate clout, Sloan's charismatic leadership and decentralized management concept, and the policy of physical decentralization of GM enterprises combined in the broad concept of the Technical Center as a specialized facility outside Detroit's city center.

Decentralization was a logical, and self-serving, end to GM's long-standing promotion of the automobile. But reassessment of its laboratory facilities was also a product of the influx of federal money for research during World War II. As early as 1942, GM management found the "cramped quarters in a congested mid-city community" inadequate for research.[94] During 1944, Sloan and Kettering formulated ideas for the new facility and a concomitant reorganization of what they named the Technical Staffs. Besides research, this included

3.13

The General Motors Laboratories in Detroit designed by Albert Kahn in the 1920s, attached to the back of the corporation's headquarters. This was a much more prestigious location than the industrial works where most corporate researchers worked, yet the building contained only a portion of the research and development staff. By the late 1940s, General Motors had research units scattered all over Detroit and beyond, and it wanted to consolidate its top scientists and engineers into a single place with room for expansion. (Photo by author.)

engineering, styling, and product study groups. (The last became "process development" by the opening of the center). Many of these other activities were spread across Detroit, and Sloan thought they should be brought to a single place outside the city but close to it. Kettering responded to Sloan by proposing a specialized complex built on a new property; Sloan concurred and dubbed the new project the General Motors Technical Center. After deliberation, GM's management determined that the property should be "outside of highly congested areas, near a railroad, twenty five to thirty minutes from the General Motors Building, and adjacent to residential areas." By December 1944, General Motors bought a half section (320 acres) in unincorporated Warren Township north of Detroit.[95] The site sat at the intersection of two section line roads (Mound Road and Twelve Mile Road) in the middle of flat, rural land "thirty five minutes by Cadillac or Chevrolet" from GM's headquarters in Detroit.[96]

The ultimate élan of the Technical Center's design, a departure from any previous research campus or building, resulted from a conscious decision on the part of GM management to pursue "an aesthetically oriented center." GM was famed for the visual design of automobiles, known as "styling." Harley Earl, head of the styling group, insisted the center be designed by an "architect of stature, and aim for a center that would be distinctive."[97] Sloan was persuaded but met resistance from board members who did not see how aesthetic considerations would add to the practicalities of the project. They wanted the center to be designed by GM's own engineers or, at most, an engineering firm. Sloan prevailed after he offered his board assurances that the design would neither interfere with the center's technical efficacy nor significantly increase costs.[98]

This aesthetic approach had precedent. Earlier factory designs by Albert Kahn and the GM Futurama exhibit at the 1939 World's Fair had shown the power of design in projecting GM's image as a modern corporation. Kahn's industrial projects of the 1930s and 1940s used standardized glass and steel members and spare structural detailing. In a Kahn design, siting and massing strikingly articulated the architecture: at the front, landscape wrapped an elegantly elongated administration building; a bridge, often lengthy and lofty, connected the administration building to the manufacturing structures; and, to the rear, files of gleaming factory sheds extended back into the site (see figure 2.7). Kahn acknowledged that his factories went beyond the necessities of industrial production to consider corporate image and self-promotion.[99] Well aware of the value of public relations, GM's pavilion designer for the 1939 New York World's Fair, Norman Bel Geddes, created a scale model of an American city in 1960 reflecting the theme of "The World of Tomorrow." Futurama showed vast green spaces beribboned with streaming highways full of GM automobiles, punctuated by gleaming modern architecture; an enthusiastic and awed public made it the most popular venue at the fair.[100] When GM unveiled plans for the Technical Center in 1945, *Architectural Record* observed, "The much heralded World of Tomorrow seems a bit less ephemeral with this vision of what one corporation promises in the way of research."[101]

Given his long-standing relationship with GM, Albert Kahn probably would have been the architect for the Technical Center, but he had died in 1942. Sloan put Earl, the corporate aesthetician, in charge of finding an architect, and he recommended Eliel Saarinen.[102] Saarinen, the first head of the Cranbrook Academy of Art founded in 1932 in Bloomfield Hills, a pastoral suburb of Detroit, had earned a national reputation as a modernist architect with his design for Cranbrook's first buildings. Saarinen, a Finnish émigré, was a futurist, fully conversant in the discourse of functional design and what he called "organic decentralization," and his idealized goals for architecture and the city meshed with the visions of GM's management. Under the auspices of his faculty position at Cranbrook, Saarinen applied his theory to the 1942 Detroit metropolitan master plan that included Warren as a dispersed urban center, an early example of the rationalist planning common in the postwar years.[103] In *The City*, published in 1943, Eliel Saarinen posited a planning process generated by "data research" and "design research." He presented design research as an activity similar to industrial science in which solutions resulted from careful assessment of experimental data.[104]

In New York on July 24, 1945, Sloan announced GM's intention to build a "huge technical center near Detroit to centralize research."[105] Hailing the new project as part of the abundant promise of the postwar world, Sloan stated, "Modern science is the real source of economic progress. . . . There can be no ceiling on opportunity if science continues to moves forward. It is to accelerate the progress of scientific advancement that the General Motors Technical Center is dedicated."[106] GM's president, C. E. Wilson (Sloan was now chairman of the board), went on to say, "We know by assembling these facilities in a coordinated center, where the environment will be especially favorable for the imaginative type of work, to see a little farther into the unknown and to convert our knowledge into practical products more quickly."[107] Kettering related that the center would house "the most theoretical scientists" and "the most practical workmen," and the gathering of talent would "work undisturbed on their developments with the benefit of the most advanced facilities and counsel of their associates."[108]

Soon after the announcement, *Architectural Record* published the startling designs of the Technical Center; futuristic renderings by Hugh Ferriss emphasized its cutting-edge style. The comparatively staid plans for the Electronics Park and the Johns-Manville Research Center published in the same issue accentuated the Technical Center's design ambition.[109] Eliel Saarinen and his partner, J. Robert Swanson, developed an initial design for the Technical Center on the Warren property. They worked on the project with Eero Saarinen, Eliel's son, who had joined the firm after studying sculpture in Paris and architecture at Yale. Eero Saarinen brought in Thomas Church, the well-known modernist landscape architect from San Francisco whom he had met through William Wurster, a trend-setting modernist architect working in California.[110]

General Motors gave "the Architect freedom in developing forward looking architectural design" to produce "coordinated uniformity of architectural treatment" with a priority of "interior flexibility."[111] The 1945 design centered on a 7-acre lake shaped as a rounded polygon; Eliel Saarinen expected the watery reflections "to give you twice as much for your money."[112] Although most of the buildings were low-rise structures in this early scheme, the 1,000-foot-long administration building extended up several floors and spanned the principal entry to form a monumental gate to the center. A prototype highway around the lake connected four groups of buildings sheathed in metal and glass. A terrace podium level connected the long fronting facades and allowed the cars to enter into ground-level garages. *Architectural Record* assessed that the "obviously whopping investment" will "represent General Motors' latest thinking in area planning and traffic control."[113] Unlike other laboratory campuses, this project was already as expressive as it was practical, as General Motors management had intended from the outset: "If the Technical Center was to be a facility, it was also to be a striking unique symbol."[114]

The commitment to ambitiously modernist design caused the project to halt in October 1946 due to the United Auto Workers' "great postwar strike" and GM's need to focus on expanding production to meet consumer demand.[115] The project resumed in December 1948, but two years later, Korean War materials restrictions caused further delays, compounded with Eliel Saarinen's death in July 1950. Eero Saarinen took over the team that now included the architect-engineers in charge of construction documents, Smith, Hinchman, and Grylls, Detroit's foremost commercial firm, and a leading local landscape architect, Edward A. Eichstedt, to supervise implementation of Church's design.[116]

Eero Saarinen developed a new scheme in lieu of the ultimately unfeasible terrace podium.[117] The design simplified the previous site plan and building design (see figure 1.5). In the final project, five complexes of buildings housed four corporate research and development divisions—styling, engineering, process development, and research—plus the Technical Center's administrative offices.[118] They surrounded a 22-acre central pool, a huge liquid quadrangle. Within the pool, a wall of fountains over 100 feet wide shot water 50 feet in the air to accent the entry drive. General Motors completed and occupied the Technical Center in stages between 1951 and 1956.

A variation on the Kahnian factory organized each building group: an extended office and laboratory structure fronted shop buildings connected by an architectural bridge. The resulting architecture appeared to be spectacularly modernist: glass and panel exteriors structured with steel and clasped with brilliant glazed-brick walls of red, yellow, orange, blue, and black. None of the structures were over three floors, eliminating the need for elevators. This gave the architects the opportunity to design uniquely exquisite staircases in each complex. Infrastructure elements—water towers, building exhausts, and fuel tanks—became sculptural highlights to the architectural massing. The styling auditorium stood alone, a great metallic dome turning one corner of the rectilinear plan. Looping drives linked both the fronts and backs of each building complex, with parking extending around the site's edge (figure 3.14).[119]

Cooperating with GM engineers, the designers contrived a number of new structural systems, some of lasting inventiveness.[120] To achieve the flexibility demanded by the client, the architects applied a 5-foot module "not only to steel construction but also to laboratory, heating, ventilating and fire protection facilities as well as to laboratory furniture, storage units, [moveable] wall partitions and so on, all of which are keyed to it."[121] General Motors considered this "standardization with precision" based on "the know-how of GM's assembly lines applied to industrial construction."[122] This extended pliability of the modular system, first used at Bell, made the Technical Center's laboratory space highly functional for decades to come.[123]

The landscape architecture also exemplified the restrained, functional palette of modernist design. It consisted of a linear bosques, verges of low evergreen planting, rectangles of lawn, and a thick forest planting of uniformly spaced trees encircling the site.[124] Trees girded the western and eastern exposures of the buildings for climate control, an issue intensified by the predominance of glass curtain walls.[125] Four weeping willow islands in the lake stood in counterpoint to the finite rectangle of its immense form. Useful in keeping maintenance costs low, the "strong orderly arrangement" also echoed the precision of the architecture.[126] Eichstedt and Church expected the maturing forest planting to "give the lawns the effect of clearings," a reference to the regional tradition of the prairie school

3.14

The General Motors Technical
Center soon after completion in
1956. The surrounding properties
as yet undeveloped, the Tech
Center extended beyond the
existing suburbs of Detroit.
However spectacular in design,
the site plan followed the typical
pattern of the corporate campus.
(General Motors LLC. Used with
permission, GM Media Archives)

of landscape design.[127] Saarinen hoped that the forest would provide another "unifying device."[128]

Church and Eichstedt intended "the spaces . . . to flow into each other without ostentation. The planting masses provided the outlines of areas that show off the building groups to best advantage from changing viewpoints."[129] In turn, according to Saarinen, the buildings formed "a controlled rhythm of high buildings and low buildings, of glass walls and brick walls, of buildings seen between the trees and buildings open to the square."[130] Their summary effect derived from the stunning combination of the fluent architectural massing, contrapuntal landscape patterning, and the clean reflective surfaces, rebounding coolly off a vast, watery foreground.

3.15
View of the pool and water tower of the General Motors Technical Center. Soon after completion of the Tech Center, the architectural photographer Ezra Stoller took a stunning set of photographs of the site for GM to use in a wide variety of publicity materials and to provide illustrations to the newspapers and journals that published numerous articles about the center. The photographs supported GM's promotion of the corporate campus as an icon of American business and industrial science. (General Motors LLC. Used with permission, GM Media Archives)

The design result was cinematic, more art direction than urban design, exhibiting a supremely dynamic sense of space. In the huge site, dramatic vistas were oblique and did not orient to culminating axial viewpoints (figure 3.15). As a contemporary critic noted, the site "should best flash by a Buick window at 35 mph. The Technical Center site module is a speedometer."[131] This Saarinen apparently intended; he designed the site "at automobile scale . . . to be seen as one drove around the project."[132]

Nevertheless, the pastoral impetus remained in conceiving the campus. As professional literature later reported, the sizable window proportions were "determined not by a standard of 'foot candles at desk level' but by the desire that the innermost draftsman be aware of the leaves of the trees."[133] The glass curtain walls exposed the site's full extent to view. Hence the design aimed "the verdant landscaping . . . inward, through glass, to the employees."[134]

By the Technical Center's completion in 1956, professional design magazines had taken exuberant notice, set off by Ezra Stoller's stunning photographs. *Architectural Forum* lauded "GM's Industrial Versailles" and covered the project's phased progress: "Finally viewed in completion, the inspired architecture of the 25 buildings is a historic symbol of today's industrial progress, also of tomorrow's ambition."[135] *Arts & Architecture* typified the hype: "Elegant and often beautiful, such

Where Today Meets Tomorrow

GENERAL MOTORS TECHNICAL CENTER

details [the glass curtain wall construction], together with exquisitely finished materials, suggest product design and manufacture as much as building. The architect has plainly created an attractive environment that plainly belongs to that part of American society whose values are increasingly determined by manufacturing and marketing techniques. Although the architect's design produces effects unrelated to the company's products, the buildings are a celebration of mass production. As such they have more than architectural significance."[136]

Arts & Architecture realized that General Motors management had a broader and much more powerful audience than Saarinen's fellow architects. The General Motors public relations staff went into high gear, producing reams of descriptive material about every facet of the colossal facility's manifold features and the astounding cleverness of its occupants. It produced two versions of the widely distributed *Where Today Meets Tomorrow: General Motors*

Technical Center—a small, handy booklet and a large, glossy picture book— each lavishly illustrated with photographs, including many of Ezra Stoller's shots of the site and architecture (figure 3.16). The text repeatedly characterized the facility as a vision of the future, the word *tomorrow* capitalized and worked into sentences at every opportunity.[137] The *General Motors Engineering Journal*, a specialized publication targeting engineering and science educators, featured more astonishing photographs, articles by the four vice presidents housed at the center, explanations of the site plan, and details of the unusual architectural elements such as the styling dome and staircases. An entire issue in 1956 made palpable the assertion by GM's president on the opening page that the center was unique "in the world . . . a vital national asset."[138] And GM targeted its own troops as well. *GM Folks*, an internal publication aimed at line employees, devoted an entire issue to the dedication of the center as a source of corporate pride and cohesion.[139]

On May 16, 1956, General Motors opened the Technical Center in ceremonies attended by over 5,000 leaders from industry, education, science, engineering, and the military. Closed-circuit television beamed the opening ceremonies to sixty-two other locations for 25,000 invited participants across the United States and Canada. The speakers were Harlow Curtice, president of General Motors (C. E. Wilson had become secretary of defense in 1953); Lawrence Hafsted, director of research and former chairman of the Atomic Energy Commission; Charles F. Kettering, the emeritus director of research; and President Dwight D. Eisenhower, who participated from the White House over closed-circuit television.

Curtice explained that "the campus-like atmosphere was sought deliberately, not to impress visitors but because we believe that such surroundings stimulate creative thinking and are conducive to good work." He went on to say that "the 'inquiring mind' approach" characterized GM's research, and "this great Technical Center will enable General Motors not only to carry on its tradition of the inquiring mind but even to speed the processes whereby many more new developments may be brought into being for the good of all." Curtice stressed the expanded role of "basic research" for "the benefit of our country and for General Motors." He hoped his audience would "come to regard the General Motors Technical Center as I do—as one of the nation's great resources—more important than the natural resources with which we have been endowed."[140]

Hafsted reiterated Curtice's call for basic research and added, "This wonderful institution which we are dedicating today is much more than a place to work. It is truly a symbol of faith of General Motors management

A brilliant end-wall faces the lake

A restful lobby welcomes the Engineering Building visitor

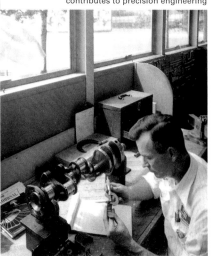

A view of patio and pool contributes to precision engineering

in the future. . . . There can be little doubt that such a magnificent facility as this will substantially contribute to our industrial progress." In full-blown Cold War mode, Hafsted reminded the audience: "We find ourselves in a race with the U.S.S.R. for continuing technological supremacy. . . . Our choice is brutally clear. As a society, we can either learn mathematics and science— or Russian."[141] Kettering was notably more light-hearted than Hafsted—the gizmo guy engineer to Hafsted's serious scientist: "The Technical Center is then after all, a facility. I think of it as a great intellectual golf course where we can go out and practice."[142]

Eisenhower let out all hyperbolic stops. He likened Sloan and Kettering to "frontiersman . . . symbolic of the United States," alluding to Meriweather Lewis and William Clark, Zebulon Pike, Ben Franklin, George Washington, Patrick Henry, Thomas Jefferson, and Abraham Lincoln. He hailed the Technical Center as "a place for leadership furthering new attacks on the technological frontier." Eisenhower asserted, "Beyond that frontier lies better and fuller employment, opportunities for people to demonstrate yet again the value of a system based on the dignity of human beings and on their free opportunities in life."[143]

The Technical Center dedication elicited effusively favorable publicity on the front pages of newspapers and the evening news.[144] *Life* spread six pages of photographs to record its "unusual beauty" under the title "Architecture for the Future: GM Constructs a 'Versailles of Industry.'"[145] *Fortune* noted that unlike other postwar research laboratories that "followed a pattern of ultramodern decor on parklike acres, far from the pressures and distractions of production departments or corporate offices," the Technical Center "conforms to the postwar fashion, but in its wedding of a great modern architect with G.M. engineering it achieves a new serene integration." It then waxed ebullient: "The achievement, which is Saarinen's, is to have held all this advanced technology under admirable control in designing an integrated series of buildings that are modern but not freakish, functional but not barren, imposing but not overblown, clean and cool in line but with an underlying warmth achieved through a bold orchestration and notable architectural use of color."[146] The *New York Times Magazine* described in detail the "campus in Technicolor," a more "pyrotechnic approach to the university atmosphere" than "the huge laboratories maintained by such veterans in the research field as General Electric and Bell Telephone Laboratories."[147] *Business Week* reported on "GM's Showplace for Stepped-Up Research," which brought "focus on the auto industry's lavish expansion in research."[148] All the accounts highlighted the Technical Center's glass and steel facades, brilliant brick, and campus-like setting (figure 3.17).

An article from the *New York Times Magazine* occasioned by the opening of the Technical Center, "Key Men of Business—Scientists," linked the utopian visions of postwar, Cold War America, and the promotion of corporate scientists and their new institution:

> The whole effort is to bring to bear a spectrum of scientific skills interacting
> to unlock nature's secrets and to apply the new knowledge in ways that can
> be translated into new products, materials and services. In the well ordered

3.17

A page from *Where Today Meets Tomorrow* that juxtaposes the three essential elements of the corporate campus: buildings set in a spacious landscape, modernist architecture, and technical facilities. The caption for the photograph of a GM engineer succinctly summarizes the rationale behind the corporate campus. (General Motors LLC. Used with permission, GM Media Archives) research center, all this goes forward in an atmosphere of calm purposefulness that enables the scientist to contribute to the coordinated undertaking without losing his sense of originality and individual achievement. . . .

For these centers are something more than bastions of progress for profit. They are the key to greater comfort, greater security, greater mastery by man of the world in which he lives. On them depends much of the speed with which we advance our standard of living and help other nations toward a brighter economic future.

And they are a vast tool in maintaining the peace—a vast source of brainpower in the time of human need. The Russians have made it clear that they intend and expect to outstrip us in the area in which we have always considered ourselves invincible—production, both of new and more destructive weapons and of all the goods that make for human well-being. Harlow H. Curtice, president of General Motors, reflects the view of most industrialists when he says it is only through facilities in which "talented young men are encouraged to think freely of problems yet unsolved and goals yet uncharted" that we can effectively meet this challenge.[149]

GM's exertions to fix a spectacular public image for the center were useful but also defensive. In 1949 *Architectural Forum* had assured its readers: "Here is an object lesson in what architecture can do on realistic grounds. The achievement is one of thoughtfulness instead of expenditure, of analysis instead of fancy."[150] By 1951 the costs of the engineering building proved so high that the architects had to redesign the styling and process buildings.[151] By 1954 $20 million had became $100 million, with $1 million for planting alone, a figure GM boasted at the center's completion as a point of pride.[152] But *BusinessWeek* astutely observed, "The architects. . . . pinched no penny, and the $100,000,000 cost estimate is surely on the low side."[153] Alfred P. Sloan Jr., in his account of his career at General Motors published in 1963, admitted to a $125 million cost and with an air of justification begins his story on the Technical Center thus: "To understand why it has been a valuable investment for the corporation, easily worth the $125 million, the reader should know something of its story." Sloan ends: "I am satisfied that the decision to provide this aesthetically pleasing and functional center for our technical talents was a sound and desirable one."[154]

After the dedication, GM publicity material, and the press coverage it fostered, consistently referred to the Technical Center as a "campus."[155] In drawing parallels with the creative and nonprofit university environment, GM addressed two key constituencies: rivals in industrial research and the public. By 1956 Bell Labs and its Summit campus dominated corporate science, providing a model imitated throughout American industry. GM could ill afford to ignore the competition, so its publicity aligned its "whopping investment" to vanguard industrial research. Popular qualms about GM's government influence, surfeit of defense contracts, contentious labor relations, and concentrated economic power would only be exacerbated with the apparent extravagance of the Technical Center. The GM "campus" evoked a public and public-minded institution rather than corporate self-indulgence.

The audacious material dimensions of the Technical Center pushed the corporate campus beyond a utilitarian corporate image to outright iconography, a means of creating and conveying ideology. In 1960 Russell Lynes, a sharp social commentator, wrote of the Technical Center in *Harper's:*

> This is what Detroit is really about. Here is know-how; here is the vision of industry; here is tomorrow today—Wednesday on Tuesday. . . . The fact that the Technical Center sits on six hundred [*sic*] acres of flat land and cost $85 [*sic*] million may be significant to General Motors but the architecture of the Technical Center should be significant to everyone. Here is unity with variation, here is consistency without boredom, seriousness without pedantry, function with playfulness. The Dream of Glory was General Motors' but the architect who told them what the dream should look like was Eero Saarinen. . . . In the days when the mansions of Grosse Pointe were built, the businessman's glorification was personal and his house was his expression of triumph. Now his glorification was corporate and it is his company's facade that matters. He doesn't build houses now: he builds whole campuses instead. Corporate ostentation affords the corporate leader the same gratification he once derived from personal ostentation and now he can call it "progress." Did the old tycoons in the Grosse Pointe mansions say: "what is good for me is good for America?" I suppose they did.[156]

The campus's compelling vision ultimately quashed Lynes's underlying uneasiness, and he was not alone. The corporate campus became a superlative vehicle to convince audiences of the social and political benefits of corporate power. It evolved from competitive edge to cultural construction.

No doubt the Technical Center almost tipped the balance between function and aesthetics, but GM's long-standing commitment to styling and the location of the styling group in the Technical Center sustained the logic of its honed design. (According to a GM vice president, the "styling guys" still guard the integrity of the site's design.[157]) While the magnitude of the Technical Center remains unmatched, future corporate campuses did emulate its modernist design, albeit more cost consciously. Yet for all of its showy "world of tomorrow" aesthetic, the Technical Center's site plan reiterated other corporate campus plans: roadways ringed the building complexes, low-rise buildings faced onto a central open space, and parking lots edged the site's perimeter (see figure 1.5). The modularity of the laboratory fixtures facilitated experimental setups, the site allowed expansion, and the prestige of the place attracted engineers and scientists. It met the requirements of flexibility, efficiency, and milieu that made corporate science profitable.

The Corporate Campus in California

As the East Coast and midwestern corporate campuses came to popular and economic prominence, the corporate campus model diffused across the American landscape to California. Southern California had become a center of the aeronautical industry in the 1930s and 1940s, and in the postwar period, it became a hub of defense-related technological research in aeronautics, electronics, computing, and aerodynamics (missiles). Key among the start–up corporations generated by the brisk business of the federal government was the Ramo-Wooldridge Corporation, formed in 1953. One of the founding partners was Simon Ramo, a decade-long veteran of General Electric's electronic research; the other partner, Dean Wooldridge, had been part of Bell Labs. (The partners made the cover of *Time* on April 29, 1957.) Ramo had concluded that GE had lagged in creating an appropriate management culture for advanced research scientists, and that AT&T Bell Laboratories accelerated success through its research administration. He described the optimal corporate research culture as "mixing formality with informality. You have to mix procedures of exchange, of information, of documentation, with means of insuring bypasses and endruns."[158] Not surprisingly, Ramo-Wooldridge completed the first corporate campus in California in 1958 and quickly followed with a second facility in 1960. They are examples of how the corporate campus proliferated through the leadership of top industrial scientists as they moved between leading companies and thus were well aware of the competitive context of industrial research.

The completion of both Ramo-Wooldridge campuses was the charge of Melville Branch, the corporate assistant for planning, who had worked with Norman Bel Geddes on GM's Futurama exhibit and at the U. S. National Resources Planning Board, which had promoted a policy of corporate dispersal. Branch wrote extensively about the connection between facilities and management based on his experience at Ramo-Wooldridge. His writings reveal that the corporate campus was seen as another manifestation of "systems engineering," the execution of complex, multiunit research and development projects, a specialty of Ramo-Wooldridge. For Ramo-Wooldridge, "research and development establishments benefit from a physical integration of structures on the site, reflecting the increasingly close interactions between scientific specializations. . . . This usually means the disposition of buildings on the land so that at least a part of each building is reasonably close to each other . . . to group them around a central mall or common area of use and intercommunications."[159] The plan provided "as much flexibility and expansion as practicable" while establishing "the backbone of the arrangement of buildings, utilities, and circulation which will maintain its efficiency, integrity, and character" as the site was modified. Security concerns, of tantamount importance given the nature of Ramo-Wooldridge's defense work, could be handled in a "relatively [unobtrusive] and pleasant manner."[160] The corporation expected the research and development scientists and engineers to respond "to spatial and visual elements," and the "most important of these is a sizeable window, which not only increases the apparent size of the room but provides an exterior outlook."[161]

The 1958 campus, just south of the Los Angles airport in Hawthorne, followed the basic pattern of its eastern counterparts, with low-rise buildings encircling a central mall, surrounded by circulation and parking. A small expanse of lawn faced the main arterial to the research and development facility, El Segundo Boulevard. The Hawthorne site, while adhering to the fundamental elements of the corporate campus, was located adjacent to a residential area, although much more baldly industrial areas were within sight. Ramo-Wooldridge's second site, in Canoga Park, an upper-middle-class suburb that epitomized affluent postwar suburban southern California, addressed this shortcoming (figure 3.18). The Ramo-Wooldridge Research Laboratories was the first use of research and development zoning in the Los Angeles region, requiring off-street parking and a minimum 100-foot setback for buildings all around the site. Designed by the architect-engineers Albert C. Martin and Associates and the landscape architect Arthur G. Barton, the project was located at the intersection of two arterials within the residential suburb. A rock and

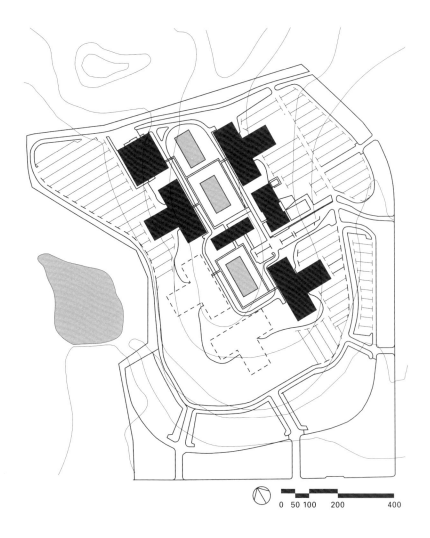

3.18
The Ramo-Woolridge Research Laboratories' corporate campus opened in Canoga Park, California, in 1960. The first example of research and development zoning in California, it introduced the corporate campus model to the American West. Unlike campuses built by established corporations in the Northeast and Midwest, Ramo-Wooldridge was a start-up that emerged as part of the rise of the defense industry in southern California.

0 50 100 200 400

planted berm edged the entire site frontage, "calculated to cut off the view of parking lots from these streets and residences, but allow the buildings to be seen in the distance." The plan for the 86-acre site included eight buildings framing a mall bisected by a central administration building. The complex opened to expansive views of the Chatsworth Reservoir and the Santa Susana Mountains, and the central open space contained planted areas and large glistening pools (figure 3.19).[162] By the time the Canoga Park research and development center opened, Ramo-Wooldridge had merged with Thompson Products, eventually forming TRW, a dominant defense and aerospace technology corporation; this site became its lead research and development center.

3.19
The Ramo-Wooldridge campus
used rock expanses to limit
irrigation costs, but the site
provided researchers
with some remarkable views of
the central quadrangle opening
out onto the Santa Susana
Mountains. (Courtesy of Northrop
Grumman Systems Corporation)

The Ramo-Wooldridge sites introduced the corporate campus model
to the American West and prompted the introduction of research and development zoning in another region of the United States. More significant,
the Ramo-Wooldridge research and development centers demonstrated that
the corporate campus was utterly systematized into corporate management,
serving the purposes of newer, innovation-based corporations, not just well-
established businesses like AT&T, General Electric, and General Motors—a
pattern that became particularly relevant in California where start-up technology corporations concentrated in the postwar era. The need for "offices with
an exterior outlook" for the scientist-engineer had become an unquestioned
part of rational corporate planning in a wide variety of corporate entities.[163]
Tellingly, the Ramo-Wooldridge campuses were financed through lending
institutions, willing to provide the corporation with capital for specialized
research and development facilities because they were a recognized part of the
business landscape.[164]

The Ramo-Wooldridge Research Laboratories campus was hailed beyond the confines of business. The influential urban planners and designers
Christopher Tunnard and Boris Pushkarev singled out the Canoga Park campus in their widely read 1964 book, *Man-Made America: Chaos or Control?*
as exemplary of comprehensively planned metropolitan expansion.[165] Local

IDEAL Suburban Living

Even though the city celebrated its 50th anniversary in 1962, more than three-quarters of Canoga Park homes have been built since 1950, when there were only 2,668 homes. Today the number of homes reaches almost the 20,000 mark. Since Canoga Park offers all the relaxation and informality of Southern California suburban living — with all the conveniences of a tremendous metropolitan area — the excitement of building fine suburban residences continues at an astounding pace.

One of Many Beautiful Local Ranches

As in all heavily populated areas in the nation, the trend is toward the sensibly paced leisurely life of the suburbs. Naturally enough, employment opportunity figures a great deal in the percentage of those who wish to escape the inconvenience of today's crowded metropolitan areas. About one-half of the total population of Canoga Park is employed in the city which, while being an astounding figure compared to many communities, only points out the logic and obvious advantages of living in this growing community.

The Canoga Park Scene — Industry and Fine Homes

4

boosters in Canoga Park included the campus as part of a 1962 promotional brochure used to attract new residents and development to the suburban community (figure 3.20). The Ramo-Wooldridge campus could rival East Coast gentility with West Coast lifestyle.

The Corporate Campus after 1960

By 1960 the term *campus* or *campus-like* became shorthand for corporate facilities in the suburbs that included at least some trimming of green around low-rise buildings. While indicating the extent to which Bell Labs's and GM's campuses were effective in winning plaudits, the term's widespread, and somewhat indiscriminate, use tends to obscure the continuing importance of the corporate campus after the 1950s in attracting top researchers to capitalist enterprises.

IN CANOGA PARK

Residentially speaking, the community has no real dividing lines. Surrounding the area are some of California's most beautiful ranches and older homes of good taste, giving Canoga Park a look and feeling of stability. Within the Community — no jerry-built tracts of endless boredom can be found — only well planned model homes designed and built to take full advantage of the fine natural setting.

For those whose livelihood finds them in the bustle and noise or nearby crowded metropolitan areas during the day, a grateful satisfaction is theirs after a few minutes drive at the end of the day. The clear and beautiful sunsets over the quiet foothills of the Santa Susana mountains lend a certain peacefulness and feeling of home to the residents of Canoga Park.

Central Mall at Thompson Ramo Wooldridge Inc.

5

Adding to this muddle, suburban manufacturing sites continued to house corporate laboratories (many of which generated quite profitable science), and some corporations never adopted the corporate campus model at all. But for many leading American firms, especially the rising tide of technology companies, the corporate campus, formulated in the Northeast and Midwest in the 1940s and 1950s, was a strategic instrument in the competition for research personnel and the fruits of their endeavors.

The importance of the corporate campus site plan, nimble laboratories, and the balance between function and aesthetics is made more obvious when considering two laboratories designed by Eero Saarinen soon after the Technical Center catapulted his architectural career: IBM's 1962 Thomas J. Watson Research Center in Yorktown Heights, New York, and the 1967 AT&T Bell Telephone Laboratories in Holmdel, New Jersey. Under the forceful guidance of the now famous Saarinen (after Saarinen's death in 1963, the work was

3.20

As this spread from a brochure produced by the local chamber of commerce in 1962 illustrates, Canoga Park's suburban neighborhoods, recreation, and the Ramo-Wooldridge research and development campus were integral to "ideal suburban living" in postwar southern California. (Courtesy of the Canoga-Owensmith Historical Society) carried on by his partners Kevin Roche and John Dinkeloo), both research labs departed from the proven site plan of the corporate campus and instead placed large single buildings of self-conscious architectural merit within very large sites. Sheathed in reflective glass, the buildings stood glinting, massive, and seemingly inviolate. Much more akin to the corporate estates housing top management that are discussed in the next chapter, grand entry drives swept through broad landscapes of lawn, trees, and water designed by Sasaki, Walker and Associates, and culminated in large, pooled parking lots. Unlike other corporate campuses, the offices and laboratories had no windows; the glass exterior walls opened only corridors to the surrounding landscape.[166] The labs turned out to be less flexible and efficient, and the casual transference of knowledge that was a hallmark of other campuses was notably absent. In the long term, neither lab generated new science to the extent expected by their corporations, and both labs later abandoned their research role.[167] The Watson Research Center at Yorktown now has a minimal research staff, but as a building named after IBM's founder and built by his son and successor, it remains a symbolic center for the corporation. The Holmdel property has been sold to a developer; not without controversy, the Saarinen building is scheduled for demolition, and the property is to be redeveloped as a mixed-use suburban development.[168]

But in northern California, IBM is representative of how the corporate campus more profitably evolved after 1960. Because it could not seem to attract the many California-trained engineers and scientists to its industrial research facilities in New York State, IBM established a research laboratory in San Jose in 1952, initially housed in a converted print plant in a downtown industrial district (IBM already had a punch card manufacturing plant in town). Forging ahead on the promising notion of the storage of electronic data on disks that could be randomly accessed, the corporation built its first California development in 1958 on a 190-acre former fruit farm in San Jose, anchoring the southern end of what became the Silicon Valley.[169] Facing Highway 101, it was an up-to-date modernist factory that included research facilities in a separate corner of the site, facing the main entrance to the complex on Cottle Road. The architecture, designed by John S. Bolles, recalled the Technical Center: color tile panels articulated low rectangular buildings. The landscape design by Doug Baylis, a former associate of Thomas Church, was quite spare but maintained the existing orchards around the perimeter.[170] The San Jose project reflected the initial influence of the architect and product designer, Eliot Noyes, engaged by IBM president Thomas J. Watson Jr. "to remodel the rather dowdy face IBM turned toward the public."[171] Known as Building 25, the research labs did include "floor to ceiling glass throughout" opening on to patios, "in true California style."[172] While often referred to as a campus because it was more attentive to architectural merit than most other industrial works (and notably more gracious than most other IBM sites at the time), the San Jose site was primarily devoted to production. It contained upward of 2,000 manufacturing workers, and *Factory* magazine awarded it Factory of the Year in 1957.[173]

Soon after, however, IBM formed the Advanced Systems Development Division and peeled off 300 top scientists from the San Jose Research Laboratories. More closely following the corporate campus exemplars of the 1950s, the company ensconced them in what one IBM engineer referred to as a "most attractive redwood building complex" surrounded by a "bucolic setting" in Los Gatos, an upscale residential suburb west of San Jose.[174] The $2.4 million complex designed by Hellmuth, Obata, and Kassebaum assembled cruciform arrangements of offices around main laboratories linked by lushly planted courtyards designed by Lawrence Halprin, who, like Thomas Church, was a leading landscape modernist. IBM executives held that "pauses are as important as the working periods . . . the opportunity for frequent respites by glancing at outdoor vistas is in accord with modern psychological theory on the nature of efficiency." Much of the 80-acre property was undeveloped, and the scientists had ample views of an idealized California landscape, as well as trails leading from the complex into meadows and woodlands.[175] During the 1960s, scientists at the Los Gatos facility conceived of digital photography storage and retrieval systems, cash-dispensing banking terminals, and public transportation fare collection systems based on cards with magnetic strips, among other innovations.[176]

IBM continued to build corporate campuses into the next two decades, each increasingly removed not just from industrial works but from the metropolitan zone altogether (figure 3.21). In 1977, as its software market became as essential as computer hardware, IBM consolidated 2,000 programmers into the West Coast Programming Center (also referred to as the Santa Teresa Laboratory) a few miles south of the 1958 factory site in San Jose. Designed by architects McCue Boone Tomsick Associates and landscape architects SWA Group, it was the first IBM site devoted exclusively to programmers. IBM defined the intent of the new center in this way: "A campus-like cluster of identifiable buildings is desired that blends with the natural environment in a pleasing and reserved fashion. The offices should be conducive to productive and creative work."[177] On a property of over 1,000 acres extending from the edge of the Santa Clara Valley floor up into the Santa Cruz Mountains, the flat 90-acre project site nestled at the base of hillsides covered

3.21

The site plan of IBM Santa
Teresa campus south of San Jose,
California, from the late 1970s.
Surrounded by a thousand
acres of open space, the IBM
site nonetheless reiterates the
corporate campus plan from
the late 1940s.

0 50 100 200 400

3.22

View of the IBM Santa Teresa
campus. At the southernmost
reaches of Silicon Valley, the site
housed IBM's top programmers
and was a particularly elegant
version of the corporate
campus. (Courtesy SWA Group,
photograph by Gerry Campbell)

with seasonal grasses (figure 3.22). Remnant fruit orchards surrounded the parking lots, and buildings clustered around a precise, central quadrangle—actually a roof deck over a large computer facility and library. The building design optimized the number of offices with "outside awareness," an overarching directive set forth by IBM, and carefully organized circulation to maintain building security.[178] The architecture, bold black-and-white banded cruciform buildings "meant to flirt with the landscape," according to architect Gerald McCue, created a "juxtaposition of the man-made form and colors to nature's."[179] The site displayed a taut, distilled, almost ethereal design of crisp concrete and lawn geometries against rolling California coastal grasslands. However exquisite the design, the essential components of corporate campus—circulating drive, multiple peripheral parking lots, buildings around a central open space—remain. By 1986 IBM completed the Almaden Research Center (ARC) for 800 research employees, mostly Ph.D.s in chemistry, computer science, engineering, mathematics, and physics (figure 3.23). Farther up into the same California hills as the Santa Teresa lab, ARC's 650 acres

3.23
IBM's Almaden Research Center in the hills above the Santa Clara Valley. Framed by hundreds of acres of pastoral hillsides, it is the latest home of IBM's premier California-based research and development staff that started out housed in a converted print plant in San Jose in 1955.

border a 1,600-acre county park, and all three properties are together managed as wildlife habitat.[180] Completely removed from the dense, congested, and smoggy Santa Clara Valley below, ARC lies in splendid pastoral isolation.

The corporate campus continues to be a mainstay of corporate building. The Boeing Longacres Campus in Renton, Washington, designed by building architects Skidmore, Owings, and Merrill and landscape architects Peter Walker and Partners, is a work still in progress, with three of a projected nine buildings complete (figure 3.24) The site plan updated familiar idioms with current concerns. Boeing was not fully aware when it bought the property that the site contained federally protected wetlands.

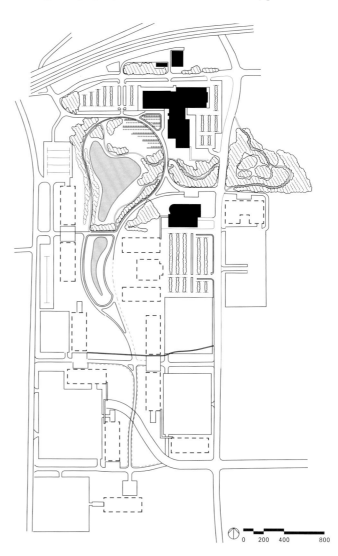

3.24

The site plan of Boeing Longacres Park in Renton, Washington. With three of twelve planned buildings completed, an ecologically correct wetland forms the central open space, though the corporate campus site plan remains the same.

Building from this constraint, the central open space became an extended, enhanced wetland, surrounded by native woodland. Although the landscape architect added another narrative to the landscape design—regionally typical orchards of apple trees oriented to call attention to a distant view of Mount Rainier—the constructed wetland formed the centerpiece of the site. The design team recommended, and Boeing agreed, that the corner of the site closest to Interstate 405 be open to views into the wetland area and that an interior drive would lead visitors along the wetland edges.[181]

The apparent story of Boeing Longacres Park is of environmental responsibility, of abiding by, even extending beyond, environmental regulations for the public good, of literally having environmental concerns at the core of corporate life. Yet in the same year that construction began at Longacres, *Fortune* designated Boeing as one of "the 10 laggards" in an "environmental scorecard," assessing the $30.4 billion company with $552 million in profits this way:

> Has insipid two line environmental policy statement; sets few numerical goals for reducing waste and pollution; hazardous waste disposal is rising, not falling; shipments of solid waste to landfills nearly doubled from 1989 to 1992; releases of toxic chemicals increased since 1987; toxic releases, adjusted for sales, are worse that the aerospace average; failed to achieve interim goal of 33% reduction of chemicals targeted in EPA's voluntary program.[182]

The Campus, the Corporation, and the City

The corporate campus so skillfully meshed the pragmatic and the prestigious that corporate management, scientists, and even the wider public came to believe that the campus milieu, particularly its ambient landscape space, was part and parcel of technological discovery. General Motors's *Where Today Meets Tomorrow* included a photograph of a GM scientist, hard at work, captioned: "A view of the patio and pool contributes to precision engineering" (see figure 3.17).[183] An extraordinary claim on scrutiny, it testifies that the landscape's "favorable influence" (to use an Olmstedian phrase) fully and unself-consciously permeated corporate capitalist science. Such an assumption underlies the proliferation of corporate campuses from Summit to Silicon Valley and beyond, the quintessential environment of twentieth-century technological research. Without a doubt, scientists solidified their corporate standing and public prominence with their relocation to the corporate campus.

Whatever its actual role in innovation, the corporate campus marked an irreversible threshold in the ongoing process of decentralization that has long shaped American cities. The corporate campus's unqualified success in attracting and retaining prized research personnel defined a new kind of suburban pastoral workplace and initiated the broad expansion of white-collar work away from traditional urban cores. By developing an exclusive suburban facility for corporate management, the corporate campus paved the way for the expansion of the other management environments of the urban periphery: corporate estates and office parks. Like the corporate campus, these development types used the landscape both to signal environmental prestige and retain targeted employees.

By adding places of white-collar employment to the suburbs, corporate campuses materially spurred American urbanism toward a dispersed, multifocal geography. Many corporations first established suburban sites for research and development and, with their success, shifted their headquarters as well.[184] In 1976, the sociologist William Whyte roundly criticized the postwar exodus of corporate management from downtowns and noticed that "moveout companies tend to be among the most technically oriented and to have a high quotient of engineers in management."[185] The corporate campus, by advancing the corporate estate, helped precipitate the retreat of top management from the city center.

Like the corporate campus, the corporate estate removed prized personnel—top management—to the suburbs and used the landscape to reinforce their status. In two seminal projects, corporate campuses provided the precedents for their design. General Foods, the first Fortune 500 company to leave Manhattan and relocate to the suburbs, scouted Summit as a possible location and retained Voorhees, Walker, Foley, and Smith to design its new headquarters. After seeing the Technical Center, the chairman of Deere & Company hired Eero Saarinen to design a new corporate office in Moline, Illinois. The definitive Deere & Company Administrative Center became the exemplar for the succeeding profusion of corporate estates in urban peripheries, as will be discussed in chapter 4.

The corporate campus also spurred the appearance of the research park. A version of the office park, the research park catered to industrial laboratories. Research parks required ample landscape perimeters around each lot, limited building heights, constricted lot coverage, and off-street parking, and strictly prohibited industrial features such as smokestacks. Initially sponsored by speculative developers and academic campuses interested in producing revenue and forming close relationships with emerging industries, research parks repackaged the essentials of the corporate campus for tenant research divisions of corporations. This will be discussed in chapter 5.

More subtle but no less telling, the corporate campus created a new rhetorical device for American businesses. As the historian Paul Venable Turner concluded of the university campus, "buildings set in the landscape" have "been a vehicle for expressing the utopian social visions of the American imagination," revealing "the power that a physical environment can possess as the embodiment of an institution's character."[186] Corporations of extraordinary power appropriated the symbolic forces of this ideal embodiment to portray a "corporate soul" and promote business as a purveyor of progressive cultural values.[187] The corporate campus humanized, sanitized, and glorified the corporate endeavor by invoking seductive American themes.

This was not an ephemeral magazine ad, but a place you could pass by, visit, walk around, and work in. Its purpose was to valorize the industrial scientist and validate the use of science for profit by asserting the pastoral ideal. To remain unswayed by the manipulative setting of the corporate campus required an acutely resistant mind-set. In persuading an admittedly receptive populace, the corporate campus reshaped the American city. Far from incidental to the ongoing process of decentralization, the corporate campus was the considered and influential invention of the most potent American corporations.

4

THE CORPORATE ESTATE
"Out of the city . . . and into the trees"

In the structure of managerial capitalism, top management was the keystone in the whole corporate organization. Corporate chiefs bore the ultimate responsibility, and reward, for increasing corporate valuation, as measured by revenues, profit margins, dividends, capital assets, and stock prices. Before the advent of the modern corporation, business owners routinely oversaw production facilities directly; the adoption of managerial capitalism removed top executives from day-to-day operations of corporations, delegating responsibility down the corporate hierarchy. As a result, executive offices no longer needed to remain physically proximate to middle and lower management offices and manufacturing plants. Capitalizing on this flexibility, corporations could distinguish top management in separate, preferred facilities.

Prior to 1945, some managerial capitalist corporations had moved their corporate headquarters to central business districts where they leased or, more rarely, constructed their own office buildings. In the city center, they had ready access to collaborators in capitalist enterprise: banks, insurance companies, stock brokerages, and large institutional and individual investors. They also could draw on the largest pool of top-flight managerial and professional labor. While some corporations still housed their executive offices in or near manufacturing plants at the end of World War II, many postwar corporate headquarters gathered together in central business districts in the largest cities. At the same time, the option to move to the urban edge emerged. For a few, the glimmering greenness of the periphery outshone the advantageous proximities of the central business district, and these corporations bought land and built their own executive facilities in the suburbs.

By the mid-1960s, a distinctive scheme had come to characterize the new suburban headquarters: low-rise modernist buildings centrally set within sites of 200 acres or more, grand entry drives culminating at reception lobbies, prominent water features, parking lots invisible to passing motorists and executive offices, and an encompassing pastoral landscape replete with sweeping vistas. These opulent projects garnered extensive media attention that drew parallels to historic estates and touted the complexes as "corporate villas," calling the new generation of executives "the Medici of our time." Observers recognized that the goals of such costly projects extended well beyond the necessities of efficient, productive workplaces.[1]

The aesthetic strategy of the new headquarters was part of the managerial imperatives of the corporation, especially the careful orchestration of corporate image. Corporations were no longer confined to the manufacture and sale of commodities; they had to market themselves in several ways. First, they had to impress investors and banks on the merits of notoriously inscrutable assessments of future performance and corporate trustworthiness. Second, they had to attract and retain the skilled senior executives who coordinated and directed diversified enterprises in a fiercely competitive environment. Third, as corporate divisions splayed out both geographically and functionally, with an increasing number of managerial specializations, employees' identification with the company became essential to counteract inclinations to view the corporation as an alienating and incomprehensible organization. Finally, the broad public viewed giant capitalist corporations as suspicious, even threatening, and their fears had to be allayed.[2]

The new suburban headquarters, like central city skyscrapers, were powerful symbols of corporate presence and financial weight to impress potential investors. The new facilities performed as a means of retaining personnel and reflecting the high status and market value of the new managerial elite. The emplacements resiliently accommodated incremental expansion of top management facilities while maintaining their aesthetic integrity. The corporate headquarters transformed the corporation into an identifiable place, creating a tangible corporate persona. This symbolic center became a source of esteem for an array of employees, as well as neighboring communities. The estates' abundant and multifaceted aesthetic pleasures provided a surprisingly convincing bulwark against unlovely capitalist realities—from cut-throat strategizing in boardrooms to distant environmental destruction. The new headquarters crafted a consummately effective corporate image that addressed disparate, even opposite, audiences: local and global, internal and external, the hoi polloi and the power players.

The headquarters did so by conjuring together two "aesthetic handles": the estate and the pastoral.[3] Their design invoked the enduring typology of the estate, indeed the villa, as an expression of power that, as James Ackerman acknowledges, "reinforces and justifies the social and economic structure and its privileged position within it while obscuring its motivation from itself and others."[4] Like its aristocratic antecedent, the new corporate estate was a manifestation of "intense, programmatic investment of ideological goals."[5] The scale and opulence of the sites testified to an incontrovertibly prestigious status and as a lavish stand-in for myriad dispersed properties. These buildings provided occasion to promote modernist architecture and exalt modernist architects, to share in the zeitgeist and cultural capital of the builder as artist. Most essential, the corporation became associated with patronage rather than mere ownership. By invoking this established ideology of beneficence, the corporate estate provided a potent instrument to mark ascendant American corporations with worldly distinction.

Concomitantly, the sites' vast and generous pastoral landscape cashed in on a different, less snobbish kind of cultural capital. They were impressive yet readily and wholly understood by American audiences, showing that gigantic corporations could live within the traditional compass of native values. That these landscapes held within them carefully placed modernist buildings, camouflaged expanses of automobile parking, and complex infrastructure embodied what Leo Marx calls "sentimental pastoralism" that "denies or masks the power of hostile [technological] forces that would impede the realization of the pastoral ideal." [6] In so doing they provided a broadly resonant alternative to the unmitigated modernity of the city skyscraper.[7]

The inventive transformation of what had been an apogee of the life of leisure and an emblematic cultural ideal into the locus of busy, unrepentant capitalist enterprise resulted from concerted effort, not forgone conclusion. Since hagiographic journalistic accounts of individual projects are ample but scholarly inquiry scant, the singular circumstances, risky strategies, and complex purposes involved in the transformative invention of these new corporate environments have been elided at best. The genre of the corporate estate evolved through the three defining projects:

the 1954 General Foods headquarters, the 1957 Connecticut General Life Insurance Company headquarters, and the 1964 Deere & Company Administrative Center.

General Foods, as the urban historian Kenneth Jackson notes, "began the outward trend in earnest" and provided a conceptual and design prototype.[8] The corporation followed the most common pattern of corporate exodus by abandoning the central business district for a prestigious suburban community. Connecticut General similarly abandoned a central business district but sought rural surroundings in the quest for efficient, horizontal work space and an encompassing ambiance designed to compensate for the loss of urban enticements. The resultant headquarters first brought together a high-modernist building and an expansive, nostalgic landscape—an abiding combination. Deere & Company left behind not a central business district but a central city industrial swath, a less acknowledged, but equally typical, pattern of executive exodus. The new Administrative Center meshed together a pastoral landscape and architectural modernity. The corporation placed the Administrative Center at the core of its corporate iconography and thus manifested the capacity of the corporate estate to act as an explicit vehicle for corporate communication and self-promoting corporate representation.

The Deere & Company Administrative Center became the exemplar for the succeeding profusion of corporate headquarters at the urban periphery. Following Deere's lead, corporations justified their copious investments by explicating their corporate estates as linchpins of intricate business relationships with employees, neighbors, stockholders, competitors, and bankers. Like the Administrative Center, subsequent corporate estates interfused building and site, concealed infrastructure, and presented carefully composed combinations of modernist buildings and pastoral landscapes.

Precedents

After 1920, as new industrial development took place chiefly in peripheral zones, suburban plants contained administrative buildings and sometimes corporate headquarters as well. Increasingly discrete from adjacent factories, these administrative or corporate offices began, by the 1940s, to appear in architectural literature as a separate building type, worthy of special design consideration. In the factory context, these buildings had to appear, if not prestigious, then suitably polite. Both *Architectural Forum* and *Progressive Architecture* singled out the Hershey Metals Products Headquarters building in Ansonia, Connecticut, completed in 1945, to exemplify this trend toward "a fresher approach."[9] *Architectural Forum* commented:

"This building successfully avoids the arbitrary planning and dull monumentality usually found in headquarters buildings for industrial groups. . . . As the plant is located near worker homes, an attempt was made to improve the appearance of the whole group by unity in architectural and landscape design."[10] These factory headquarters began to deploy such niceties as sweeping entry drives through ample, gently graded front landscape of turf and trees and large but confined parking lots placed away from the front facade.

By the 1940s, many small-scale insurance offices had moved from the central business district to residential suburbs as well.[11] These unassuming buildings were set within a few acres of landscaped property, adjacent to or within neighborhoods, in order to "fit pleasantly into a residential area . . . with familiar materials and with reliance on good taste and good proportions."[12] By the early 1950s, these insurance offices had spearheaded relocations from the central business district to suburban sites.[13] *Business Week* reported the reasons for these moves out of New York:

> (1) There's just not enough downtown space in the right places, and it doesn't look like there will be; (2) rents and real estate prices on good locations look prohibitive, especially to smaller companies; (3) the commutation problem is getting worse; (4) it's getting harder to hire first class personnel to work in some of the more unsightly, congested New York areas; (5) management thinks workers will be happier looking at trees instead of grimy buildings and listening to birds instead of honking taxis.[14]

The pioneer insurance offices had mostly female clerical staffs, a need for efficient paper processing, and limited purchasing and sales activities that made downtown locations essential.[15] The ensuing estates would reflect the parameters of the smaller enterprises. General Foods succeeded several pioneer insurance companies in moving to White Plains from New York City and, like them, emphasized congruence with the existing suburb. Like its lesser competitors, the insurance giant Connecticut General went to the suburbs in search of efficient paper-processing space for its overwhelmingly female staff.[16]

Nonetheless, the most salient antecedent of the corporate estate is the corporate research campus discussed in chapter 3. The expansive, costly, and purpose-built campuses integrated sizable landscapes with large low-rise buildings. The campuses had already confronted the challenge of developing an appropriate suburban facility for the higher echelons of corporate management. Their design used the landscape to signal environmental prestige and retain a targeted employee group—scientists lured from university campuses and competing industrial laboratories. The setting sold the corporation, a lesson not lost on the owners and designers of the corporate estates. In two cases, the link between the corporate research campus and the corporate estate is explicit: the architect of the Bell Labs went on to design the General Foods headquarters, the first corporate estate, and the architect of the General Motors Technical Center subsequently designed the Deere & Company Administrative Center, the most influential model of the corporate estate.

The design schemes of the factory headquarters, pioneer insurance buildings, and corporate campuses all contained integrated landscape spaces and employed a common, if occasionally diluted, pastoral in their articulation. Their significance lies in the inclusion of landscape for a new purpose: corporations considered the designed landscape essential to the functioning of their management facilities. The corporate estate transformed the pastoral of these prototypes into an intensified, bucolic idyll, at once familiar and new.

Inventing the Idea: General Foods

The move of General Foods, a Fortune 500 company, from Manhattan to White Plains in 1954, augured the new concept of the corporate estate. Since 1921, General Foods had occupied leased offices at 250 Park Avenue that the company had expected to accommodate its needs "almost indefinitely." By 1937 the company had taken over "more and more floors" within the office building, and by 1945 it had expanded to 383 and 385 Madison Avenue.[17] The 1,300 corporate employees were now housed in three buildings, and the company expected expansion into even more buildings and floors given the rapidly expanding economy. By any standard, the office arrangement was inefficient and probably counterproductive, but the corporation could not find better quarters in Manhattan. By 1949 the company established a committee to "explore every aspect of the problem."[18]

Initially the committee cast a wide net, considering the Midwest sites of General Foods manufacturing plants and other distant locations.[19] But in the end, the corporation's long-standing banking partners in New York and the city's pool of qualified personnel dissuaded the company from locating outside the metropolitan area. Nonetheless, the task force considered Manhattan itself to be saddled with significant "discomforts caused by dirt, dust, noise, and the ever increasing problem of traffic congestion."[20] In addition, the concern to avoid atomic "target areas" as a result of the increase in civil defense activities probably also influenced the decision to leave New York's central business district. [21]

The corporate task force considered Long Island City, Brooklyn, Staten Island, the Bronx, and Hoboken but found that their "partly industrial" character "would not suit our needs." The task force then focused on "the perimeter of the metropolitan area," considering the suburban communities of Garden City and White Plains, both in New York; Summit, New Jersey; and Stamford, Connecticut.[22] All were connected to New York City by rail and contained commercial centers to provide shopping and basic services. Each of these communities was what might be termed a country club suburb: upper middle class, devoid of obvious ethnicities, near the estates of the very rich, attended by golf courses, and ideally pastoral. None of these places had seen the full impact of suburbanization: functioning farms remained interspersed among pockets of residences, adjacent parkways had not yet become expressways, and nearby countryside was still the venue for Sunday outings. This was the rural edge as much as the suburban fringe.

Significantly, Summit was the location of AT&T Bell Laboratories, designed by the architects Voorhees, Walker, Foley, and Smith and the landscape architects the Olmsted Brothers. During the period when General Foods moved from Manhattan, the eventual corporate president, Charles G. Mortimer, was implementing the strategy of managerial capitalism and used the occupation of the new building as an opportunity to extend a decentralized corporate structure.[23] The new headquarters paralleled both the management concept and the environmental context of Bell Labs, and, unsurprisingly, Voorhees, Walker, Foley, and Smith became the architects and landscape architects for the new General Foods suburban establishment.

White Plains, north of New York City in Westchester County, "won out as the best of the perimeter locations."[24] Like most other corporations contemplating a development project, General Foods hired an intermediary consultant to scout out possible locations and avoid land speculation. In White Plains, William L. Butcher, the chairman of the local County Trust Company, helped the process of site selection considerably, advantageously connecting General Foods's secret representatives with local politicians, particularly Edwin G. Michaelian, mayor of White Plains.[25] After the war, Butcher and Michaelian had set about attracting what they termed "depression-proof industries" to Westchester County, specifically targeting insurance companies.[26] A quarter of a century later, after the county had become nationally known as the home of numerous corporate headquarters, Michaelian described the General Foods deal as "the real breakthrough."[27] As described in chapter 2, the evolution of the corporate estate in Westchester County began as a fiscal compromise to maintain, as much as possible, an uncluttered, bucolic, nineteenth-century elite landscape threatened by the dissolution of the upper-class estate and the loss of their hefty taxes revenues yet increasingly burdened by the costs of public services demanded by the ever increasing numbers of suburban home owners. This concurred with General Foods's desire to build in a location with prestige that was markedly not industrial. In this milieu, the corporate estate of low-rise buildings, arcing entry drives, and pastoral landscapes is a recognizable iteration of the landscapes it replaced.

On January 12, 1951, General Foods announced to its employees that the company had taken an option on a parcel in White Plains just within the city limits.[28] Dense woods covered half of the 46-acre former farm edged along one side by the Central Westchester Parkway, soon to become an expressway extension of the New York Thruway. The tract was also next to a city ballpark and two hospitals, St. Agnes Hospital and the New York Hospital, a site Frederick Law Olmsted had designed in the previous century. The sloping property had views of the surrounding rolling woodlands. The General Foods management presented the site to its employees in a brochure that declared, "We're Sitting Pretty." An aerial photograph pointed out nearby woods and lakes, with the new headquarters as part of a community built among the trees.[29]

Purchase of the property by General Foods depended on a zoning reclassification to allow the new development. Although *Business Week* reported that "natives of Westchester are happy about the whole thing," this was far from the case.[30] Michaelian, who became county executive in 1958 and guided Westchester's development through the 1960s and early 1970s, presided as mayor over the rezoning hearing, which he later recalled as the most contentious of his career.[31] Nevertheless, the Common Council approved the rezoning, though with restrictions, on June 4, 1951, and on June 6, the General Foods board of directors authorized the land acquisition and funds for the building design.[32]

As a first priority in working with Voorhees, Walker, Foley, and Smith, the General Foods engineers "agreed very early in the proceedings that the building should in effect 'crown the hill' thus assuring the availability of vistas for all sides of the structure."[33] The engineers intentionally maximized "all possible desirable views" out from the new complex.[34] The building had to conform to the 45-foot height limit, setback requirements, and off-street parking provisions imposed by the city's development restrictions. The resulting 357,000-square-foot complex was a "low, rambling, earth-hugging type of construction" of three buildings: a main south building and two wings, east and west, forming a U around a central courtyard formally planted with a short allée and flowering trees (figure 4.1).[35]

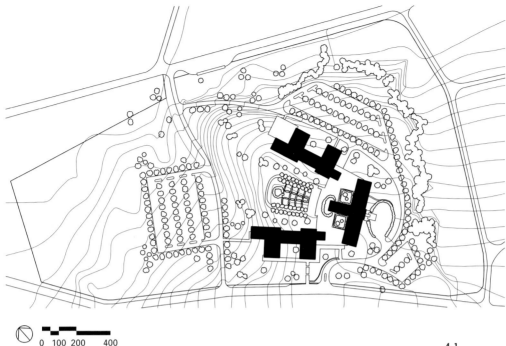

0 100 200 400

4.1

The site plan of the General Foods Headquarters, While Plains, Westchester County, New York, which opened in 1954. Although other corporate estates would be more distinguished in terms of landscape and building architecture, the site plan would essentially be the same: an entry drive, a centrally set complex of buildings in a large, primarily green site, and two large blocks of parking. Like all other corporate estates, the social milieu of the new suburban headquarters was noticeably upscale, devoid of obvious ethnicities, and very distant from any suburban industrial zone.

A driveway extended from the widened and realigned North Street on the west side of the site and ended on an oval turnaround in front of the south building. Two large parking areas, one downslope on the east, the other farther downslope on the north, accommodated 650 cars, enough for half of the employees as the company initially expected most would take public transit. [36] The construction mostly removed the existing woods, but the site design preserved a perimeter of trees on the southern and eastern sides of the site, with smaller groves to the west and north, as well as a "few good specimen trees" where possible.[37] Lawn covered what landscape space remained.

The steel frame building itself employed the most up-to-date mechanical and electrical systems, including air-conditioning.[38] The buildings' exterior finishing, according to the corporate engineers, "was the subject of a great deal of discussion." After discarding stone as too costly, the company settled on a conventional brick veneer, common in many of the buildings designed by the Voorhees firm. The company pointedly decided against a modernist glass and steel aesthetic in order to not appear too incongruous with the colonial and colonial revival styles of the prevailing local architecture, a savvy decision in light of its lukewarm reception in White Plains.[39]

Although the landscape had a modest conception, it was a major marketing point in the corporation's effort to retain employees and get them to follow the company to White Plains. Besides including various financial incentives, the concerted campaign described the move as "out of the city . . . and into the trees."[40] In publications directed to employees, sketches of the proposed building always included encircling trees, and the site's descriptions repeatedly mention views of wooded areas.[41] The 1952 brochure, "GF Moving Day and You," emphasized the "spacious" character of the building and site, the opportunity to provide natural light with "the absence of other people's skyscrapers," and the cafeteria with "a pleasant outlook over gardens and hills." The shallow building footprint provided one window per two employees—to provide "a job with a view," in the words of a *Business Week* article describing the move.[42] Charles G. Mortimer, the president of General Foods, in his speech to employees on their arrival in White Plains in March 1954, pointed to the new office's efficiency, comfort, and natural lighting; in-house cafeteria; ample parking; and the landscaped site in which "we shall . . . find ourselves working in a parklike setting and a more peaceful atmosphere with reduced nerve strain on everyone."[43] The company plainly hoped that the views and surroundings would compensate for the disruption and change brought about by the move. The May 1954 *GF News* declared on page 1:

> And for the first time ever they [General Foods headquarters employees] have a new home designed and built to fit their needs, with comfortable working and living space, and a view of the wooded hills of Westchester County. The move has brought many changes, some immediately welcomed—like a chance to stroll on tree-lined paths at noon—and some that will take a little getting used to—like the distance from the big city.[44]

The campaign proved effective, and General Foods lost only 140 of its 1,200 employees.[45] Thirteen years later, Mortimer boasted of low turnover rates, an explicit goal of the suburban relocation.[46]

The architectural restraint, central courtyard, and self-contained site planning of the new headquarters recall the laboratory campuses of the postwar years, of which Voorhees was a specialist.[47] Yet the complex was notably more prominent than the laboratory campuses, with its bulky, ostentatious massing and eye-catching venue (figure 4.2). On completion of the complex, *Fortune* dubbed it "imposing."[48] By 1957, once the New York Highway Authority revamped the Cross Westchester Parkway into the Cross Westchester Expressway, an extension of the New York Thruway, the office building, perched on its hill at a curving interchange, became readily apparent. The building was an unprecedented element in suburban

4.2
The General Foods Headquarters
after the completion of the Cross
Westchester Parkway, a section
of the New York Thruway, and
an expansion of the original
buildings with a new arcing
structure facing the highway.
The new highway made the site
even more noticeable, while also
connecting the headquarters to
the larger metropolitan region.
The corporation also significantly
extended the parking lots as the
corporation needed to provide
more parking as the staff grew
and as a greater percentage of
employees drove to work. One
of the significant advantages of
large suburban sites was room for
expansion. (Courtesy of Westchester
County Historical Society)

Westchester that placed a dramatic architectural and landscape image along a road-way traveled by increasing thousands of cars a day in the country's most important metropolitan region.[49] As *Fortune* noted soon after completion of the Thruway, "Industrialists are increasingly aware of the felicity of their positions along the new highway."[50] By 1964, a north building enclosed the courtyard and presented to the highway a huge arcing sweep of building facade faced in white marble.[51]

In a 1967 *Fortune* interview, Mortimer expressed complete satisfaction with the decision to leave Manhattan for White Plains.[52] However costly the move (besides all the employee subsidies and new taxes, the corporation had to hire new staff—gardeners, motor pool, building engineers and maintenance, and the entire restaurant crew), the corporation found more benefits than accounting alone could tote.[53] No longer a central business district tenant, the corporation commanded its own domain and expected its employees would become local property owners as well. General Foods in White Plains was a corporate reflection of the idealized, and much promoted, suburban strivings of their employees. [54]

Although the 1954 General Foods headquarters can be seen as a derivative of corporate laboratory campus, with a staid landscape and architectural conception, its overt attention to creating an impressive public facade anticipated the more grandiose conceptions of the corporate estates in the years to come. Subsequent versions of the corporate estate were more expansively executed, but the basic site plan scheme of General Foods—a low-rise, centrally sited building; entry drive; two large parking lots peripheral to the building's entrance facade; an enveloping landscape setting—remained the same. Following General Foods, the conviction that suburban headquarters would deliver spatial self-sufficiency, employee loyalty, public favor, and competitive prestige drove the corporate estate's ever more generous configurations.

The Modernist and the Pastoral: Connecticut General Life Insurance Company

The 1957 headquarters of Connecticut General Life Insurance Company, built in the countryside near Bloomfield, Connecticut, redefined the architectural character and landscape scale of the corporate estate. Since the 1920s, the corporation had occupied an office building in the well-established insurance center of downtown Hartford. It expanded that office in 1938, but by 1947, with a doubling of its insurance business to over $2 billion, the company began a process of space assessment. Under the leadership of president Frazar B. Wilde, the corporation took a cue from the efficiency models that had transformed industrial production decades earlier and were already influencing insurance management. Connecticut General reconceived the processing of insurance records as a huge, horizontal, factory-style enterprise.[55] According to Wilde, the corporation then underwent

> a period of painful appraisal of its proper location in metropolitan Hartford. . . . We did not emerge from this analysis of our problem without confusion and with complete conviction. In close balance of the pros and cons our decision to move was influenced in the end more by the need for land than any other single factor. The need for land arose out of our conception of what would be the most efficient home office plan. . . . What acreage does is to permit future expansion with a minimum of building difficulties and to provide employee facilities, especially parking, on a basis which is normally not possible in a more central location.[56]

The corporation determined that the only suitable site for this horizontal processing was a relatively unrestricted suburban location. By 1950 it had purchased a 280-acre parcel of countryside in Bloomfield, a small community 5 miles outside Hartford.[57]

A firm believer in extensive committee deliberation and action, Wilde determined that the design team would have to be able to work closely with representatives of the corporation and himself, the self-admitted "majority of one" in the chain of corporate command.[58] In 1953, after a year's selection process, the corporation chose the architecture firm of Skidmore, Owings, and Merrill, with Gordon Bunshaft and William S. Brown in charge of the building design, Joanna Diman as the in-house landscape designer, and Isamu Noguchi as the artist of sculptural and landscape elements. Bunshaft and Brown were fresh from the enormous critical and corporate success of Lever House in Manhattan. Bunshaft, in particular, was popularly known as a "stubborn, top flight designer . . . who keeps one eye cocked on Corbusier's concern with related forms, the other on Mies van der Rohe's precise, modular construction." Though Wilde did not like modernist architecture, he was convinced as a "good insurance man" that the high modernist design, indeed a sophisticated abstraction of the industrial factory, would deliver "flexibility, high-grade materials for low maintenance, and qualities of beauty and humanity that would attract and hold clerical employees (mostly young women) in labor short Hartford."[59] At the same time, Wilde was a famed hiker of New England wildlands and "an ardent naturalist" who wanted to "prevent the destruction of wildlife cover on the Bloomfield site."[60]

Wilde feared that in the rural move, he would lose many of his employees, particularly the 1,200 young, unmarried, high school graduates who composed not only the majority of the 1,600 women employees but also of the 2,000 total employees. As *Fortune* characterized it, "The original feminine reaction to the site: 'Bloomfield? Why there are cows out there!'" He compensated by planning an unprecedented set of employee amenities. As reported by *Fortune*:

> In or around the building will be: a large cafeteria, snack and soda bar, ping-pong tables, shuffleboards, barbershop, beauty parlor, cardroom, lounge, game room, ice-skating pond (with swans in the summer), variety store, lending library (with record section), pickup, order, and delivery service (for dry cleaning, shoe repair, flowers, and groceries), gas station (for general service and minor repairs), 400-seat auditorium, twelve bowling alleys, two softball diamonds, four tennis courts, six horseshoe pits, lawn games, picnic grounds with barbecue pits, and a quiet room for noontime meditation.[61]

In addition, the company initially paid half the cost of bus travel to and from Hartford because most of its clerical workers did not own cars.[62] Like the welfare capitalist factories from earlier in the century, the corporation provided an astounding scope of amenities to its employees, in many ways creating an all-inclusive environment, with the services of the city in an ideal rural setting.

At the same time that Wilde was concerned about the welfare of his staff, the final plan of Connecticut General confronted the issue of establishing hierarchy within a horizontal plan. In what *Fortune* would dub the "Battle of the Wing," the architects argued for a separate executive wing, largely on the aesthetic ground that it would articulate the overall massing of the building—creating a white-collar iteration of the administration building to the clerical "factory." The executives on the building committee, and Wilde himself, were uncomfortable with the blatantly hierarchical concept, the misgivings expressed by references to "ivory tower" and "executive privileges."[63] *Fortune* reported:

> What weighed most heavily on the executives was the psychological effect their new quarters might have on both employees and customers. Would employees resent preferential executive treatment—or expect it? Would customers downgrade executives who didn't have executive suites? . . . The argument hit its peak following a public viewing of the [building] model [in May 1954] and a series of individual attempts to explain the need for the wing to wives, employees and clients. Said a Philadelphia client, cuttingly, "Well, I suppose it makes some sense, but in our part of the country we are more democratic than that and just don't believe in a separate club for officers." The company committee, by now seriously upset, began to explore methods of doing away with the wing.[64]

An alliance of the junior executives and the architects constituted the faction in favor of the wing, though they faced opposition from Wilde himself. Ultimately Skidmore, Owings, and Merrill threatened to "withdraw from the project if it was forced to abandon the wing."[65] Surprisingly, in mid-1954, after eleven months of wrangling, Wilde capitulated. Although the *Fortune* article does not record the eventual employee reaction, the executive wing distinction became standard in many subsequent corporate estates, and in almost all those designed by Skidmore, Owings, and Merrill (see figure 4.15).

The eventual plan of Connecticut General centered the building in the expansive pastoral (see figure 1.6). A grand entry drive extended from what was once a country road and culminated in a tight oval drive in front of the executive wing. A driveway enclosed the center of the site, and linked to it were subsidiary entry drives from surrounding secondary roads. The 1956 building complex consisted of a main three-story building with four interior courtyards that housed most of the 2,000-person corporate staff, including the 1,600 women clerical workers; an executive wing that faced the front of the site toward the main entrance; and a cafeteria wing cantilevered over a reflecting pool facing the rear of the site toward the scenically constructed landscape. A terrace, designed by Isamu Noguchi, edged the rear of the building, interpreted as a "moat between technology and nature."[66] Two parking lots flanked the main building with entries from the enclosing driveway. A service drive extended around the east parking lot to a basement-level service dock. A short drive from the west parking lot connected to the executive parking directly under the executive wing.

A modular modernist design, the exterior of the building was sheathed in strips of aluminum and sheets of glass on a base of granite. The windows looked outward to the landscape, extending the building space to the horizon, or inward onto courtyards—three designed by Noguchi and a fourth designed by Bunshaft himself. The interior spaces, without permanent partitions or structural columns, flowed uninterrupted toward floor-to-ceiling windows, never more than 60 feet away from any point in the building (see figure 2.12). As *Architectural Forum* observed soon after the building's dedication, "It is significant that an insurance company lives here, for insurance companies—second only to royalty—are the world's biggest dealers in symbols. They have to be: their product is an intangible, security. How do you go about looking secure? . . . In architecture security is symbolized no longer by a massive arch, but by a long free span." The Connecticut General employees became "swaddled in space," both interior and exterior (see figure 2.13).[67]

Of the 280-acre site, the building and parking lots would occupy less than 50 acres, leaving the majority of the existing meadows and woodlands to be enhanced by the landscape design (figure 4.3). The landscape design melded the found qualities of the site—large oak trees, woodland areas, meadows—with carefully deliberated constructions: a dammed stream formed a lake to accommodate excess site runoff and created an oak-studded island as a view for the cafeteria, reminiscent of the aristocratic estate of England's Blenheim; the edges of the woodland were thinned and other trees added to form a savanna-like forest edge; the building itself was "carefully sited on a low ridge to preserve a number of large oak trees."[68] Meandering pathways looped through and around the lake area, happening on a sculptural family group by Noguchi that Wilde liked but also thought "a puzzlement."[69] The result, according to a contemporary account, was "the English kind of countryside that Constable painted and Thomas Hardy wrote about: ancient, thrilling oaks, meadows, rows of ridge lines rising like wave crests from shallow misty valleys."[70]

Wilde's qualms about the move turned out to be largely unfounded: employees responded positively to the new work setting. The corporation lost less than 2 percent of its employees as a result of the move and "found hirings

up 70% and turnover down 20%."[71] Future suburban corporate headquarters would also contain many employee amenities, but none would match the array of Connecticut General. By March 1958, Wilde, addressing the Princeton University Conference "Environment for Business and Industry," confidently stated, "We can report no regrets. The values we had hoped to derive by going to the countryside have materialized."[72]

Inadvertently or not, the articulation of the executive wing reinforced a gendered division of space. As *Architectural Forum* reported in 1957, "The gleam and stylishness of the interiors have made the young girls doing clerical work—the building's main population—dress up, their superiors say. On the long open floors, men are occasional angular figures, sternly silhouetted, against the petticoated skirts."[73]

A sense of space that, according to *Architectural Forum*, was a "denial of barriers" enveloped rigid corporate and gender divisions. The site conception, inevitably associated with suburban domesticity, was probably not a conscious appropriation of the idealized women's environment of the 1950s. Yet the landscape reidentified the business environment into an apparently friendly, conformist suburban neighbor, complete with backyard amenities, altogether fitting for the female employees.

Like the General Motors Technical Center that opened in the same year, the building received extensive popular and professional press attention. *Life* lauded it as "one of the finest office structures in the country," *Time* as a "building with a future," *Newsweek* as an "important departure from the monolithic piles which corporations once favored."[74] The press had picked up on Wilde's clearly stated intent: "This is a building that we believe may exert an influence on the office of the future, perhaps even on the city of the future."[75] As *Life* magazine reported in a five-page spread, "Symposium in a Symbolic Setting: Fine New Building Meets Challenge of City Crisis," Wilde inaugurated his building with a three-day symposium attended by "400 architects, city planners, and other urban specialists," and as they met to "discuss the tangled problems of metropolitan growth, snarled highways and city disintegration, they gathered in a place that had successfully met some of the challenges they were going to discuss" (see figure 1.2).[76] Seemingly without irony, *Life* quoted Lewis Mumford, one of the many legendary attendees: "The problem of maintaining the city in a state of health rests on . . . making it possible for the pedestrian to exist. . . . Instead of planning motor cars to fit our life, we are trying to plan our life to fit the motor car."[77]

Neither the corporate executives nor the designers of the Connecticut General Headquarters understood the full import of the automobile. They provided parking spaces for fewer than half the employees in two parking lots cheek by jowl with the sleek building, a serious blemish according to *Architectural Forum* that nevertheless concluded, "The building's lean gleam will outlast the car's fat shine."[78] Within a year, the parking lots expanded to almost a one-to-one ratio to the employees as fewer and fewer sought alternative means of transportation; a multistory parking garage was an eventual addition. Wilde later stated, "We accepted that most people wanted to drive to work."[79]

With Connecticut General, the corporate estate evolved in two significant ways. First, Wilde envisioned the Connecticut General headquarters as a clarion call for change in corporate building, indeed a new vision of the city. His audience extended well beyond his employees and stockholders, suggesting the potential for corporate promotion and utility in this new kind of setting (figure 4.4). Second, Wilde's belief in the superior functionalism of the architecture,

4.3

The Connecticut General Life Insurance Company headquarters, in Bloomfield, Connecticut, outside Hartford, which opened in 1956. Two hundred eighty acres acres of lush, bucolic topography surrounded the celebrated Skidmore, Owings, and Merrill modernist building, though observers noted that the huge, adjoining parking lots detracted from the building's aesthetic. This photograph, taken soon after the building opened, also shows the expansion of the parking areas on the upper right, necessary because more and more employees drove their automobiles to work. Eventually Connecticut General built a parking garage to accommodate their expanded parking needs (see figure 1.8). (Ezra Stoller © Esto)

4.4

Skidmore, Owings, and Merrill followed Connecticut General with a series of corporate estates in the late 1950s and early 1960s that used similar design strategies. Two examples are the Reynolds Metal Company, Richmond, Virginia, from 1957 (top), designed with the landscape architect Charles Gillette, and the Upjohn Corporation Headquarters, Kalamazoo, Michigan, from 1961 (bottom), designed with the landscape architects Sasaki, Walker, and Associates. (Ezra Stoller © Esto)

along with a very American concern for preserving the landscape, led to a landmark combination of structure and site—high modernist building and big pastoral landscape.[80] If the structure defined modernity, the site recollected the very landscape that rapid suburbanization was replacing (see figure 2.13). But this was borne out of Wilde's idiosyncratic preferences, and the awkward handling of the parking lots underscores the separate footings of the architecture and landscape. Though Wilde and his designers did not understand the integrative potential of this duality, others would.

The Definitive Estate: Deere & Company Administrative Center

As if in response to Mumford's jeremiad and to *Architectural Forum*'s critique, carefully tucking away of "the car's fat shine" was integral to the definitive Deere & Company Administrative Center in Moline, Illinois. The exemplar for all subsequent corporate estates, it brought together landscape, site plan, and architecture into an elegant and commanding solution. Deere definitively proved the corporate value of the high-image, high-style suburban headquarters.

In May 1955, William A. Hewitt became president of Deere & Company, then second to International Harvester in the farm machinery business and distinctly lagging in the emerging global market. In his first decade as president, Hewitt would transform the company; it became the global leader in agricultural machinery and a dominant multinational corporation.[81] By autumn 1955, Hewitt had authored a strategic plan to bring about industry leadership "in six key indices—sales, profit ratios, quality, new designs, safety of operations, and excellence in employee, dealer, stockholder, and public relations." As a key part of the strategy, Hewitt included, "Build a new office building."[82] Wayne G. Broehl, who wrote the best-regarded history of Deere & Company, assessed that this "in retrospect turned out to implant a signal Hewitt mark on the entire company."[83] Hewitt realized that the company's Moline location needed an extra draw in the competitive labor market of the booming postwar economy and a consolidated image to create a global corporation.[84] A year before the completion of the General Motors Technical Center and Connecticut General headquarters, Hewitt's document decisively relegates Deere's engineers to "handle power houses, foundries, supervision of factory layouts and purchase of machine tools *but not* architecture," and specifically describes the new office as a "campus."[85] It evidences Hewitt's fundamental conception of the company's new work environment as a superlative land-scape, not as an utilitarian structure.

Initially Hewitt obtained "a big box of architects' prospectuses" from his friend, the top Ford executive Robert McNamara, a classmate at Berkeley and Harvard Business School, who had recently directed the completion of a new administration building.[86] But Henry Dreyfuss, the long-standing product design consultant who had modernized the look of the Deere & Company products, most notably the streamlined tractor of 1938, guided Hewitt to two recent projects Dreyfuss considered "superb models to emulate": the Massachusetts Institute of Technology Auditorium and the General Motors Technical Center, both designed by Eero Saarinen.[87] As Hewitt recounted in his 1964 inaugural speech: "Henry said if we were interested in an architect whose work will last and still be excellent 25 or 50 years from now, we should seriously consider Eero Saarinen."[88] Hewitt visited both projects, meeting Saarinen at the Technical Center.[89] Hewitt, who according to *Time* spent two months in Europe every year, collected art, and enjoyed "expensive suits and first class living," was impressed.[90] As Hewitt described it, "Then and there I decided Eero Saarinen was the man for the job."[91]

Hewitt and Saarinen convened in Moline in August 1956 to visit and discuss possible sites. Deere & Company owned a large swath along the Mississippi River in Moline, covered with an accretion of 100 years' worth of factories, offices, warehouses, and outbuildings; it was the site of the original 1847 factory that produced the famous prairie-breaking steel plow and established the company. These were the "works" from which Hewitt wanted to remove his executives and upper corporate administration (see figure 2.2). The company also owned an undeveloped riverside property a mile to the east of the works, but Hewitt and Saarinen discarded it for aesthetic reasons. It was edged by railroad tracks and a junkyard, the river prospect apparently in no way a compensation.[92] As they looked for other sites not owned by the company, Saarinen assessed that "he had never seen a community that offered so many problems in regard to having potential sites marred by the nearness of shacks, trailer camps, cemeteries, cheap commercial buildings and other unattractive blight."[93] Compounding the gritty aesthetic realities of a nineteenth-century factory town was the devastating effect of dutch elm disease, which by the late 1950s had destroyed almost all of the city's elms, impugning Moline's 1930s appellation of Elm City.[94]

Searching beyond the city limits, Hewitt and Saarinen found a potential site south of East Moline: bluffs above the Rock River valley extending down through a ravine to level agricultural fields.[95] Comprising four farms totaling 720 acres, the site contained some existing trees and views over the valley that promised the kind of elegance Hewitt was looking for.[96] Hewitt himself lived on a "farm" with 130 arabian horses along the Rock River.[97] To verify the site's potential, Hewitt and Saarinen boarded a utility repair lift to better see what the view might look like from the new building's upper floors.[98] The message of the glinting Technical Center, assimilated by both Hewitt and Saarinen, was the summary, unfettered totality of its environment and a site that did not merely contain buildings but performed in dynamic equivalency with them.

The Deere & Company corporate board did not match Hewitt's enthusiasm for a new building, resisting abandonment of the company's traditional residence and wary of appearing pretentious to their farmer customers. But with "his personal credibility on the line," Hewitt sold the idea of the building, the site, and the architect to his cautious board. Broehl claims: "It is probably not excessive to say that at this meeting Hewitt turned this insular, Midwestern farm implement company in a new direction, pointing it towards a new role as one of the world's best known multi-national corporations."[99] Hewitt wanted pre-eminence, and like countless other leaders before him whose estates he had no doubt seen on frequent European sojourns, he needed a symbolic consolidation of his power.[100] In January 1957 the board approved Hewitt's new building and his architect. In the 1957 annual report to stockholders, Hewitt announced the purchase of the site and justified the new administrative center:

> The location will make it possible to consolidate in one area employees
> scattered in seven buildings, some which are rented and some as old as
> seventy-six years. The new administrative center will increase the efficiency
> of the many departments now operating with space and communication
> problems. Moreover the existing parking problem will be eliminated and
> land will be available for future expansion.[101]

All of these efficiencies could have been accomplished, and much more cheaply, at the vacant central Moline site that the company already owned. But Hewitt's choice, with Saarinen's advice, was to abandon central Moline for a potentially more stately setting outside the city limits.[102] This choice belies simplistic strides toward efficiency and indicates Hewitt's aspiration to create an elite environment to announce Deere's arrival in the global market and attract, and keep, executive personnel—an environment certainly based on the new architecture, but much more fundamentally based on the aesthetics of landscape.

After purchasing the land in the summer of 1957 for an average price of $600 an acre, Hewitt called Saarinen back to Moline to site the new building. Saarinen chose the location with the most expansive views over the Rock River valley at the site's highest elevation. According to Hewitt, Saarinen "wrote down our requirements: an office building for 800 to 1,000 people, a cafeteria, and executive dining room, a 400 seat auditorium and a large product display area, all accessible under cover for protection during the winter, plus capacity for further expansion."[103] Saarinen later characterized the program as "not a complicated one. It was to be a 'headquarters' for the people who worked in it and also a proud central home for every person in the far-flung organization who would visit it individually or in groups."[104]

In August 1957, Hewitt wrote to Saarinen "to set down a few fundamental ideas that may be helpful to you in creating a new headquarters for Deere & Company." Hewitt emphasized his lack of preconceptions about what the design of the building should be, which he saw as Saarinen's responsibility, and then stated:

> The men who built this company and caused it to grow and flourish were men of strength—rugged honest, close to the soil. Since the company's early days, quality of product and integrity in relationships with farmers, dealers, suppliers, and the public in general have been Deere's guiding factors.
>
> In thinking of our traditions and our future, and in thinking of the people who will work in or visit our new headquarters, I believe it should be thoroughly modern in concept, but at the same time, be down to earth and rugged.[105]

Saarinen's first inspiration was to raise a "rugged" concrete building: a pyramid inverted, on the highest bluff overlooking the valley floor. Hewitt found it wanting.[106] According to Saarinen's associate Paul Kennon, Saarinen returned to his office and began work on a steel frame building lower down in the valley "that was absolutely sympathetic with the trees."[107] To Saarinen "the broad ravines seemed the finest, most pleasant, and most human site" for the building.[108] Three weeks after the aborted inverted pyramid, Saarinen requested that Hewitt visit his office in Bloomfield Hills, Michigan. As Hewitt remembered it in 1977, Saarinen showed him a model of the new scheme "complete with land contours, trees, shrubs and a pond." The main steel frame administration building straddled the valley floor facing the flat farm fields and the Rock River valley (figure 4.5). A fourth-floor bridge connected it to the product display building extending up the valley's side; a corresponding extension on the opposite side of the valley accommodated future building expansion. (Roche and Dinkeloo, the principals who took over Saarinen's practice after his death, completed the extension in 1972.) In place of the inverted pyramid, a parking lot occupied the highest point of the site so that the circulation

moved, almost counterintuitively, down toward the building—from parking lot, through a product display and auditorium building, across a glass-enclosed bridge, and on into the main administration building. Hewitt, satisfied that it met the company's program, gave the go-ahead to develop the design.[109]

Saarinen's next move was to earn him an assured place in the history of twentieth-century architecture, a clearly stated goal on his part.[110] Instead of the lustrous metal that he used in other buildings before and after, Saarinen trussed the edifice in the obtrusively industrial Cor-Ten steel, which rusts to a protective finish. Saarinen described his decision:

> Deere & Company is a secure, well-established, successful farm machinery company, proud of its Midwestern farm-belt location. Farm machinery is not slick, shiny metal but forged iron and steel in big, forceful, functional shapes. The proper character for the headquarters' architecture should likewise not be slick, precise glittering glass and spindly metal building, but a building which is bold and direct, using metal in a strong, basic way.

4.5
The 720-acre site outside Moline, Illinois, of the Deere & Company Administrative Center. The former agricultural land was planted with many new trees to wrap the headquarters in woodlands. In marked contrast to Connecticut General, the two large parking lots are carefully subsumed within the landscape, one barely visible at the far right of the photograph. (Photo by David MacTavish, used by permission)

Having decided to use steel, we wanted to make a steel building that really was a steel building (most so-called steel buildings seem to me to be more glass buildings than steel buildings, really not one thing or the other). We sought an appropriate material—economical, maintenance free, bold in character, dark in color.[111]

After presenting the preliminary design in June 1958, Saarinen engaged Hideo Sasaki to be the project's landscape architect.[112] Once involved, Sasaki confirmed Saarinen's imaginative leap that the building should straddle the valley. He met with Saarinen and the project team on site and worked on the exact placement of the building.[113] As part of the site planning process Sasaki raised balloons to outline the building configuration and placement. This enabled the design team to fully integrate the building and site (figure 4.6).[114]

An unpaved, gravel road, Coal Town Road, crossed the site, "full of chuckholes and impassable in winter."[115] Running across the mouth of the ravine, it divided the site's hilly upland from the flat fields edging the Rock River. The original site plan included a laboratory for research and development on the opposite side of the road from the Administrative Center, with the presumption that prototype farm machinery could be tested on the fields. Eventually the company considered even the experimental use of machinery "too dirty" for the public eye, and this portion of the site plan never went beyond the schematic phase.[116]

4.6

The Administrative Center buildings sited across the ravine of the Deere & Company property. Although Eero Saarinen initially wanted to top the highest hill on the site (where the parking lot now is visible in the upper right of the photograph) with an inverted pyramid, William Hewitt, Deere's chief executive officer, did not like the concept. Saarinen then proposed straddling the ravine and Hewitt concurred; the landscape architect Hideo Sasaki raised helium-filled balloons projecting the corners and perimeters of the building to determine exactly the most elegant place to site the structures. (Environmental Design Visual Resources Center, University of California, Berkeley)

Although the fundamental site scheme was Saarinen's, Sasaki extended, articulated, and refined the role of the landscape design in the concept of the headquarters. Saarinen wanted an unprecedented intimacy between the building and the landscape. Sasaki and his project manager, Stuart Dawson, would grade, plant, and form water to achieve a synthesis of building and landscape both serene and striking (figure 4.7). Sasaki took the timid square of water centered on the building facade that Saarinen included in the 1958 presentation and re-formed it into a prominent water feature with an upper pond eased against the building and a lower pond stretching along the ravine bottom. Sasaki intended the upper pond to be noticeably manicured, edged in a sinuous border of gravel, with an island of weeping willows and surrounded by magnolias.[117] In the final design, a terrace extended from the center of the building facade to form a straight edge against the upper pond. Underneath the terrace, the executive dining room stretched out from the building's lowest floor, so that the water surface

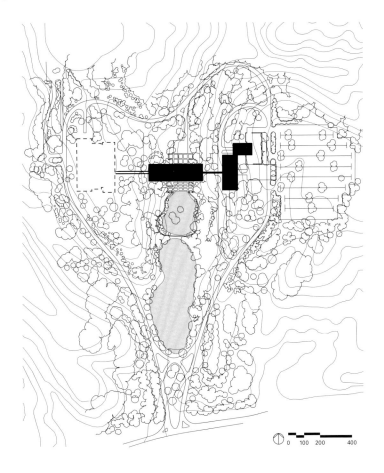

4.7

As the site plan makes clear, the carefully interwoven composition of architecture, topography, planting, and pond of the Deere & Company Administrative Center created the summary aesthetic effect of this quintessential, and highly influential, exemplar of the corporate estate. Like the corporate campus, the site plan also took into account further expansion of the building.

skims across at eye level from the interior. Although the upper pond gives the appearance that the building forms a dam, the site drainage flowed in the opposite direction. The upper pond is fed by city water and rebounded the rust and gold patterning of the building facade. The lower pond both extended the water feature to set a dramatic foreground to the building from the entry sequence and solved a site problem created by the placement of the building. Wedged across the bottom of the ravine, the building blocked a creek, disrupting the drainage pattern of the watershed. Hence, the lower pond formed a retention basin to a large culvert that extended from the upper ravine, around the building, and emptied into the lower pond.[118] (The building flooded during its construction, underscoring the potential hazards of the siting.) In addition, the lower pond cooled the air-conditioning system, always under duress in any glass-enclosed modernist building, with delicate grids of spray fountains lowering the water temperature on hot days.[119]

The dramatic entry drive beginning at Coal Town Road, paved and later renamed John Deere Expressway, presented the entire landscape (figure 4.8). Dawson worked and reworked the interior road system through an iterative process of repeated grading and modeling.[120] This evolutionary process resulted in a roadway that is an active element in the experience of the landscape, orchestrating the views to maximum effect. The looping driveway lassoed the building complex, moving from the ravine bottom at the road intersection, rising along the ravine embankments and revealing stunning views across the ponds to the building facades, banking upward into the woodland landscape, eventually arriving at the principal parking lots disclosed at the last possible moment, and then dropping back down again to encircle the building complex at the rear to provide service access. A subsidiary looping drive to the exhibition building and auditorium, part of the first phase of building, exited off the main drive on the east side.

Besides the manicured upper pond, Sasaki conceived of the rest of the landscape as a native woodland: oaks and maples, complemented with understory shrubs and contrasted with meadows of unmown grasses. Only 30 acres immediately surrounding the building and upper pond were to be mown and obviously tended; the remaining 690 acres were to be left as they grew. Although the existing trees on site inspired Saarinen's concept of the building (after his death, Hewitt dedicated a large oak Saarinen particularly admired as a memorial), the site was sparsely wooded to begin with, and in the first years, over a thousand trees were lost to dutch elm disease.[121] The landscape concept required tree planting to an extent unprecedented in Dawson's experience, with thousands of trees planted in the first years and assiduous replacement as necessary in

4.8
View of the drive into the Deere & Company Administrative Center that demonstrates how the design of the grading, planting, and roadway precisely maximized the aesthetic effect of the landscape surrounding the headquarters. (Photo by author)

the years thereafter. Not all the trees were strictly locally indigenous, *native* being a looser term in 1960 than today, indicative of American species more than anything else. As Stuart Dawson characterized it, the design was the inevitable result of Saarinen's interest in having a building in the woods. According to Dawson, because of the building's emphatic architectural statement, the landscape was not supposed to be perceived as designed.[122] Rather, the building would be seen as having emerged from a locally familiar, if intensified, landscape. Nonetheless, this exclusively deciduous landscape did elicit protests from the board and employees, who were concerned about a bleak and dreary winter vista. Nevertheless, with Hewitt's support, Sasaki's concept prevailed.

In spite of this controversy, Dawson understood the landscape design as "refining not testing philosophies."[123] It would function peculiarly and particularly to smooth the way for Saarinen's daring building, which went beyond the new modernist aesthetic of the era to an even more provocative expression of functionalism and mass-produced, industrial materiality. Saarinen used the cage of Cor-Ten steel not only as an exterior manifestation of the structural members but to form exterior louvers over the banks of glass wrapping the building's seven floors. As Saarinen explained: "Having selected the site because of the beauty of nature, we were especially anxious to take full advantage of views from the offices. To avoid curtains or Venetian blinds, which would obscure the views, we worked out a system of sun-shading with metal louvers and specified reflective glass to prevent glare."[124] Saarinen also considered that the glass-paneled bridge connections between the main building and the wings "should give the users a wonderful sense of actually being up in the trees."[125]

Saarinen's choices for the exterior manipulation of the Cor-Ten certainly expressed the building's horizontal straddle of the ravine, binding it into the surrounding landscape. It also made for a uniquely, even overwhelmingly, rusty building. After the building's completion, the rust's organic, earthy patina would elicit fortuitous recollections of both the surrounding tree trunks and the color of plowed fields, but at the outset, the unproven concept was easily perceived as bizarre. Hewitt later recalled his engineers' reactions: "[They] were a little alarmed, thinking 'We've been warning farmers against rust for 120 years, and now Hewitt wants to build a big rusty building—and make us work in it.'"[126] Displaying a rare loyalty, Hewitt did not waver in his support of Saarinen. As Dawson assesses it, "There was not another industrialist who would have agreed to a rusty building."[127]

Hence the landscape had a dual role. In emphasizing the seamlessness between interior and exterior space, a common goal of the modernist architectural aesthetic greatly stressed by Saarinen, the landscape enveloped the building, becoming part of the materiality of the building itself, finishing the building's interiors in the way paint and molding, frescoes and tapestries would have in previous architectural generations. In risking the censure, even ridicule, of the company's board, employees, and customers for the building's unprecedented extrapolation of modernist materiality and function, the landscape was soothingly recognizable, harking on, albeit in a most refined edition, a hundred years' worth of public parks, Victorian manors, college campuses, scenic preserves, country clubs, and golf courses, and the "pleasing prospect" of woodlands among the fertile fields of an ordinary American rural landscape—all readily seen in and around Moline. This was not self-conscious. In retrospect, Stuart Dawson characterizes the design as a "natural solution" not modeled on any particular landscape, emulating no specific antecedent.[128]

In his history of the company, Wayne G. Broehl, underscores that most of upper management fretted that employees, the public, and Deere's farmer customers would regard the headquarters as a pretentious folly. In particular, they expected farmers to find the center too "urban." As Broehl states, "Only when the building was up and occupied would these subtle nuances of employee and public reaction become clearer."[129] Completion of the building was slow and certainly further impeded by Saarinen's death in 1961, shortly after construction began. On April 30, 1963, at the annual meeting of stockholders at the central Moline offices, Hewitt announced the expectation that the meeting would be held at the new administrative center the following year. He went on to reiterate to the gathered stockholders that the buildings that they found themselves in were "grossly inadequate for today's operations" and that the new center "has been planned painstakingly for our needs and should pay its way in increased effectiveness."[130] Seven years after engaging Saarinen, Hewitt was careful to justify his reasons for the move once again.[131]

On April 9, 1964, the *Moline Dispatch* reported that the copper sculpture of a deer leaping over a log—the "Leaping Deer" trademark—which had stood on top of the company's central Moline brick office building since shortly after 1900, would find a new "home in a wooded area south of the display building at the new administrative center" (see figure 2.2).[132] The headquarters moved to the new building on April 20.[133] The year before, Deere had become the biggest producer of agricultural machinery in the world for the first time in its history. In a speech to his employees, Hewitt declared the hope that the new management setting would provide "additional inspiration to all of us to be bold, ingenious and creative, to use our imagination in new ways to keep John Deere out in front as a leader" (figure 4.9).[134]

On June 5, 1964, Hewitt inaugurated the building with what *Business-Week* would nationally report as "Moline's Biggest Bash."[135] Hewitt jetted in

4.9

The entry view of the Deere & Company Administrative Center. Used on countless publications including annual reports, corporate brochures, and now Web sites, the Administrative Center became the icon of the global corporation for both internal and external audiences. (Photo by author.)

over 300 high-echelon corporate executives, including the reigning regent of American business, David Rockefeller, president of Chase Manhattan Bank.[136] The bash was a tremendous success, garnering both local and national publicity. Hewitt began the ceremonies acknowledging the assembled worthies and giving tribute to Saarinen. Henry Dreyfuss, Deere's long-standing industrial designer, followed Hewitt's welcome with hopeful superlatives:

> Perhaps the best way I can convey what I mean is to say—if the first John Deere were to walk in at this moment, I believe he would recognize this building as his own. The honest directness and the imagination that inspired him to throw aside tradition and use what in his day was an extreme material—(imagine using steel for a plow)—is echoed throughout this building, inside and outside, from top to bottom—even in the material from which it has been built. . . . For all its size and daring use of the site, this is a building that beckons and welcomes you. The men and women who will work here will give it life and warmth. The design in steel and glass will give them and their work inspiration, will permit imagination, will inspire courage of conviction—and they in turn, will contribute warmth and spirit and the love of the tradition that for nearly 130 years has made this a great company.[137]

But it was the speech of well-known economist Gabriel Hauge, advisor for economic affairs to President Eisenhower, president of Manufacturers Hanover Trust Company of New York City, and that same year appointed as director of the Council of Foreign Relations, that captured the more subtle symbolic purposes of the building. After quoting the English philosopher Alfred North Whitehead, "A great society is a society in which its men of business think greatly of their functions," Hauge went on to state:

> The firm of Deere & Company is well and widely known. Its product line has been ratified by the custom accorded it in the markets it serves. The company has been endorsed by people who make judgments about investing their money. And it seems to me that here today we have seen evidence of businessmen—Bill Hewitt and his associates—thinking greatly of their functions. We know they can produce handsomely to meet the needs of their customers. Now we know something more about their success from this handsome house which they have fashioned as the headquarters of their world wide operation.
>
> . . . The creation of wealth is not necessarily a lovely process. People can get hurt, skills can be rendered obsolete, investment can lose value,

natural resources have to be put to the uses of man, and in the process beautiful landscapes have to be scratched, trees have to be cut down. All this isn't necessarily a lovely process.

It does seem to me however that . . . we are witnessing an impressive manifestation of the business community thinking greatly of its functions. I speak now not only of all the efforts that businessmen contribute in their communities unrelated to their own activities, but also of pursuing and seeking excellence in the way this enterprise has achieved it in this great new nerve center for Deere & Company. As I heard Bill Hewitt talk about the problem that was posed by challenging tradition in pulling together all the parts of Deere here in this building . . . my thoughts went back to another saying . . . and it is this: "From the altar of the past, carry away, not the ashes, but the fire."[138]

The rhetorical prospect of the Administrative Center enacted a mythic, prelapsarian American landscape, which Deere's steel plow had so neatly sliced apart.

The internal concerns the company leadership harbored throughout the eight-year process of bringing the project to fruition disappeared with the occupation of the building and its attendant accolades. C. R. Carlson, "one of the more conservative of the older board members," wrote to Hewitt just one day after taking up residence in the center. After describing his long history of working in facilities that were "comfortable and livable" at best, but more often "cheap and badly constructed . . . makeshift," Carlson reveled in his new surroundings: "I must say that the surroundings are wonderful and the building itself is an excellent one in which to work. . . . I am sure that it is going to be conducive to better work on the part of all of us who have the privilege of working here."[139]

This reaction could be expected as part of initial enthusiasms, yet the positive responses continued over the long term. The sociologists Mildred Reed Hall and Edward T. Hall conducted three surveys of employees from all ranks of the headquarters staff: in April 1964 before the move; in October after occupancy; and finally in 1969, five years after the move. As at Connecticut General, the female employees dressed better in the new building; attracting new high-quality personnel became easier, and ads that included pictures of the center had notably high response rates (figure 4.10). The employees found the site and landscape to be the most positive element of the Administrative Center. After the 1969 survey, Hall and Hall commented:

The most striking thing about the general response to the building was the continuing awareness and sensitivity to the beauty of the site. Again and again we heard remarks about the building's beautiful surroundings and grounds. Most people mentioned this as the thing they liked most about the building. Appreciation for the beautiful pastoral setting more than offset the rare negative responses to the out-of-town location which we had heard in our interviews five years earlier.[140]

Though the employees responded positively to the building as a functional, efficient, and effective working environment (countered only by the now familiar complaints about glass-skinned buildings regarding temperature control and lack of privacy in the open plan work areas), it was the building's setting that engaged employees' imaginations and fostered their sense of attachment to their workplace.

Hall and Hall reported as well that visiting farmers, Deere customers through several generations, were "among the most enthusiastic visitors to the building." Distributors and dealers brought in clients by the busload and used "the building as a selling point for Deere's products."[141] Hall and Hall estimate that between 1964 and 1973, over 700,000 people visited the site, and it

4.10
An ad for the Deere & Company Administrative Center in *Destination Quad Cities*, a 1997 visitors' guide to the Moline area. Subsequent to this ad, the corporation renamed the site the Deere & Company World Headquarters. (Ad courtesy of Deere & Company, Moline, Illinois)

It's not just another day at the office

"In concept, in character, in intellectuality, it stands alone — a symbol of industrialism enriching rather than destroying the landscape..." Walter McQuade, architectural critic

Deere & Company Administrative Center is one of the 16 most highly acclaimed office buildings in America. A steel and glass masterpiece only an Eero Saarinen could conceive.

- *An awe-inspiring architectural gem in a pure, pastoral, 1,000-acre setting overlooking the Rock River Valley.*
- *Twin lakes alive with swans and oriental goldfish. Plus a willowed island featuring a bronze sculpture by world-renowned sculptor, Henry Moore.*
- *Atrium with 57-foot skylighted ceiling.*
- *Agricultural museum featuring a 2,000-item, 3-dimensional 19th century mural by Alexander Girard.*
- *Display of current and historical John Deere farm, industrial, and lawn care equipment.*
- *Film at 10:30 a.m. and 1:30 p.m. weekdays, except holidays. Display floor open 9 a.m. to 5:30 p.m., including weekends and holidays. Located 7 miles southeast of downtown Moline on John Deere Road.*

At John Deere, every day is special. Come see for yourself.

continues to attract 25,000 people a year.[142] Although the center is clearly private property, no gates or barriers close it off, and visitors freely wander through the grounds during daylight hours. The product display building is open seven days a week, and farmers from all over the country stop by to take a look at the products. Today, if you buy a $250,000 harvester built at Deere's East Moline plant, the company treats you to lunch in the executive dining room gazing out over Sasaki's ponds (figure 4.11).

Sasaki and Dawson had intended the majority of the grassland to appear prairie-like. But because Deere had entered the tractor mower business in 1963, the site immediately became a proving ground for Deere's products—all 720 acres a testament to their effectiveness. The landscape took on the appearance, as Dawson describes it, of a "golf course" rather than a native landscape.[143] Visitors could experience the neat result of Deere's labor-saving devices in person. As Deere had participated in the mechanization of the farm, making possible single farms of large acreage, so Deere's landscape presented the mechanized estate, its vast lawn expanses no longer dependent on fleets of gardeners, and grazing cattle or sheep.

Hall and Hall concluded, "We discovered in the course of the Deere study that what the building communicates is as important in its consequences as anything else we were able to identify." It communicated to employees (and one can safely presume others as well) corporate pride, industry leadership, and the expectation of top work performance of products and personnel.[144] The degree to which the landscape was essential in this communication cannot be parsed, but the Deere employees' overwhelming consciousness of the aesthetic value of the landscape places it at a fundamental level of perception.

The center also proved to be usefully photogenic. By the time of the opening ceremonies, Deere & Company had produced a large-format booklet, "Challenge to the Architect: Deere & Company Administrative Center," quoting Hewitt and Saarinen on their goals for the building and displaying extensive photographs of its vistas—exterior shots of the building and surrounding landscape or interior shots culminating in views of the expansive grounds.[145] Both *Time* and *BusinessWeek* articles announcing the opening included views of the building with its foreground ponds; *Time*'s close-ups of the unusual construction showed it intertwined with the branching trees that "wave just outside the horizontal steel louvers."[146] Since its opening, corporate brochures, annual reports, and promotional materials of all kinds have prominently featured exterior vistas of the Administrative Center. A 1980 brochure, "Character of a Company," with a stunning centerfold view of the building, across the ponds, framed by the bucolic landscape, typified the use to which Deere & Company put the aesthetic

4.11
View from the interior of the
executive dining room of the
Deere & Company Administrative
Center, on the lowest floor of the
main building, level with the water
in the ponds. (Photo by author)

value of the center. The text unequivocally declared, "There is no more visible expression of the special character of John Deere than the Administrative Center in Moline, Illinois."[147]

To the local community, the opening of the center signaled a telling fidelity to Deere's traditional home even though Moline's downtown would decline with the removal of the corporate offices.[148] On the inauguration day of the center, the editorial page of the *Moline Dispatch* found it "immensely heartening to see these new buildings as a solid expression from Deere that this community is facing the future with high promise and honest optimism."[149] By 1989 the same newspaper would report the Deere Administrative Center as the "'All Time Favorite Building' in the 'Best of the Quad Cities' reader's survey" in an article entitled, "Architectural Gem Blends into Countryside."[150] Like Deere's corporate broadsheets, local booster publications inevitably featured views of the center and its grounds.

The project won many awards, including the American Institute of Architects' First Honor Award, the Architectural League of New York's Collaborative Medal of Honor, and the American Society of Landscape Architects' Honor Award. Architectural and design magazines acclaimed the new center, with lush photographs illustrating its salient features.[151] In *Architectural Forum,* Walter McQuade hailed the "depth of feeling in Deere which makes it much less transitory than most modern architecture . . . a symbol of industrialism, enriching rather than destroying the landscape by contrast."[152] The critic John Jacobus, in the British publication *Architectural Review,* went well beyond the usual puffery, viewing Saarinen's work with a jaundiced eye, particularly his "endless solecisms" and his undisguised ambition to be historically significant. Jacobus nonetheless assessed the import of the project:

> The office building on a rural or suburban site is, of course, one of the most frequently encountered programmes in post-war American architecture. Most of such buildings have been, stylistically of a pronounced urban flavour; neither Wright nor Goff nor Paolo Soleri nor any other architect of a romantic, organic or earthy orientation has influenced the architecture produced by this migration of the office to the countryside which has become, it is true, partly overrun with asphalt parking areas and networks of feeder roads. Yet its public, "display" side has often been handsomely landscaped by way of compensating for the mutilation caused by the automobile. Part of the charm of John Deere comes from the steep, accidented site, which contrasts with the usual prairie-like site for buildings of this genre. This location ensured greater intimacy and privacy, and helped to encourage a concentrated eight-storey block instead of the customary two- or three-level structure. In this way the horizontal ennui of GM or of SOM's Connecticut General or Upjohn (Kalamazoo) is avoided, and Saarinen's building seems less like the inevitable spatial extension of a shapeless parking mall than is sadly the case in most of these big offices structures, which are inherently vulnerable to the sneering criticism of being nothing more than reclining skyscrapers in form.[153]

In 1993 the Administrative Center won the American Institute of Architects' twenty-five-year award for exemplifying "design of enduring significance."

Hewitt and his designers pulled off a remarkable feat. They were able to win the approbation of cultural critics, hard-headed capitalists, staid colleagues, wary employees, Deere's legendarily thrifty customers, and the folks in Moline. As an estate, the Administrative Center identified the potentially anonymous corporation as both local gentry and global player, a point of native pride and worldwide status. Saarinen's building reflected an international aesthetic discourse about abstraction, functionality, pure form, and absolute space usually confined to an allied cohort of designers and their patrons. The pastoral landscape, in active complement, reflected, a century after Olmsted, a democratic arcadia, appealing to everyone who visits it and a prophylactic against the potential excessive modernity of the architecture *and* the corporate institution it housed. The Administrative Center was simultaneously elite and populist, exclusive and community minded, luxurious and efficient, imposing and welcoming.

The Administrative Center's endurance as the model of the corporate estate stemmed from the positive image it conveyed to an array of audiences. The corporate estate artfully subjugated "disagreeable facts" with aesthetic pleasures and dispatched, if momentarily, the "moral ambiguities" of managerial capitalism.[154] Its incarnation of sentimental American pastoralism slyly placed the machine in the garden, but the garden also became a machine, producing persuasive representations to be appreciatively consumed by the corporation's resistant and receptive attendants. Indeed, it became, in Hewitt's words, "thoroughly modern in concept, but at the same time down to earth and rugged."[155]

The Corporate Estate after Deere

By all accounts, Deere confirmed the presumptions about the advantage of the corporate estate. Conventional wisdom became received wisdom. Coinciding with Deere & Company's ascendancy, and thus inevitably underscoring it, the Administrative Center served as an archetype for all future corporate estates. Subsequent corporate estates, while showing differences in detail, essentially followed Deere's pattern of a large pastoral site enveloping a modernist structure, one or two large parking lots visually subsumed into the landscape, a presentational entry drive, and an expanse of reflective water. Following the Deere model, the purpose of the corporate estates was to provide a recognizable seat for a globalized corporation, an apparatus of public relations, and an apposite site of executive offices. Like the corporate campus, the high-profile, popular, and business success of the early East Coast and Midwest corporate estates spurred followers in other corporations and spread the model to other regions across the United States. Among the next-generation corporate estates, the site plan remained remarkably consistent, though new thematic articulations emerged peculiar to corporate preferences or needs.

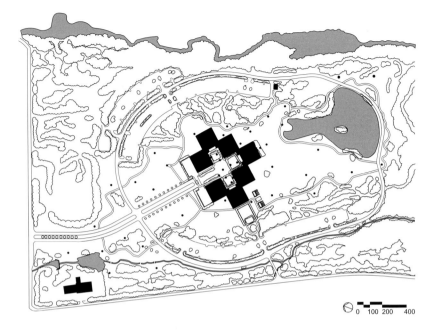

0   100   200   400

4.12
The site plan of the 1970 PepsiCo World Headquarters and Donald M. Kendall Sculpture Garden designed by the building architect Edward Durell Stone Sr. and the landscape architect Edward Durell Stone Jr. and the garden designer Russell Page. Each dot represents a sculpture connected through the site by a "golden path" designed by Page. It is just down the road in Harrison, New York, from the original corporate estate, General Foods. The site plan adheres to the same basic site organization, with two large parking lots surrounded by thick groves, ensuring invisibility from the buildings and sculpture gardens.

Driven by the tastes of chief executives, suburban headquarters became explicit vehicles to display the corporation's aesthetic patronage. Most exemplary of this is the 1970 PepsiCo World Headquarters in Harrison, New York, just down the road from the General Foods 1954 headquarters (figure 4.12) Donald Kendall, CEO and chairman of PepsiCo, had been collecting large works of modern sculpture since 1965. Another Manhattan emigrant, he had conceived the headquarters' grounds on the 112-acre former polo field as a sculpture garden that would encourage and welcome visitors. The architect, Edward Durrell Stone Sr., designed a building complex consisting of seven three-story buildings joined at their corners around a cruciform courtyard. The site, designed by the architect's son, Edward Durrell Stone Jr., surrounded the building with a great lawn encircled by a woodland edge. An axial parkway ended at the courtyard, and a looping drive led to two parking lots hidden among the woods. (figure 4.13)

After Stone Jr. completed the initial landscape design, the British garden designer Russell Page worked with Kendall to site many additional sculptures and articulate gardens within the landscape. He designed the "golden path," a gravel walk that led visitors through the gardens and past the sculptures (figure 4.14).[156] The headquarters essentially functioned as a local public park, as anyone was (and is) free to wander the grounds right up to the building. A brochure available to visitors stated that Kendall "imagined an atmosphere of stability,

4.13

View of PepsiCo World
Headquarters from the sculpture
garden. (Photo by author)

creativity and experimentation that would reflect his vision of the company."[157]
The sculpture garden, now named after Kendall, provided the corporation with
a unique public presence.

With the political tumult of the late 1960s, largely concentrated in center
cities, and increasingly skeptical receptions in the highest-end suburbs, many corporations used their suburban headquarters as an opportunity to decrease their
visible profile, fully subsuming their headquarters within densely landscaped
properties. The 1971 American Can headquarters in Greenwich, Connecticut,
designed by the architects Skidmore, Owings, and Merrill and the landscape architects Sasaki, Dawson, and Demay, secreted the corporate estate within wooded
terrain (figure 4.15). Though the headquarters is glimpsed from a passing highway, the design downplayed the entry from a collector road, from which the headquarters remained invisible. The parking underneath the structure minimized
the impact of the new complex on the 175-acre former estate, previously zoned
residential.[158] The 1976 headquarters of Richardson-Merrell, a pharmaceutical

company, in Wilton, Connecticut, designed by Kevin Roche John Dinkeloo and Associates, reiterated American Can's site solutions by means of a long, shallow structure tucked deep into the existing woodlands (figure 4.16). Although the site contained an open meadow closer to the road, the corporation chose to go upland, into the forest, so that the building straddled a creek ravine—undoubtedly a costlier alternative.[159]

The 1982 Union Carbide Corporation World Headquarters in Danbury, Connecticut, took the corporate pastoral enclave to an extreme. Also designed by Roche Dinkeloo, the headquarters lay within a 674-acre site (figure 4.17). Kevin Roche convinced the corporation to "democratize" office layouts (rigidly hierarchical in their Manhattan headquarters) so every office provided a view of the surrounding woodland. Five stories of parking formed the center of the edifice, and spokes of offices encrusted the exterior. A series of ramps worthy of GM's Futurama exhibit of the 1939 World's Fair moved the employees and their 3,000 cars through the building.[160]

4.14
The "golden path" connects the artworks of the Donald M. Kendall Sculpture Garden. Unlike most other corporate estates, PepsiCo allows the public to freely park and wander through the site, though no doubt the site and its sculpture collection are under surveillance. (Photo by author)

4.15

The American Can corporate estate from 1971. The company placed its headquarters well within a densely wooded site and eliminated exterior parking lots altogether by placing them under the building. As corporations left what they perceived as turbulent urban areas in the late 1960s and early 1970s and ventured into ever more exclusive communities like Greenwich, Connecticut, it suited both the local residents and the corporation to retreat from public view as much as possible. (Ezra Stoller © Esto)

The defense systems contractor TRW (an early adopter of the corporate campus discussed in chapter 3) bought a thickly wooded residential estate in Lyndhurst, Ohio, outside Cleveland, tore down the existing house, and built a new headquarters. The scheme, designed by the building architects Lohan Associates and the landscape architects Sasaki Associates, went to unprecedented lengths to manage and preserve trees on site.[161]

The ability of suburban sites over central business district locations to effectively remove the corporation from public access and view, while maintaining an elite ambience, was a significant corporate advantage in a politically and socially turbulent age. Unlike Connecticut General, Deere & Company Administrative Center, and PepsiCo, these sites were not open to general visitors, and, indeed, most suburban corporate headquarters built since the mid-1970s require permission to enter.

After Earth Day and the rise of the contemporary environmental movement, many corporate estates explicitly used their landscape spaces to orchestrate an environmentally positive image of their businesses. The first corporate estate on the West Coast, and still the only one that rivals in scale and grandeur its East Coast and Midwest counterparts, the 1971 Weyerhaeuser Corporate Headquarters outside Tacoma, Washington, further articulated the corporate estate as a vehicle for public display (figures 4.18 and 4.19). In addition, by reforesting the

site, the timber and forest products company was also repositioning its corporate
image, in part to reflect the more considered forest practices that it was implementing on its properties (an effort that culminated in a subsequent advertising campaign promoting Weyerhaeuser as "The Tree Growing Company").[162]
Charles Bassett of Skidmore, Ownings, and Merrill, a former associate of Eero
Saarinen, worked with Peter Walker of Sasaki, Walker and Associates on the
project for George Weyerhaeuser Jr., grandson of the company's founder. Like

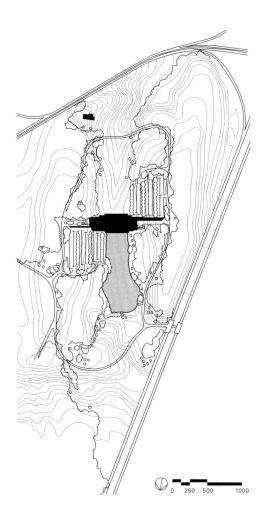

4.18

The site plan of the Weyerhaeuser Corporate Headquarters that opened in 1971 outside Tacoma, Washington. The design makes the most of the fundamental elements of the corporate estate, with dramatic use of topography to sculpt terraces of parking up the sides of the valley, a huge building bridging the valley floor, and vistas of meadow, lake, and forest opening to the two highways edging the site.

Deere, the building straddled a valley, damming a lake edged in wetland plants on one side and facing an open wildflower field on the other. The two parking lots terraced down the valley sides to meet the structure's floors, layered up from the valley. The restored woodland edge enclosed the long valley view.[163] Framed by forest, meadow, and wetland, the palatial vista from two adjoining highways particularly pleased George Weyerhaeuser.[164]

Through the 1980s, corporations used corporate estates to "showcase . . . commitment to the environment."[165] In a state where the efforts of Lady Bird Johnson had built a widespread consciousness of the native Texas prairie, Frito-Lay selected 213 acres in Plano with the potential "to give the entire project a true North Texas regional flavor," as a corporate executive put it, and landscaped the site with regional native plants.[166] The pharmaceutical company Merck

promoted its headquarters on 460 acres in Whitehouse Station, New Jersey, as an "ecological laboratory," eschewing lawns, transplanting large trees, and placing parking underneath the offices (figure 4.20).[167]

By the 1980s, the corporate estate attempted to address public disenchantment with unfettered suburban expansion and the alienating sameness of modernist corporate developments. Many projects embodied the preoccupations of postmodernist design that became popular in the 1980s, like the new General Foods headquarters, the second in Westchester County.[168] Other corporate estates combined consciously historicist architecture of the rural mansion or villa with a regionalist landscape design. For corporations, this trend—what might be called Palladio meets the prairie school—implied a commitment to place in the hopes of quelling local opposition and an effort to become a more congenial, if nonetheless formidable, neighbor. The Codex World Headquarters in Canton, Massachusetts, prompted vociferous local protest, and ultimately the permission to build on the site had to be granted

4.19
The design of the Weyerhaeuser corporate estate planned for intensive planting of the degraded site with trees, grasses, and aquatic plants, creating an idealized vision of a Northwest landscape. Even the building dripped with vines, growing in long planter boxes that wrapped the exterior edge of each of the building's concrete floors. Weyerhaeuser was the first corporate estate on the West Coast, and still the only one that matches the scale of its East Coast and Midwest counterparts. (Photo courtesy of Weyerhaeuser Archives)

4.20

As corporate estate site plans increasingly eliminated parking lots by placing them underneath or atop buildings, landscape space could permeate the corporate offices to an ever greater extent. At Merck World Headquarters, opened in 1990, an interior courtyard preserved old trees on the site, and the site design used regional, native plants as part of an environment-conscious policy adopted by the corporation. The site also included an ample array of services for employees, from fitness centers to convenience stores, harkening back to the 1956 Connecticut General Life Insurance Company headquarters. (Courtesy of Kevin Roche John Dinkeloo and Associates)

4.21

The Codex corporate estate located between Route 128 (now part of Interstate 95) and the Blue Hills Reservation, with Boston visible in the far distance. (Courtesy of Koetter Kim & Associates, Inc.)

by Governor Michael Dukakis. Codex, a high-technology corporation, had resided for two decades in various research and development parks near Boston's Route 128 (discussed in the following chapter). The new site was also on Boston's Route 128 but at its less-developed southern end, adjacent to one of the Boston Metropolitan Park System's original, beloved open spaces planned by Charles Eliot: the Blue Hills Reservation (figure 4.21). The design, by the architects Koetter, Kim, and Associates and the landscape architect Laurie Olin, incorporated historic structures and patterns (a racetrack, stables, field walls) rather than obliterating them, in the hopes of seeming more sensitive to the site's legacy.[169] Olin chose materials and forms to recollect the local vernacular landscape that he described as "resisting" generic formulas (figure 4.22).[170] Likewise, the local residents vehemently opposed the Becton Dickson Headquarters in Franklin Lakes, New Jersey; the mayor ran and won on a platform to stop the headquarters. In response, the vice president charged with the project explained that the corporation decided to avoid "the appearance of grandeur and affluence. . . . We wanted a country house."[171] The eventual design, master planned by the landscape architect Morgan Wheelock, with architecture by Kallman, McKinnel, and Wood, produced a headquarters of Edwardian propriety.[172] Stylistic concessions aside, the corporations once again forged ahead against local resistance, as they had since the 1950s.

Persuasive Generosity

By the 1990s, scores of big businesses built corporate estates in the United States. After Saarinen's death, Kevin Roche John Dinkeloo and Associates designed at least a dozen suburban headquarters for corporate clients, and Skidmore, Owings and Merrill produced a similar collection of landmark suburban structures; other architects followed suit. The invention of the corporate estate certainly needs to be seen in the context of the postwar dominance of modernist architecture in which structures of metal and glass were free from the dictates of the street and the city and embodied a new, historically unfettered future. These architects were keenly interested in playing out these ideas on the ground, and they met their match in the nation's top executives.

The Sasaki firm and its various offshoots were by far the dominant landscape architects of corporate estates.[173] In a time of much more miserly aspirations in the collective public landscape, when the nation as a whole privileged the production of the private suburban space over public space, urban or

suburban, these were the largest commissions of the postwar era, for clients who outstripped any others in terms of social status and financial clout. The designs did not significantly transgress the boundaries of the Olmstedian landscape aesthetic, but applied that aesthetic to a new kind of project and new purposes. In an opposite but complementary tack to modernist architecture, this nostalgic pastoral was also essential to the invention of the corporate estate.

While these designers had the ability to make tangible the ambitious, even audacious, reach of American corporations in the decades after World War II, the determined interest to embody the corporation in a new way lay with the corporate leadership. Like the factories of early industrialization, corporate estates became emblems of American capitalism. Their grand scale and design extend well beyond the necessities of effective work spaces, parking accommodation, and congruent suburban appearance. The coursing driveways, au courant architecture, lavish water features, and vistas over hundreds of sylvan acres identified the corporate estate as an elite environment suitable for a potent managerial class. Nonetheless, the appealing intensity and extent of the corporate estates' landscapes provided a primed populace with well-appreciated and approachable enjoyments.

The advent of the corporate estate manifested a particular moment of American economic history. Profits were ample, global competition modest, and internal politics favorably inclined to the corporate enterprise. These corporations were thoroughly American in ownership, management, and outlook, rooted in a nation that loved to turn its back on cities and stake a claim on the suburban pastoral idyll—isolated, proprietary, verdant, and disengaged from civic space. As a consequence, these corporations were far from the Medicis of our time, as the Medicis and their sort, however profligate their private pleasure grounds, bred a particular form of collective, decorative urbanity that remains enviable.

With greater amplitude than the corporate campus, the corporate estate transformed the anonymous corporation into a tangible symbol of the greatness of American capitalism astride the world. This symbolic center became a source of esteem for an array of employees, as well as neighboring communities. The corporate estates could be adjusted for both corporate and contextual conditions while consistently asserting a pleasurable aesthetic effect. Their "pleasing prospects" resonated with a range of targeted audiences: internal and external, resistant and receptive, parochial and worldly. Corporations understood that the landscape exposition of the corporate estate conveyed a persuasively generous perspective of the corporate endeavor.

4.22

Although the Codex site design kept many features of the old horse farm, the local community protested the intrusion of massive building and parking structures on the bucolic landscape of this still relatively rural portion of the periphery of Boston. This kind of protest was typical of many communities since the advent of pastoral capitalism that always, in the end, reluctantly accepted corporate developments. Four years after moving in to the facility in 1986, Codex underwent restructuring and vacated the site—an unimaginable turn of events in the 1950s. The building is now owned by Medical Information Technology. (Courtesy of Koetter Kim & Associates, Inc.)

5

THE OFFICE PARK

*"Looking over the tree tops
instead of the car tops"*

In 1950, Associated Reciprocal Exchanges, one of the business insurance firms that spearheaded the establishment of suburban headquarters in Westchester County along with General Foods, moved "lock, stock and president" from Manhattan to Port Chester, New York. The company built a modest three-story brick structure, laid out a surrounding lawn, and maintained the existing woodland around the edges of the site. Associated Reciprocal Exchanges expected the move to save money, but by 1951, the project proved to be less fiscally advantageous than expected. *Business Week* reported that "skyrocketing" construction costs and added outlays for maintenance, food services, and employee transit subsidies proved financially burdensome.[1] By 1955 the company had moved back to Manhattan, where it leased downtown office space.[2]

Not all firms, even if they were established and profitable, could sustain the added expenditure of building and maintaining their own facilities because custom-built offices were pricey. If it had moved in the 1960s, Associated Reciprocal Exchanges would have had a more cost-effective choice in bucolic Westchester: an office park, with space for lease in a suburban setting modeled on the residential subdivision. The office park was the response of speculative developers to the suburban workplace preferences first seen in the corporate campus and corporate estate.

Office Parks for an Expanding Regional Economy: Corporate Branch Offices, Back Offices, Service Corporations, and Start-Ups

While research divisions were consolidated into the corporate campus and top management into the corporate estate or downtown skyscrapers, the third tier in the managerial capitalist hierarchy dispersed into a multitude of regional offices. Corporate branch offices carried out the day-to-day business of the corporate enterprise under the direction of upper management. These lower management offices, close to manufacturing facilities and warehouses, provided services to a local customer base. In the expanding economy of the postwar era, branch offices multiplied significantly and enabled corporations to gauge and create national markets. These branch offices, which oversaw production, distribution, and completed sales, were essential to corporate profitability. Indeed, a hallmark of managerial capitalism is the organization of coordinated hierarchical corporate operations across geographically expansive territory.[3]

In addition to the growth of lower management divisions, the postwar expansion of industrial corporations, banks, and insurance companies required large staffs of clerical workers engaged in record-keeping activities because the number and scale of transactions had increased significantly. By the late 1950s, management relegated the primarily female workers involved in the paper processing of business documents to "back offices," functionally separate from central management. In addition to the large clerical staffs required for data management, as it later became known, back office activities needed large storage areas for paper records and later for computers, which through the 1970s were bulky contraptions.[4]

In addition to multiplying branch offices of national corporations and expanding back office functions, postwar prosperity generated innumerable start-up corporations. New companies that provided specialized services for other corporations, such as insurance, engineering, marketing, design services, data processing, law, and accounting, proliferated.[5] Government spending for research and development also fueled the rapid growth of new high-technology firms and high-technology subsidiaries of established corporations.[6]

None of these new kinds of office tenants merited the kind of investment in property and construction implied by corporate campuses or corporate estates. Regional managers and back office staffs were too low in the corporate hierarchy, and service corporations and high-technology firms were too new and dependent on corporate and government contracts to be sure of their long-term viability. Both corporate campuses and estates required considerable lead time between the decision to build and occupancy—not advantageous in the immediacy of market opportunities out of which these kinds of regional corporate offices grew.

At the outset, these expanding offices of the postwar economy had three choices of location. First, they could locate in the central business district. Many found it advantageous to do so, but the central business district also presented significant drawbacks. In downtowns they competed for high-priced space with more prestigious corporate echelons, banks, and large insurance companies. Branch offices served regional customers, particularly suburban and rural manufacturing concerns, and by the 1950s, the escalating congestion of downtowns impeded mobility. Branch offices had less need to be near center city banks and insurance companies, as those business connections were more critical to headquarter offices. For back office functions, the predominance of expensive, small floor plate, multistory, elevator structures was an impediment to efficient processing and storage of paperwork and, later, computing. In addition, corporations perceived that their desired labor force for back offices—white, middle-class women—would be found in increasing concentrations in the suburbs and not the center city.[7]

Second, during the 1940s small office buildings began being constructed in the retail zones of residential suburbs, specifically geared to branch offices and small service corporations. Although they were widespread enough as a phenomenon to be recognized as a particular building type by architectural periodicals, these buildings had several disadvantages. In retail areas, parking was limited, and tenants and their clients competed with shoppers for on-street parking. Transportation connections to the center city existed, but peripheral connections did not, restricting regional access. As small, individual buildings in tightly controlled residential suburbs, they were expensive to build, had unsure tenancy, and were inadequate for larger staffs.[8]

Third, they could locate in newer planned industrial districts at the urban periphery. Post-1920s industrial districts were more orderly than their predecessors. Speculative developers subdivided land, established zoning and title, and put in roads and rail spurs to create what they came to call industrial parks with ready lots for sale or lease for manufacturing and warehouse uses. Though quite

bare-bones, they provided coordinated infrastructural systems, limited building densities, and buffer space between tenants and flanking adjacent land uses. Once they were established, construction on individual lots proceeded expeditiously in industrial parks.[9] In the postwar era, marketing for industrial parks emphasized their restrictions and inclusion of green space (figure 5.1). The 1945 *New York Times* advertisement for the Elston-Central Industrial District near Chicago exhorted: "Locate your plant in this new industrial park! . . . In this new

industrial park, types of businesses and plant design will be rigidly restricted. Broad lawns and terraces will make it truly a garden spot—an inspiration to achieve the utmost quality and efficiency."[10]

Many lower management echelons found places in these new, less noxious industrial suburbs where relatively wide, efficient office buildings of one to three stories could be set out on the ample properties as part of allied industrial plants or as detached nonindustrial buildings. In some cases, such industrial site office buildings were designed with attention to both building design and landscape architecture (figure 5.2).[11] In the San Francisco Bay Area, this expansion of office uses in industrial districts accounted for the first wave of midcentury management suburbanization, not the headquarters exodus that was typical of New York City. In particular, the high-technology firms of the Bay Area emerging in the late 1940s and 1950s located in peripheral industrial districts.[12] Besides the ease and flexibility of construction in these districts, security concerns and the call for dispersal from the center city favored peripheral locations, especially for firms with extensive government contracts. But these manufacturing and warehousing district offices had one significant and unacceptable drawback— they placed management employees in an industrial, blue-collar context.

The office park and its variations emerged to meet the demand created by regional corporate offices and address the status concerns of corporate employees. Like the industrial parks on which they were modeled, office parks were speculative developments for multiple tenants with strict construction guidelines, but unlike them, they were located in upscale residential suburbs and catered to white-collar management tenants. (As noted in chapter 1, office parks can be referred to in various ways: as business parks, executive parks, and corporate parks, for example. Confusingly, some early office parks were even called industrial parks, like the Stanford Industrial Park discussed below, but they can be categorized as office parks because of their location, uses, and restrictions.) Rapid expansion of such office parks was hastened by the construction of federally funded airports and highways, particularly peripheral beltways. They were also facilitated by shifts in the fiscal management of suburbs and the invention of new zoning regulations in suburban jurisdictions. Although they were preceded by the corporate campuses and corporate estates on the suburban periphery of American cities, office parks became the most widespread type of suburban business landscape.

Changing Suburbs and Office Parks

In the postwar era, the development of diverse tax bases provided by retail and commercial sectors became an essential strategy for the fiscal survival of burgeoning residential suburbs. Suburban residents required a full complement of public services, placing ever greater budget demands on their local governments. The fiscal share carried by residential taxes did not meet the costs of services, but raising tax rates was politically impossible. Nonresidential uses offered fiscal relief but posed political challenges. Suburban home owners were wary of commercial uses, especially large employment centers that risked compromising the pastoral tranquility of their communities. The more exclusive the residential community, the more acute was the resistance.[13]

Local governments responded to this fiscal pressure with new zoning strategies. Zoning had developed in the 1920s to restrict and separate uses, particularly to control uses such as industry and rental housing near choice residential developments. In the postwar era, suburban jurisdictions deployed zoning to make office uses acceptable to their residents.[14] One of the first, Menlo Park, California, exemplified the trend. In 1948 it zoned 26 acres as an "Administrative, Executive, Professional, and Research" zone. The zoning restricted lots to a minimum of 2 acres and 40 percent maximum building coverage and required one off-street parking space for every 250 square feet of building, deep setbacks, and landscaping of all open areas. The city expected the code to eliminate all on-street parking for employees and the ample land-scaped space to harmonize with surrounding residential development. A report to the Menlo Park Planning Commission stated: "This was an invitation to large companies to build their offices in the country. At the same time it was a clear statement that it is possible to build office buildings in what are essentially residential neighborhoods without detracting from either one." Relocating from downtown San Francisco, the first occupant of the zone was the office of *Sunset Magazine*, the influential shelter magazine that enthusiastically promoted the suburban lifestyle in the West. The office, designed by noted Bay Area building architect Cliff May and landscape architect Thomas Church, was a case study of the new suburban workplace: offices all in one story, architecture that was akin to a ranch house, plenty of free off-street parking for employees and visitors, and an ample garden setting. Within five years, branch offices of two insurance companies and an engineering manufacturing corporation followed—each with landscape surrounds designed by another noted Bay Area landscape architect, Geraldine Knight Scott (figures 5.3 and 5.4). By 1953 the city extended the zoning to encompass 70 acres.[15]

Key changes in postwar transportation systems transformed the location options for suburban offices. The construction of beltways and radial highways to form metropolitan networks significantly increased regional accessibility. By the mid-1950s, new highways were underway to ring the Bay Area, Boston, Atlanta, Washington, D.C., Chicago, Dallas, and Houston, and by the 1960s, most other large metropolitan areas as well. Besides the regional connections, these beltways were often coordinated with new peripheral airport construction, such as Dulles Airport in Washington, D.C., or expansion of existing airports such as Chicago's O'Hare. The combination of highway access to airports and hubs of highways and beltways significantly facilitated regional automotive mobility and access to airplane travel. New high-tech firms and corporate branches needed regular visits to Washington to nurture government contracts. Branch offices of large corporations and service corporations required executives to travel back and forth to distant corporate headquarters as well as move among regional business contacts. For all these enterprises, including back office staffs, regional connectedness expanded the suburban labor pool.

Suburban tax structures, new suburban office zoning, and regional transportation systems opened the door for developers to devise the speculative office park based on older industrial parks (which were themselves speculative responses to the suburban factory). Rather than industrial suburbs, developers placed office parks in upper-end residential suburbs.[16] As *Business Week* succinctly described, "Office parks

5.3

An early example of offices in the suburbs, Allstate Insurance set up a branch office in Menlo Park, California, in 1950. The zoning code adopted by the city in 1948 required deep landscape setbacks, low-rise buildings, and abundant off-street parking. The effect was a set of offices that looked like postwar suburban ranch houses and meshed well with surrounding residential development. (Geraldine Knight Scott Collection [2000-3], Environmental Design Archives, University of California, Berkeley)

are the brainchildren of suburban real estate promoters who were inspired by industrial parks. . . . But office parks are strictly for executives and white-collar workers."[17]

The developers of office parks used a subdivision strategy initially formulated for residential suburbs: the planned unit development (PUD). Filed with local governments as part of the land subdivision process, PUDs set covenants, codes, and restrictions that extended well beyond the broad requirements of zoning. They regulated uses and types of tenants with such specificity that, like the architectural and racial restrictions of residential PUDs, ensured a specific class context. The regulations set out specifications on building height, bulk, materials, and styles of initial construction and future modifications. Likewise, prescription for green surrounds codified setbacks around the edge of the development and adjacent roadways, landscape perimeters to buildings and parking lots, and concealment of infrastructure.[18] Extending the aesthetic and social

5.4
The open space setbacks of the
Menlo Park offices, designed by
Bay Area landscape architect
Geraldine Knight Scott, were
generous enough to provide
employees with croquet courts,
shady picnic areas, and broad
views of lawn—inconceivable
workplace amenities for office
workers before the postwar era.
(Geraldine Knight Scott Collection
[2000-3], Environmental
Design Archives, University of
California, Berkeley)

strictures to office developments that proved so lucrative to developers in residential PUDs was the singular insight of office park developers. This facilitated their acceptance by exclusive residential suburbs and extended their marketability to potential business tenants.

While taking social and aesthetic cues from residential suburbs, office park developers also incorporated the profitable flexibility of tenancy agreements that was typical of industrial parks. As was the practice in industrial parks, developers did not build out all possible structures immediately, but responded to demand in a phased construction process. Tenancy could take one of several forms. Tenants could occupy a building or part of a building put up by the developer and simply rent office space. Office park developers could "build to suit" for a particular tenant with long-term lease agreements, but ownership would remain with the developer. Occupants could establish very long-term leases on a lot or buy it outright and build their own building. The last option was typical of corporate occupants that expected extended occupation and had staffs large enough to fill entire buildings. In most cases, office parks offered all of these options within one development. Management and maintenance of the office park as a whole remained with the developer, who enforced controls to ensure a predictable environmental result and protect real estate values.[19]

Office parks translated the basics of the corporate campus and corporate estate into a lucrative speculative development initially built by local developers, not large corporations. A diffuse phenomenon, office parks appeared in regional business centers as much as well-known headquarters cities. As corporations moved manufacturing to the South and West and new semiconductor companies formed new industrial clusters in Massachusetts, Texas, and California, office parks also appeared.[20] Flexible and adaptable for a range of operations, office parks eventually became the dominant form of suburban corporate workplace.

Birmingham and Waltham: The First Office Parks

The Jackson Company created the first office park in Mountain Brook, Alabama, a suburb of Birmingham. Planned and begun in 1951, the new project was called, simply, "The Office Park," thus naming this entire genre of suburban development. Birmingham had become a regional industrial center for steel manufacturing during the late nineteenth century and by the 1920s had diversified into a broad range of industrial concerns, with a downtown that "boasted the largest and tallest offices buildings in the South." Mountain Brook, home to the upper crust, was the city's most elite segregated suburb and designed in the Olmsted mode in 1926.[21] Both the developer and tenants of The Office Park considered the prestigious pastoral quality of the surrounding community to be the primary asset of the park.[22]

The Office Park was located on a new limited-access highway that connected downtown Birmingham, 5 miles distant, and the airport, a factor that tenants found favorable. The 70-acre site was wooded and sloping (figure 5.5). The site plan, devised by Jackson in-house, maintained a perimeter of woods around the site and terraced the office lots down the slope. Each office lot contained a building of a maximum of two stories covering no more than 25 percent of the parcel, surrounded by parking. Strips of landscape edged each building, lined the principal roadway through the site, and covered the slopes to enclose each office lot. In the parking lots, additional planting strips broke up the expanses of asphalt between rows of parking spaces. The parking lot planting strips, or parking berms, became a distinctive, even identifying feature of the office park. Protective covenants determined parking ratios, building heights, lot coverage, and allowable uses. The developers established an architectural control committee to approve signs, landscaping,

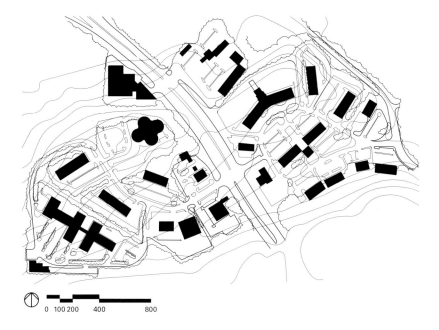

0 100 200 400 800

5.5
The site plan of The Office Park, Mountain Brook, Alabama, outside Birmingham. Begun in 1951, an era of increasing public advocacy for civil rights, the development was an alternative to downtown offices and instead located in a segregated suburb outside the center city. At the same time, the development had to adhere to Mountain Brook's assiduously guarded pastoral setting. Surrounding each office structure with small expanses of off-street parking and landscape verges edging the buildings, lots, and roadways provided suburban continuity.

and architecture. Tenants occupied the first office units in 1952, and by 1969 the office park was 85 percent occupied.[23]

An insurance corporation, Middlesex Mutual Trust Company, developed the second office park, Hobbs Brook Office Park in Waltham, Massachusetts, in 1955. It was sited along Route 128, Boston's new beltway. Middlesex built the office park as both a speculative development and to house two of its subsidiaries, the Boston Manufacturers Mutual Insurance Company and Mutual Boiler Insurance Company, both employing extensive clerical staffs. Douglas, Orr, deCrossy, Winder, and Associates planned the 85-acre site, Andersen, Beckwith, and Haible designed the first building, and Kelsey-Highlands Nursery did the landscape design. The covenants defined the allowable office uses and, in keeping with local zoning in Waltham, restricted building footprints to 20 percent coverage, required 25 percent of the lot to be landscaped, limited height to two stories, or 35 feet, and required one parking space per 250 square feet of office space.

The insurance firm credited the "personnel problem" with their decision to move from a central Boston location. As they put it, "We have been successful in hiring a more desirable type of person than was consistently available in Boston at substantially less expense. We are satisfied too that our good location in a basically selective community has had a strong impact on

our productivity." The company noted that employee turnover decreased, and they no longer had to deal with "congestion problems."[24] A 1957 *Architectural Record* article discussed the elegant new insurance building, but the development type was so unfamiliar that the article presumed that no other buildings would be placed on the property. By 1968, three other office structures, including a research and development firm, occupied the site, with space for several more.[25]

As illustrated by the Mountain Brook and Waltham office parks, developers expected office parks to be built out incrementally over a number of years, even decades. The standard method of financing office parks was a twenty- to thirty-year mortgage. Initial cash flows were needed to service the debt, but developers expected rents to rise with economic expansion and as site improvements (including securing the zoning and planning agreements) increased the value of the land. Office parks provided significant long-term profits to their investors in terms of both rental income over time and increased equity in the property (which enabled them to borrow more money if need be). Developers could also generate income from the office park as leasing agents and property managers, negotiating rental agreements and supervising maintenance of the buildings, roadways, parking lots, and landscape.[26]

In office parks, the strips of green surrounding buildings, lining roadways, and forming the parking berms carried the weight of establishing an ambient and coordinated suburban verdure, a pinched yet present pastoral aesthetic (figure 5.6). Given the lengthy time frame for full build-out, empty building lots were an enduring presence. While working within the development envelope prescribed by the covenants, codes, and restrictions, buildings responded to individual clients and differed considerably in detail. Yet the distinguished architects who worked on corporate campuses and estates during the same period were not working on office parks, so buildings tended to be generic. In addition, parking was off street, in discrete, spacious parking lots adjacent to buildings, and provided at no cost to employees and visitors. Generally developers in the 1950s provided one parking space for every 250 to 300 square feet of office space, a standard that remains the same today. Given that a standard parking space is 9 by 19 feet and requires an adjacent turning lane of 12 feet plus some additional width for interior circulation, office park parking lots surfaces were approximately the same square footage as adjacent buildings. These expanses of asphalt challenged the suburban aesthetic.

The pastoral landscape space of the office park, however tightly apportioned, gave it coherence and consistency with surrounding residential development. This was essential; both surrounding suburban communities and tenants looking for indicators of "quality" demanded it. Cory Jackson, the developer of the Mountain Brook Office Park, identified this effect as "looking over the tree tops instead of the car tops."[27]

The Research Park

A variant of the office park appeared in the 1950s that specifically targeted emerging high-technology firms. The research park was devised by both private developers as for-profit investments and universities as either for-profit or nonprofit ventures. Integral to the definition of the research park is an explicit, or at least geographic, association with one or more universities.[28] Although the private developer version of the research park eventually came to have limited appeal (by 1990 nonprofit entities, including state and local governments, sponsored 85 percent of the research parks in the United States), the university-affiliated research park came to have global renown.[29]

Boston-based Cabot, Cabot & Forbes (CC&F), a real estate management firm of long standing and blue blood, developed a series of precedent-setting

Gerald Blakeley of Cabot, Cabot & Forbes, who saw the opportunity presented by the junction of burgeoning industrial research activities in the Boston area and the new Route 128 beltway around Boston that opened up tracts of countryside for new development. He conceived of a polished, upscale form of the industrial park that would appeal to corporations engaged in research and development. Blakeley is standing in front of one of his research park projects. (Courtesy of Cabot, Cabot & Forbes, photo by Carleton W. Patriquin)

industrial, research, and office parks along Route 128, the first limited-access metropolitan beltway. The highway was planned but not under construction in 1947 when CC&F hired Gerald Blakeley, the entrepreneurial son of an MIT engineering professor who had done consulting work for Johns-Manville.[30] Blakeley understood that the highway, devised to divert through traffic around Boston, opened up new land for development with excellent automobile and truck access (figure 5.7). He conceived of an updated version of the industrial park, with stricter restrictions, ample landscape surroundings, and located not at the industrial periphery near working-class districts, but in the bucolic residential suburbs that edged the future Route 128. Blakeley targeted CC&F as the developer to carry out his idea because of the estimable social standing and political influence of the founders and partners.[31]

The first CC&F project, the New England Industrial Center, was on a 158-acre site in Needham that opened in 1952, close by the estate of one of the firm's partners. Cabot, Cabot & Forbes did not have initial support for rezoning from residential to industrial use. Like other suburban communities,

Needham resisted the incursion of commercial developments, and Blakeley carried out "missionary work" with local organizations such as women's clubs and the Rotary, stressing the tax benefits and assuring local residents that the project would not detract from the town's residential quality. In addition to 40-foot minimum setbacks, landscaping requirements, and maximum 50 percent lot coverage, the uses were limited to light manufacturing, prototype manufacturing, wholesaling, and offices. The Boston real estate community considered the project a risk. According to one of the firm's members, "There wasn't a real estate broker in Boston who didn't think we were nuts."[32] The park was organized for long-term land leases, and by 1957 all but 10 acres of the park were occupied; Blakeley had produced a 500 percent return on

5.8

As this ad made clear, the 1950s electronics industry, including research and development, relied on highly trained women workers. By the 1950s, the kind of skilled, educated "girl" that corporations wanted was increasingly found in the suburbs. (Courtesy of AT&T Intellectual Property. Used with permission)

Cabot, Cabot & Forbes's Waltham Research and Development Park built along Route 128. Route 128's first office park, the Hobbs Brook Office Park, was off the next exit along the highway. (Courtesy of Cabot, Cabot & Forbes, photo by Carleton W. Patriquin)

CC&F's initial investment. Ten years after the opening, the park also provided 10 percent of local tax revenues.[33]

The proliferating high-technology research firms in the Boston area became key tenants of the Blakeley-type industrial parks. During World War II, the Boston area had been a focus of government-sponsored high-technology defense research centered at Harvard and MIT. In the first two decades after the war, the Boston region became a dominant high-technology hub of government laboratories, research units of established corporations, and a slew of new companies formed by alumni of Harvard and, particularly, MIT. In addition, the specialized, skilled workers assembling technology components were primarily women, who were moving to suburbs in increasing numbers (figure 5.8).[34]

Quickly realizing their target market, CC&F opened the first so-named research park on Route 128 in 1955, the Waltham Research and Development Park, next door to the Hobbs Brook Office Park (figure 5.9). Although the development covenants allowed the same uses as their previous industrial parks, the allowable lot coverage was considerably less, 20 to 33 percent instead of 50 percent.[35] CC&F opened the Lexington Office Research Park in 1958, a further permutation of its lucrative scheme, and quickly followed up with the Bedford Research and Office Park in 1959. The covenants allowed

the same range of uses but limited coverage to 25 percent.[36] By 1960, CC&F had ten parks either completed or under construction along Route 128; by 1968 eighteen were in place.[37] With each park, building densities decreased, reflecting ever greater emphasis on a pastoral context that harmonized a wide range of building types and uses, including "light manufacturing, proto-type production, and offices" (figure 5.10).[38]

CC&F originally thought that it could attract existing corporate research and development departments. Although two corporations built what were essentially corporate campuses within CC&F research parks, during this period of expansive economic growth established corporations preferred to build corporate campuses as their own facilities on their own properties.[39] Instead, the range of uses in research parks perfectly suited upstart high-technology firms that were rapidly developing, testing, and manufacturing prototype electronic products while creating an entirely new industry and industrial cluster.[40] These firms were not in a position to split production from management and research and yet needed a demonstrably middle-class context to attract high-technology

5.10

The Sylvania Electric facility within the Waltham Research and Development Park. (Courtesy of Cabot, Cabot & Forbes, photo by Carleton W. Patriquin)

scientists and engineers and mostly female assembly workers. As the *New York Times* reported, CC&F's Route 128 research parks gave high-technology "executives and researchers a campus atmosphere."[41] It also made the developments more appealing to suburban jurisdictions and home owners. As a vice president of CC&F explained, the research park "appeals to people to whom 'Industrial' is a dirty, smoke belching word. It is current, sophisticated, and perhaps, above all patriotic."[42] With their flourishing success along Route 128, by 1960 CC&F had comparable projects under development in the King of Prussia suburb of Philadelphia and the suburbs of Los Angeles and San Francisco.[43]

In the Boston area, the CC&F research parks were not explicitly allied with the universities that fostered the nascent high-technology industry, but the research parks' advent was related to the proximity of major academic research institutions such as MIT. More or less contemporary with the CC&F projects, two university-affiliated research parks appeared as well: the Stanford Industrial Park in Palo Alto, California (renamed the Stanford Research Park in the 1970s), and the Research Triangle Park of Raleigh, Durham, and Chapel Hill, North Carolina. Their success spawned a host of other university-affiliated research parks that eventually edged out private sector developers.

Stanford University developed the first university research park on part of their vast land holdings on the San Francisco peninsula. Because of the terms of Leland Stanford's endowment, the university could not sell any of its 8,800 acres, but it could lease and develop them. Cash poor, the university embarked on a development program in 1947 to generate income under the leadership of Alf Brandin, the university's business manager. Projects included a shopping center, housing, and areas for industrial uses. At the university's request, the local jurisdiction, Santa Clara County, zoned 50 acres between the city of Palo Alto and the rolling hills to the west as light industrial. The zoning designation dictated the development should have "minimum one-acre building sites, 40 percent maximum lot coverage, and one car per three hundred square feet" of floor space and limited uses to what the university referred to as "smokeless" industry.[44] Brandin credited an influential Stanford alumnus with suggesting the university's conception of the industrial land as a residential suburb, "parklike" and without fences.[45] By this time as well, Menlo Park, adjacent to Stanford, had enacted its precedent-setting zoning to accommodate suburban offices.

At the same time, the dean of engineering, Frederick Terman, who founded Stanford's electrical engineering department in the 1930s and eventually became provost in 1955, aggressively sought to connect the university with the up-and-coming high-technology industry of the San Francisco peninsula. Terman eschewed traditional demarcations between pure research and for-profit research. Most famously, in 1939 he gave a few hundred dollars of seed money to two of his brightest students, William Hewlett and David Packard. Having spent the war years on the East Coast overseeing government-sponsored research at Harvard, Terman understood that high-technology research and development would increase after the war and that Stanford could benefit intellectually and financially from close contacts with industry. By 1946 the university had already established the nonprofit Stanford Research Institute with the intent of "commercialization of our innovations," though initially not electronics; the institute had moved from the Stanford campus into a decommissioned army hospital in Menlo Park in 1947. Terman focused on a precursor of the microwave tube, traveling-wave tube technology, which had been invented at Bell Labs. Recognized for his foresight and leadership, Terman not only believed in institutional connections such as the Stanford Research Institute that brought academia and business together; he thought physical proximity enabled interchange. Terman saw the designated industrial lands as an opportunity to consolidate Stanford's ties to the soon-to-be flourishing electronics industry.[46]

Varian Associates, a new microwave tube technology corporation started in 1948 by Russell Varian and Sigurd Varian, approached Stanford to be the first tenants in the industrial zone. As Stanford engineering graduates who had spent the war years in New Jersey doing military radar research with a team of Stanford scientists yearning "longingly for California," the Varians had close personal and professional connections to Terman. In a move congruent with their East Coast counterparts, they relocated the administrative and research staffs from their San Carlos industrial site, 10 miles north of Palo Alto.[47] While maintaining their San Carlos plant, they proposed a noticeably more polished facility designed by Eric Mendelsohn, the refugee Bauhaus architect who spent his last years in San Francisco, and landscape architect Thomas Church, the renowned modernist (figure 5.11). The choice of both designers indicates the Varians' interest in elevating the working environment for their management and research personnel; although they were very cost conscious, they specifically requested that the building not have an "industrial character." The building resembled an extended western ranch house, with a porch colonnade wrapping the entire perimeter and a low-pitched hip roof enclosing the extensive mechanical rooftop equipment required for the laboratories. The site plan displayed a classic modernist design strategy, canting the orthogonals of the building 45 degrees to the square of the 10-acre lot and placing it in the center.[48]

5.11

The Varian Associates project in the Stanford Industrial Park in 1960. The site illustrates the minimal embellishments of the early projects in the research park. (Courtesy of the Palo Alto Historical Association)

Construction at the Varian Associates site was underway in 1951, and in the same year, the university officially designated the area as the Stanford Industrial Park. With this designation, the university reserved the right to review all proposed construction plans and approve of all tenants. In 1953 the industrial park was incorporated into Palo Alto and its zoning added to Palo Alto's municipal regulations, with additional requirements for a 90-foot landscape setback along roadways and the placement of parking behind structures to screen it from view.[49] From then on, as the park expanded, the additional acreage became incorporated into the city of Palo Alto.

By 1955 the size of the park was 220 acres and included sites for Eastman Kodak, General Electric, Houghton Mifflin, Scott Foresman, Admiral Corporation, Preformed Line Products, Beckman Instruments, and, most notably, Hewlett-Packard, which had amply profited during the war years. Like Varian Associates, Hewlett-Packard (HP) reiterated the pattern that had taken place in the East and Midwest and repositioned its managers and researchers out of their production site by the Palo Alto railroad tracks uphill into the Stanford Industrial Park. The move was intended to reflect "the company philosophy that people require attractive and pleasant surroundings to attain maximum job satisfaction and to perform to the best of their abilities."[50] The headquarters, completed in 1960, displayed an elevated level of design with building architecture by Clark, Stromquist, and

Sandstrom and landscape architecture once again by Thomas Church that "exuded the optimism of the opening of the electronics age."[51] Canted on site at 45 degrees like the Varian building, the HP complex was like a small version of a corporate campus, complete with cafeteria and buildings surrounding a well-designed central open space that Church conceived of as a "worker's playground" and included "horseshoe pits, volleyball and badminton courts" (figure 5.12).[52]

By 1960, the park had grown to 345 acres and included a sizable acreage devoted to Lockheed Missile and Aircraft. At that point, Stanford proposed to add another 250 acres and accommodate a tenant, the Ampex Corporation, on 80 acres edging up the hillsides of the university property. But local residents balked. Like so many of the other suburban residential communities into which corporations wished to expand, they had been suspicious and wary of Stanford's plans from the beginning. Local activists put the annexation through a contentious referendum that ultimately swung in Stanford's favor but reflected a reality of the Stanford Industrial Park. It was not planned as a coherent development, and its regulations were "lenient and sketchy."[53] As a 1961 critic noted, "Much has been made by Brandin and other university officials concerning the esthetic [sic] quality of these smokeless plants. Yet although it is true that the 40 percent

5.12

The Stanford Industrial Park in 1960, with Palo Alto beyond. The new Hewlett-Packard facility is visible at the center of the photograph, the canted foursquare of buildings surrounding an interior courtyard. The photograph shows the rather spare and sparse quality of the park in its first two decades. (Courtesy of the Palo Alto Historical Association)

ground coverage and mandatory landscaping represent higher standards than in conventional developments, very few structures can be described as handsome; some are extremely coarse. Furthermore, even 40 percent of ground coverage—a figure that may seem satisfactory on paper—proved too generous a concession on the part of the university. The sites are much too crowded."[54]

Far from the elevated standards the university claimed, the Stanford Industrial Park was more industrial than park and did not approach the development standards being promoted in corporate campuses, suburban office zoning, office parks, research parks, or even the more stringent industrial parks. Without the influence of the university, the project would likely not have been approved in such an elite setting as Palo Alto, and without the intensity of development, the project might not have attracted tenants and become financially viable. (For instance, Varian Associates would have needed almost twice as much land for their complex if they had followed the zoning of one of the CC&F research parks.) Ampex ultimately pulled out of the project as a result of the protests; later, when Stanford again proposed extending the industrial park, local hill preservation advocates sued. As a result, site coverage decreased to 20 percent, and by the end of the 1960s, Stanford became more stringent in reviewing the uses and designs of tenants. By that time, enough of the park had been developed at the higher rate, and a desirable concentration of companies had made the cost of the lower density competitive. Not until the 1970s, however, when the park had grown to over 600 acres, did Stanford codify standards and rename the site the Stanford Research Park.[55]

Stanford Research Park is now part of the creation narrative of Silicon Valley, and its existence has come to be seen as sui generis.[56] As the Stanford Industrial Park, the electronics industry, and Stanford itself evolved in the 1950s and 1960s, the mythic initiative of the park and its creators became both lore and a marketing tool. (Brandin even claimed he invented the term industrial park.[57] In fact, it existed in American manufacturing suburbs for at least three decades before 1950.) Stanford Industrial Park was (and often still is) presented as the genesis of the entire concept of high-technology scientists and engineers working in a green, select, suburban context—a "campus-like" atmosphere—an idea that Terman reinforced. Yet work at the Bell Labs corporate campus dominated electronic research and development through the 1950s and beyond, churning out more patents than any other enterprise. Terman, like every other electronic scientist working in the 1940s and 1950s, could not have avoided knowing about it. Indeed, by 1955, the Bell Labs transistor came west in the person of its co-inventor, William Shockley, who set up shop south of Palo Alto in Mountain View. (The next generation of high-technology entrepreneurship was located there and in Sunnyvale, in industrial and office parks.) While Terman rightly claimed that his entrepreneurial vision of high-technology industry and academic cooperation was fulfilled in the ascendancy of Varian, Hewlett-Packard, and the astounding number of successful companies that eventually formed on the San Francisco peninsula, most of the initial tenants of the Stanford Industrial Park were local branches of established corporations, and many were not high-technology firms at all. Stanford Industrial Park was a speculative, for-profit development—surprisingly, a rather sparely pastoral one in its first two decades—that met an existing trend to place corporate management in general, and scientists and engineers in particular, in exclusive residential suburbs.

One can even see that Hewlett-Packard's famously nonhierarchical style of "management by walking around" had antecedents in Bell Labs management with "no chains of command clanking in the corridors."[58] Like Bell's campus, the top management and researchers in HP's small-scale complex within the Stanford Industrial Park relied on its "campus-like" context to reinforce the casual transference of knowledge that facilitates invention. But HP and all the other firms locating in what would become the Silicon Valley did indeed have an advantage over their Northeast and Midwest counterparts: the absurdly clement weather of the San Francisco Peninsula that made going in and out and around buildings a nonissue, if not a pleasure. It made the promise of the pastoral corporate workplace that much more real. Annalee Saxenian, in her seminal study contrasting the electronics industries of Route 128 and the Silicon Valley, attributes Silicon Valley's dominance to a corporate culture that stresses communication over competition. While Silicon Valley's entrepreneurs readily met in a myriad of informal and social settings in their work and leisure places, easily sharing information, Route 128's rarely strayed out of their offices. No doubt this is the result of the more conspicuously hierarchical, suspiciously competitive culture of the New England firms, as Saxenian observed.[59] But one cannot help surmise that the habit of ease of movement and communication in the Silicon Valley might begin with the "workers' playgrounds" themselves, and in this the Stanford Industrial Park can claim originality.

What the Stanford Industrial Park most famously did was make the corporate campus fiction an actuality. Location within university lands and the frequent exchange with the Stanford faculty and students promised as part of tenancy in the park reduced the level of dissemblance associated with working on a "campus" that was really part of a capitalist enterprise. Terman tried to remove any last stigmas associated with for-profit scientific research. Placing industrial researchers literally within the university realm was essential in that process.

Coeval with the conception of the Stanford Industrial Park, a coalition of political, academic, and development interests formed to establish a research center in North Carolina. By the late 1940s, Howard W. Odum, the renowned University of North Carolina, Chapel Hill, sociologist, comprehended the implications of the flow of research and development dollars from the government and private industry. Aware of what Stanford was doing, but in an opposite tack from Terman, he was concerned that the university be shielded from compromising profit motives and remain in the realm of pure research. Odum conceived of a separate research institution sponsored by the University of North Carolina and North Carolina State College at Raleigh and two of the state's black colleges, the Agricultural and Technical College at Greensboro and North Carolina College at Durham. He proposed the institute be located between Raleigh, Durham, and Chapel Hill close by the Raleigh-Durham airport. The institute could carry out contract research while preserving the integrity of the universities' mission. In 1953, the universities' administration did not accept Odum's initial proposal, and he died in 1954, but his academic colleagues continued to look for an opportunity to bring his idea to fruition.[60]

While Odum and his colleagues had proceeded on the academic front, a local developer and contractor, Romeo Guest, was attempting to attract the laboratories of northeastern corporations to the area. An MIT graduate, Guest was well aware of the success of research-oriented real estate in metropolitan Boston and understood that the nexus of universities in central North Carolina might be marketable to research and development enterprises. Extremely well connected, Guest began discussing his idea for a concentration of research facilities between Raleigh, Durham, and Chapel Hill with state politicians and university faculty and, in 1953, coined "Research Triangle" to describe the zone centered around the Raleigh-Durham Airport between the three cities. By 1954, Guest nationally distributed a brochure describing the Research Triangle, *Conditioned for Research*, which emphasized the nearby universities, the abundance of educated labor, and an "ideal" setting for facilities "on acres and acres of beautiful rolling land" (figure 5.13).[61] He lobbied the top university administrators at Duke University, NC State, and UNC, and in 1955 he met with the governor, Luther Hodges, to promote the idea; Hodges made it his own. North Carolina ranked second from the bottom in per capita income in the United States, and though the state's universities produced excellent graduates, the best ones left North Carolina for employment elsewhere. Hodges saw the opportunity to reverse that trend and bring a new set of corporate interests to North Carolina, besides its established industries of textile mills, furniture production, and tobacco.[62]

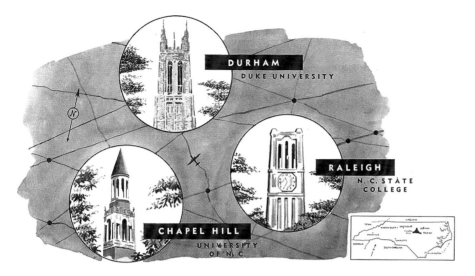

The initial conception of the Research Triangle was as a for-profit speculative development for Guest and other investors. The state would play a critical role in stewarding the project and supplying infrastructure, and the universities would raise private and foundation funds to establish a research center in the triangle as an anchor development. Hodges and Guest assembled a set of investors and bought almost ninety parcels; eventually the property encompassed 5,000 acres of pine woodlands interspersed with agricultural fields (figure 5.14).[63] In 1958 the project was significantly restructured. The investors were bought out, and the Research Triangle Park became a venture of the nonprofit Research Triangle Foundation established by Duke, UNC, and NC State. Besides overseeing the foundation and the park, the universities formed the nonprofit Research Triangle Institute, to do contract research, located on 157 acres at the center of the park near the airport. George Herbert, the former executive associate director of the Stanford Research Institute, assumed leadership of the Research Triangle Institute.[64] The institute fulfilled much of Odum's original vision, except that Duke University, a private, all-white university, was included and North Carolina A&T and North Carolina College were left out. While this is easy to understand as a manifestation of the southern color line, it is not so different

5.14

The site of the Research Triangle Park in 1959. Woods covered much of the site, which had very little infrastructure to support the kind of development envisioned by the promoters of the park. (Courtesy of the Research Triangle Foundation)

from the exclusionary interests that New York City corporations had in moving to Westchester in the search for employees of "a better type."

From the outset, the Research Triangle Park focused on serving research divisions of established corporations, not nurturing start-ups. Hodges saw it as a way of generating economic development and high-quality jobs.[65] In 1959 the state created the Research Triangle Regional Planning Commission to undertake the planning, implementation, and regulation of the park's development and ongoing maintenance. The state completed new access highways to and through the park, forming its basic layout (figure 5.15). Since the park encompassed an unprecedented acreage, land costs were relatively modest, and the foundation did not need to make a profit, the development guidelines for the park were unusually restrictive. Purchased lots (there were no leases) were permitted only 5 percent coverage, and uses were narrowly limited to research. Deep landscape perimeters preserved woodlands on all sides. No structures could be visible from

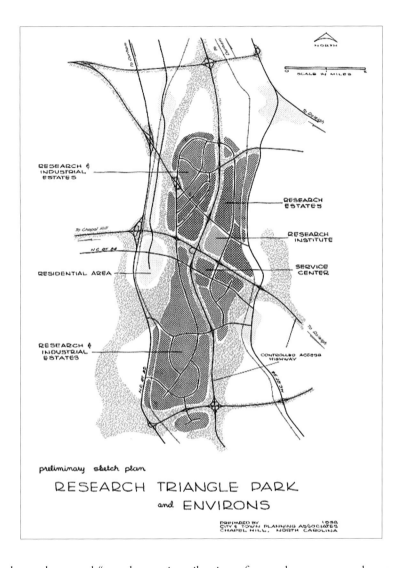

RESEARCH & INDUSTRIAL ESTATES

RESEARCH ESTATES

RESEARCH INSTITUTE

RESIDENTIAL AREA

SERVICE CENTER

RESEARCH & INDUSTRIAL ESTATES

CONTROLLED ACCESS HIGHWAY

preliminary sketch plan

RESEARCH TRIANGLE PARK
and ENVIRONS

PREPARED BY 1958
CITY & TOWN PLANNING ASSOCIATES
CHAPEL HILL, NORTH CAROLINA

5.15
An initial plan for Research Triangle Park from 1958. With wending roadways, broad swaths of woodlands, and "estates" for research, the park took advantage of the existing rural qualities of the site, significant public subsidies for infrastructure, and inexpensive land costs to create an overwhelmingly pastoral context for its tenants. (Courtesy of the Research Triangle Foundation)

the roadways and "no odors, noise, vibrations, fumes, dust, gases, smoke, etc. permitted to cross property lines."[66]

The Research Triangle Institute was the initial 1960 occupant, followed by Chemstrand laboratory (a fiber and polymer research division of the Monsanto Corporation), two small laboratories, and a field station of the U.S. Forest Service. Given the laggardly pace of development by 1965, the Planning Commission extended lot coverage to a still remarkably low 15 percent and allowed some limited manufacturing activities in conjunction with research activities.[67] That year the Johnson administration, in a political payback to Governor Terry

Sanford, announced that the Environmental Health Sciences Center (later renamed the National Institute of Environmental Health Sciences) would be placed in the park, and IBM bought 400 acres for a research and production facility.[68] The Research Triangle Park then developed rapidly, and by 1978, *Science* announced, "Research Triangle Park Succeeds Beyond Its Promoters' Expectations."[69] It attracted chemical, electronic, material science, pharmaceutical, and biotechnology research from major national and international corporations, significantly diversifying its corporate base. It is now the largest research park in the United States (6,600 acres), employing the most employees (40,000), and by one estimate has the highest percentage of scientists and engineers (33 percent) (figure 5.16).[70]

In spite of the fact that the establishment and expansion of the Research Triangle Park had no apparent opposition, it was planned and controlled with far greater stringency than Stanford Industrial Park. Distinct from other suburban corporate landscapes, it was not associated with any specific high-end residential

5.16

Today the Research Triangle Park is the largest research park in the United States and one of the largest in the world, covering over 6,000 acres. Even with low densities and generous woodland buffers, it still has new development sites on offer. (Courtesy of the Research Triangle Foundation)

area, though many sprang up as a result of the economic growth generated by the park. The development guidelines guarded the pleasing visual rurality of the landscape, at least the view from the road, but this contrasted sharply with the intensely technocratic capitalism carried on within the sites. Occupants confirmed that the perceived prestige and the quality of their sites were by far the most important reasons for locating in Research Triangle Park.[71] In a regionally unglamorous location, not the realm of start-ups and venture capitalists, and so sprawling as to defy perception as a place-based entity, it received, and continues to receive, far less notice than what is arguably its lesser competitor, the Stanford Research Park.

The Stanford Research Park and the Research Triangle Park became two models of university-affiliated research park development. Stanford was a for-profit venture, part of an amplification of the university's capital portfolio intended to serve an existing regional market; the Research Triangle Park was a nonprofit investment intended to boost a region's lagging economy by creating highly attractive conditions for outside investors. Both models would be used by the scores of research parks developed in subsequent decades in both the United States and abroad.

Expansion of the Office Park

By the end of the 1950s, the market for exclusively white-collar facilities in the suburbs spurred for-profit private developers to expand their investment in office parks. By 1960 they had established office parks in Omaha, Nebraska; St. Paul, Minnesota; and Kansas City, Missouri, as well as additional ones in Birmingham and Waltham; by 1965 in suburban Atlanta, Georgia; Oklahoma City; Mobile, Alabama; Tucson, Arizona; Englewood, Colorado; Asheville, North Carolina; San Mateo, California; Kansas City, Kansas; Chattanooga, Tennessee; Wellesley, Massachusetts; El Paso, Houston, and Dallas, Texas; and Oakbrook, Illinois.[72] That same year the trend prompted *Industrial Development and Manufacturers Record* (a corporate real estate development journal) to initiate an annual office park report. It identified office park locations as "cities which serve as regional capitals for commerce, finance, and industry." The personnel of corporate expansion and decentralization, "middle executives and their staffs . . . a sales force or regional administrative operation," tenanted the projects, as well as corporate service business such as insurance, accounting, architectural, and engineering firms. The journal delineated the typical features of office parks besides a maximum 25 to 33 percent lot coverage:

> They are self-contained areas with internal street patterns and access . . . usually small tracts of less than 75 acres. . . .
>
> . . . A great deal of attention is given to landscaping and land-use to provide a controlled environment. . . . This controlled environment characteristic expresses itself in such performance standards and deed covenants as setback and landscaping requirements, design and construction control, sign restrictions, and off-street parking requirements. . . . The self-contained nature of parks with the above restrictions creates quiet campus-like environments, quite different from the usual bustle of downtown locations.

The journal observed that new office parks were located near arterial roads leading to the central business district and "near or in better residential areas of the city." While the article noted that being out of the "traffic-jammed" downtown was "a definite, clear-cut advantage," this precluded "convenient public transportation of office staff." Once again, "lower turnover among employees" was a major benefit of the office park. The article concluded, "The attractiveness of a controlled environment, apart from the normal strains of the downtown locations, is a definite asset of an office park."[73]

That same article also pointed to a notable geographic trend—the early development of office parks around cities in the Southeast. In light of the civil disobedience of the civil rights movement that focused on public space, commercial venues, and public transportation in southeastern urban centers, the "controlled environment" of the office park with private streets and no public transportation could be seen as an "asset" that extended well beyond efficiency. In cities like Atlanta or Birmingham in 1965, making an employment center accessible only by automobile drastically filtered the employee pool along racial lines.

As office parks proliferated, developers increasingly understood the marketing value of landscape design; developers hired the veteran designers of corporate campuses and estates. Sasaki, Walker and Associates designed "a truly campus-like atmosphere" in Atlanta's first office park, the 1965 Executive Park, adjacent to an interstate exit. The project was preceded by Peachtree Industrial Boulevard, an industrial park developed in immediate postwar years that brought branch plants of such national corporations such as General Electric, Deere & Company, General Motors, and Eastman Kodak. Atlanta had also completed a major upgrade of its airport in 1959 and had a beltway under construction, enabling the Executive Park tenants to easily connect to regional clients and back to headquarters offices. The developer, Michael Gearon, fined contractors $1,000 for every existing tree that was destroyed during construction, a clear valuation of the pastoral qualities of the site. *Business Week* reported: "Office buildings of striking modern architecture, one four stories tall, nestle in a sylvan setting off boulevards that wind through 144 acres of a former dairy farm." Gearon reasoned, rightly it turned out, that cities like Atlanta were primed for office park development because sluggish growth had left large, undeveloped tracts close to the central business districts; Executive Park was just eight miles from the downtown. It was a quick success, a "developer's dream," attracting thirty-seven tenants in thirty months, 90 percent of them national corporations. The density of the office park increased, with building heights rising to as many as eight stories.[74] By 1972 thirty-nine office parks had located in suburban Atlanta, and between 1964 and 1974, almost two-thirds of new office space in the Atlanta region was constructed in the suburbs.[75]

By 1968 the Urban Land Institute (ULI), a development industry research association, published the first office park planned unit development (PUD) ordinance (modeled after residential planned unit development) in its widely distributed series, *New Zoning Landmarks*.[76] That same year, ULI first included office parks as "a newly emerging type of commercial development project" in the widely used industry reference, *Community Builders Handbook*.[77] A subsequent analysis by ULI used the comprehensive term business parks to discuss the diverse types of office parks appearing in the suburbs.[78] These variations emerged because the industrial park and office park, formerly discrete, became conflated by the mid-1960s. Slow-growing industrial parks set aside zones for white-collar offices; for example, the 200-acre Bohannon Industrial Park in Menlo Park, California, opened in 1954, but by 1969 introduced a sector of exclusively office uses.[79]

By the late 1960s, the expansion of suburban white-collar workplaces made office parks a "sure bet in most places" for investors. *Business Week* reported that the "controlled environment" of the office park attracted not only "the service departments of downtown companies" but top management as well. Office parks allowed corporations to avoid the hassles and cost of building their own headquarters while occupying a separate establishment rather than several anonymous floors in a downtown skyscraper.[80] The tenants in office parks, while all white collar, were extremely various. For instance, Oak Brook Office Park, which opened in 1960 in a Chicago suburb, contained tenant businesses ranging in size from fewer than 10 people to more than 700 employees by 1969. They included sales offices of national corporations, insurance firms, finance companies and accountants, employment and real estate agencies, architects, and lawyers. Most of the firms had relocated from the central business district. Notably, Oak Brook Office Park was one part of a larger comprehensive suburban development that included "executive homes," a shopping center, a light industrial district, and extensive open space amenities, including fox hunting, country clubs, and a forest preserve. The office park was part of a larger prestigious community.[81]

A Longer, Greener View

By the early 1980s, with urban highway networks essentially complete, office parks proliferated in the suburbs. While mortgage lending for local developers continued to be a source of investment capital, joint ventures between local developers and well-capitalized financial institutions became common. Commercial banks, insurance companies, cash-rich corporations, and pension funds partnered in office parks, and in 1980 the federal government deregulated savings and loan corporations so that they could lend insured savings to speculative developers.[82] With the influx of risk capital, a two-decade track record of profitability, and the continuing expansion of suburbs in American metropolitan areas, office parks became a particular focus of real estate investment. Office park projects enlarged significantly in scale and often included supporting uses, such as hotels, restaurants, retail, and day care centers. A 1968 national survey of office parks found that typical building lots were 4 acres in size and ranged from 1 to 7 acres, the total size of an office park was about 70 acres, and the expected build-out was several hundred thousand square feet of office space.[83] In the 1980s office park projects began to contain building lots of 20 to 40 acres and extend over hundreds of acres; target square footages of 1 to 5 million were customary, and 10 to 15 million square feet were not uncommon.[84]

Traffic patterns, utilities, and, above all, the parking had to work in the expanded parks of the 1980s, but they were a given. Office park owners increasingly focused on the landscape as "a function of why people moved to the suburbs in the first place . . . to enjoy a pastoral environment," while generic architecture proved quite adequate. An office park entrepreneur explained to a national convention of fellow office park developers:

> It is not like a downtown setting where you have a high-rise building dominating the site, with very little open land round it. There people notice and recall the design of the structure. But in the suburbs where you may have a

six-story building and two or three two-story buildings there is not enough
building mass to do anything noteworthy in architectural terms.

Here people are most impressed with the landscaping, the visual
appeal. They remember how they got in and out, how they moved around,
how the park looks. When they say the park looks "pretty" they do not
mean the buildings.[85]

While in practice small-scale buildings can certainly be distinguished, this statement underscores how fundamental the pastoral space of the office park was to
its promotion in the real estate market; the quote was highlighted in the second
major publication on office park development. Not surprisingly, landscape architects became the key planners and designers of office parks during this period.

In the expanded office park terrain, the new designs relaxed the pastoral
squeeze and allowed a more generous effect. Principal roadways of office parks became multilane arterials with landscape medians and generous verges of green—"a
scenic parkway" in the case of Corporate Woods outside Kansas City, Kansas—and
the whole complex might include site amenities such as trails, parks, recreation
facilities, even golf courses (figure 5.17). The landscape design, in combination
with distinctive signs identifying the park, what developers call the signage system,
provided orientation through the vast projects and an address for the business
tenants (figure 5.18). A combination of signage and particularly showy landscaping adorned the principal entrances and the freeway or arterial frontages of office

5.17

As seen here in the Arvida Park of
Commerce in Boca Raton, Florida,
designed by the SWA Group,
office park developers added
landscape amenities to their
projects, such as parkways and
golf courses, through the 1980s
and early 1990s. These extended
landscape features were integral
in marketing these speculative
projects in an increasingly
competitive market, as office parks
became a common constituent of
the suburbs. (Courtesy of SWA
Group, photo by Gerry Campbell)

5.18
As is typical of office park developments of the past three decades, the Arvida Park of Commerce signage system allowed tenant corporate offices to create a recognizable address while adding to the general sense of order and environmental control within the office park. (Courtesy of SWA Group, photo by Gerry Campbell)

parks.[86] With 1 million square feet of office space, the Cornell Oaks Corporate Center in Washington County, Oregon, designed by the landscape architects Mitchell Nelson Group, exemplified the more generous, even elegant, landscape of office parks (figure 5.19).[87] Schemes also maximized pastoral effects by clustering buildings along green spines such as EDAW's design for Dulles Corner in suburban Washington, D.C., where multistoried buildings edged a "Central Park," a telling reference to Olmsted.[88] Useful for promotion, the new office parks created a longer, greener view, uninterrupted by parking lots.

As office parks proliferated, developers vied for prospective tenants, and the landscape design bore the burden of attracting them. At Hacienda Business Park in Pleasanton, California (at the eastern reaches of the Bay Area metropolitan zone, 30 miles east of San Francisco), the developers conceived of an astounding 12 million square feet of office space for 40,000 workers as a "self-contained city" to be built out over a thirty-year period.[89] In a joint venture representative of the period, the Prudential Insurance Company, a national insurance corporation, owned 83 percent of the property; Callahan-Pentz, a local developer, owned the balance and was charged with the day-to-day tasks of development. (They had successfully partnered on three previous developments). Sites within the park were offered in a wide range of options: "straight land sales, speculative office projects, build-to-suit leases, build to sell, land sales to other developers."[90] The developers geared the park's visual appeal to the streetscape (figure 5.20). The 860-acre project was visible from the adjoining Interstate 580 and close by the intersection of another one. The landscape architects, POD, Inc., and the graphic designer, Michael Vanderbyle, designed gateway arches integrating colonnades of custom lights, signage, tilted quarter rounds of lawn, and arcing lines of trees placed at the peripheral entrances of the office park and at key orienting intersections. The arches became the symbol of Hacienda, adorning stationery and pervading promotional materials.[91] The developers reasoned, "We wanted to create a statement people won't forget. . . . Corporate facility people tour the state in a 72 hour period. They will see numerous projects and go back to their offices with stacks of brochures—they never forget Hacienda."[92]

These massive office park projects necessitated much more complex site engineering, traffic management, political agreements, and long-term governance structures than the earlier generation of office parks. Within two years after the land purchase for Hacienda was complete, in 1980, the developer and the local city and county authorities moved expeditiously to establish a range of mechanisms to facilitate the park's development. The city of Pleasanton adopted the developers' subdivision plan and development guidelines as an amendment to its general plan and zoning ordinances and certified an environmental impact report (EIR)

5.19

As "looking over tree tops instead of car tops" became more important in marketing office parks, landscape architecture was ever more essential to their development. Cornell Oaks Corporate Center, in the suburbs of Portland, Oregon, typifies the large-scale post-1980s office park with ample, substantially planted parkways, parking lot berms, medians, and verges. While the lots await development, the amplitude of greenery (comparatively much less expensive to construct) compensated for the decades- long incremental build-out of office buildings, creating a recognizable place even without structures. (Courtesy of Maul Foster Alongi)

5.20

The Hacienda Business Park archways, part of a marketing strategy to make the business park memorable to prospective corporate tenants scouting for office locations. (Photo by author.)

required under California law for a project of this scale. The city also established the largest assessment district in California, the North Pleasanton Improvement District, to finance the infrastructure. As a former seasonal wetland prone to flooding, the site required comprehensive regrading in which higher elevations were cut and the lower elevation filled, and flood control channels were consolidated and rerouted. The expected traffic necessitated improvements to existing arterials and streets, the upgrade of two freeway interchanges and the construction of two entirely new ones, over 10 miles of new streets within the project, and two new fire stations. The developers also established the Hacienda Business Park Owners Association to maintain the streets and landscaping within the office park (the streets had been deeded to the city as public property); to run a design review committee in charge of upholding the park's detailed covenants, codes, and restrictions; and to operate the developer-built Hacienda Child Care Center.[93]

Like many other communities before them, Pleasanton residents expressed dismay over the scale of the development and the apparent inevitability of a project that would house a workforce of 40,000—2,000 more than lived in Pleasanton at the time. Even before their land assembly from six property owners was complete, and anticipating local opposition, the development team hired a polling group to canvass Pleasanton and assess the political obstacles to the project; in response, the developers organized an aggressive public relations campaign and a speakers bureau to promote the project. Nonetheless, a local citizens' group, Citizens for Balanced Growth (CBG), sued the city and developer in 1982 over the validity of the EIR and general plan amendment. While the court upheld the environmental findings, it invalidated the general plan amendment, and the city had to rewrite the entire general plan to incorporate Hacienda's zoning and guidelines and certify a new EIR. CBG then placed the project on a referendum in 1985, but the developers won by a 65 to 35 percent margin.[94]

Comparable to the large-scale residential development that preceded them in postwar suburbs, these massive office park projects of the 1980s were far from being purely private speculative enterprises (figure 5.21). An extensive public

5.21

The Hacienda Business Park in Pleasanton, California. At 860 acres, almost the same size as New York's Central Park, the scale is very typical of office parks after 1980. The AT&T Center discussed in chapter 6 is in the upper right of the office park just below the freeway. (Terraserver)

financial and jurisdictional apparatus supported them, and the local political elite worked effectively to quash grassroots opposition. By the time the Bay Area Rapid Transit (BART) broke ground for a new station at Hacienda in 1991, an additional public investment that the developers lobbied for, the public had to be regarded as a sub rosa partner in the project.

This snug relationship between the developer and the public jurisdictions governing the property mitigated the risks associated with the immense speculative investment. The suburban office market softened in the late 1980s as a result of overbuilding; market absorption simply could not keep pace with the rate of office development. As early as 1988, suburban Atlanta had an office vacancy rate of over 23 percent, and by the early 1990s, the national average of suburban office vacancies was over 20 percent—and these statistics did not consider the many unbuilt parcels in most post-1980 office parks.[95] The empty offices, the savings and loan collapse, and the restructuring of risk capital in its wake had considerable effects on office parks like Hacienda: parcel development slowed, capital flows to repay loans ebbed, and financial restructuring was difficult to come by. But by then, the public interest lay with the financial success of the office park, and Pleasanton moved to rezone sections of the park for housing for which risk capital was still available. New public facilities were also constructed in the office park: the Pleasanton post office, the Alameda County Superior Court, the Livermore-Pleasanton Municipal Court, a community college branch, and a middle school.[96] The rezoning and public facilities carried the project through to the more expansive economic times of the late 1990s, when office construction resumed throughout the Bay Area.[97] By 1999 the original joint venture partners had sold the last of their properties, and by 2005 only a few parcels remained empty.[98]

As in earlier office parks, the generous pastoral effects of the parkways and parking lot berms served to give the park coherence during a long build-out period and visual consistency around diverse building types, including housing, which was not expected at the outset. But the amplitude of Hacienda's pastoral landscape constructed well ahead of most of the office park buildings through the auspices of a public finance district also served as a buffer against the vagaries of economic cycles. Joe Callahan, a partner and the public relations and management lead in the project, later said that this "allowed us to create the illusion, and reality, of a major location."[99] In negotiating their way through an economic downturn, a "major location" enmeshed in the budgetary structures of public entities that corresponded to a physical reality of archways and greenswards proved to have surprising leverage in the supposedly clear-cut calculations of the bottom line; Hacienda survived. By 2007 Hacienda contained 475 companies, at least 75 of them publicly traded corporations, and comprised headquarters, major regional offices, and large back offices of over 40 corporations, including Roche Holding AG, Oracle, Kaiser Permanente, Safeway, Walmart, Shaklee, Cisco, Dahlin Group, AT&T, Sun Microsystems, and Simpson Manufacturing, some occupying upward of 1 million square feet.[100]

The amplitude of post-1980 office parks also began to extend, at least for a time, the aesthetics of office parks beyond the Olmstedian pastoral. Postmodernist singularity served developers seeking to distinguish projects in ubiquitously undulating suburbs. THK Associates designed the master plan for the 180-acre Greenwood Plaza, an office park in suburban Denver, in 1970. Over the next decade, the office park innovated a water reuse and recharge system that integrated a number of retention ponds as features in its pastoral landscape. By the early 1980s, the landscape design resulted in lowered utility fees, conserved water, and a familiar but generic appearance. In 1982 when new owners developed the next two buildings in the project, they commissioned SWA Group to complete the landscape design (figure 5.22). The two glass box office buildings sat in the middle of the lot and faced each other across a courtyard above a parking garage. The design surrounding the two buildings looked like the rest of office park: parking berms, clusters of trees, a pond with a little bridge. The interior courtyard was designed by George Hargreaves, then with SWA Group.[101] In a marked challenge to the prevailing forms of Olmstedian pastoralism, the skewed yet obvious geometries and bold color palette signaled the advent of postmodernism in American landscape architecture. The developer got a uniquely hallucinatory vision that became known as Harlequin Plaza (figure 5.23). In *Landscape Architecture*, a local landscape architect wrote: "Harlequin Plaza is in opposition to everything I know about program, process, and product. But maybe it is for these exact oppositions that I find it so invigorating, refreshing, and stimulating—a wonderful surprise."[102] Hargreaves went on to form his own firm, gain international standing in the profession of landscape architecture as a leading postmodernist, and chair the department of landscape architecture at Harvard.

Similarly, the developers intended for Solana to stand out in Dallas–Fort Worth's vast suburban market. Straddling two suburbs, Westlake and Southlake, the plan for the 900-acre site (the scale of Central Park) proposed 7 million square feet of office space, a hotel, and commercial services. The joint developers, Southwest real estate entrepreneurs Maguire Thomas Partners and IBM (the lead tenant, slated to occupy 3 million feet of office space), hired the Offices of Peter Walker and Martha Schwartz to devise the site concept and master plan.

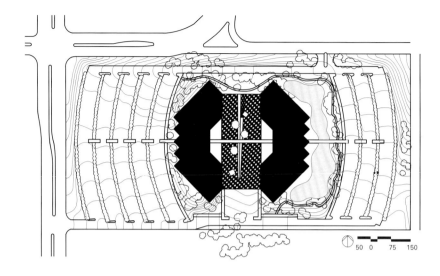

Walker was a veteran designer of corporate campuses and estates, and Schwartz, like Hargreaves, was a leader in postmodernist landscape architecture. They led a team of designers, including Legorreta Arquitectos from Mexico City, to devise a plan that integrated the site's rolling oak-studded grassland and made use of the metaphor of a Mexican hacienda in the site design—a historicist referent that typified postmodernist design (figure 5.24). A huge purple pylon framed by diagonal parallels of trees sat at the freeway interchange that accessed the office

park. Within the office park, wide wildflower meadows, clean orthogonals of lawn and gravel, orchards of regularly planted trees, canals, and a water feature that alluded to a wending prairie stream surrounded structures of massive, vibrantly colored walls.[103] The Texas architectural critic David Dillon dubbed it "Vaux on the prairie," referring to André Le Nôtre's famous seventeenth-century palace grounds, Vaux-le-Vicomte outside Paris. Solana received worldwide notoriety in publications from Japan, Germany, Great Britain, and Italy.[104]

The marketable, photo-op, postmodernist design of office parks transformed landscape architecture, but the pastoral design of office parks has prevailed through all attempts at stylistic reinterpretation. By 2005 new owners of the office park replaced Harlequin Plaza with a much more staid design (although the name lives on), and Maguire reworked Solana to display a conventional pastoral landscape and, like Hacienda, weathered Dallas–Fort Worth's glutted market by inserting suburban housing within the office park.[105] At Solana, IBM never really took up residence because its OS2 computer operating

5.24

The developers of Solana, straddling the towns of Westlake and Southlake, Texas, sought to reorient the familiar pastoral landscape aesthetic and generic modernist architecture of the office park toward a bolder, more distinctive design composed of emphatic large-scale landscape geometries complementing a set of vividly hued monumental buildings. (Courtesy of PWP Landscape Architecture) system fizzled in the software market; more than twenty years into the project; only 2.7 million square feet of the projected 7 million have been built. Solana's largest occupant, Sabre Corporation, which had eventually taken over as anchor tenant, was enticed by a ten-year 90 percent property tax abatement offered by the city of Southlake in 2002 and extended again in 2005.[106] As of spring of 2009, Sabre did not plan to renew its lease, and Maguire Properties was in serious financial trouble; it used the undeveloped part of the site to raise hay and was hoping to drill natural gas wells for additional revenue generation.[107] It is unlikely that Solana has made a return on investment; in any case, the pastoral proved not so easily dislodged (figure 5.25).

Much more significant, the large-scale, large-parcel office park changed the calculated advantage of corporate campuses and estates for American corporations. By the 1980s, U.S. companies contended with increased global competition and a more volatile economic climate, for better and worse. Exemplary of the new value-minded corporate builders was Microsoft, an ascendant corporation by any standard. After leasing buildings in an office park in Bellevue, Washington, named Corporate Campus East, Microsoft occupied its first custom-built structure in 1986: four buildings in Redmond on a large, build-to-suit parcel in an existing office park developed by a local entrepreneur.[108] The complex of cruciform buildings surrounding a small, central open space functioned as both research and development center and corporate headquarters.

5.25

In spite of international press coverage, Solana has not been an economic success, and much of the site has reverted to a much more familiar pastoral landscape. (Courtesy of PWP Landscape Architecture)

The corporation dubbed the structures the "Microsoft Corporate Campus" but began buying buildings only five years after occupying the site (figure 5.26). As the company expanded over the next three decades, Microsoft leased and bought up adjacent office parcels, built new structures, razed existing buildings to build new facilities, and extended to other office parks across an adjacent highway, a process that is still ongoing. The corporation expects to house 12,000 employees in 10 million square feet.

As it built out, Microsoft added increasingly lush and ample landscape spaces between the buildings, devoted space to recreation, and developed a unifying signage system recognized worldwide as a shorthand for the corporation (figure 5.27).[109] (If Microsoft is in the news, a view of one of its signs announcing "Microsoft Corporate Campus" almost inevitably accompanies the stories.) The office park configuration allowed Microsoft to build an estate-scale campus on the installment plan, eschewing grandiose and irretrievable expenditures, extended construction time lines, and rigid building configurations. It is a hybrid of the most advantageous qualities of the corporate campus, estate, and office park that provides flexibility, a prestigious milieu, and cost-effectiveness and likely epitomizes the continuation of suburban corporate landscapes into the foreseeable future. Like its tonier predecessors from which its key elements are derived, the Microsoft Corporate Campus stands as a symbolic and actual center for a far-flung and indubitably far-reaching corporation.

An American Versailles?

The anecdote that opens chapter 1 of this book is about the Solana office park development. In the words of one of the principals of the landscape architecture firm, Solana was to be "the American Versailles." That particular landscape vision did not come to fruition, but, arguably, office park developers through the latter half of the twentieth century, and ongoing, commanded a surfeit of capital, property, and political influence that could be made manifest by grandiloquent reorganization of the landscape. They gathered into their courts of green verges representatives from corporations of global reach that collectively affect every life on the planet.

In any metropolitan periphery in the United States, office parks are seen consistently and ubiquitously near higher-income residential areas, while corporate campuses and estates are more exceptional, even if more noteworthy. Through dowdy and modish renditions, the office park has relied on landscape articulation for promotion and, ultimately, visibility in the marketplace. Within codified standards, it could be adapted for a remarkable variety of corporate scales, uses, and levels while inserted seamlessly within the suburban milieu.

As economic growth emerged not from belching smokestacks and banging assembly lines but from binary code and biochemistry, the office park proved to be particularly adaptable to technological, information, and service ventures. These postindustrial enterprises began, incorporated, and went public entirely in city peripheries quintessentially defined by a peculiarly American concern for the pastoral. The inexorable import of the office park is that the ubiquitous, trenchant suburban aesthetic, with its implications of conformity and stability, could frame a wide array of capitalist enterprises to the seeming satisfaction of most everyone concerned.

With the office park, the standardization of production and product that directed the evolution of industrial capitalism extended to broad swaths of the national urban landscape. Office parks controlled every aspect of experience—access, orientation, materiality, and visual field—staging managerial capitalism's optimized workplace. As a kind of pinnacle of the landscape of automobility, even walking through an office park appears to defy its rigorous regulation. Devoid of the spontaneity, diversity, and happenstance that were previously integral to the geography of commerce (and is still visible in the downtowns of some cities), office parks corporatized not just office space but the peripheral expansion of American metropolitan zones.

5.27
The Microsoft Corporate Campus now occupies several million square feet on both sides of the freeway through Redmond. As it took over more office park parcels, the company added landscape areas (including some playfields) and constructed a handsome system of low signage walls that identified which parts of the office parks are part of Microsoft's facilities—a cost-effective corporate campus on the installment plan. (Used with permission of Microsoft)

6

GLOBAL PASTORAL CAPITALISM

"You will feel like you are in heaven"

If you log on to Google Earth and type in the address of the Google corporate headquarters, the globe on the main screen begins a dizzying turn, and after a few clicks hones in on a site in Mountain View, California.[1] The Google headquarters displays contemporary design gestures: buildings of juxtaposed deconstructed geometries, a witty panoply of vibrant colors, a vegetable garden, and greenhouse gas–conscious solar panels arrayed across rooftops. Zoom back a bit, leave the gestures aside, and the site plan is familiar: a central open space surrounded by low-rise buildings, peripheral drives, and parking, all edged by the green undulation of grass and trees—rooted in decades of corporate campus construction that began with AT&T Bell Labs, inventors of the transistor that makes all this laptop navigation possible (figure 6.1). Zoom back a bit farther and the larger setting of the Google Campus is also familiar—an office park, first seen in Birmingham, Alabama, over half a century ago (figure 6.2).

Close Google Earth and turn to the Google Web page, and the search engine will turn up countless sites (including Google's own) extolling Google Campus's

6.1

The Google Campus, Mountain View, California. Like Bell Labs and the GM Technical Center, the campus has a central open space, surrounded by low-rise buildings and peripheral parking and driveways, a form invented in the Northeast in the 1940s. (Terraserver)

6.2

Unlike the corporate campuses of the 1940s through the 1970s, the Google Campus is part of a preexisting office park, a type of development seen in the suburban zones of most metropolitan areas since the 1960s. Google has expanded far beyond the site known as the Google Campus and occupies many of the surrounding office buildings. It has taken over more and more office park lots as the company has grown, a cost-conscious form of pastoral capitalism. (Terraserver)

"unique" atmosphere of creativity and efficiency, many employee perquisites, an apparent lack of hierarchy, the great cafeteria, superior work spaces, cool design, and outdoor spaces to bask in the sun and think "Googley" thoughts. In an all-too-familiar refrain, *Fortune* (now online, of course) praises the campus as a place where "ideas bubble up from the lightly supervised engineers, none of whom worry too much about their projects ever making money."[2] The accolades echo, no doubt unwittingly, the 1929 memos among the AT&T Bell Labs executives as they conceived their beyond the state-of-the-art suburban research facility with "a suitable restaurant," the business literature buzz about Connecticut General's 1954 Bloomfield headquarters "ringed with amenities," and, in some way or another, descriptions of every other pastoral capitalist landscape of the past sixty years. Dig a little deeper into the blogosphere and some curled-lip posting will point out that the "Googleplex" was originally built, all the way back in 1997, as the research and development campus of SGI (Silicon Graphics Incorporated).[3]

The Google Campus is exemplary of American suburban corporate landscapes at the beginning of the twenty-first century: a corporate campus abandoned by its original occupants, reused as a suburban corporate headquarters, within an office park—a trifecta of optimized pastoral capitalism.

Global Competition and Pastoral Status

Optimization became essential as the triumphant postwar march of American managerial capitalism began to dissipate in the 1980s. While many American corporations continued to inhabit corporate campuses and estates, they did so under new conditions of downsizing and reorganization as global competition increased, hostile or friendly takeovers consolidated former competitors, investors demanded increased stock value over profits, top management introduced leaner management structures, and many parts of the corporate hierarchy were outsourced to consulting firms rather than remaining integral parts of a unified management. Corporate structures were increasingly volatile as employee ranks shrank and grew in abrupt cycles unknown in the comparatively stable American economy of the 1950s and 1960s. Suburban corporate landscapes, formed in the crucible of American corporate dominance, were reshaped in the image of the new corporations. Nowhere did this become more obvious than in the destiny of some of the much-heralded corporate estates of previous decades.

In 1970, American Can moved into its secreted, custom-designed 605,000-square-foot headquarters on 155 woodland acres in Greenwich,

Connecticut (see figure 4.15) By the early 1980s, the corporation was in the process of divesting itself of its original corporate enterprise, packaging and canning, and transforming itself into a financial services enterprise. In 1983 American Can announced it was leaving the property. Although the stated reason was that corporate employees could not find affordable housing in upscale Greenwich, downsizing had reduced the corporate workforce from 2,000 to 1,200 people. Almost half the building was empty, but under the original zoning agreement worked out with Greenwich when the building was constructed, American Can could not lease space to another business.

In 1985 when American Can sued Greenwich in order to lease parts of the building and won the right to bring in two other occupants, the town of Greenwich appealed the ruling. Still in the headquarters in 1986, American Can was bought for $570 million by Triangle Industries, which that same year bought American Can's competitor, the National Can Company, for $460 million, escalating Triangle Industries' debt to $2 billion. Down to 1,000 corporate employees, American Can then sold the building for $170 million to a real estate investment firm and took a ten-year lease on 300,000 square feet, providing "a significant amount of capital to help finance future growth," according to an American Can vice president. Renaming itself Primerica to reflect its departure from the packaging industry and down to 270 employees in 1987, the corporation still could not sublease the empty part of the building due to ongoing litigation with Greenwich over the number of tenants allowed in the building. In 1988 Pechiney S.A., a French state-owned metals conglomerate, bought Triangle Industries, and Primerica vacated the building a year later.

In 1993 a legally required property tax revaluation in Greenwich reduced assessments on office properties by 40 percent due to increasing vacancies, and the town's tax burden shifted to home owners—the exact opposite of the tax advantages that had convinced suburban jurisdictions like Greenwich to accept these developments in the first place. Needless to say, this created contention in the suburban community. That same year Connecticut governor Lowell Weicker offered $8 million in grants to Witco Corporation to relocate its 800-person staff from Manhattan and $1.2 million to Armonk Lists Company to move 175 employees from two locations in Armonk, New York, to the property, renamed the Greenwich American Center. Without the generous state subsidies, the site would have remained a "corporate white elephant."[4] Now part of an international property development and management corporation specializing in top-flight corporate offices in the United States and Europe (and soon to venture into India), Greenwich American Center is marketed as providing "appealing pastoral views from all four sides."[5]

Out among the cows when it opened in 1956, the landmark corporate estate of Connecticut General Life Insurance Company became surrounded by suburban development in subsequent decades (figure 6.3). Renamed Cigna when the corporation merged with the Philadelphia-based Insurance Company of North America in 1982, it kept 4,500 employees at the Bloomfield site while top management moved to Philadelphia. Between 1996 and 2001, the company spent $7.6 billion purchasing its own stock to sustain its value. In 1999, Cigna divested itself of its casualty and property insurance divisions, concentrating on health insurance, retirement planning, and employee benefits. That same year, it began a $1 billion upgrade of the entire corporate information technology system, expecting to be able to trim its workforce, but the system cost the company millions of customers and loss of stock value. Beginning in 2000, Cigna became the subject of a myriad of lawsuits over managed care, some brought by state governments.[6]

Cigna, which needed cash, found the development market for the Bloomfield site too lucrative to pass up, and in 2000 it proposed selling off all but 30 of 280 acres in Bloomfield for housing, a golf course, four large office buildings, and a hotel. Once praised as a model of efficiency, Cigna's building was deemed too costly to refurbish at a price of $40 million, so it would be demolished and Cigna would lease back one of the new office buildings from the developer. Employees did not care to make "work their whole world," being "more concerned about a diverse workforce, competitive salaries and things like parking," according to Cigna's assistant general counsel. He went on to say, "People moved paper around like a human conveyor belt. We don't work like that anymore." But throughout the years, Cigna had maintained the site as open space for the local community and, coupled with the architectural significance of the building, the proposed demolition raised an outcry among local residents. Preservation activists argued that the building and site be declared a historic landmark: "Frazar Wilde's plan redefined the American workplace."[7] The National Trust for Historic Preservation declared the site one of "America's 11 Most Endangered Places" in 2001. Bloomfield politicians, unwilling to upset the town's largest taxpayer, supported the redevelopment plan and noted that the corporation could "close up shop and move back to Philadelphia." As of 2002, the development was slated to go forward, but a coalition of local activists and some politicians sought a solution where the building could be maintained as a conference center and given tax breaks as a historically significant structure. But no developer came forward in response, and Cigna was to vacate the building in 2005. By that time, Cigna's fortunes had revived enough to acquiesce to the

6.3

Connecticut General Life Insurance Company headquarters, 1965. Almost a decade after its opening, the corporate estate was still surrounded by rural land, though new residential development is visible at the top right of the aerial. (Digital Collection, 1965 Aerial Surveys of Connecticut, Connecticut State Library)

pressure to rehabilitate and reinhabit the building, but it did sell off most of the surrounding property to developers, who built a golf course, a luxury hotel, and high-end condominiums (figure 6.4).[8] The "building with a future" of the 1950s was disposable by the end of the century, reluctantly saved as a relic of an expired corporate past.

By the 1990s, the long-term investment in purpose-built facilities for corporate staffs on corporate-owned properties required the kind of surplus funds, unified management, and confidence in the future that many, if not most, American corporations could no longer muster.[9] Instead, the prestige and scale of the post-1980s office park began to supplant the logic of the corporate campus and corporate estate. At Hacienda Business Park, AT&T was an initial tenant, moving a major regional office from downtown San Francisco in 1984 (see figure 5.21). In 1986 the Hacienda developers broke ground on the 1.1

6.4

The Cigna (as the corporation is now known) office building today. Under financial pressure and surrounded by suburban development, the corporation subdivided its property and sold it for development. Only after considerable public pressure did the company agree to keep the building. (Terraserver)

million-square-foot AT&T Center, a built-to-suit corporate campus within the office park, which opened in 1988 with ceremonies attended by California senator (and future governor) Pete Wilson. Its fortunes on the decline, AT&T soon abandoned the center. In 1994 the corporate headquarters of PeopleSoft, a global enterprise software corporation founded in 1987, moved to the site. (Eventually AT&T either moved or eliminated 4,000 jobs in Hacienda.) By 2002 PeopleSoft had expanded its facilities, including a new auditorium.[10] In 2005 PeopleSoft merged with Oracle after a two-year takeover battle characterized by *BusinessWeek* as "bitter and bizarre."[11] Now a much-reduced Oracle staff remains in two smaller buildings, while Kaiser Permanente health care has occupied part of the square footage. The more grandiose developer-built office parks with large build-to-suit parcels offer a singular corporate advantage in a competitive global economy—pastoral status with an exit strategy.

Pastoral Capitalism Goes Global

At the same time that American corporations began to be challenged by global competitors in the 1980s, American corporations' model of pastoral capitalism began to be adopted abroad. Although residential suburbs in the three decades after World War II were not solely American artifacts, the suburban offices of white-collar employment were an exclusively American phenomenon. In the rest of the world, corporate management resided either in offices near industrial plants or in city business districts, as it had in the United States before World War II. By the 1970s, this began to change as American corporations established substantial overseas facilities based on their homeland counterparts, European corporations built facilities based on American models, and the office park materialized as the landscape of choice for globalized managerial capitalism.

In the early 1970s, IBM built a corporate estate for its European headquarters outside Portsmouth, in southern England. Alongside the M27 motorway, which provided broad views into the site, the building rested on filled marshland once expected to accommodate the northern expansion of Portsmouth's harbor. Designed by architects and engineers Arup Associates and landscape architect Anthony Paul, the site displays the vocabulary of stateside comparables: a generous expanse of pastoral lakes, trees, and grass facing the adjoining motorway, buildings of notable architectural distinction, carefully orchestrated circulation, and a block of large parking facilities completely hidden from public view. Striking to contemporary British reviewers was the site's quality of a "defensive isolated island" and its lack of close-by urbane amenities, a mark of "puritanical American corporatism" (figure 6.5).[12] Whatever skepticism the project generated at its inception, the project became Portsmouth's touchstone for participation in the global economy, touted on the Web sites of public jurisdictions and private interests alike.[13] Like the 1954 General Foods Headquarters in Westchester County, New York, the IBM headquarters catalyzed later development of adjacent corporate estates, office parks, and corporate campuses.

Similar to many American corporations, Volvo built a corporate estate in the wake of an ambitious corporate reconception. In the early 1980s, the car and engine manufacturing company had merged with a Swedish holding company of diverse global enterprises, and the company reconstituted its top management. In a move that paralleled Deere & Company thirty years before, Volvo resited its management facility from central Göteborg, the industrial center that employed 20,000 Volvo factory workers, to a wooded peninsula beyond the edge of town. The American architectural firm Mitchell/Giurgola Architects was

charged with providing "a catalyst" for the 100 top-level managers—"a place to think and plan rather than a place to write paychecks." The headquarters, shielded by woodlands and reached by a circuitous entry drive, had spectacular seaward views and, in the tradition of Scandinavia's world-renowned modernists Gunnar Asplund and Alvar Aalto, the architecture had "classical, medieval, and vernacular" allusions.[14] It is reminiscent of Deere in both conception and execution: a bucolic woodland site in detached isolation from nearby factory works that unfurls a sternly elegant headquarters along a presentational drive. The Volvo estate underscores the global adoption of the intertwined principles of American corporate management and corporate building.

Though they intentionally stood out in the international business landscape, corporate estates were not a wide-ranging occurrence outside the United

6.5

IBM European Headquarters, Portsmouth, United Kingdom. Though skeptically received in the early 1970s by British commentators and local governments, the IBM headquarters catalyzed a string of new suburban corporate developments in the vicinity, as did the early pastoral capitalist projects in the United States. (© Peter Cook/VIEW)

States (figure 6.6).[15] Instead, the office park, and its many variants, became pervasive, first in Britain and then elsewhere. Similar to the United States, the United Kingdom had an established convention of industrial parks (referred to as industrial estates) that extended back at least to the 1930s.[16] By the late 1970s, as peripheral highways extended around and connected major metropolitan areas, the British economy began to convert from an industrial to a service economy.[17] By one estimate, between 1971 and 1982, the Southeast, that is, the sector of the United Kingdom in and around London, lost 500,000 manufacturing jobs while gaining the same number of service sector jobs.[18] For obvious reasons, the United Kingdom was also an easy embarkation point for globalizing American corporations. These factors combined with Britain's three-century tradition of prizing the bucolic pastoral landscape above all others (and from which

Americans had derived their own pastoral attachments) and the "sceptred isle" office park was inevitable.

A series of events involving IBM and Cambridge University spurred the development of the office park in Britain and beyond. In the late 1950s, IBM moved to establish its first major research center outside the United States and originally wanted to locate near Cambridge and its world-famous university. Wary that a research and development facility would detract from Cambridge's celebrated historical charm and adhering to postwar land use regulation that prohibited industrial development in and around the city, the local planning authorities refused permission.[19] IBM first leased and later bought the Hursley estate in Hampshire, near Winchester, which had been a grand country house during the Edwardian era but lay in a deteriorated state after being requisitioned during World II as an aeronautical engineering outpost of Vickers Aircraft. IBM tore down leftover makeshift structures, removed toxics from the site remaining from the aeronautical activities, and made extended efforts to contain and minimize impacts from its research activities. IBM built new structures in a cluster around the original house, rehabilitated the house as offices and conference rooms, installed peripheral parking lots, and restored the extensive grounds, planting many new trees—in effect reproducing the corporate campus model for the first time outside the United States.[20]

Set on 100 acres of Jane Austen's native county, Hursley Park drolly repatriated American corporate pastoral taste to its ancestral grounds, but Cambridge's rebuff of IBM's research center became a turning point in the process of establishing the office park in Britain, and, thereafter, the rest of the world. Cambridge's rejection spurred an ongoing discussion during the 1960s about the place of new high-technology research and development among Cambridge University officials, the town council, and local planning authorities. The university had been producing science applied to profitable enterprise for many decades, but in the wake of the automobile manufacturing that had intruded on the hallowed elite environs of Oxford in the 1930s and 1940s, Cambridge and surrounding Cambridgeshire instituted strict prohibitions on industrial land uses in the early 1950s, with central government concurrence. At the same time, as a result of both its intellectual and urban milieu, Cambridge provided its graduate scientists and engineers with a setting and lifestyle they found very amenable, and so they tended to remain in the vicinity after obtaining degrees, maintaining close ties to the university. Furthermore, Cambridge was a prime location of British government laboratories. By the late 1960s, this concentration

6.6

Bouygues SA, a global construction firm, built the first (and so far the only) corporate estate in France, 3 miles from Versailles. Kevin Roche John Dinkeloo and Associates, veteran designers of American corporate estates, designed a huge complex on the 70-acre site, named Challenger by the corporation. Although the accomplished British landscape architect Peter Shepheard designed a landscape plan, little of it was carried out, and the palatial building stands on mostly open lawn. (Courtesy of Kevin Roche John Dinkeloo and Associates) of cleverness was ramping up innovative applied technology, but Cambridge's cosseted townscape had little to offer in terms of appropriate facilities.

By 1969 the university promoted a reassessment of the planning strictures and formed a faculty committee chaired by the physicist Sir Nevill Mott, a scientist whose own work was very much linked to the transistor research at Bell Labs; he later shared a Nobel Prize with a Bell Labs scientist, Philip Warren Anderson. The Mott committee proposed a solution that would mediate between enterprise and environs—a "science park" that would be conducive to high-technology research and development, modeled on American predecessors of the 1950s, like the Stanford Industrial Park. Trinity College of Cambridge University owned a suitable 108-acre parcel on the north side of town, adjacent to the intersection of a limited access roadway and a planned motorway connecting Cambridge and London's Stanstead Airport. It was part of an original agricultural land grant to the college by Henry VIII, but had more recently been degraded as an armored tank storage lot during World War II; the college was seeking alternative revenue generation.[21]

Trinity College proposed the Cambridge Science Park in 1970 and acted as developer to oversee the installation of roads, a decorative lake restructured from an old gravel pit, and the "generous provision of trees and open water and construction of mounds." Lot coverage was kept to less than 20 percent, building

6.7
The Cambridge Science Park is a recognizable iteration of the office park site plan. Like Stanford Research Park, this was a for-profit venture by one of Cambridge University's colleges and is credited with instigating an economic agglomeration known as Silicon Fens. (Courtesy of Cambridge Science Park)

heights to two stories, and occupants to those directly associated with applied scientific research and supporting uses. The landscape provisions were essential ingredients to make planning authorities accede to the new development and to attract branches of internationally based firms to establish Cambridge "listening posts" (figure 6.7).[22] With ongoing management by Trinity College, the project was built in phases, and occupancy was initially slow because the development type was unfamiliar (the first tenant was Laser-Scan, a spin-off from Cambridge University's Cavendish Laboratories, Britain's premier physics laboratory). By 1985, the Cambridge Science Park stood at the center of a venture capital–fueled high-technology hub known as the Cambridge Phenomenon—a smaller-scale English version of Silicon Valley and Route 128 (figure 6.8). In a process similar to its American predecessors, the Cambridge Science Park proved to be the first of numerous new science and business parks in the Cambridge region, now known as Silicon Fens—some built by Cambridge colleges, most built by private developers, housing a few home-grown start-ups but many international corporate branches. Its success led to the establishment of thirty other science parks near British universities by 1985.[23]

Like the adoption of pastoral capitalism in the United States, successful, highly publicized projects like the Cambridge Science Park bred new projects ever farther afield as a replicable development type with consequential economic

6.8
Like its American counterparts, the Cambridge Science Park contains low-rise buildings, plenty of parking, and ample, well-maintained grounds. (Courtesy of Cambridge Science Park)

Stockley Park in the London
borough of Hillingdon. Although
the ample landscape space is
typical of many office parks,
the joint public and private
development in this case enabled
the remediation of a severely
degraded and contaminated site.
The office park project provided
a key link in the London greenbelt
between two existing open spaces
and provided golf courses, bridle
trails, footpaths, and playing fields
as public amenities. (Terraserver)

outcomes. By the late 1970s, office parks not affiliated with academic institutions first emerged in regional economic centers across the United Kingdom, as they had in the United States.[24] Like their American models and the Cambridge Science Park, motorways edged the sites that contained ample landscape space, included parking lot berms, and provided one parking space for every 300 square feet of floor space. Designed by landscape architects Brian Clouston and Partners, outside Bristol in southwest England, Aztec West set the trend for a new wave of speculative, developer-built office park expansion in Britain. At 168 acres and a build-out of 2.27 million square feet, it was the largest private landscape project in Britain since the eighteenth century. Digital Equipment Corporation, the Boston-area high-technology firm and a two-plus-decade resident of Route 128 research parks, was the second tenant. By 1985 Bristol was recognized as a center of global branch offices, and, with Aztec West, the office park became a widely accepted, investor-driven development type in Britain.[25]

Developers' keen interest in this new kind of speculative development supported the Thatcher government's deregulation of the national zoning code in 1987, catalyzing an escalation in office park development. (Compared to the United States, the United Kingdom has significantly more stringent development regulations, and before 1987, any change in internal office building configuration or use would require a permitting process.) By 1989, the first office park developments, more commonly known in Britain as business parks, were followed by some 575 other projects with potential for over 250 million square feet at build-out. Of these, 107 were more than 50 acres in extent, and 28 planned for potential office square footages of 1 million to 3 million.[26]

Most of the British business parks developed in regional centers, but Stockley Park was a notable exception. Located on the northwest periphery of London not far from Heathrow Airport, the 350-acre project remediated a toxic and polluted former landfill as a joint enterprise among private partners, an academic pension fund, and the London Borough of Hillingdon. In a highly atypical development, the investors directed the designers, the architects, and engineers Arup Associates and Clouston to develop a plan that included a public golf course, walking and biking trails, public stables, and habitat restoration, all connected to a regional greenbelt (figure 6.9). Opened in 1989 with the Prince of Wales in attendance, the project attracted attention for both the scale of the office development, 1.5 million square feet, and as an early example of what is now called brownfield redevelopment.[27] Although other British projects more closely followed American models in their dearth of civic features, the remediation and public open space elements of Stockley Park were in marked

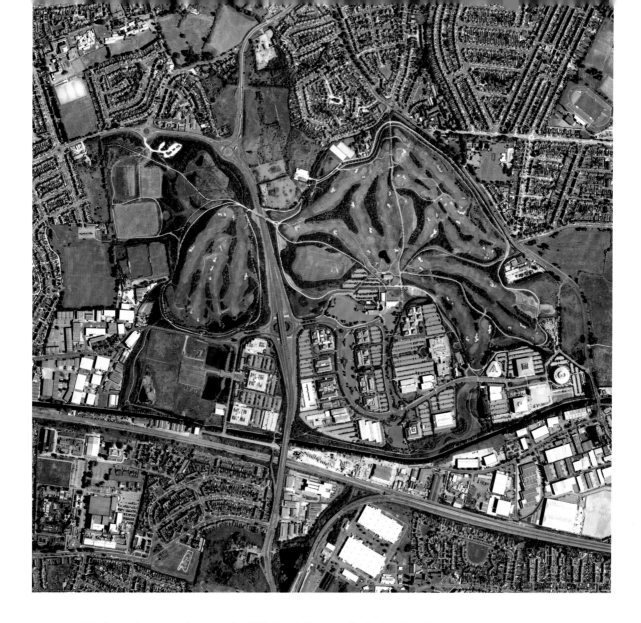

contrast with the environmental approach of Hacienda Business Park, developed in the same decade, that filled existing seasonal wetlands and made much more minimal concessions to the public realm (figure 6.10).

In France as well, an IBM research and development center prompted the development of an American-style research park. Designed by the noted modernist Marcel Breuer, IBM's La Gaude facility outside Nice on the French Riviera, opened in 1961 and consisted of a single three-pronged building, shaped to provide views over 34 acres planted with olive groves. The research center was not

6.10

Stockley Park with restored wetlands that remediate site contaminants while providing a marketable image of the office park. (© Dennis Gilbert/VIEW)

quite an American-style corporate campus (it contained no central open space) but nonetheless was unique in France as a bucolic setting for corporate offices.[28] By the early 1970s, after the Cambridge Science Park proposal, French local and national authorities approved of a nearby science park, Sophia Antipolis, promoted by a well-connected local politician and the head of IBM La Gaude, an initial member of the board of directors. Like Cambridge Science Park, the promoters modeled it after Stanford Research Park, noting that the French project shared a similar, aesthetically notable, bioregional context of mild weather, hilly terrain, and closeness to the sea (figure 6.11). Run by a foundation as a nonprofit enterprise, Sophia Antipolis is a recognizable reiteration of the office park form with the addition of a generous buffer circumscribing two-thirds of the site. Sophia Antipolis housed

a host of international corporate branches—among the first tenants were IBM, Texas Instruments, and Digital Equipment Corporation—and became the center of France's so-called Telecom Valley. But it also housed classic back-office corporate functions typical of office parks, like the reservations center of Air France, employing large numbers of women with technical expertise.[29] Unlike Cambridge Science Park (which, like Stanford Research Park, was a profit-making enterprise) the nonprofit Sophia Antipolis did not immediately spur private, speculative development in office parks, which did not appear in France until the end of the twentieth century.[30]

Not surprisingly given their historical ties to Britain and its idealized landscape, developers in Anglophone Australia, Ireland, and South Africa opened office parks by the early 1990s, entirely comparable to British and American models.[31] The notable proliferation of office parks in postapartheid South Africa has parallels to office park development in Birmingham and Atlanta in the 1950s and 1960s that, by dint of their peripheral location and lack of accessibility by public transport, filtered employees along racial lines.[32] In the more spatially constrained, highly regulated cities of continental Europe and Japan, zones of low- to medium-rise, large floor plate office buildings outside central business districts termed office parks or science parks appeared, but with minimal, if any, landscape areas and without large areas of surface parking. Variously successful as enterprise zones, they were well connected by public transportation, and the terms seemed to denote a position outside of the central business district, not low-density offices with large expanses of landscape space.[33] An exception to this in continental Europe, German redevelopment programs used low-density office park development as a focused strategy to rehabilitate and reuse postindustrial sites in depopulating, economically depressed regions, particularly in the Ruhr Valley, where the generous landscape provisions specifically functioned to remediate toxic sites.[34]

In the developing world, the office park proliferated most often under the rubric of science, software, and technology parks. Abetted by the promotion of the seemingly unparalleled technological and economic productivity of Route 128 and Silicon Valley, a host of analytical literature describing the positive effects of agglomeration in the Boston and the San Francisco Bay Area, and the characterization of their set of conurbations and cultures as "technopoles," global decision makers, including the government officials of developing nations, looked to these places as fonts of capitalist wisdom.[35] What they saw in Waltham and Palo Alto were the Cabot, Cabot & Forbes research parks and the Stanford Research Park—low rise, low density, plenty of parking, an ambient layering of green—housing staffs of highly educated, knowledgeable, skilled workers, and leaders of technological innovation (figure 6.12). And, as witnessed by the Cambridge Science Park, these positive economic and environmental results could apparently be recreated elsewhere, at least to some extent. In reality, agglomeration effects are elusive, and capturing the alchemy of Route 128 and Silicon Valley is no easy matter. Nonetheless, the developing world seized on the research or office park as the most obvious and reproducible element of successful high-technology regions.

Science, software, and technology park initiatives in the developing world transposed the physical particulars of the Route 128 research parks, the Stanford Research Park, and the Cambridge Science Park to new venues, with the promise of technological innovation, global market competitiveness, and national development. An early and influential example was the Singapore Science Park, a development begun in 1980 by the Singapore government through the auspices of the Jurong Town Corporation, a state-sponsored development corporation. Planned in three phases, it covered 163 acres accessed by adjacent expressways and surrounded by a ridgeline nature park. In conceiving the project, the developers focused on the park's physical image. Intended to foster local entrepreneurship and innovation and to funnel applied technology from local academic

institutions, in reality the Singapore Science Park (not unlike the reality of the Stanford Research Park) became tenanted with branch offices of global corporations, some not engaged in research at all. The park was first and foremost a development whose tenants found a suitable and prestigious place for their corporate staffs—in the words of the local newspaper, "lush green to nurture the brainy with its oasis like landscaping" (figure 6.13) The importance of the "lush green" was underscored in 2007 as Ascendas (the subsidiary of Jurong Town Corporation created to oversee the SSP's management and continuing development) began a $400 million renovation of "green fingers" wending between buildings and nature trails linking various parts of the Singapore Science Park and the nature park, all to create "lifestyle elements aimed at enhancing its serene campus ambience . . . a spectacular green backdrop for R&D technology to flourish."[36]

While the term "science park" is widely used in China, Taiwan, and Korea, thus far these developments house primarily export-oriented manufacturing with some associated research and development, similar to peripheral planned industrial districts in the developed world.[37] This is likely to change, especially in China, where the central government is making concerted efforts to foster

6.12
The Stanford Research Park today, built out and with mature landscaping, the Hewlett-Packard building at top. (For contrast to the Stanford Research Park in 1960, see figure 5.12.) Seized on as a global model because of its association with Silicon Valley, the particular circumstances that gave rise to the Silicon Valley economic phenomenon are difficult to replicate. Nevertheless, in countless projects across the world, Stanford Research Park's site plan is imitated in the hope of repeating Silicon Valley's success. (Imagery by Pictometry International Corporation)

The Singapore Science Park
reiterated the forms and features of
American office parks. Although it
generated far less local corporate
business and innovation than
expected, it was successful
in attracting branch offices of
established corporations, as did the
early office parks of Birmingham,
Boston, and the Bay Area. Like
its American predecessors, the
Singapore Science Park used lush
landscape and a signage system
to create a sense of status and
orderliness that appealed to global
corporations. (Wikimedia Commons)

homegrown innovation and attract management divisions of global corporations. Singapore Science Park's Ascendas has become a prime investment partner
in Chinese science and business park proposals geared toward corporate offices
such as the Dalian Software Park, master-planned by British design consultants
to include four development zones and a forest park outside the northeastern
city of Dalian.[38]

As India emerged as a global participant in the electronic and software
industries in the 1990s, technology parks and corporate campuses became both
the setting and symbol of India's increasingly influential role in the international
electronics and digital markets. Exemplary are the developments in Bangalore,
in the Indian state of Karnataka, once renowned as the Garden City of India.
In 1976 the state government established the Karnataka State Electronics Development Corporation Limited (KEONICS) to promote the expansion of the
electronics industry. By the early 1980s, KEONICS had purchased 332 acres
of land 18 kilometers outside Bangalore's city limits and planned a technology park dubbed Electronics City, which attracted global companies like

6.14

The Wipro campus in Bangalore, India. Like postwar firms in the United States, Indian high-technology companies have built corporate campuses to attract and retain educated personnel and to impress competitors and collaborators. (Courtesy of Wipro)

Hewlett-Packard, Siemens, and Motorola as well as Indian corporations like Wipro. In 1991 the central government provided significant tax incentives to export-oriented software development corporations, relaxed laws restricting foreign ownership, and established Software Technology Parks of India (STPI) to support technology park expansion and infrastructure. STPI funded targeted infrastructure improvements, and Electronics City became a prime location for global corporations, including Indian ones like Infosys, to build Bangalore campuses. With increasing economic success, software corporations also built freestanding, purpose-built corporate campuses in Bangalore, most notably Wipro in 2002.[39] A Wipro's real estate manager explained: "As the firm has grown, we now have to consider the image we portray to our overseas clients when they visit. A campus has become a necessity" (figure 6.14).[40]

The development of Electronics City and other pastoral workplaces has been credited with making a dent in the "brain drain" of educated Indians to the developed world seeking both economic rewards and better working and living conditions.[41] As an Indian engineer who migrated from Ahmedabad to Bangalore blogged: "After entering into any of the IT related company campus, you will feel like you are in heaven."[42] As the blogger and others have observed, the "divide" between the corporate workplaces and the larger landscape of Bangalore is extreme. A long history of poor infrastructure and negligible city services for ordinary residents has been leapfrogged by self-contained, state-sponsored infrastructure systems for transportation, water, energy, and sewerage that form a central part of the marketing campaigns of Electronics City and its offshoots. Vast disparities in economic, political, and social capital between those within and without the high-technology firms are exemplified by the contrast between the lustrous green and glass landscape of international corporations and the modest vernacular neighborhoods, often the remains of preexisting agricultural villages, that surround them.[43] As STPI has now been used as a model in other developing nations, other parts of the globe will likely replicate the same disparate geographies.[44]

In India, the divide is liable to continue to grow. In a deal brokered between the prime ministers of India and Singapore, a joint development between a local development agency and Ascendas (developers of the Singapore Science Park) opened another major technology park in Bangalore, the International Technology Park, in 1995 to be the "icon of India's IT success story." With explicit marketing of landscape image and lifestyle and an ultimate build-out of 2.3 million square feet in architecturally consistent midrise buildings over 70 acres (Electronics City is noted for its highly diverse structures), the project's Web site promotes it as a "World in a Park" where "world-class business infrastructure amidst wide green spaces provides the optimal environment for Fortune 500 corporations, MNCs [multinational corporations] and leading local corporations located in the park."[45]

Capitalist Magic: Gazing at Greenness

If the declarative pastoral rhetoric of supposedly bottom-line capitalist enterprises seems mind-boggling—GM Technical Center's "view of patio and pool contributes to precision engineering"—as it resurfaces half a century later and halfway around the world, this is indicative of how the purported magic of gazing at greenness has so thoroughly permeated corporate management, first in the United States and now internationally. Science parks in Singapore look the way they do because of the preferences and prejudices of postwar American corporate leaders, thoroughly steeped in a deep cultural fount of pastoral ideology.

The economic geographers Michael Storper and Michael Manville observed in an article that explores aesthetic preference in business location, "Beauty is more a residential than business amenity. Firms are unlikely to choose an urban area based on its aesthetic qualities. Silicon Valley overflows with business but it's no one's idea of an architectural treasure."[46] Architectural, arguably not, but to any visitor who has experienced Silicon Valley's hills and dales, where billowing oaks and swaying eucalyptus permeate residential districts, a robust network of public open spaces that would win the approval of Olmsted is close at hand, and corporate offices are lushly ensconced in layers of trees, grass, and shrubs, it is a place of remarkably consistent pastoral pleasures. And it is these "pleasing prospects," some of which they have created, that corporations for the past sixty years have been convinced are essential to their function. One has to presume that IBM has not kept a thousand acres of prime California real estate surrounding the laboratory of its research engineers and scientists for no reason at all.

Pastoral capitalism is a major venture in suburbanity, as influential and widespread as residential suburbs. Yet unlike residential suburbs, this type of metropolitan development did not originate as an ideal promoted by designers, advocated by reformers, and coveted by consumers. Distinct from many inventions of twentieth-century city building, these suburban developments were not present in a preexisting canon-in-waiting or the stuff of conjectural expositions about the future of the metropolis. Pastoral capitalism originated with corporations as they reconceived their corporate structures, turned away from the city, and tracked the flow of elites and capital to the verdant urban periphery, a process that is ongoing and now worldwide. The designers involved in these projects brought to the table the vocabulary of the pastoral landscapes and modernist buildings, the ability to concretize ideas, and expertise in implementation, but these suburban forms were the visions of capitalists and emerged from a capitalist imperative.

This spatial order's appeal is perfectly obvious, even sensible. Pastoral capitalism makes managerial capitalism work as a standardized set of dispersed environments to carry on profitably segmented corporate operations—at this point functional, predictable, and proven. These places brought scientists to Summit and now keep the brainy in Bangalore—they meet the expectations of elite corporate workers. The projects with summary aesthetic refinements are very pleasing, and the ones with more generic articulations are pleasant enough. Most assuredly, they are always orderly, contain exceedingly serviceable infrastructure, and are meticulously maintained. They play an obvious part in the creation of wealth.

Viewed in this way, pastoral capitalism is a predictable part of an evolution of the industrial and postindustrial city over the past century. Dispersed development can be seen as a long-term historical phenomenon in which metropolitan zones evolve toward moderated, functional densities and the highly concentrated urban patterns of the first part of the twentieth century were an anomaly of industrialization. At the periphery, pastoral capitalism is part of the trend toward suburban land use diversity, particularly over the past three decades, which is mirrored by a center revived by lower densities and increased homogeneity of land uses.[47] As Robert Bruegmann contends in *Sprawl: A Compact History,* the decision to privilege "mobility, privacy, and choice" in city building is functional, nonelitist, and inevitable.[48]

Bruegmann is part of a larger cohort of scholars and critics reconsidering the suburbs not as the center city's culturally and socially impoverished outlier of enforced conformity and consumerist values, but as an understandable and desirable reshaping of the city into a differently legible, accessible, and manageable pattern of specialized land uses that emerged from new social and economic forces.[49] The old city has a bird's-eye diagrammatic clarity as a whole; the suburbs have a diagrammatic clarity in their constituent parts that suburban residents link together as a coherent experience as they move through the suburbs by automobile.[50] The corporate campus, corporate estate, and office park are exemplary, if not a kind of apotheosis, of this suburban reordering. From the perspective of the old city, they are indecipherable; from the new suburban order, they have unassailable logic and coherence.

The reassessment of the low-density urban periphery extends to the recognition that suburbs are an alternative economic geography that significantly dominates the economic activity of metropolitan regions. The presence of pastoral capitalism has enabled the suburbs to attain this economic dominance in two essential ways. As discussed in chapter 2, corporate centers and business properties render fiscal supports for suburban residential services that cannot be funded entirely through home owner property taxes. In this way, the accelerated suburban residential expansion in the United States would not have been possible without pastoral capitalism, especially in suburban communities that found the prospect of industrial development abhorrent. This is an upward spiral of development that shifted the economic center of gravity to favor suburban city building. Suburban residential expansion needed a concurrent expansion of public services, the suburban milieu and labor pool attracted corporations, public jurisdictions first facilitated and then incentivized the construction of tax-lucrative corporate employment centers, employment centers created yet more demand for residential development, and so on. At some point as well, the sheer question of scale comes into play, as the working population, square feet of corporate space, and number of jobs well outpace even thriving center cities.[51]

This revised suburban history has seen the suburbs as much more receptive to social complexity than the stereotypical postwar white, middle-class, nuclear family residing in a single-family house. Extending back to the ethnically diverse industrial suburbs of the early decades of the twentieth century to the lively "ethnoburbs" of the early twenty-first century, the suburbs have defied social homogeneity more than might be expected, especially in recent decades.[52] And while multinational corporations were the realms of white middle- and upper-middle-class men in the 1950s, they have more recently been one of the more stalwart defenders of affirmative action in the face of political disenchantment, advocates of a diverse workforce in a global economy.[53]

This understanding of the historical and extant suburbs is valid yet limited. The advent of the pastoral corporation removed leaders of postwar capitalism from the heart of the American city—a categorical abandonment by powerful, self-interested, and economically generative entities essential to civic health. By any measure, American center cities experienced disinvestment and decline in the postwar perod, and the long-term effects of this was obvious for decades in many places, like Moline, Durham, Birmingham, and Hartford, notwith-standing very recent efforts at selective downtown revitalization.[54] One can only imagine the much more dire consequences of this kind of abandonment in the cities of developing world.

In tandem with center city decline, suburban corporate landscapes locked into place the last keystone of the immense, and ever-growing, automobile-dependent suburb with all its attendant difficulties. The smooth rides of beltways and freeways have become nightmarish roils of traffic that make downtown congestion of the 1950s seem quaint in comparison. The pastoral workplace, even more than the pastoral dwelling, precludes the concentration of population that makes public transportation feasible for governments and users.[55]

Even more fundamental to thinking about the condition of the suburbs today is that the elemental imprint of broad-scale postwar suburbanization was the result of concerted efforts of racial- and class-biased public and private interests.[56] This was not a values-neutral reordering of city space. Postwar sub-urbanization took the form of enclaves—sovereign, specialized land uses with limited automobile connections to other suburban sectors and often buffered by a landscape edge—the better to create autonomy, privacy, and segregation. So while the suburbs as a whole may have even more diverse residents today, the specialized spatial enclave remains a ubiquitous suburban unit and has implications for racial, ethnic, and class disparities.[57]

By definition, corporations are institutionally guarded, and the prized insularity and privacy of the suburbs, long noted as a characteristic of residential suburbs, suit the corporate endeavor as well.[58] In whichever form they take—corporate campus, corporate estate, or office park—they create enclaves for like-minded members of the corporate enterprise. Limited entries from public roadways, long driveways, self-contained infrastructure, expanses of parking lots, buildings of inscrutable uses, and ubiquitous pastoral surrounds can all be seen as both reflecting and reinforcing an autonomous identity where engagement beyond the corporate office is an optional effort.

This separatist, not just suburban, geography of business is the crux of the matter, with consequences for the governance, form, and equity of metropolitan regions. Center city corporate management in the early twentieth century participated in the advocacy for urban reforms that transformed the American city for the better. Dedication to city affairs was inevitable as corporate offices stood directly on streets and corporate workers walked at least some distance through the city to work; participation in the functional and aesthetic improvement of the collective public realm was in corporations' own self-interest while broadly beneficial to city residents. The separatist enclave of corporate management in the suburbs has no such burden; its logic is based on independence from larger metropolitan realities and the power of selective participation in issues of collective governance. If all you see in your workday are your coworkers and all you see out your window is the green perimeter of your carefully tended property and the "carapace of the automobile" insulates you both to and from work, the notion of a shared responsibility in the collective metropolitan realm is predictably distant.[59]

First in the United States, and now globally, governments have been complicit in the face of this intent. The overt and covert fiscal favoritism to already stupendously moneyed corporations through publicly financed infrastructure, direct subsidies, tax incentives, and regulatory facilitation extended pastoral capitalism well beyond the limits afforded by private investment alone. The regulatory process has guarded too little of the public trust in molding suburban corporate developments, disregarding the ultimate environmental implications of low-density, auto-dependent extensions of metropolitan areas for corporate offices. No matter if corporations and real estate markets collapse, governments seem determined to prop up pastoral capitalism's continued existence, eliding the detrimental impacts to present and future metropolitan regions and the global environment as a whole.

The persistence of this separatist geography is an essential problem for the future reform of the suburban landscape—the expectation that the process of suburban densification can ultimately be a solution to an unsustainable metropolitan form. In all types of city building, the initial scheme of land division—the site plan—is profoundly resistant to change.[60] This is all the more obvious in suburban corporate landscapes where the enclave pattern, even with densification, resists being reshaped into a more highly connected landscape where auto dependence can be superseded by mass transit, pedestrian, and bicycle connections (figure 6.15). While a couple of proposals in continental Europe and China hold out sustainable office parks as components of "green urbanism," the larger trend of corporate investment remains committed to management facilities of spendthrift resource consumption.[61]

It might be easy to see the global ubiquity of pastoral capitalism as an indication of a kind of "dumb" repetition of a type of built environment. Though initially unproven, as it became present in the metropolitan landscape, pastoral capitalism became the object of thoughtless imitation, normalized as part of the city building process through zoning, financing, and real estate marketing. How much the landscape of pastoral capitalism contributed to corporate success over

6.15

The X-shaped building at the center of the image is the former TRW headquarters (discussed in chapter 4). With corporate restructuring, the property was subdivided and sold off. Remarkably, the initial imprint of the enclave pattern of the headquarters remains, as a large lifestyle center was inserted in the site below the former headquarters, new residential development and golf courses surround the site, and a medical office of the Cleveland Clinic took over the old headquarters. All of these uses are utterly disconnected from each other, making it impossible to move between them in anything but an automobile. (Terraserver)

the past six decades is difficult to calibrate, but pastoral capitalism's endurance across time, geography, and global cultures has to be indicative of a concordance with corporate impetus. The notion of corporate hegemony is well understood as part and parcel of political and economic systems. But that hegemony also manifests itself as part of a metropolitan spatial order that supersedes established urban orders in cities across the world, trumping regional idioms. It allows corporate entities to exercise maximum control over their environments and personnel, and obviates their responsibility for shared governance, and financing, of the collective public realm.

Beyond claims of management efficiencies, pastoral capitalist landscapes situate corporate endeavors as existentially positive, subsuming the unpleasant realities of the institutions they house. Emblems of an Ivy League college, an aristocratic estate, or tidy green park place a pleasing, even nostalgic, frame around the very entities that are responsible for much that is disconcerting about the contemporary world—exploitative labor relations, shameful material inequities, baneful transportation impacts, scary technology, profligate dealings, and ongoing environmental destruction. Like the Bangalore blogger, we might be forgiven for thinking that immersion in a lush, well-tended corporate landscape is a paradisiacal experience. Pastoral corporate landscapes suspend our lurking misgivings about the avid purveyors of global capitalism with a steadying pastoral sheen.

The gradual transference of the pastoral aesthetic from common ground to capitalist tool is a cynical end of what had been optimistic means. Fredrick Law Olmsted intended that the pastoral public park, at its best, would be a reliable common ground in an era of consequential and contested change in American life accompanying the rise of industrial capitalism and modern urbanization. However paternalistic, the intent was to provide an everyday environment conducive to social, physical, and mental health. The nineteenth-century advocacy of designed landscapes as instruments of progressive betterment primed the public to consider these landscapes with favorable regard. The appropriation of the pastoral by corporations initially seemed to extend rather than compromise the public park's civic legacy. The steps from humane workplace to corporate solipsism were incremental; capitalists directed pastoral persuasions first toward employee compliance, then their own aggrandizement, and finally to dissemblance.

The landscapes of pastoral capitalism are part and parcel of corporate ideology, reinforcing the self-regard of the corporate management and mystifying the unpleasant actualities of corporate power. Reforming pastoral capitalism will require more than a less complacent public sector, though that would be a considerable start. To question imperatives of capitalism these days seems like the stuff of an unfortunate blowhard uncle at Thanksgiving dinner who makes the rest of the table stare hard at their wine glasses or sneak a tidbit to the dog. But really, might we ask more of corporate governance than abdication from the collective, public sphere and a suspension of environmental accountability for the landscapes they inhabit? A broader realization among politicians, developers, financiers, planners, designers, and the wider public about the power of the suburban corporate site plan to thwart a restructured, resource-efficient, civic-minded metropolitan landscape is essential to activate the public sector in the public interest.

For their part, corporations could ask themselves whether an unquestioned nineteenth-century taste for retreat and verdant isolation applied to the workplace is the way forward on a planet of perilously compromised resources. A reasonable interest in status, flexibility, and efficient operations can be redirected to new urban forms and to retrofitting existing ones. The power of redirection in corporate building is not in the hands of countless people making countless decisions. Rather, a couple of thousand corporate leaders, maybe even fewer, could usher in a new kind of corporate building, as indeed a handful did in the mid-twentieth century.

NOTES

Chapter 1

1. The literature on the suburbs is extensive but scant in the specifics discussed in this book. Basic survey texts on the history of suburbanization are Kenneth Jackson, *Crabgrass Frontier: The Suburbanization of the United States* (New York: Oxford University Press, 1985); Robert Fishman, *Bourgeois Utopias* (New York: Basic Books, 1987); and John R. Stilgoe, *Borderlands: Origins of the American Suburbs, 1920–1939*, (New Haven, CT: Yale University Press, 1988). Jackson briefly singles out the exodus of corporations from the central business district as part of the final postwar phase of suburbanization in chapter 14 "The Drive-in Culture of Contemporary America" (268–269). Fishman generally discusses suburban employment within the final chapter, "Rise of the Technoburb," but makes no specific mention of suburban corporate landscapes (182–208). Stilgoe focuses on residential suburbanization as does Dolores Hayden in *Building Suburbia: Green Fields and Urban Growth, 1820–2000* (New York: Vintage Books, 2004). Hayden's *A Field Guide to Sprawl* (New York: Norton, 2004) contains an aerial view of an industrial park but not management offices. Journalistic observations of the suburban phenomenon such as Joel Garreau, *Edge City: Life on the New Frontier* (New York: Anchor Books, 1991), and James Howard Kunstler, *Home from Nowhere: Remaking Our World for the Twenty-First Century* (New York: Simon and Shuster, 1996), are engaging but ahistorical. Richard Walker's "A Theory of Suburbanization: Capitalism and the Construction of Urban Space in the United States," in *Urbanization and Urban Planning in Capitalist Society*, ed. Michael Dear and A. J. Scott (New York: Methuen, 1981), 383–429, is an elegant, lucid, and still useful analytical summary of seminal geographic and economic geography research on the suburbs up to 1980.

2. Decentralization research focuses on metropolitan location and distribution. For two succinct analyses, see B. Berry and Y. S. Cohen, "Decentralization of Commerce and Industry: The Restructuring of Metropolitan America." in *The Urbanization of the Suburbs*, ed. Louise H. Masotti

and Jeffrey K. Hadden (Thousand Oaks, CA: Sage, 1973), and particularly Gary Pivo "The Net of Mixed Beads: Suburban Office Development in Six Metropolitan Regions" *APA Journal* 56, no.1 (1990): 457–458. A recent addition to the suburban literature that illuminates a more complex view of the all-too-often-stereotyped suburbs and reproduces many primary source documents is *The Suburban Reader*, ed. Becky M. Nicolaides and Andrew Wiese (New York: Routledge, 2006), but it has only one excerpt discussing suburban white-collar employment centers from Peter O. Muller, *The Outer City: The Geographical Consequences of the Urbanization of the Suburbs* (Washington, DC: American Association of Geographers, 1976). Mueller correctly distinguishes suburban headquarters and office parks. Peter G. Rowe's chapter, "Corporate Estates," in *Making a Middle Landscape* (Cambridge, MA: MIT Press, 1991), is a purportedly historical examination of a similar subject. Based on a cursory examination of a few projects published in design magazines and architectural project books, it makes no distinction between factory administration buildings and suburban corporate headquarters of exclusively management uses, confuses the corporate research campus and corporate estate and their very different purposes and circumstances, and entirely ignores the office park. Chapter 3 in John R. Findlay's *Magic Lands: Western Cityscapes and American Culture after 1940* (Berkeley: University of California Press, 1992) on the Stanford Industrial Park is an informative case study but does not address the related national trends. Similarly, Margaret Pugh O'Mara's "Uncovering the City in the Suburb: Cold War Politics, Scientific Elites, and High Tech Spaces," in *The New Suburban History*, ed. Kevin M. Kruse and Thomas Sugrue, (Chicago: University of Chicago Press, 2006), 35–56, insightfully discusses the suburbanization of knowledge workers in the Cold War era, but it is largely without description of the resulting built environments. Robert Bruegmann, *Sprawl: A Compact History* (Chicago: University of Chicago Press, 2005), notes the central importance of the office park in suburban expansion and the puzzling paucity of research about it. (70–71, 243).

3. Manuel Castells and Peter Hall, *Technopoles of the World: The Making of Twenty-First Century Industrial Complexes* (New York: Routledge, 1994), 1.

4. Alfred Dupont Chandler Jr. is the essential historian of the managerial capitalist corporation and the evolution of the management hierarchy. A prolific scholar, his seminal text on managerial capitalism is *Strategy and Structure* (Cambridge, MA: Harvard University Press, 1962). Two of his other books are *The Visible Hand: The Managerial Revolution in American Business* (Cambridge, MA: Harvard University Press, 1977), and *Scale and Scope: The Dynamics of Industrial Capitalism* (Cambridge, MA: Harvard University Press, 1990), particularly chaps. 2, 3, and Conclusion.

5. Jackson, *Crabgrass Frontier*; Robert Lewis, ed., *Manufacturing Suburbs: Building Work and Home on the Metropolitan Fringe* (Philadelphia: Temple University Press, 2004).

6. Robert Brenner, *The Economics of Global Turbulence: The Advanced Capitalist Economies from the Long Boom to the Long Downturn, 1945–2005* (New York: Verso, 2006).

7. Gérard Duménil and Dominique Lévy, *The Economics of the Profit Rate: Competition, Crises, and Historical Tendencies in Capitalism* (Northampton, MA: Edward Elgar, 1993); Gérard Duménil, Marc Glick, and Dominique Lévy, "The Rise of the Rate of Profit during World War II," *Review of Economics and Statistics* 75, no. 2 (May 1993): 315–320.

8. Robert A. Beauregard, *Voices of Decline: The Postwar Fate of U.S. Cities* (New York: Routledge, 2003), 45–57; Robert M. Fogelson, *Downtown: Its Rise and Fall, 1880–1950* (New Haven, CT: Yale University Press, 2001).

9. Fishman, *Bourgeois Utopias*; Jackson, *Crabgrass Frontier*; Fogelson, *Downtown*; Richard Longstreth, *City Center to Regional Mall: Architecture, the Automobile, and Retailing in Los Angeles, 1920–1950* (Cambridge, MA: MIT Press, 1997); Mark Gottdeiner, *Planned Sprawl: Private and Public Interests in Suburbia* (Thousand Oaks, CA: Sage, 1977); John R. Logan and Harvey L. Molotch, *Urban Fortunes: The Political Economy of Place* (Berkeley: University of California Press, 2007); Greg Hise, *Magnetic Los Angeles: Planning the Twentieth-Century Metropolis* (Baltimore, MD: Johns Hopkins University Press, 1997); Robert A. Beauregard, *When America Became Suburban* (Minneapolis: University of Minnesota Press, 2006). For an illuminating set of quantifying charts on the rapid decentralization between 1950 and 1970, see Bruegmann, *Sprawl*, 62–63.

10. Becky M. Nicolaides, *My Blue Heaven: Life and Politics in the Working Class Suburbs of Los Angeles, 1920–1965* (Chicago: University of Chicago Press, 2002); Andrew Wiese, *Places of Their Own: African American Suburbanization in the Twentieth Century* (Chicago: University of Chicago Press, 2004); Nicolaides and Wiese, *The Suburban Reader,* chaps. 7, 14.

11. A numbers of recent scholars have noted that metropolitan forms have been persistently mischaracterized as concentric bands of decreasing density gradients around the central business districts. Instead, since the nineteenth century, cities have actually been less orderly and contiguous than metropolitan models have implied. See Richard Harris and Robert Lewis, "Constructing a Fault(y) Zone: Misrepresentations of American Cities and Suburbs, 1900–1950," *Annals of the American Association of Geographers* 88, no. 4 (1998): 622–639; Bruegmann, *Sprawl*, 39–41.

12. In the 1950s "congestion" was cited over and over again as one of the great disadvantages of center city location for new corporate offices. For two of myriad examples, see "Should Management Move to the Country?" *Fortune* 46, no. 6 (December 1952): 143; Elizabeth James, "Why Move to White Plains," *GF News* 15, no. 5 (May 1954): 12–13.

13. Jackson, *Crabgrass Frontier*; Fogelson, *Downtown*.

14. Fogelson, *Downtown;* Beauregard, *Voices of Decline* and *When America Became Suburban*; Logan and Molotch, *Urban Fortunes*.

15. Fishman, *Bourgeois Utopias;* Jackson, *Crabgrass Frontier;* Beauregard, *When America Became Suburban;* Logan and Molotch, *Urban Fortunes;* Gottdeiner, *Planned Sprawl;* Marion Clawson, *Suburban Land Conversion in the Unites States* (Baltimore, MD: Johns Hopkins University Press for Resources for the Future, 1971); Marc Weiss, *Rise of the Community Builders: The American Real Estate Industries and Urban Land Planning* (New York: Columbia University Press, 1987); Robert Self, *American Babylon: Race and Struggle for Postwar Oakland* (Princeton, NJ: Princeton University Press, 2003); David M. P. Freund, "Marketing the Free Market: State Intervention and the Politics of Prosperity in Metropolitan America," in Kruse and Sugrue, *The New Suburban History,* 11–32.

16. Self, *American Babylon;* Freund, "Marketing the Free Market"; Arnold Hirsch, "Less Than *Plessy:* The Inner City, Suburbs, and State Sanctioned Residential Segregation in the Age of *Brown,*" in Kruse and Sugrue, *The New Suburban History*, 32–56; Douglas S. Massey, *American Apartheid: Segregation and the*

Making of the Underclass (Cambridge, MA: Harvard University Press, 1993); Thomas Sugrue, *The Origins of the Urban Crisis: Race and Struggle in Postwar Detroit* (Princeton, NJ: Princeton University Press, 1996). See also Nicolaides and Wiese, *The Suburban Reader*, chaps. 8, 11.

17. For an excellent, succinct case study of the sorting in suburbs of previously mixed urban land uses, see Robert Fishman, "On Big Beaver Road: Detroit and the Diversity of American Metropolitan Landscapes," *Places* 19, no. 3 (Spring 2007): 42–47.

18. Raymond Williams, *The Country and the City* (New York; Oxford University Press, 1973); Tom Williamson, *Polite Landscapes: Gardens and Society in Eighteenth-Century England* (Phoenix Mill, Gloucestershire: Sutton Publishing, 1995).

19. A. J. Downing, *Landscape Gardening and Rural Architecture* (1876; repr. New York: Dover, 1991); Dell Upton, *Architecture in the United States* (New York: Oxford University Press, 1998), 111–121. For an extended discussion of the American pastoral aesthetic discussed briefly here, see James S. Duncan and Nancy G. Duncan, "The Narrative Structures: The Cultural Codes of a Landscape Aesthetic," in their *Landscapes of Privilege: Aesthetics and Affluence in an American Suburb* (New York: Routledge, 2004), 14–36.

20. Duncan and Duncan, "The Narrative Structures."

21. Frederick Law Olmsted, "The Winning Design by Olmsted and Vaux," reprinted in *Forty Years of Landscape Architecture: Central Park*, ed. Frederick Law Olmsted Jr. and Theodora Kimball (Cambridge, MA: Harvard University Press, 1973), 41–48.

22. Duncan and Duncan, "The Narrative Structures."

23. Frederick Law Olmsted, reprinted in *Civilizing American Cities: Writings on City Landscapes*, ed. S. B. Sutton (Cambridge, MA: MIT Press, 1971), 96.

24. Roy Rosenzweig and Elizabeth Blackmar, "The 'Many Sided, Fluent, Thoroughly American' Park" in their *The Park and the People: A History of Central Park* (Ithaca, NY: Cornell University Press, 1992), 307–339. Geoffrey Blodgett, "Frederick Law Olmsted: Landscape Architecture as Conservative Reform," *Journal of American History* 62, no. 4 (March 1976): 869–889.

25. Upton, *Architecture in the United States*; Gwendolyn Wright, *Building the Dream: A Social History of Housing in the United States* (New York; Pantheon Books, 1981); Dolores Hayden, "Building the American Way: Public Subsidy, Private Space," in *The Suburban Reader*, ed. Nicolaides and Wiese, 273–281; Hayden, *Building Suburbia*.

26. Duncan and Duncan, "The Narrative Structures."

27. Chandler, *The Visible Hand*, 497; see also Gardiner Means, *The Corporate Revolution in America*, (New York: Crowell-Collier, 1962).

28. Marx, "Does Pastoralism Have a Future?" 218; cf. Marx, *Machine in the Garden*.

29. I have written about suburban corporate landscapes in two previous publications: "Campus, Estate, and Park: Lawn Culture Comes to the Corporation." in *J. B. Jackson and the American Landscape,* ed. Paul Groth and Chris Wilson (Berkeley and Los Angeles: University of California Press. 2003), 255–274, and "The Corporate Estate in The United States, 1954–1964: 'Thoroughly modern in

concept, but . . . down to earth and rugged,'" *Studies in the History of Gardens and Designed Landscapes* 20, no. 1 (January–March 2000): 25–56. Parts of chapter 4 draw upon the latter article.

30. Robert E. Lang, "Office Sprawl: The Evolving Geography of Business" (Washington, DC: Brookings Institution, October 2000), http://www.brookings.edu/~/media/Files/rc/reports/2000/10metropolitanpolicy_lang/lang.pdf (accessed October 2004).

Chapter 2

1. Dell Upton, *Architecture in the United States* (New York: Oxford University Press, 1998), 215–218; Carol Willis, *Form Follows Finance: Skyscrapers and Skylines in New York and Chicago* (Princeton, NJ: Princeton Architectural Press, 1995), 147–155.

2. Richard Walker, "A Theory of Suburbanization: Capitalism and the Construction of Urban Space in the United States," in *Urbanization and Urban Planning in Capitalist Society*, ed. Michael Dear and A. J. Scott (New York: Methuen, 1981), 396.

3. Roland Marchand, *Advertising the American Dream: Making Way for Modernity* (Berkeley and Los Angeles: University of California Press, 1985).

4. Robert Beauregard, *Voices of Decline* (New York: Routledge, 2003); Robert Gottlieb, *Forcing the Spring: The Transformation of the American Environmental Movement*, (Washington, DC: Island Press, 2005), chap. 2.

5. Wayne G. Broehl, *John Deere's Company: The Story of John Deere's Company and Its Times* (New York: Doubleday, 1984), 614–615.

6. "Should Management Move to the Country?" *Fortune* 46, no. 6 (December 1952): 143; Lathrop Douglass, "New Departures in Office Building Design," *Architectural Record* 102, no. 40 (October 1947): 119–146.

7. L. Andrew Reinhard and Henry Hofmeister, "Modern Offices: New Trends in Office Design," *Architectural Record* 97, no. 3 (March 1945): 99.

8. General Foods, *GF Moving Day and You* (New York: General Foods, 1952), 9.

9. "Should Management Move to the Country?" 166.

10. Michael Johns, *Moment of Grace* (Berkeley and Los Angeles: University of California Press, 2003), 8–9.

11. "Should Management Move to the Country?" 168.

12. Philip Herrera, "That Manhattan Exodus," *Fortune* 76, no. 6 (June 1967): 144.

13. Roger J. O'Meara, "Executive Suites in Suburbia," *Conference Board Record* 9, no. 8 (August 1972): 9–10.

14. Richard Reeves, "Loss of Major Companies Conceded by City Official," *New York Times*, February 5, 1971, 33.

15. Quoted in Tracy B. Augur, "Decentralization: Blessing or Tragedy?" in *Planning 1948: Proceedings of the Annual National Planning Conference Held in New York City, October 11–13, 1948* (Chicago: American Society of Planning Officials, 1948), 28.

16. Eliel Saarinen, "Detroit Planning Studies," *New Pencil Points* 24, no. 120 (December 1943): 51.

17. Harold Hauf, "City Planning and Civil Defense," *Architectural Record* 108, no. 8 (December 1950): 99.

18. Philip D. Reed, "General Electric's Decentralization Plan," *American City* 63 (October 1948): 7.

19. "Big Industry Moves to the Country," *Architectural Forum* 95, no. 2 (July 1951): 146; "Electronics Park, Syracuse, New York," *Architectural Record* 105, no. 20 (February 1949): 96–103; "GE Gets Small-Business Touch," *Business Week*, April 19, 1952, 118, 120, 122–124.

20. "Should Management Move to the Country?" 168.

21. Charles G. Mortimer, *A Fresh Chapter* (New York: General Foods, 1952), 5–6.

22. Kraft Foods (parent company of General Foods), employee interview with the author, June 19, 1997.

23. Fortune, "Should Management Move to the Country?" 166, 168.

24. "First Insurance Home Office in City to Open Monday," *Westchester Reporter Dispatch*, April 23, 1953, n.p.

25. "Why Companies Are Fleeing the Cities," *Time*, April 26, 1971, 86–88; Reeves, "Loss of Major Companies"; O'Meara "Executive Suites"; Herbert E. Meyer, "Why Corporations Are on the Move," *Fortune* 92, no. 5 (May 1976): 255–258, 266.

26. Elizabeth James, "Why Move to White Plains," *GF News* 15, no. 5 (May 1954): 12–13; Elizabeth James, "What Is a Headquarters," *GF News* 15, no. 5 (May 1954): 1.

27. Graham Romeyn Taylor, *Satellite Cities: A Study of Industrial Suburbs* (New York: Appleton, 1915); cf. Margaret Crawford, *Building the Workingman's Paradise: The Design of American Company Towns* (New York: Verso, 1985).

28. George C. Nimmons: "Modern Industrial Plants, Part I," *Architectural Record* 44, no. 5 (November 1918): 415–421; "Modern Industrial Plants, Part II," *Architectural Record* 44, no. 6 (December 1918): 532–549; "Modern Industrial Plants, Part III—Plans and Designs," *Architectural Record* 45, no. 1 (January 1919): 27–43; "Modern Industrial Plants, Part IV, Discussions of the Various Types of Windows for Industrial Buildings," *Architectural Record* 45, no. 2 (February 1919): 148–168; "Modern Industrial Plants, Part VIa, The Excessive Turnover of Labor and the Influence of Employee's Welfare Work in Reducing It," *Architectural Record* 45, no. 4 (April 1919): 341–355; "Modern Industrial Plants, Part VIb, The Excessive Turnover of Labor and the Influence of Employee's Welfare Work in Reducing It," *Architectural Record* 45, no. 5 (May 1919): 451–470; and "Modern Industrial Plants, Part VII, Sears, Roebuck & Co.'s Plant, Chicago," *Architectural Record*. 45, no. 6 (June 1919): 506–525. See also Taylor, *Satellite Cities*.

29. Nimmons, "Modern Industrial Plants, Part VI-b," 451. He goes on to list "architecturally designed buildings . . . working conditions . . . food and lunching facilities . . . recreation and entertainment,"

including "outdoor athletic fields, playgrounds, walks and gardens," medical facilities, "education," employee benefits, and "housing." (451–454) As an architect, Nimmons would naturally emphasize design issues, but it is remarkable that he does give site design issues emphasis over building design.

30. Nimmons, "Modern Industrial Plants, Part VIb," 437.

31. Kenneth Jackson, *Crabgrass Frontier: The Suburbanization of the United States* (New York: Oxford University Press, 1985), 84; Richard Walker and Robert Lewis, "Beyond the Crabgrass Frontier; Industry and the Spread of North American Cities," in *Manufacturing Suburbs: Building Work and Home on the Metropolitan Fringe*, ed. Robert Lewis (Philadelphia: Temple University Press, 2004), 16–31.

32. "Building in One Package: How the Austin Company Solves Some of Industry's Unique Problems and Applies the Same Approach to Special Buildings of All Kinds," *Architectural Forum* 82, no. 2 (February 1942): 115.

33. Albert Kahn Associated Architects and Engineers, "The Design of Factories Today,' *Architectural Record* 98, no. 5 (November 1945): 121–122.

34. Walker and Lewis, "Beyond the Crabgrass Frontier."

35. General Foods, *GF Moving Day and You,* 9. On the assiduously guarded pastoral character of Westchester County, see James S. Duncan and Nancy G. Duncan, *Landscapes of Privilege: Aesthetics and Affluence in an American Suburb* (New York: Routledge, 2004).

36. Becky M. Nicolaides and Andrew Wiese, eds., *The Suburban Reader* (New York: Routledge, 2006), 114.

37. "Explains Plans of Laboratory," *Newark News*, August 1, 1930, n.p.

38. "Big Development in Murray Hill by Bell Telephone Laboratories," *Summit Herald*, August 1, 1930, 1.

39. Michael Mudd, "William L. Butcher: Three Decades Building Westchester," *Westchester Commerce and Industry*, January 23, 1977, H3; Edwin Michaelian quoted in Milton Hoffman, "Michaelian Was There at the Beginning," *Westchester Commerce and Industry*, January 23, 1977, H4.

40. "Zoning Map of the Borough of New Providence," *Summit Herald and Summit Record*, February 24, 1933, insert.

41. Lawrence G. Foster, "'Research Row' Rustic Location of Labs along the Lackawanna Aids Industrial Giants in 'Wooing the Muses,'" *Newark Sunday News*, November 13, 1949, 12, 21.

42. Mudd, "William L. Butcher"; Hoffman, "Michaelian."

43. "Office Building near Waltham, Massachusetts," *Architectural Record* 121, no. 2 (February 1957): 178; Fred F. Stockwell, "Hobbs Brook Park Office Buildings," *Urban Land* 20, no. 4 (April 1961): 3.

44. "Offices Move to the Suburbs," *BusinessWeek,* March 17, 1951, 82.

45. Robert O. Self, "Prelude to a Tax Revolt: The Politics of the 'Tax Dollar' in Postwar California," in *The New Suburban History*, ed. Kevin M. Kruse and Thomas J. Sugrue (Chicago: University of Chicago Press, 2006) 147; John R. Logan and Harvey L. Molotch, *Urban Fortunes: The Political Economy of Place* (Berkeley and Los Angeles: University of California Press, 2007).

46. Self, "Prelude to a Tax Revolt," 147–149.

47. Daniel Bell, *The Cultural Contradictions of Capitalism* (New York: Basic Books, 1976), 11, 77, 94–95.

48. "G.M. Technical Center," *Architectural Forum* 91, no. 1 (July 1949): 71; exemplary of the GM publicity, General Motors Public Relations, *Where Today Meets Tomorrow: General Motors Technical Center* (Detroit: General Motors Corporation, 1956).

49. *Deere & Company Administrative Center*, video viewed at the Deere & Company Administrative Center Display Building, June 1997.

50. "Should Management Move to the Country?" 164.

51. Jackson, *Crabgrass Frontier*.

52. "The Power of a Road," *Fortune* 56, no. 4 (October 1957): 285.

53. William Story, "Advertising the Site through Good Design," *Landscape Architecture* 49, no. 3 (Spring 1959): 144–145.

54. David A. Granley and Charles E. Jolitz, "The New General Foods Headquarters: Its Design and Construction—Part Two," *GF Technical Bulletin* 6, no. 2 (June 1952): 2.

55. Sharon Zukin, *Landscapes of Power* (Berkeley and Los Angeles: University of California Press, 1991), 142–145.

56. W. Brewster Snow, *The Highway and the Landscape* (New Brunswick, NJ: Rutgers University Press, 1959), 157.

57. Peter Walker, designer of many corporate projects, avers that this coy manipulation of infrastructure technology was the modernist, "functional" element of these landscapes in lieu of their somewhat dated pastoral design. Peter Walker, interview with the author, November 1997.

58. "Insurance Sets a Pattern," *Architectural Forum* 107, no. 3 (September 1957): 127.

59. J. Ross McKeever, *Business Parks, Office Parks, Plazas and Centers* (Washington, DC: Urban Land Institute, 1971), 18.

60. Elizabeth James, "Why Move to White Plains," *GF News* 15, no. 5 (May 1954): 13.

61. Walker, "Theory of Suburbanization," 401; Barbara Baran, "Office Automation and Women's Work: The Technical Transformation of the Insurance Industry," in *High Technology, Space, and Society*, ed. Manuel Castells (Thousand Oaks, CA: Sage, 1985), 143–71; Kristin Nelson, "Labor Demand, Labor Supply and the Suburbanization of Low-Wage Office Work," in *Production, Work, and Territory*, ed. Allen J. Scott and Michael Storpor (Winchester, MA: Allen and Unwin, 1986), 149–171.

62. Story, "Advertising the Site," 145.

63. Franklin L. Hunt, "New Buildings of Bell Telephone Laboratories," *Journal of Applied Physics* 14 (June 1943): 251; Mervin J. Kelly, "The Bell Telephone Laboratories—An Example of Creative Technology," *Proceedings of the Royal Society of London Series A* 203, no. 10 (October 1950): 291.

64. Fortune, "Should Management Move to the Country?" 170.

65. "Building with a Future," *Time*, September 16, 1957, 91.

66. Herrera, "That Manhattan Exodus," 109.

67. Mildred Reed Hall and Edward T. Hall, *The Fourth Dimension in Architecture* (Santa Fe, NM: Sunstone Press, 1975), 61.

68. Ibid., 58.

69. "Should Management Move to the Country?"; Herrera, "That Manhattan Exodus"; O'Meara, "Executive Suites"; Meyer, "Why Corporations Are on the Move"; "Why Companies Are Fleeing the Cities"; Herbert E. Meyer, "Simmons Likes it Down South," *Fortune* 93, no. 5 (May 1976): 255–258, 266

70. Roland Marchand, *Creating the Corporate Soul* (Berkeley and Los Angeles: University of California Press, 1998).

71. Ibid., 362.

72. Walker, "Theory of Suburbanization," 397.

73. J. B. Jackson, "The Popular Yard," *Places* 4, no. 3 (1987): 26, 30.

74. Leo Marx, "Does Pastoralism Have a Future?" in *The Pastoral Landscape*, ed. John Dixon Hunt (Washington, DC: National Gallery of Art, 1992), 213.

75. Walker, "Theory of Suburbanization," 392.

Chapter 3

1. Kenneth A. Meade, "The Shortage of Scientific and Technical Personnel: What Industry Is Doing about It," *Science*, May 2, 1947, 457, 458, 460. Like other industrial companies in the years immediately following World War II, General Motors quickly grasped the potential of research, especially defense research, as an ongoing enterprise in and of itself and the related dilemma of attracting qualified personnel. General Motors could point to the proposed Technical Center as the premier setting for this new version of the corporate scientist.

2. A. R. Raskin, "Key Men of Business—Scientists," *New York Times Magazine*, May 13, 1956, 15.

3. Francis Bello, "The World's Greatest Industrial Laboratory," *Fortune* 58, no. 5 (November 1958): 148–157.

4. George Wise, *Willis R. Whitney, General Electric, and the Origins of U.S. Industrial Research* (New York: Columbia University Press, 1985); Deidre Laporte, "Bell Laboratories: The Beginnings of Scientific Research in an Industrial Setting," *Annals of the New York Academy of Sciences,* eds. Joseph W. Dauben and Virginia Staudt Sexton (New York: New York Academy of Sciences, 1983), 85–100; Leonard S. Reich. "Irving Langmuir and the Pursuit of Science and Technology in the Corporate Environment," *Technology/Culture* 24, no. 2 (1983): 199–221; David F. Noble, *America by Design: Science, Technology and the Rise of Corporate Capitalism* (New York: Knopf, 1977), particularly chaps. 1–3.

5. Alfred Dupont Chandler Jr., *Strategy and Structure* (Cambridge, MA: Harvard University Press, 1962), *The Visible Hand: The Managerial Revolution in American Business* (Cambridge, MA: Harvard University Press, 1977), and *Scale and Scope: The Dynamics of Industrial Capitalism* (Cambridge, MA: Harvard University Press, 1990), particularly chaps. 2, 3, and Conclusion.

6. Laporte, "Bell Laboratories," 85–100; Reich, "Irving Langmuir," 199–221; Noble, *America by Design*.

7. Noble, *America by Design*, chap. 4, on industrial scientists as proponents of welfare capitalism. Noble focuses on labor relations and commercial practices and does not discuss changes in the factory. David E. Nye, *Image Worlds: Corporate Identities at General Electric* (Cambridge, MA: MIT Press, 1985); George C. Nimmons, "Modern Industrial Plants, Part VIa, The Excessive Turnover of Labor and the Influence of Employee's Welfare Work in Reducing It," *Architectural Record* 45, no. 4 (April 1919): 341–355, and "Modern Industrial Plants, Part VIb, The Excessive Turnover of Labor and the Influence of Employee's Welfare Work in Reducing It," *Architectural Record* 45, no. 5 (May 1919): 451–470; Graham Romeyn Taylor, *Satellite Cities: A Study of Industrial Suburbs* (New York: Appleton, 1915); Margaret Crawford, *Building the Workingman's Paradise: The Design of American Company Towns* (New York: Verso, 1985).

8. Wise, *Willis R. Whitney*, 259–260, quoted 213, 222.

9. Kenneth Jackson, *Crabgrass Frontier: The Suburbanization of the United States* (New York: Oxford University Press, 1985), 84.

10. For summaries of the principles of suburban factory design, see "Building in One Package: How the Austin Company Solves Some of Industry's Unique Problems and Applies the Same Approach to Special Buildings of All Kinds," *Architectural Forum* 82 no. 2 (February 1942): 113–117; Albert Kahn Associated Architects and Engineers, "The Design of Factories Today," *Architectural Record* 98, no. 5 (November 1945): 120–138.

11. Rebecca S. Lowen, *Creating the Cold War University* (Berkeley and Los Angeles: University of California Press, 1997), 7–16, 43–66.

12. David Kaiser, "The Postwar Suburbanization of American Physics," *American Quarterly* 56, no. 4 (December 2004): 870–878.

13. Paul Venable Turner, *Campus: An American Planning Tradition* (Cambridge, MA: MIT Press, 1984). Of course, many American universities were located in urban settings, but as Turner makes clear, influenced by the ideal set forth by Thomas Jefferson's plan for the University of Virginia, Americans do not see the city as the optimal setting for higher learning. Even many urban campuses try to preserve or insert green surrounds; see for instance Columbia University in New York City.

14. Kaiser, "The Postwar Suburbanization of American Physics," 870–878. Kaiser also discusses the emphasis on ethnic and social homogeneity in the selection of employees with a doctorate in physics.

15. Ibid, 861–863.

16. Nye, *Image Worlds,* 18–20. Nye incorrectly identifies NELA as the National Electric Light [sic] Association, but otherwise his account is accurate. See also Wise, *Willis R. Whitney,* 257–258; John Winthrop Hammond, *Men and Volts: The Story of General Electric* (New York: McGraw-Hill,

1941), 340–344; General Electric, *A Century of Progress: The General Electric Story, 1876–1978* (Schenectady, NY: General Electric, 1981): 55.

17. Florence Dempsey, "Nela Park: A Novelty in the Architectural Grouping of Industrial Buildings," *Architectural Record* 35, no. 6 (June 1914): 468–503.

18. Montgomery Schuyler, "A New Departure in 'Big Business,'" *Architectural Record* 35 no. 6 (June 1914): 505–507.

19. After the government forced GE to dissolve NELA, the corporation maintained Nela Park as a marketing and occasional research facility without publicizing its GE connection. Nye, *Image Worlds*, 18–20; Wise, *Willis R. Whitney*, 257–258.

20. Quoted in Noble, *America by Design*, 115. Jewett studied at the University of Chicago under Albert A. Michaelson, the first American Nobel laureate in physics. Franklin L. Hunt, "New Murray Hill Laboratory of Bell Telephone Laboratories," *Journal of Applied Physics* 14, no. 6 (June 1943): 250–251. Bello, "World's Greatest Industrial Laboratory," 155.

21. H. D. Arnold, "Report on 'An Acreage Laboratory,'" July 19, 1929, Murray Hill file, AT&T Archives, Warren, NJ (hereafter cited as AT&T).

22. J. F. Dawson, "Report of Conference, Bell Telephone Company Laboratories," July 8, 1930, Records of the Olmsted Associates, Series B, Box 491, Job File 9218, folders 1 and 2, Manuscript Division, Library of Congress (hereafter cited as ROA).

23. H. D. Arnold, "Report on 'An Acreage Laboratory,'" 4–6.

24. Ibid.; H. P. Charlesworth memo to Dr. Arnold Jewett, "Laboratories Expansion Program—Suburban Activities," August 21, 1929, AT&T.

25. J. E. Moravec to Olmsted Brothers, February 20, 1931, ROA.

26. "Big Development in Murray Hill by Bell Telephone Laboratories," *Summit Herald*, August 1, 1930, 1; Dawson, "Report of Conference."

27. H. P. Charlesworth to J. E. Moravec, memo, October 7, 1932, AT&T; Dawson, "Report of Conference." Voorhees, Gmelin, and Walker was well known for its central business district buildings, particularly the Barclay-Vesey Building for New York Telephone. Ralph Walker won the AIA Centennial Medal of Honor in 1957. See Ralph Walker, *Ralph Walker Architect* (New York: Henahan House, 1957); Richard Guy Wilson, "Ralph Walker," *The AIA Medal* (New York: McGraw-Hill, 1984), 184–185.

28. Dawson, "Report of Conference."

29. C. R. Parker, "Report of Visit Bell Telephone Laboratories," July 17, 1930, ROA.

30. "Plan Big Plant Near Summit," *Newark News*, July 29, 1930, clipping file, New Providence Historical Society.

31. "Big Development," 1.

32. Ibid.

33. The *Newark News* of same day summarized Jewett's characterization of the development, including the involvement of the Olmsted Brothers, and published the same list of local company officers and scientists. "Explains Plans of Laboratory," *Newark News*, August 1, 1930.

34. Jackson, *Crabgrass Frontier*, 172–189.

35. Cf. Turner, *Campus*.

36. "Zoning Map of the Borough of New Providence," *Summit Herald and Summit Record*, February 24, 1933, insert.

37. F. B. Jewett to H. P. Charlesworth "Outside Laboratory—Murray Hill," memo, August 26, 1930, AT&T; H. P. Charlesworth to J. E. Moravec, memo, October 7, 1932, AT&T.

38. H. V. Hubbard to S. F. Voorhees, October 5, 1939, ROA.

39. Don Graf, "Murray Hill Unit, Bell Telephone Laboratories, Inc.," *Pencil Points* 23, no. 8 (August 1942): 34–71; Walker, *Ralph Walker Architect*, 176–193.

40. Ibid.

41. Initially a fence enclosed only three sides of the site, leaving the front open, but concerns for security once war broke out led to complete site closure. See notes on plan 9218-53, "Fencing Plan," December 15, 1939, Olmsted Archives, Frederick Law Olmsted National Historic Site, National Park Service (hereafter cited as OA).

42. C. D. Haines to C. R. Parker, October 5, 1939, ROA. See also Parker's notes on plan 9218–15, October 11, 1939, OA.

43. See Parker's notes on plan 9218–15, October 11, 1939, OA.

44. Graf, "Murray Hill" 36–70. The complex bore a marked resemblance to Eliel Saarinen's architecture at Cranbrook, particularly the 1931 Kingswood School for Girls. The buildings created courtyards with irregularly spaced openings very similar to the scheme at Bell, but more graciously executed. See Turner, *Campus*, 215–248, and Diana Balmori, "Cranbrook: The Invisible Landscape," *Journal of the Society of Architectural Historians* 53, no. 1 (March 1994): 30–60.

45. Ben Smith to C. R. Parker, February 2, 1940, ROA.

46. In a testy letter to Bell Labs president O. E. Buckley terminating their services on the project, the eminent principal of Olmsted Brothers, Henry V. Hubbard, acknowledged the overt disputes with the architects that "annoyed and perhaps embarrassed" Bell executives but defended their advocacy of "informal treatment" of the landscape to be "in keeping with the surrounding countryside." H. V. Hubbard to O. E. Buckley, December 2, 1942, ROA. Given the tensions between them, the architects did not ask Olmsted Brothers to join the design team for the second building at Murray Hill completed in 1949.

47. The Voorhees firm also self-published a large-format book with many large photographs based on Graf's *Pencil Points* article. It does not mention Olmsted Brothers either. See Don Graf, *Convenience for Research* (New York: Voorhees, Walker, Foley, and Smith, 1944).

48. "Workshop for Bell Scientists: A $3,000,000 Phone Laboratory," *Newsweek*, August 4, 1941, 44–45.

49. Graf, "Murray Hill," 69.

50. "Modern Laboratory," *Life*, September 18, 1944, 79, 81, 82.

51. Hunt, "New Murray Hill Laboratory," 257.

52. "The Bell Telephone Laboratories at Murray Hill, N.J.," *Science*, June 1, 1945, 554–555.

53. Mervin J. Kelly, "The Bell Telephone Laboratories—An Example of Creative Technology," *Proceedings of the Royal Society of London Series A* 203, no. 1074 (October 1950): 291.

54. Ibid.

55. "At Bell Labs, Industrial Research Looks Like Bright College Years," *BusinessWeek,* February 6, 1954, 74–75.

56. Bello, "The World's Greatest Industrial Laboratory," 148–149.

57. Bell Laboratories, *Welcome to Murray Hill* (Murray Hill, NJ: Bell Laboratories, [1972]).

58. Lawrence Foster, "Research Row: Rustic Location of Labs along the Lackawanna Aids Industrial Giants in 'Wooing the Muses,'" *Newark News Sunday*, November 13, 1949, 12, 21.

59. "At Bell Labs," 74.

60. All featured in the November 1945 *Architectural Record.*.

61. For an account of GE's research approach, see Wise, *Willis R. Whitney*.

62. Wise, *Willis R. Whitney*, 211, 212, 259–260; Laurence Hawkins, *Adventure into the Unknown: The First Fifty Years of the General Electric Research Laboratory* (New York: Morrow, 1950), 84.

63. Kendall Birr, *Pioneering in Industrial Research* (Washington, DC: Public Affairs Press, 1957), 163–164.

64. "$8,000,000 Plant to Spur Research," *New York Times*, June 1, 1945, 13; "General Electric Research Laboratory," *Architectural Record* 108, no. 1 (July 1950): 124–127. GE management chose the site because the river provided water for processing and cooling and a place to dump "purified wastes." The location also provided access to transportation: river barges and a railroad branch along the river edge. Most important, the site had plenty of room for expansion. Hawkins, *Adventure into the Unknown*, 123.

65. Hawkins, *Adventure into the Unknown*, 121–127; "General Electric Research Laboratory."

66. Birr, *Pioneering in Industrial Research*, 172–173. Just before the war, the Electronics Department consolidated both "works laboratories" (laboratories that were attached to factories that dealt with immediate production problems) and parts of the original Research Laboratory at the Schenectady facility.

67. "GE Laboratory to Speed Research in Post-War Use of Electronics," *New York Times* August 12, 1945, 5.

68. Birr, *Pioneering in Industrial Research*, 172; "GE Plans Big Syracuse Output," *New York Times*, September 23, 1945, 32; "Big Industry Moves to the Country," *Architectural Forum* 95, no. 2 (July 1951): 146.

69. Edward H. Laird, "Electronics Park: An Industrial Center for the General Electric Company," *Landscape Architecture* 38, no. 1 (October 1946): 14–16; "Electronics Park, Syracuse, New York," *Architectural Record*, 105, no. 2 (February 1949): 96–103.

70. Laird, "Electronics Park," 16.

71. Turner, *Campus*, 245.

72. Quoted in Charles Haines, "Planning the Scientific Laboratory," *Architectural Record* 108, no. 1 (July 1950): 107. Haines worked on Bell Labs as part of the architectural team of Voorhees, Walker, Foley, and Smith.

73. "Big Industry Moves to the Country," 146–148.

74. Philip D. Reed, "General Electric's Decentralization Plan," *American City* 63 (October 1948): 7.

75. Ibid., 145; "Electronics Park, Syracuse, New York," 97; "GE Gets Small Business Touch," *Business Week*, April 19, 1952, 118–130.

76. "Big Industry Moves to the Country"; "New View of Metals," *Business Week*, August 27, 1955, 158; "Industrial Group on the Campus Plan"; Laird, "Electronics Park"; "Electronics Park, Syracuse, New York."

77. "Research: How Can It Be Controlled?" *Business Week*, June 5, 1954, 80–86.

78. "New View of Metals," 158.

79. Although I cannot document this, Manville was one county over from Bell Labs (though admittedly a world away). The movable walls used at Bell were filled with asbestos, and these kinds of walls were a Johns-Manville product. I would surmise that in manufacturing and installing the movable partitions for Bell that Johns-Manville management might have seen the advantages of separating research functions.

80. "Chronology: Company's Rise and Fall," *Bridgewater Courier News*, May 14, 1995, A-4; Research and Archeological Management, *Somerset County Cultural Resource Survey, Phase I* (Somerville, NJ: Somerset County Cultural Heritage Commission, 1989); J. H. Van Horn, *Historic Somerset* (Somerville, NJ: Historic Societies of Somerset County, 1965).

81. "History of Manville, 1939–49," *Somerset Star Herald*, May 5, 1954, 3; Johns-Manville, "Anniversary Issue," *Johns-Manville News Pictorial* (January 1958): 11.

82. Quoted in "Johns Manville Starts Expansion," *New York Times*, September 7, 1945, 29.

83. "New J-M Expansion Predicted by Brown, Center Is Dedicated," *Manville News*, May 26, 1949, 1; "Manville Builds New Home for Industrial Research," *Business Week*, November 8, 1947, 44.

84. "Manville Builds New Home for Industrial Research."

85. "Research and Manufacture Combined under One Roof," *Architectural Record* 98, no. 5 (November 1945): 112–113; "Large Corporation Builds a Research Campus in New Jersey," *Architectural Record* 106, no. 4 (October 1949): 108–114; Clifford F. Rassweiler, "The Johns-Manville Research Center Six Years Later," *Architectural Record* 118, no. 3 (September 1955): 222–224.

86.   Rassweiler, "The Johns-Manville Research Center," 224.

87.   Craig Calhoun and Henryk Hiller, "Coping with Insidious Injuries: The Case of Johns-Manville Corporation and Asbestos Exposure," *Social Problems* 35, no. 2 (April 1988): 162–181. Since the 1930s Johns-Manville had a specific corporate strategy to prevent the dissemination of research indicating the connection between asbestos exposure and asbestosis and cancer.

88.   General Motors Public Relations, "General Motors Builds Its First 50 Million Cars" (Detroit: General Motors, 1955), 4.

89.   Ibid., 5.

90.   For views and description of this building, see "Building for the General Motors Company, Detroit, Mich. Albert Kahn Architect," *American Architect—Architectural Review*, November 21, 1921, 392–394; "The Durant Building," *Architecture and Building* 52, no. 4 (April 1920): 37–39.

91.   "Research Staff Picture History," *Michigan Tradesman* 73 (May 1956): 32–33.

92.   Cf. Alfred P. Sloan Jr., *My Years with General Motors* (New York: Doubleday, 1963); Chandler, *Strategy and Structure* and *The Visible Hand.*.

93.   "New Frontier," *New York Times*, May 14, 1945, 16:3.

94.   General Motors Public Relations Staff, *Where Today Meets Tomorrow: General Motors Technical Center* (Detroit: General Motors Corporation, 1956), 6,5.

95.   Sloan, *My Years with General Motors*, 300–304.

96.   Fortune, "G.M. Technical Center," *Fortune* 44, no. 6 (December 1951): 82.

97.   Sloan, *My Years with General Motors*, 304. Earl significantly influenced the design outcome of the Technical Center. Earl, who joined GM in 1927 as head of the new art and color section, was the vice president in charge of the styling staff. He designed the highly successful 1927 Cadillac LaSalle with flying wing fenders and windows to make the car look longer and lower (the beginning of streamlining, a process still ongoing in car design). Earl originated the use of car colors other than black and conceived of the yearly car model; both became standards for the car industry and immeasurably contributed to GM's marketing success. He pioneered the production of "dream" cars—what today are called concept cars—to test public tastes for future model year proposals. Earl arguably invented car styling, understanding that automobiles had an allure beyond their handy convenience. He started with a staff of ten and commanded a thousand employees by the opening of the Technical Center. For a summary of his styling philosophy, see General Motors Public Relations, *Styling: The Look of Things* (Detroit: General Motors, 1956).

98.   Sloan, *My Years with General Motors*, 304–305.

99.   Members of Albert Kahn Associated Architects, "The Design of Factories Today," 120–126. After completion of the Technical Center, the architect Eero Saarinen asserted that its "architecture really carries forward the tradition of American factory buildings which had its roots in the Middle West in the automobile factories of Albert Kahn." Eero Saarinen, *Eero Saarinen on His Work*, ed. Aline Saarinen (New Haven, CT: Yale University Press, 1962), 24.

100. Roland Marchand, *Creating the Corporate Soul: The Rise of Public Relations and Corporate Imagery in American Big Business* (Berkeley and Los Angeles: University of California Press, 1998), 301–311.

101. "General Motors Technical Center," *Architectural Record* 98, no. 5 (November 1945): 98–103.

102. Sloan, *My Years with General Motors*, 305. For more on Eliel Saarinen, see David G. DeLong, "Eliel Saarinen and the Cranbrook Tradition in Architecture and Urban Design," in *Design in America: The Cranbrook Vision, 1925–1950* (New York: Harry Abrams, 1983), 47–90.

103. Eliel Saarinen, "Detroit Planning Studies," *New Pencil Points* 24, no. 12 (1943): 51. The Detroit plan was published in *New Pencil Points* in three installments: December 1943, January 1944, and February 1944.

104. Eliel Saarinen, *The City* (Cambridge, MA: MIT Press, 1943).

105. "General Motors Speeds Research," *New York Times*, July 25, 1945, 23.

106. Quoted in General Motors Public Relations, "Technical Center History," 1956, 3–4, UAW Research Department, Accession No. 350, Box 89, file GM Research Activities—Technical Center, Warren Michigan, 1956, Archives of Labor and Urban Affairs, Wayne State University (hereafter cited as UAW).

107. Quoted in "General Motors Speeds Research."

108. Quoted in ibid.

109. "General Motors Technical Center," *Architectural Record* 98, no. 5 (November 1945): 98–103. The issue was dedicated to laboratory buildings, and besides the Technical Center, it included photographs, drawings, and descriptions of the "campus" of General Electric Electronics Park and the "quad" of the Johns-Manville Research Center, besides a couple of specialized individual laboratory buildings on industrial sites. Although the landscape architects Wilcox Laird were mentioned in a caption of the photograph showing the Electronics Park's model, Thomas Church was the only landscape architect included in the bold-type list up front under the article title. He was listed right after the architects, Saarinen & Swanson, and before Hugh Ferriss, who had done the renderings published in the article.

110. Susan B. Riess, interviewer, "Elizabeth Bower Church: A Life by the Side of Thomas Church," in *Thomas D. Church, Landscape Architect, Volume II* (Berkeley: Regents of the University of California, Berkeley, 1978), 514–515.

111. General Motors Corporation, "A History of the Development and Construction of General Motors Technical Center, Warren Township, Mocomb County, Michigan," General Motors Technical Center, 1956, internal memo reviewed by the author at the General Motors Technical Center, May 2007.

112. Quoted in Edward A. Eichstedt, "Current Work in Progress: Landscape at the General Motors Technical Center," *Landscape Architecture* 42, no. 4 (July 1952): 176.

113. "General Motors Technical Center," 99, 101.

114. General Motors Public Relations, "Technical Center History," 5.

115. Sloan, *My Years with General Motors*, 305.

116. The project started in the Saarinen and Swanson office that included Eliel Saarinen and J. Robert Swanson, as well as Eliel Saarinen's son, Eero. During 1947 they formed the partnership Saarinen, Swanson, and Saarinen. Swanson left and formed his own firm in the same year, and the father and son formed Saarinen, Saarinen Associates. After the elder Saarinen's death in 1948, the son formed Eero Saarinen and Associates. Charles Eames, "one of [Eero] Saarinen's closest friends," wrote in *Architectural Forum* in 1971: "Eliel, in association with his son Eero, did design a first version; but a second version—three years later—and its subsequent development were the work of Eero, with the critical support and stringent conscience of his father." Charles Eames, *Architectural Forum* 134, no. 5 (June 1971): 21–28. According to Church's wife, Betsey, Church went to Michigan numerous times and worked closely with Eero Saarinen on the project. Riess, *Thomas D. Church,* 514. Edward Eichstedt, a local landscape architect, was brought in to complete the contract documents, select materials, and do field supervision.

117. Saarinen, *Eero Saarinen on His Work*, 24.

118. Although all four were research and development units, the research division engaged in pure research, unencumbered by specific applicability, and it therefore carried the most prestige.

119. For a description and discussion of the design of the Technical Center, see "G.M. Technical Center," *Architectural Forum* 91, no. 1 (July 1949): 70–78; "General Motors Technical Center," *Architectural Forum* 95, no. 5 (November 1951): 111–123; Eichstedt, "Current Work in Progress," 166–168; "GM Nears Completion," *Architectural Forum* 101, no. 5 (November 1954): 100–119; "GM's Industrial Versailles," *Architectural Forum* 104, no. 5 (May 1956): 122–129; "Technical Center for General Motors Warren, Michigan," *Arts & Architecture* 74, no. 5 (May 1957): 25.

120. Frederick G. Tykle and Ervine E. Klein, "Unique Architectural Elements of the GM Technical Center," *General Motors Engineering Journal* 3, no. 3 (May–June 1956): 69–77; Saarinen, *Eero Saarinen on His Work*, 26. Among the new systems were: exterior glazed brick; neoprene fenestration and panel gaskets based on car window gaskets; 2-inch prefabricated porcelain-laminated sandwich panels for both interior and exterior walls; and plastic ceiling panels hung underneath fluorescent lighting, producing shadowless lighting for work areas.

121. Saarinen, *Eero Saarinen on His Work*, 24.

122. General Motors Public Relations, "Technical Center Architecture," 2.

123. Scott G. Knowles and Stuart W. Leslie, "'Industrial Versailles': Eero Saarinen's Corporate Campuses for GM, IBM, and AT&T," *Isis* 92, no. 1 (March 2001): 10.

124. The landscape required 13,000 trees, some 600 fully grown; 3,180 shrubs; and 55,941 ground cover plants. Also, uplights illuminated 280 trees at night. The entire landscape was irrigated by an underground system. Lawn covered 155 of the 320 site acres. General Motors Public Relations, "Technical Center Shorts," press release, 1956, 2, Box 89, folder GM Research Activities-Technical Center 1956, UAW; Eichstedt, "Current Work in Progress," 167.

125. "G.M. Technical Center," *Architectural Forum*, 71.

126. Eichstedt, "Current Work in Progress," 167.

127. Ibid. The work of Jens Jensen and O. C. Simonds typifies the prairie school of landscape design of the early twentieth century, much influenced by northern European concepts. Betsey Church,

Church's wife, speculated that the landscape design of the Technical Center showed the influence of Alvar Aalto's landscape design in Finland, particularly the idea of a building placed in the clearing of a regularly planted forest. Riess, *Thomas Church, Vol. 2*, 515.

128. Saarinen, *Eero Saarinen on His Work*, 24.

129. Ibid.

130. Ibid.

131. "GM Technical Center," 100.

132. Saarinen, *Eero Saarinen on His Work*, 24.

133. "G.M. Technical Center," 71.

134. "GM Nears Completion," 109.

135. "GM's Industrial Versailles," 123.

136. "Technical Center for General Motors Warren, Michigan," 25.

137. General Motors Public Relations, "Where Today Meets Tomorrow."

138. Tykle and Klein, "Unique Architectural Elements of the GM Technical Center," 69–77

139. *GM Folks* 19, no. 6 (June 1956). Issue devoted to the opening of the General Motors Technical.

140. Harlow H. Curtice, "Accelerating the Pace of Technological Progress," in *The Greatest Frontier* (Detroit: General Motors Corporation, 1956), 7, 10, 11.

141. Lawrence R. Hafsted, "The Future Is Our Assignment," in *The Greatest Frontier*, 13, 15.

142. Charles F. Kettering, "Let's Turn Around . . . and Look at the Future," in *The Greatest Frontier*, 23–24.

143. Dwight D. Eisenhower, "The Rich Reward Ahead," in *The Greatest Frontier*, 26–27.

144. "G.M. To Dedicate Technical Unit," *New York Times,* May 13, 1956, F1; "Curtice Bids U.S. Spur Technology," *New York Times,* May 17, 1956, 1. Several people have told me that they remember watching the Technical Center coverage on the evening news as children in the 1950s.

145. "Architecture for the Future: GM Constructs a 'Versailles of Industry,'" *Life*, May 21, 1956, 102–107.

146. "G.M. Technical Center," *Fortune*, 82.

147. Raskin, "Key Men of Business," 15, 38.

148. "GM's Showplace for Stepped-Up Research," *Business Week*, May 12, 1956, 103.

149. Raskin, "Key Men of Business," 15.

150. "G.M. Technical Center," *Architectural Forum*, 71.

151. General Motors Technical Center, "History of the Development," 2.

152. Eichstedt, "Current Work in Progress," 166.

153. "GM's Showplace for Stepped-Up Research," 103.

154. Sloan, *Eero Saarinen on His Work*, 305.

155. Strikingly, neither the 1945 corporate announcement nor the first publication in *Architectural Record* of the project makes any comparison to university sites, a difference made more notable in the latter by the side-by-side publication of the Electronics Park and the Johns-Manville Research Center. From then on, publications eschewed the term until the completion of the center. The first reference to the Technical Center as a campus is the 1952 article by Edward Eichstedt published in *Landscape Architecture* on his and Church's ongoing work: "The general effect is similar to a well-planned university group comprising separate colleges." Eichstedt, "Current Work in Progress," 166.

156. Russell Lynes, "After Hours: The Erosion of Detroit," *Harper's* 220, no. 1316 (January 1960): 23–25. Lynes is the author of *The Tastemakers* (New York: Grosset and Dunlap, 1949) whom Pierce Lewis commends: "Nobody has written more perceptively and engagingly about [taste in America] than Russell Lynes." Pierce Lewis, "American landscape Tastes," in *Modern Landscape Architecture: A Critical Review*, ed. Marc Treib (Cambridge, MA: MIT Press, 1993): 2–18.

157. D. Dan McCarthy, interview with the author, GM Technical Center, Warren, Michigan, June 2007.

158. Oral history project of the National Air and Space Museum, interview by Martin Collins with Simon Ramo, June 27, 1988, Los Angeles, California, http://www.nasm.si.edu.research/dsh/TRANSCPT/RAMO1:HTM. (accessed March 4, 2008).

159. "About the Author" (about Melville Branch, author of article), *Princeton Engineer* 18, no. 1 (October 1957): 76; Melville C. Branch Jr., "Planning Environment for Research and Development, Part II: The Planning Process," *Princeton Engineer* 18, no. 2 (November 1957): 26.

160. Melville C. Branch Jr., "Planning Environment for Research and Development, Part I: Environment," *Princeton Engineer* 18, no. 1 (October 1957): 24.

161. Ibid., 25.

162. M. C. Branch and Arthur G. Barton, "Research and Development Fitted into a Residential Community," *Landscape Architecture* 50, no. 4 (Summer 1960): 204–211.

163. Branch, "Planning Environment for Research and Development—Part I: Environment," 29.

164. Ibid., 24.

165. Christopher Tunnard and Boris Pushkarev, *Man Made America: Chaos or Control? An Inquiry into Selected Problems of Design in the Urbanized Landscape* (New Haven, CT: Yale University Press, 1963), 294.

166. "Research Center, Yorktown, N.Y.," *Architecture & Building News* 221, no. 26 (June 1962): 923–926; "Unique Cross-Curve Plan for IBM Research Center," *Architectural Record* 129, no. 7 (June 1961): 137–146; "Research in the Round," *Architectural Forum* 114 (June 1961): 80–85; "Bell Labs Mirrored Superblock," *Architectural Record* 132, n. 11 (October 1962): 145–152; "The Biggest Mirror Ever," *Architectural Forum* 126, no. 3 (April 1967): 33–41; "Bell Telephone Laboratories Holmdel," *Architectural Design* 37, no. 7 (August 1967): 355–356, 339.

167. Knowles and Leslie, "'Industrial Versailles,'" 17–19, 27–28.

168. Ron Emrich, "Holmdel Consultant Calls for Bell Labs Demolition, McMansions, Golf Course," *Preserve NJ*, March 4, 2009, http://preservationnj.wordpress.com/2009/03/04/holmdels-consultant-calls-for-demolition-of-bell-labs-mcmansions-golf-course (accessed September 13, 2009).

169. David W. Kean, *IBM San Jose: A Quarter Century of Innovation* (San Jose, CA: International Business Machines Corporation, 1977), 1–45; Almaden Research Center "History of the Almaden Research Site," http//:www.almaden.ibm/almaden20/history.shtml (accessed March 13, 2008).

170. "IBM's New Corporate Face," *Architectural Forum* 106, no. 2 (February 1957): 106–115; "IBM's New Industrial Campus," *Architectural Forum* 108, no. 6 (June 1958): 104–107.

171. 1957 IBM description of Cottle Road Research Labs quoted in Almaden Research Center, "History of the Almaden Research Site."

172. "I.B.M. Banishes Dowdiness." *Fortune* 59, no. 6 (June 1957): 129–135; "IBM's New Corporate Face."

173. Kean, *IBM San Jose*, 121, 47.

174. Ibid., 78–79.

175. "Changes in the Office Environment: Research Facilities," *Progressive Architecture* 46, no. 7 (July 1965): 155.

176. Kean, *IBM San Jose*, 79–82.

177. IBM, "Statement of Requirements, Santa Teresa Laboratory," in Gerald M. McCue, "IBM's Santa Teresa Laboratory: Architectural Design for Program Development," *IBM Systems Journal* 17, no. 1 (1978): 22, http//:www.research.ibm.com/journal/sj/171/ibms (accessed March 13, 2008).

178. McCue, "IBM's Santa Teresa Laboratory"; "IBM's Santa Teresa Laboratory," *Architectural Record* 162 no. 2 (August 1977): 91–104; "IBM West Coast Programming Center," *Process: Architecture* 85 (October 1989): 74–77.

179. Hugh Geddes, "Industrial Parkland: Landscapes of a New Aristocracy" (master's thesis, University of California, Berkeley, 1986), 88.

180. Almaden Research Center, "History of the Almaden Research Site"; Almaden Research Center, "Quick Facts about the Almaden Site," http//:www.almaden.ibm.com/almaden20/quick.shtml (accessed March 13, 2008).

181. Philip Enquist, Interview with the author, June 1993; Skidmore, Owings & Merrill, *Longacres Park Master Plan: The Boeing Company*. (San Francisco: Skidmore, Owings, and Merrill, 1991).

182. Faye Rice, "Environmental Scorecard: The 10 Laggards," *Fortune* 128, no. 2 (July 1993): 122.

183. General Motors, *Where Today Meets Tomorrow,* n.p.

184. Roger J. O'Meara, "Executive Suites in Suburbia," *Conference Board Record* 9 no. 8 (August 1972): 10–11.

185. William Whyte, "End of Exodus: The Logic of the Headquarters City," *New York*, September 20, 1976, 89.

186. Turner, *Campus*, 305.

187. Marchand, *Creating the Corporate Soul*, 357–363.

Chapter 4

1. Jory Johnson, "Pastures of Plenty: Thirty Years of Corporate Villas in America," *Landscape Architecture* 80, no. 3 (March 1990): 51–52. For a small selection of similar historical allusions, see Fred Koetter, "The Corporate Villa," *Design Quarterly* 135 (1987): 3–32; Robert Campbell, "Intimations of Urbanity in a Bucolic Setting," *AIA Journal* 77, no. 1 (January 1988): 72–77; Gina Crandall "In Capability," *Landscape Architecture* 74, no. 3 (May–June 1984): 29–32.

2. Alfred Dupont Chandler Jr., *The Visible Hand: The Managerial Revolution in American Business* (Cambridge, MA: Harvard University Press, 1977), 497.

3. John Dixon Hunt, "Pastorals and Pastoralisms," in John Dixon Hunt, ed., *The Pastoral Landscape* (Washington, DC: National Gallery of Art, 1992), 16. Hunt refers to the repeated use of the "aesthetic handle" of pastoralism in the American landscape, including corporate headquarters.

4. James Ackerman, *The Villa: The Form and Ideology of Country Houses* (Princeton, NJ: Princeton University Press, 1990), 10. Here Ackerman is acknowledging the Marxist analysis of Reinhard Bentmann and Michael Muller in *The Villa as Hegemeonic Architecture,* first published in German in 1970 and translated by Tim Spence and David Craven (Atlantic Highlands, NJ: Humanities Press, 1992). In the first chapter, Ackerman discusses the ideology of the villa as "a concept or myth [of city dwellers] so firmly rooted in the unconscious that all who hold it affirm it as an incontrovertible truth . . . through which over the course of millennia persons whose position of privilege is rooted in urban commerce or industry have been able to expropriate rural land, often requiring for the realization of the myth, the care of a laboring class or slave" (p. 10).

5. Ackerman, *The Villa*, 286.

6. Leo Marx "Does Pastoralism Have a Future?" in *The Pastoral Landscape*, ed. John Dixon Hunt (Washington, DC: National Gallery of Art, 1992), 218. Marx discusses sentimental pastoralism in regard to nineteenth-century American landscape painters. In accounting for sentimental pastoralism, he quotes Ralph Waldo Emerson's commendation in "The Poet" (1844) to the artist "who reattaches things to nature and the Whole,—reattaching even artificial things, and violations of nature, to nature, by a deeper insight—disposes very easily of the most disagreeable facts." Marx first explained American pastoralism in his landmark work of literary analysis, *The Machine in the Garden: The Pastoral Ideal in America* ((New York: Oxford University Press, 1964).

7. For a discussion of the use of the skyscraper as an urban image, see Kenneth Turney Gibbs, *Business Architectural Imagery in America, 1870–1930* (Ann Arbor: University of Michigan Press, 1984), and Carol Willis, "Form Follows Finance: The Empire State Building," in *The Landscape of Modernity*, ed. David Ward and Oliver Zunz (Baltimore, MD: Johns Hopkins University Press, 1992).

8. Kenneth Jackson, *Crabgrass Frontier: The Suburbanization of the United States* (New York: Oxford University Press, 1985), 268.

9. T. Creighton, "Pearl Harbor to Nagasaki: A Review of Architectural Progress during the War Years," *Progressive Architecture* 27, no. 1 (January 1946): 42–81.

10. "Headquarters Building for the Hershey Metals Products Co.," *Architectural Forum* 83, no. 2 (August 1945): 108–110.

11. "Insurance Company Home Offices," *Pencil Points* 23, no. 1 (January 1942): 7; "Office Building—North American Life and Casualty," *Architectural Forum* 90, no. 1 (January 1949): 76–81; "Designed to Be Functional in Plan Quiet in Expression—Home Office Building for Phoenix Insurance Co.," *Architectural Record* 102, no. 6 (December 1952): 126–135.

12. "Designed to be Functional in Plan," 128.

13. "Offices Move to the Suburbs," *BusinessWeek*, March 17, 1951, 79–84.

14. Ibid., 80.

15. "Office Building—North American Life and Casualty," 76; "Offices Move to the Suburbs," 82.

16. Besides the factory headquarters and insurance companies, two publishing corporations had moved their entire operations out of Manhattan prior to 1940. Doubleday & Company moved to the commercial center of Garden City, Long Island, in 1910 and Reader's Digest moved to northern Westchester County in 1936. Searching for a nostalgic American environment, Reader's Digest's owners Dewitt and Lila Wallace built a large neocolonial building, recalling both Independence Hall and the Governor's Palace in Williamsburg, and set it within estate-like grounds. The establishment contained its entire national operation. Although Reader's Digest's mailing address is famously the small town of Pleasantville, the offices are actually near Mt. Kisco, a fashionable area for New Yorkers' country retreats, eight miles from Pleasantville and even today in a quiet village, not the suburbs. Reader's Digest's self-contained operations, small economic influence, and owner-driven peculiarities make it a notable anomaly but not a trendsetter.

17. Charles G. Mortimer, *A Fresh Chapter* (New York: General Foods, 1954), 1. (General Foods internal brochure courtesy of the General Foods Public Affairs).

18. Ibid., 2.

19. General Foods, *GF Moving Day and You*, 9; General Foods, "Goodbye to Subways? GF Takes Option on Site for New General Offices," *GF News Letter*, 12, no. 2 (February 1951): 2.

20. General Foods, *GF Moving Day and You*, 9, 12.

21. *Fortune* reported that of twenty-two companies that consulted with an expert on land acquisitions in suburban Westchester County, each "privately revealed that, among other things, it wanted to avoid target areas," though only one would admit this on record. Since the General Foods move was one of the subjects of the article and its land acquisition corresponds in time with the description, it is likely that it was one of the companies. "Should Management Move to the Country?" *Fortune* 46, no. 6 (December 1952): 166.

22.   General Foods, *GF Moving Day and You*, 9, 12.

23.   "Mortimer of General Foods," *Fortune* 50, no. 3 (September 1954): 132.

24.   General Foods, *GF Moving Day and You*, 12.

25.   Michael Mudd, "William L. Butcher: Three Decades Building Westchester," *Westchester Commerce and Industry*, January 23, 1977, H3.

26.   Milton Hoffman, "Michaelian Was There at the Beginning," *Westchester Commerce and Industry*, January 23, 1977, H4.

27.   Quoted in Mudd, "William L. Butcher," H3.

28.   General Foods, "Goodbye to Subways?" 2.

29.   General Foods, *GF Moving Day and You*, 10–11.

30.   "Offices Move to the Suburbs," 82.

31.   Hoffman, "Michaelian Was There at the Beginning," H5.

32.   General Foods, "Follow-Ups; Moving Story," *GF News*, 12, no. 7 (July–August 1951): 2.

33.   David A. Granley and Charles E. Jolitz, "The New General Foods Headquarters: Its Design and Construction—Part Two," *GF Technical Bulletin* 6, no. 2 (June 1952): 3.

34.   Ibid., 4.

35.   General Foods, *GF Moving Day and You*, 26; Granley and Jolitz, "The New General Foods Headquarters: Its Design and Construction—Part Two," 4.

36.   General Foods, *GF Moving Day and You*, 23; Granley and Jolitz, "The New General Foods Headquarters: Its Design and Construction—Part Two."

37.   General Foods, *GF Moving Day and You*, 23.

38.   David A. Granley and Charles E. Jolitz, "The New General Foods Headquarters: Its Electrical Distribution System," *GF Technical Bulletin*, 6, no. 3 (September 1952): 6–8; David A. Granley and Charles E. Jolitz, "The New General Foods Headquarters: Its Heating, Ventilating, and Air Conditioning Systems," *GF Technical Bulletin* 6, no. 4 (December 1952): 4–7.

39.   Granley and Jolitz, "The New General Foods Headquarters: Its Design and Construction—Part Two," 4.

40.   Elizabeth James, "Why Move to White Plains?" *GF News* 15, no. 5 (1954): 12–13.

41.   General Foods, *GF Moving Day and You*; General Foods, "'54 in White Plains," *GF News* 13, no. 5 (May 1952): 3; General Foods, "We Move Our General Offices to White Plains," *General Foods Annual Report* (Fall 1954): 12–13; General Foods, "Moving Out," *GF News* 15, no. 4 (April 1954): 3; General Foods, *General Foods* (White Plains, NY: General Foods, [1954]).

42.   General Foods, *GF Moving Day and You*, 26–28, 31; "Company Flees Maddening Crowd," *Business-Week*, March 27, 1954, 53.

43.   Mortimer, *A Fresh Chapter*, 8.

44. Elizabeth James, "What Is a Headquarters?" *GF News*,15, no. 5 (May 1954): 1.

45. General Foods, *General Foods*, 2.

46. Philip Herrera, "That Manhattan Exodus," *Fortune*, June 1, 1967, 109.

47. "Voorhees Walker Foley & Smith," *Architectural Forum* 101, no. 5 (November 1954): 140–147.

48. Fortune, "Should Management Move," 142.

49. Sharon Zukin, *Landscapes of Power* (Berkeley and Los Angeles: University of California Press, 1991), 142–145.

50. "The Power of a Road," 285.

51. "Office Buildings," *Architectural Record* 130, no. 4 (April 1963): 181–182.

52. Herrera, "That Manhattan Exodus," 109. Given the investment that corporations made to move to suburban sites, its unlikely that any executive would publicly admit a mistake, but Mortimer was clearly satisfied.

53. General Foods, *GF Moving Day and You*, 30.

54. James, "Why Move to White Plains?" 13.

55. "A Dramatic New Office Building," *Fortune* 56, no. 3 (September 1957): 164–166.

56. Frazar B. Wilde, "Welcome," in *The New Highways: Challenge to the Metropolitan Region* (Hartford: Connecticut General Life Insurance Corporation, 1958), 1–2.

57. "A Dramatic New Office Building," 164–166; "Insurance Sets a Pattern," *Architectural Forum* 107, no. 3 (September 1957): 119.

58. "A Dramatic New Office Building," 166–167.

59. Quoted in "Building with a Future," September 16, 1957, 91.

60. H. M. Horner "Introduction," in Frazar B. Wilde, *Time Out of Mind* (New York: Newcomen Society of North America, 1959), 6; "A Dramatic New Office Building,"165.

61. "A Dramatic New Office Building," 230.

62. Ibid., 233.

63. Quoted in ibid., 169.

64. Ibid., 169.

65. Ibid., 228.

66. "Insurance Sets a Pattern," 115.

67. Ibid., 114.

68. Jory Johnson, *Modern Landscape Architecture* (New York: Abbeville Press, 1991), 88.

69. Quoted in "Building with a Future," 91.

70. "Insurance Sets a Pattern," 113.

71. Ibid., 233; "Building with a Future," 91.

72. Quoted in Charles Moore, "Environment and Industry," *Architectural Record* 124, no. 1 (July 1958): 162.

73. "Insurance Sets a Pattern," 126–127.

74. "Symposium in a Symbolic Setting," *Life,* October 21, 1957, 49–54; "Building with a Future," 86–91; "For Corporate Life '57," *Newsweek*, September 16, 1957, 114–115.

75. "Building with a Future," 86.

76. "Symposium in a Symbolic Setting," 49.

77. Ibid., 54. For a full transcript of the speeches and papers of the symposium, see Connecticut General Life Insurance Company, *The New Highways: Challenge to the Metropolitan Region* (Hartford: Connecticut General Life Insurance Company, 1958), a mimeographed compilation. An edited version of the concluding session specifically about Hartford, not included in the mimeograph, with a background paper by Wilfred Owen of the Brookings Institution, was published under the same title by Connecticut General in 1959, presumably to influence local and state highway planning.

78. "Insurance Sets a Pattern," 127.

79. Quoted in Moore, "Environment and Industry," 162.

80. SOM followed Connecticut General with a series of suburban headquarters buildings very similar to those of Connecticut General: Kimberley-Clark Corporation, Neenah-Menasha, Wisconsin, 1957; Reynolds Metal Company, Richmond, Virginia, 1957, with Charles Gillette; General Mills, Golden Valley, Minnesota, 1959; and Upjohn Corporation, Kalamazoo, Michigan, with Sasaki, Walker and Associates, 1961. All are on smaller sites with flat topography and pastoral effects.

81. Wayne G. Broehl, *John Deere's Company: The Story of Deere & Company and Its Times* (New York: Doubleday, 1984), 607, 614–615. Broehl was the Benjamin Ames Kimball Professor of the Science of Administration at the Tuck School of Business, Dartmouth College.

82. Quoted in Broehl, *John Deere's Company*, 615.

83. Ibid.

84. Mildred Reed Hall and Edward T. Hall, *The Fourth Dimension in Architecture* (Santa Fe: Sunstone Press, 1975), 13.

85. Quoted in Broehl, *John Deere's Company*, 617.

86. William Hewitt, "The Genesis of a Great Building and of an Unusual Friendship," *AIA Journal* 56, no. 19 (1977): 36. The Ford headquarters was, and still is, a classic SOM downtown skyscraper of the 1950s—only in the middle of a stretch of lawn near Greenfield Village. Currently the back section of the site is a small, public arboretum and a speculative office park, presumably owned by Ford. See Architectural Forum, "Ford Builds a New Automobile City," *Architectural Forum* 93, no. 12 (December 1950): 102–107.

87. Broehl, *John Deere's Company*, 617.

88.   William A. Hewitt, "Opening Remarks," in *Deere & Company Administrative Center* (Moline: Deere & Company, 1964), 2 (company brochure recording inaugural ceremonies and speeches, courtesy of the Rock Island County Historical Society).

89.   Broehl, *John Deere's Company*, 638.

90.   "Green, Yellow & Gold," *Time,* May 24, 1963, 93.

91.   Hewitt, "Genesis of a Great Building," 36.

92.   Broehl, *John Deere's Company*, 638.

93.   Quoted in ibid.

94.   Bess Pierce, *Moline: A Pictorial History* (Virginia Beach, VA: Donning Co., 1981), 141.

95.   Broehl's account of the site selection, based on records in the Deere & Company Archives, differs from Hewitt's recollections that he set forth in a 1977 speech in front of the AIA's College of Fellows, later adapted into an article for the *AIA Journal.* In the speech, Hewitt states that he invited Saarinen to "Moline to look at four sites we had scouted out, none of which we owned. They were all large, partly hilly and wooded" (Hewitt, "The Genesis of a Great Building," 37). Perhaps Hewitt had discounted the river site even before Saarinen's visit. Hewitt and Saarinen may have had to consider the existing company property, or at least appear to do so, to placate the parsimonious board.

96.   Hewitt, "Genesis of a Great Building," 36; Broehl, *John Deere's Company*, 638.

97.   "Green, Yellow & Gold," 93.

98.   "'Dying to See Mural' Says Aline Saarinen," *Moline Dispatch*, June 5, 1964, 3; Hewitt, "Genesis of a Great Building," 36.

99.   Broehl, *John Deere's Company*, 639–640.

100.   Hewitt spent two months a year in Europe. "Green, Yellow & Gold," 93.

101.   William A. Hewitt, "The President's Letter," in *Deere & Company 1957 Annual Report* (Moline: Deere & Company, [1958]).

102.   The decision to move out of central Moline was much to its detriment, as smaller businesses and the local hotel shut down. Deere has recently reinvested in downtown Moline as part of an urban revitalization effort undertaken by the city. It donated a site for a new convention center and arena, built the new offices of its health insurance company (that it later sold), and developed a new farm machinery museum at the former location of the old plow works. Part of the riverside industrial swath is still devoted to an up-to-date plow factory that never left central Moline. Although the company demolished most of the factory works in the early 1990s, the original Deere & Company factory building still stands.

103.   Hewitt, "Genesis of a Great Building," 36.

104.   Quoted in Deere & Company, *Challenge to the Architect: Deere & Company Administrative Center* (Moline: Deere & Company, 1964), 7.

105.   William A. Hewitt to Eero Saarinen, August 23, 1957, reprinted in Deere & Company, *Challenge to the Architect: Deere & Company Administrative Center* (Moline, IL: Deere & Company, 1964), 5.

106. Walter McQuade, "John Deere's Sticks of Steel," *Architectural Forum* 121, no. 1 (1964): 77; Hewitt, "Genesis of a Great Building," 36.

107. Paul Kennon interviewed by Tsukasa Yamashita in "Eero Saarinen and His Works," *Eero Saarinen* [extra edition of] *Architecture + Urbanism*, no. 163 (April 1984): 235. Although the influence of the unique integration of Japanese architecture and landscape seems palpable in the building and the site, neither Saarinen nor Hewitt in any published account makes reference to this. According to Stuart Dawson, Hideo Sasaki thought he was hired because Saarinen wanted a "Japanese feel" to the upper pond, though notably, according to Dawson, Saarinen never overtly referred to the landscape as a Japanese garden in either correspondence or conversation. Hideo Sasaki was born and raised in the United States, and the initial conception of the landscape was a native midwestern deciduous woodland (interview with Stuart Dawson). Paul Kennon, an architect who worked with Saarinen on Deere, claimed in the interview about Saarinen in *Architecture + Urbanism*, a Japanese publication, that Saarinen visited Japan between the presentation of the inverted pyramid scheme and the steel frame structure in the valley scheme, and that the new proposal "came out of his visit to Japan." Kennon recounts: "Then he [Saarinen] made a trip to Japan and he visited his friend [Kenzo] Tange. He came back from his trip and he walked into the studio and looked at the huge John Deere model and he looked at it and said it doesn't work, the land and the trees. He took his hand and wiped it off and said let's start clean, fresh, and he threw it away. Every tree was then located. . . . Then he started to place buildings on the land, they were very simple buildings but with the weathering steel, and the way the sunshade began to work I thought it had a very oriental quality to it and I think he was very much influenced by that trip to Japan" (235). Cesar Pelli, also a member of Saarinen's office at the time, recounted in the same series of interviews: "I do not know because we never talked about this but there is [a] little Japanese attitude in John Deere, the tree house tradition, Katsura Place. . . . Also the buildings feel like a series of pavilions on the ground, very lightly. It's not a sense of western buildings. . . . But Eero never, [sic] these things if he did them were only because he absorbed them and they came through him, and would not know where they came from." Cesar Pelli interviewed by Tsukasa Yamashita in "'Eero Saarinen and His Works," *Eero Saarinen*, 228. According to Hewitt, the new design, presented with a large and extensive site model "complete with land contours, trees, shrubs and a pond. . . . essentially what was built," was ready three weeks after the failure of the first proposal, a tight schedule at best, but Saarinen was known for extreme work habits (Hewitt, "The Genesis of a Great Building," 36).

Neither Hewitt nor Saarinen made any reference to a visit to Japan in any published account of the evolution of the building design. A tongue-in-cheek letter exchange between Hewitt and Saarinen in 1960 over the furnishing of the building complicates this confusion regarding the Japanese influence on the design of the headquarters. Hewitt quoted Saarinen's part of the exchange in his speech at the opening day ceremonies in 1964 and again at the convocation of the AIA fellows in 1977. To spur Saarinen's slow delivery of the design of the interiors and furnishing, Hewitt wrote Saarinen pretending to recommend "some truly hideous Victorian furniture" with pictures from the magazine *Connaissance des Arts*. Saarinen wrote back a letter that Hewitt quoted in full in both speeches, apparently equally in jest: "I am a great admirer of Japanese residential architecture. The interiors of the Katsura Palace are among the most beautiful in the world. The absolutely simple interiors, the modular divisions in the wall and the standardized floor mats give a room real spatial dignity's. . . .We have been working on models of the executive area, and they show real promise of achieving the interiors of the same quality as the Katsura Palace, the Silver Palace and others. It would be a shame to spoil them with furniture." Saarinen goes on to suggest a boardroom of lacquer trays, floor seating, pillows for the older members with "creaking knee joints," and geisha girls proffering refreshments (Hewitt, "Opening Remarks," 3–4; Hewitt, "Genesis of a Great Building," 37, 56). The profoundly ironical tone of the letter and the relish with which Hewitt quoted to his inaugural audience "this amusing letter of which I [Hewitt] am very fond" counters the assertion of admiration for Japanese design. (Hewitt, "Opening Remarks," 3). It seems a peculiar undermining of what would seem to be the essence of the building. The quibbling on both Saarinen's and Hewitt's part may be explicable given the historical era. Hewitt was a veteran of the Pacific theater, and a dozen years out from World War II, it may simply have been impolitic for the head of a major American corporation or his architect to acknowledge the influence of a so recently despised enemy.

108. Eero Saarinen, *Eero Saarinen on His Work, ed.* Aline B. Saarinen (New Haven, CT: Yale University Press, 1962), 76.

109. Hewitt, "Genesis of a Great Building," 36.

110. Saarinen, *Eero Saarinen on His Work*, 14.

111. Ibid., 77.

112. Sasaki had worked with Saarinen at the Yale Hockey Rink. He and his partner, Peter Walker, had done landscape revisions at the General Motors Technical Center.

113. Stuart Dawson interviewed by the author, Berkeley, California, September 17, 1997.

114. Dawson interview; Jory Johnson, *Modern Landscape Architecture*, 32.

115. Hewitt, "Opening Remarks," 2.

116. Dawson interview.

117. Ibid.

118. Ibid.

119. Ibid.; Johnson, "Deere & Company, Moline Illinois," 38. Peter Walker, when asked what was modernist about these landscapes, pointed to these kinds of technological innovations and functions of landscape features, apparently in keeping the functionalist notions of modernist design. Sasaki, according to his partner Walker, brought site planning "to the table" and understood the implications of engineering—air conditioning, parking, roads, fire protection, drainage—in the surrounding landscape (Peter Walker, interviewed by the author, November 12, 1997). For a further discussion on Hideo Sasaki, his design philosophy, and his contributions to the practice of landscape architecture, see Peter Walker and Melanie Simo, *Invisible Gardens: The Search for Modernism in the American Landscape* (Cambridge, MA: MIT Press, 1994), 209–257.

120. Dawson interview.

121. Johnson, Modern Landscape Architecture, 36; Dawson interview.

122. Dawson interview.

123. Ibid.

124.   Saarinen, *Eero Saarinen on His Work*, 76.

125.   Eero Saarinen quoted in Deere & Company, *Challenge to the Architect: Deere & Company Administrative Center*, 8.

126.   Hewitt, "Genesis of a Great Building," 37.

127.   Dawson interview.

128.   Dawson, when pressed on the point of models and influences, particularly of Connecticut General, stresses, "The last thing you wanted to do was imitate anybody else" (Dawson interview). Peter Walker, Dawson's colleague who went on to design a number of other corporate estates, says of Dawson that he had spent time going around and looking at the local Boston Park System, designed by the various generations of Olmsteds, and since his modernist education lacked other historical training, this had a profound effect on his work.

129.   Broehl, *John Deere's Company*, 640.

130.   William A. Hewitt, "President's Address," in *Deere & Company: Report of the Annual Meeting of Stockholders* (Moline: Deere & Company, 1963), 6.

131.   At this same meeting, Hewitt reported to his stockholders Deere's entrance into "the general consumer field with one of our machinery products" with "a small 7 horsepower lawn and garden tractor," a venture that would have telling consequences on the character of the landscape design of the new administrative center. Ibid.

132.   "Deere Deer Comes Down," *Moline Dispatch*, April 9, 1964, n.p.

133.   "Deere Administrative Center to Open Officially Tomorrow," *Moline Dispatch*, June 4, 1964, 5.

134.   Letter from William A. Hewitt to "John Deere Employees and Their Families" [1964], courtesy of the Rock Island County Historical Society, Rock Island, Illinois; Deere & Company, *Administrative Center*, video at the Deere & Company Administrative Center Display Building, viewed June 1997.

135.   "Moline's Biggest Bash," *BusinessWeek*, June 20, 1964, 62–64;.

136.   For a complete list, see *Deere & Company Administrative Center* (Moline, IL: Deere & Company, 1964). Deere & Company brochure recording inaugural ceremonies and speeches.

137.   Henry Dreyfuss speech reprinted in *Deere & Company Administrative Center*, 5.

138.   Gabriel Hauge, speech reprinted in *Deere & Company Administrative Center*, 17.

139.   C. R. Carlson to William A. Hewitt, April 20, 1964, quoted in Broehl, *John Deere's Company*, 671.

140.   Hall and Hall, *The Fourth Dimension in Architecture*, 58.

141.   Ibid., 61, 37; Genevieve Sorter Capowski, "Designing a Corporate Identity," *Management Review* 82, no. 6 (June 1993): 38.

142.   Hall and Hall, *The Fourth Dimension in Architecture*, 39.

143.   Dawson, who continues to consult with Deere, has reduced the mown acreage to 200 and is returning the remaining acreage to a native grass landscape. Dawson interview.

144. Hall and Hall, *The Fourth Dimension in Architecture*, 10, 29, 61.

145. Deere & Company, *Challenge to the Architect*.

146. "Plowmen's Palace," *Time*, August 7, 1964, 64–65; "Moline's Biggest Bash," 62–64.

147. Deere & Company, *Character of a Company* (Moline: Deere & Company, [1980]), 18–20.

148. See note 102.

149. "The Deere Center: Symbol of Strength," *Moline Dispatch*, June 4, 1964, 24.

150. "Architectural Gem Blends into Countryside," *Moline Dispatch*, August 20, 1989, 3.

151. McQuade, "John Deere's Sticks of Steel"; "Deere and Co., USA," *Architectural Design* 35, no. 8 (August 1965): 404–409; John Jacobus, "John Deere Office Building, Moline, Illinois, USA," *Architectural Review* 137, no. 819 (May 1965): 364–371; "Saarinen's Deere Building Opens," *Progressive Architecture* 45, no. 7 (July 1964): 64; "Offices, Moline, Illinois," *Architecture & Building News* 227, no. 21 (May 1965): 979–84.

152. McQuade, "John Deere's Sticks of Steel," 77. This quotation by McQuade is often used in corporate publications and advertising featuring the Administrative Center.

153. Jacobus, "John Deere Office Building," 128.

154. See note 6.

155. William A. Hewitt to Eero Saarinen, August 23, 1957 reprinted in Deere & Company, *Challenge to the Architect*, 5.

156. Johnson, "Pepsico, Purchase, New York," *Modern Landscape Architecture*, 17–27; Catherine Howett, "Pepsico Reconsidered," *Landscape Architecture* 79, no. 3 (April 1989): 82–85; PepsiCo, *Donald M. Kendall Sculpture Gardens* (Purchase, NY: PepsiCo, 1997).

157. PepsiCo, *Donald M. Kendall Sculpture Gardens*.

158. "Headquarter Offices for American Can Are a Model of Restraint," *Architectural Forum* 134, no. 1 (January–February1971): 28–34; "Pastoral Palazzo," *Architectural Review* 149, no. 889 (March 1971): 137–146; "American Can Company," *AIA Journal* 59, no. 5 (November 1973): 120–138; Ada Louise Huxtable, "It's So Peaceful in the Country," *New York Times*, January 17, 1971, D29.

159. "Richardson-Merrell Headquarters Wilton, Connecticut," *Architectural Record* 159, no. 2 (February 1976): 82–85.

160. Nory Miller, "Kevin Roche, John Dinkeloo and Associates: Union Carbide Corporation World Headquarters," *GA Document*, no. 9 (February 1984): 24–27; Andrea Dean, "Corporate Contrast in the Suburbs," *Architecture: AIA Journal* 74, no. 2 (February 1985): 60–69; "Restructuring the Corporate Habitat," *Architectural Record* 171, no. 12 (October 1983): 52–57.

161. Herbert L. Smith, "Image Identity and Appeal," *Architectural Record* 174, no. 13 (November1986): 85–103; Robert Bruegmann, "The Corporate Landscape," *Inland Architect* 33, no. 5 (September–October 1989): 33–42; Dawson interview 1997.

162. Mark B. Milstein and Stuart Hart, "Weyerhaeuser Company: The Next 100 Years" (Washington, DC: World Resources Institute, 1987), http://pdf.wri.org/bell/case_1-56973-233-7_full_version_english.pdf (accessed January 6, 2010).

163. "Weyerhaeuser Corporate Headquarters," *Process: Architecture*, no. 85 (October 1989): 44–45; "Wide Open Spaces," *Industrial Design* 19, no. 2 (March 1989): 37–42; Roger Montgomery, "A Building That Makes Its Own Landscape," *Architectural Forum*, 136, no. 2 (March 1972): 22–27.

164. Walker interview.

165. Kay Tiller, "Frito Lay Prairie Campus," *Landscape Architecture* 78, no. 3 (April–May 1988): 42.

166. Quoted in ibid., 43.

167. James Howard Kunstler, "Merck: The Corporate Landscape Goes Native," *Landscape Architecture* 83, no.12 (December 1993): 60–62; Anne Raver, "Corporate Cottage Deep in the Forest," *New York Times*, December 22, 1991, 57.

168. "A Change in Direction for Kevin Roche?" *Architectural Record* 166, no. 20 (August 1979): 93–96; Mildred F. Schmertz, "Building a Corporate Image," *Architectural Record* 172, no. 10 (September 1984): 103–119; Gina M. Crandall, "In Capability," *Landscape Architecture* 74, no. 3 (May–June 1984).

169. Grace Anderson, "A Corporate Villa," *Architectural Record* 175, no. 13 (November 1987): 120–131; Robert Campbell, "Intimations of Urbanity in a Bucolic Setting," *Architecture: AIA Journal* 77, no. 1 (January 1988): 72–77; Jory Johnson, "Codex World Headquarters: Regionalism and Invention," *Landscape Architecture* 78, no. 3 (April-May 1988): 58–63; Laurie Olin, "Regionalism and the Practice of Hanna/Olin, Ltd.," in *Regional Garden Design in the United States*, ed. Therese O'Malley and Marc Treib (Washington, DC: Dumbarton Oaks, 1995); Koetter, "The Corporate Villa," 3–32.

170. Olin, "Regionalism and the Practice."

171. Quoted in Mildred Schmertz, "Recollection and Invention," *Architectural Record* 176, no. 1 (January 1988): 65.

172. Ibid.; Robert Campbell, "Arts and Crafts Spirit Pervades Corporate Offices," *Architecture: AIA Journal* 77, no. 1 (January 1988): 72–77; Ellen Posner, "Harmony, Not Uniqueness," *Landscape Architecture* 79, no. 4 (May 1989): 43–49; Johnson, "Becton Dickson," in *Modern Landscape Architecture*, 155–163; Stephen Kliment, "Rooms with a View," *Architectural Record* 181, no. 11 (November 1993): 80–85.

173. The Sasaki-related firms are as follows. The original firm was Hideo Sasaki and Associates of Cambridge and Watertown, Massachusetts, formed in 1953. In 1958 the firm became Sasaki, Walker and Associates. Peter Walker took a branch of the office to San Francisco in 1959. In the mid-1960s the Watertown office became Sasaki, Dawson, DeMay Associates and the San Francisco office remained Sasaki, Walker and Associates. By 1975 the San Francisco office had moved to Sausalito; it became the SWA Group completely separate from the Watertown office, which became Sasaki Associates. Peter Walker left the SWA Group in 1983 and formed a partnership with Martha Schwartz, The Offices of Peter Walker and Martha Schwartz (they completed Solana, discussed in the next chapter). That ended in the early 1990s, and Walker formed another firm: Peter Walker and Partners, now known as PWP Landscape Architecture. All of the various versions of the firms have extensive

experience designing corporate estates, corporate campuses, and office parks. See Melanie Simo, *The Offices of Hideo Sasaki: A Corporate History* (Berkeley, CA: Spacemaker Press, 2001, 86).

Chapter 5

1. "Offices Move to the Suburbs," *BusinessWeek,* March 17, 1951, 82–84.

2. "The Record Reports," *Architectural Record* 108, no. 6 (December 1955): 9.

3. Alfred Dupont Chandler Jr., *Strategy and Structure* (Cambridge, MA Harvard University Press, 1962)*, The Visible Hand* (Cambridge, MA: Harvard University Press, 1977), and *Scale and Scope* (Cambridge, MA: Harvard University Press, 1977). Raymond Vernon, *Metropolis 1985: An Interpretation of the Findings of the New York Metropolitan Regional Study* (Cambridge, MA: Harvard University Press, 1960), 68–85.

4. Vernon, *Metropolis 1985,* 123–126.

5. Ibid., 115; Barbara Baran, "Office Automation and Women's Work: the Technical Transformation of the Insurance Industry," in *High Technology, Space, and Society*, ed. Manuel Castells (Thousand Oaks, CA: Sage, 1985), 143–171; Kristin Nelson, "Labor Demand, Labor Supply and the Suburbanization of Low-Wage Office Work," in *Production, Work, and Territory*, ed. Allen J. Scott and Michael Storpor (Winchester, MA: Allen and Unwin, 1986), 149–171.

6. Annalee Saxenian, *Regional Advantage: Culture and Competition in Silicon Valley and Route 128* (Cambridge, MA: Harvard University Press, 1994, 1996), 11–28; Stephen Strickland, "Whither R&D," *Industrial Development and Manufacturers Record* 134, no. 8 (August 1965): 10–24. Strickland was the chief clerk of the Select Committee on Government Research in the early 1960s.

7. Donald L. Foley, "Factors in the Location of Administrative Offices with Particular Reference to the San Francisco Bay Area," *Papers and Proceedings of the Regional Science Association Second Annual Meeting, December, 1955, Vol. 2*, ed. Gerald A. P. Carruthers (Cambridge, MA: Regional Science Association, 1956), 318–326; Donald L. Foley, *The Suburbanization of Offices in the San Francisco Bay Area* (Berkeley: Regents of the University of California, 1957), Vernon, *Metropolis 1985*, 118–126; Gerald Manners, "The Office in the Metropolis: An Opportunity for Shaping Metropolitan America," *Economic Geography* 50, no. 2 (April 1974): 96–101.

8. "Small Business Buildings, Locations Factors: Decentralization, Zoning, and Parking," *Architectural Record* 107, no. 1 (January 1950): 103–111.

9. Greg Hise, "'Nature's Workshop: Industry and Urban Expansion in Southern California," in *Manufacturing Suburbs: Building Work and Home on the Metropolitan Fringe,* ed. Robert Lewis (Philadelphia: Temple University Press, 2004), 178–199; Victor Roterus, *Planned Industrial Parks* (Washington, DC: Housing and Home Finance Agency, 1960?); William Bredo, *Industrial Estates: Tool for Industrialization* (New York: Free Press, 1960). Bredo was a senior economist with the International Industrial Development Center of the Stanford Research Institute.

10. Display ad 357—no title, *New York Times*, July 22, 1945, 56, http://proquest.umi.com/pqdweb?did= 94858163&sid=1&Fmt=10&clientId=1566&RQT=309&VName=HNP (accessed May 15, 2005).

11. Two projects of this sort designed by a leading modernist building architect, William Wurster, and the leading modernist landscape architect, Thomas Church, are the Shuckl Canning Company administrative offices in Sunnyvale attached to their factory and the Pacific headquarters for the Insurance Company of North America occupying its own lot. Both moved from downtown San Francisco. "Office Building for the Shuckl Canning Co.," *Architect and Engineer* 154, no. 2 (August 1943): 12–17; "Country Office Building," *Arts & Architecture* 61, no. 6 (June 1944): 19–21; "Big Business Moves to the Country," *Architectural Record* 110, no. 3 (September 1951): 160–163. As a building type, there is evidence that this pattern existed elsewhere. See, for instance, a warehouse and administrative branch office in Cicero, Illinois, for Roebling, a manufacturer of wire and cable. "Warehouse and Branch Office," *Progressive Architecture* 29, no. 8 (August 1948): 61–66.

12. Foley, *The Suburbanization of Administrative Offices*.

13. Frederick P. Clark, "Office Buildings in the Suburbs," *Urban Land* 13, no. 7 (July–August 1954): 3–10; "More Payrolls for a Bedroom Community," *Urban Land* 12, no. 5 (May 1953): 3–4.

14. "Office Buildings"; "More Payrolls."

15. "Commerce in Menlo Park," *Urban Land* 12, no. 6 (June 1953): 3–4. For description of two of the office buildings, Sunset Magazine and Magna Engineering Corporation, see "Small Office Buildings 3. Ranch House Plan," *Architectural Forum* 96, no. 2 (February 1952): 114–116; "Three Small Buildings for Suburban Businesses 1. Sprawling Plan Exposes All Offices to Country Atmosphere," *Architectural Forum* 98, no. 6 (June 1953): 156–158. Design documents of the projects are also contained in the Geraldine Knight Scott Archives, College of Environmental Design Archives, University of California, Berkeley.

16. "Wooing White Collars to Suburbia," *BusinessWeek*, July 8, 1967, 96–98; George B. Long Jr., "Office Park Development," *Urban Land* 32, no. 1 (February 1973): 10–17.

17. "Wooing White Collars to Suburbia," 97.

18. J. Ross McKeever, ed., *The Community Builders Handbook* (Washington, DC: Urban Land Institute, 1968), 241–243; National Association of Industrial and Office Parks Educational Foundation, *Creating, Understanding and Enforcing Industrial and Office Park Protective Covenants* (Arlington, VA: National Association of Industrial and Office Parks, 1985).

19. "Office Parks: First Annual Report," *Industrial Development and Manufacturers Record* 134, no. 9 (September 1965): 9–14.

20. The postwar formation of new industrial clusters is discussed in Michael Storpor and Richard Walker, eds., *The Capitalist Imperative: Territory, Technology, and Industrial Growth* (New York: Basil Blackwell, 1989).

21. Blaine A. Brownwell, "Birmingham Alabama: New South City in the 1920s," *Journal of Southern History* 38, no. 1 (February 1972): 23–25.

22. J. Ross McKeever, *Business Parks, Office Parks, Plazas, and Centers* (Washington, DC: Urban Land Institute, 1971), 35.

23. Ibid., 16–17, 21–22, 45–46, 83–84, 123.

24. Fred F. Stockwell, "Hobbs Brook Park Office Buildings," *Urban Land* 20, no. 4 (April 1961): 3.

25. "Office Building near Waltham, Mass.," *Architectural Record* 121, no. 2 (February 1957): 177–183; McKeever, *Business Parks*, cover, 57–58, 124.

26. McKeever, *Business Parks*, 40–41.

27. Quoted in ibid., 18.

28. Michael I. Luger and Harvey A. Goldstein, *Technology in the Garden: Research Parks and Regional Economic Development* (Chapel Hill: University of North Carolina Press, 1991), 28–30.

29. Ibid., 53.

30. The Johns-Manville corporate campus is discussed in chapter 3.

31. Freeman Lincoln, "After the Cabots—Jerry Blakeley," *Fortune* 62, no. 5 (November 1960): 171–173.

32. Ibid., 174, 176; "Mills Now Built on a 'Package Plan,'" *New York Times*, January 3, 1956, 79.

33. Lincoln, "After the Cabots," 178.

34. R. C. Estall, "The Electronic Products Industry of New England," *Economic Geography* 39, no. 3 (July 1973): 189–216; Saxenian, *Regional Advantage*, 12–20; Susan Rosegrant and David R. Lampe, *Route 128: Lessons from Boston's High-Tech Community* (New York: Basic Books, 1992), 74–143.

35. "Fourth Annual Survey of Research Parks," *Industrial Development and Manufacturers Record* 134, no. 8 (1965): 33–34; photo and caption, Bredo, *Industrial Estates*, 13.

36. "Fourth Annual Survey of Research Parks," 33–34.

37. Lincoln, "After the Cabots," 172; Henry R. Leiberman, "Technology: Alchemist of Route 128," *New York Times*, January 8, 1968, 139.

38. R. John Griefen, "A Research Park Does Not Live by Research Alone," *Urban Land* 24, no. 3 (March 1965): 3–5.

39. Ibid., 3–4.

40. Estall, "The Electronic Products Industry"; Storpor and Walker, *The Capitalist Imperative*; A. J. Scott, *New Industrial Spaces: Flexible Production and Regional Development in North America and Western Europe* (London: Pion Limited, 1988), chap. 7.

41. Lieberman, "Technology: Alchemist of Route 128," 139.

42. Griefen, "A Research Park Does Not Live by Research Alone," 3.

43. Lincoln, "After the Cabots," 172, 184.

44. Luger and Goldstein, *Technology in the Garden*, 131; "Working in the Suburbs," *Architectural Forum* 114, no. 1 (January 1960): 61.

45. Luger and Goldstein, *Technology in the Garden*, 127.

46. Saxenian, *Regional Advantage*, 20–24; Stewart W. Leslie and Robert H. Kargan, "Selling Silicon Valley: Frederick Terman's Model for Regional Advantage," *Business History Review* 7, no. 7 (Winter 1996): 435–437; Timothy J. Sturgeon, "How Silicon Valley Came to Be," and Stuart W. Leslie "The Biggest 'Angel' of Them All: The Military and the Making of Silicon Valley," both in *Understanding Silicon Valley: The Anatomy of an Entrepreneurial Region*, ed. Martin Kenney (Palo Alto: Stanford University Press, 2000); "SRI Mission and Values," http://www.sri.com/about/card.html, and "SRI's History and Innovations Timeline," http://www.sri.com/about/timeline/ (both accessed October 13, 2008). SRI initially focused on material science for consumer products such as new plant sources for rubber production and formulations for laundry detergents.

47. John R. Findlay, *Magic Lands: Western Cityscapes and American Culture after 1940* (Berkeley and Los Angeles: University of California Press, 1992), 136; Russell Varian, "The Founding of Varian Associates" [1958], http://www.varianinc.com/cgi-bin/nav?corp/history/founding&cid=KLJQJIOPFJ (accessed October 13, 2008).

48. "For Electronic Research and Development," *Architectural Record* 116, no. 1 (July 1954): 156–161.

49. Luger and Goldstein, *Technology in the Garden*, 131, Margaret Pugh O'Mara, *Cities of Knowledge: Cold War Science and the Search for the Next Silicon Valley* (Princeton, NJ: Princeton University Press, 2005), 119.

50. "HP Timeline 1950s," http://www.hp.com/hpinfo/abouthp/histnfacts/timeline/hist_50s.html (accessed 13 October 13, 2008).

51. Richard Jonca, David J. Neuman, and Paul Venable Turner, *Stanford University* (New York: Princeton Architectural Press, 2006), 99.

52. Church quoted in Findlay, *Magic Lands*, 138; "HP Timeline—1950s."

53. Stanford had commissioned the architecture firm of Skidmore, Owings, and Merrill to develop a master plan in 1953 for development, but it primarily focused on the housing and retail components and minimally dealt with the industrial area. In any case, the university officials did not agree with the master plan and ignored it. Findlay, *Magic Lands*, 128–129, 133.

54. "Working in the Suburbs," 61.

55. Richard Walker, *The Country in the City: Greening the San Francisco Bay Area* (Seattle: University of Washington Press, 2007), 100–101; Findlay, *Magic Lands*, 135–136; Luger and Goldstein, 126.

56. Findlay, *Magic Lands*, 117–145; O'Mara, *Cities of Knowledge*, 118–124. As Timothy J. Sturgeon points out, the electronics industry was also well established before World War II rather than being "invented" by Frederick Terman. Sturgeon, "How Silicon Valley Came to Be."

57. Luger and Goldstein, *Technology in the Garden*, 127.

58. "HP Timeline 1940s," http://www.hp.com/hpinfo/abouthp/histnfacts/timeline/hist_40s.html (accessed February 1, 2010); "At Bell Labs, Industrial Research Looks Like Bright College Years," *BusinessWeek,* February 6, 1954, 75.

59. Saxenian, *Regional Advantage.*

60. Louise R. Wilson, *The Research Triangle of North Carolina: A Notable Achievement in University, Governmental, and Industrial Cooperative Development* (Chapel Hill, NC: Colonial Press, 1967), 4–9.

61. C. M. Guest and Sons, *Conditioned for Research* (Greensboro, NC: C. M. Guest and Sons, 1954).

62. Wilson, *The Research Triangle*, 9–13; Luger and Goldstein, *Technology in the Garden*, 77–78.

63. Wilson, *The Research Triangle*, 13–15; David Havlick and Scott Kirsch, "A Production Utopia? RTP and the North Carolina Research Triangle," *Southeastern Geographer* 44, no. 2 (2004): 266.

64. Wilson, *The Research Triangle*, 15–18; Luger and Goldstein, *Technology in the Garden*, 77–79.

65. Luger and Goldstein, *Technology in the Garden*, 76–77.

66. Luther J. Carter, "Research Triangle Seeks High-Technology Industry," *Science*, November 12, 1965, 869; Board of Directors, Research Triangle Park, minutes of July 23, 1959, quoted in Havlick and Kirsch, "A Production Utopia?" 269.

67. Carter, "Research Triangle Seeks High-Technology Industry," 867, 869.

68. Ibid., 869; Albert N. Link and John T. Scott, "The Growth of Research Triangle Park," *Small Business Economics* 20, no. 2 (2003): 169.

69. Luther J. Carter, "Research Triangle Succeeds beyond Its Promoters Expectations," *Science*, June 30, 1978, 1469.

70. Link and Scott, "The Growth of Research Triangle Park," 167; Luger and Goldstein, *Technology in the Garden*, 83–84.

71. Luger and Goldstein, *Technology in the Garden*, 85–86.

72. McKeever, *Business Parks*, 45–67; "Office Parks: First Annual Report," 13–14.

73. "Office Parks: First Annual Report," 9–13.

74. "Notes of the Business Landscape, Atlanta 'Really Springing,'" *Fortune* 56, no. 6 (1957): 265–266; "Office Parks: First Annual Report," 12; "ID's Second Annual Report Office Parks for Industry," *Industrial Development and Manufacturers Record* 135, no. 9 (September 1966): 22–23; McKeever, *Business Parks* 51, 123; "Wooing White Collars," 98.

75. Manners, "The Office in the Metropolis," 95–97.

76. Lenard L. Wolffe, *New Zoning Landmarks in Planned Unit Development* (Washington, DC: Urban Land Institute, 1968).

77. McKeever, *Community Builders Handbook*, 24.

78. McKeever, *Business Parks.*

79. Ibid., 48.

80. "Wooing White Collars," 97–98.

81. McKeever, *Business Parks*, 53; David B. Knight and Tatsuo Ito, "Office Parks: The Oak Brook Example," *Land Economics* 48, no. 1 (1972): 67.

82. Barbara Lewis, "Joe Callahan; Visionary with a Penchant for New Projects," *Hacienda Network*, July 24, 2007, 2–3; National Association of Industrial and Office Parks Education Foundation, *Office Park Development: A Comprehensive Examination of the Elements of Office Park Development* (Arlington, VA: National Association of Industrial and Office Parks, 1984), 177–190.

83. McKeever, *Business Parks*, 15–16.

84. For instance, in a 1995 survey of the twenty-five largest office parks in the Washington, D.C., metropolitan area, the average planned square footage was 5.7 million square feet, and the target square footages ranged from 2.9 million to 16 million. Gail Lawyer, "Largest Office Parks Planned in the Metro Area," *Washington Business Journal*, May 14–20, 1995, 36, 38.

85. Quoted in National Association of Industrial and Office Parks Education Foundation, *Office Park Development*, 42.

86. Ibid., 6.

87. "Cornell Oaks Corporate Center," *Landscape Architecture* 78, no. 8 (December 1988): 96.

88. William J. Thompson, "Dulles Corner," *Landscape Architecture* 78, no. 8 (December 1988): 82–87.

89. Quoted in David Beers, "We Have Seen the Future and It Is Pleasanton," *San Francisco Examiner Image Magazine*, January 18, 1987, 14.

90. Judy Kalvin, "Hacienda: A Textbook Case in Community Relations," *Corporate Design and Realty* 4, no. 7 (September 1985): 29.

91. Ibid.; POD, Inc., *Hacienda Business Park* (San Francisco: POD, Inc, 1985), landscape architecture firm cut-sheet; Beers, "We Have Seen the Future."

92. Quoted in Kalvin, "Hacienda," 31.

93. Ibid., 29, 31–32; Barbara Lewis, "Hacienda Celebrates Silver Anniversary," *Hacienda Network*, July 24, 2007, 1; Barbara Lewis, "Joe Callahan"; Hacienda Network, "Hacienda 25th Anniversary," *Hacienda Network*, July 24, 2007, special pullout section.

94. Beers, "We Have Seen the Future"; Kalvin, "Hacienda," 29; Lewis, "Hacienda Celebrates" and "Joe Callahan," 2.

95. BOMA [Building Owners and Managers Association] International Research Department, *Building Owners and Managers North American Office Market Review: Mid Year 1988* (Washington, DC: BOMA Research International, 1988); "Office and Industrial Vacancies," *Mortgage and Real Estate Executive Report*, April 1, 1995, 6–7.

96. Lewis, "Hacienda Celebrates" and "Joe Callahan"; Hacienda Network, "Hacienda 25th Anniversary."

97. "Office and Industrial Vacancies"; Tim Venable, "Not Overbuilt Anymore: Industrial Parks Lead Robust Real Estate Recovery," *Site Selection* 40, no. 6 (1995): 902–904, 906, 908–909, 911; Donald R. Ciandella, "Lagging New Supply, Rising Demand Invigorates Office Sector," *National Real Estate Investor* 38, no. 7 (July 1996): 37–38, 40, 42–45, 91.

98. Lewis, "Hacienda Celebrates."

99. Quoted in Lewis, "Joe Callahan," 2.

100. Hacienda Network, "Hacienda 25th Anniversary"; Marion Steward, "Hacienda Index," *Hacienda Network*, July 24, 2007, 7, 9.

101. Barbara Goldstein, "Harlequin Plaza," *Landscape Architecture* 73, no. 40 (July–August 1983): 56–59; Sutherland Lyall, *Designing the New Landscape* (New York: Van Nostrand, 1991); Joie Horanic, "Re-Using Scarce Waters for Suburban Offices," *Landscape Architecture* 70, no. 4 (July 1980): 389–391.

102. Cathie Mitchell, "Black Tie and Terrazzo," *Landscape Architecture* 73, no. 4 (July–August 1983): 59.

103. Joel W. Barna, "Solana in the Sun," *Progressive Architecture* 70, no. 4 (April 1989): 65–74; Marita Thomas, "Superb Teamwork Forges 'Age-Proof' IBM Center," *Facilities and Management* 8, no. 2 (February 1989): 48–55; David Dillon, "And Two in the Country," *Landscape Architecture* 80, no. 3 (March 1990): 62–63.

104. Lotus International, "Dal Parco al Giardino = From Park to the Garden," *Lotus International*, no. 87 (1995): 34–61; "Solana," *Baumeister* 187, no. 4 (1990): 32–34; Alan Phillips, *The Best in Science, Office and Business Park Design* (London: B. T. Batsford, 1993); "I fasti dell'ellectronica = The Glorious Deeds of Electronics," *Architettura* 36, no. 10 (October 1990): 724–726; "IBM Southlake and Village Center, Solana, Westlake and Southlake, Texas," *GA Document*, no. 24 (August 1989): 20–24.

105. Greenwood Village, Colorado, "Honoring Our Heritage, Harlequin Plaza," http://www.greenwoodvillage.com/index.asp?nid=513 (accessed May 5, 2008); Dan Marcec, "Developing a New Landscape: Mixed-Use Projects Are on the Rise in the Dallas Area," *Texas Real Estate Business* (January 2007), http://www.texasrebusiness.com/articles/JAN07/cover1.html (accessed May 6, 2008).

106. Marcec, "Developing a New Landscape"; City of Southlake, "Incentives History," January 11, 2002, http://www.ci.southlake.tx.us/search/default.aspx?QueryExpr=sabre (accessed May 5, 2008); City of Southlake, *Sabre Holdings' Headquarters: Project Profile*, February 2, 2005, http://www.ci.southlake.tx.us/search/default.aspx?QueryExpr=ontacts (accessed May 5, 2008).

107. Maura Webber Sadovi, "Tough Times Pressure Maguire to Restructure Debt on Texas Complex," *Wall Street Journal,* April 22, 2009, http://online.wsj.com/article/SB124035983163841451.html (accessed January 13, 2010).

108. The developers were Wright Runstad & Company, and the building was designed by the Callison Partnership. "Design '89: NAIOP Annual Design Development Awards," *Development* 20, no. 60 (November 1989): 42; Wright Runstad & Co., "Wright Runstad & Co., Historical Timeline: Microsoft Corporation Headquarters, 1986–94," http://www.wrightrunstad.com/AboutUs/Timeline/Timeline4_1.htm (accessed May 20, 2008).

109. Scott Williams, "Microsoft Buys Another Building," *Seattle Times*, March 14, 1991, http://community.seattletimes.nwsource.com/archive/?date=19910314&slug=1271531 (accessed May 10, 2008); Hinanee Gupta, "Microsoft to Add 1,000 Mostly in the Redmond Area," *Seattle Times*, May 21, 1990 http://community.seattletimes.nwsource.com/archive/?date=19900421&slug=1067553 (accessed May 10, 2008); Brier Dudley, "Microsoft expansion to ripple through the Region," *Seattle Times*, February 10, 2006, http://community.seattletimes.nwsource.com/archive/?date=20060210&slug=microsoft10 (accessed May 10, 2008); Todd Bishop, "Microsoft Reimagines [sic] Its Corporate Home," *Seattle Post-Intelligencer,* January 27, 2005, http://seattlepi.nwsource.com/business/209568_msftcampus27.html (accessed May 10, 2008); Benjamin J. Romano, "Microsoft Campus Expands, Transforms, Inside and Out," *Seattle Times*, November 23, 2007, http://seattletimes.nwsource.com/html/microsoft/2004007121_microsoft11.html (accessed May 10, 2008). For an interactive map of the growth of the Microsoft Corporate Campus since 1986, see http://seattletimes.nwsource.com/news/local/microsoftcampus/microsoftcampus.html (accessed May 10, 2008).

Chapter 6

1. The address of the Google headquarters is 1600 Amphitheater Parkway, Mountain View, California 94043.

2. Adam Lashinsky, "Chaos by Design," *Fortune Online,* October 2, 2006 http://money.cnn.com/magazines/fortune/fortune_archive/2006/10/02/8387489/index.htm (accessed May 4, 2008).

3. An exemplary site and postings can be seen at Rob Pegoraro, "Gawking at Google," http://blog.washingtonpost.com/fasterforward/2008/01/gawking_at_google.html (accessed May 4, 2008). On the design of the original Silicon Graphics campus by STUDIOS Architecture and SWA Group, see Michelle Martin, "An Instant Landmark in Silicon Valley," *World Architecture*, no. 68 (July–August 1998): 67–71.

4. James Feron, "Companies Leave City and Find New Troubles," *New York Times*, October 11, 1983, B4; Eleanor Charles, "American Can Selling Its Campus," *New York Times*, August 17, 1986, R6; "Fire Closes Primerica Office," *New York Times,* October 22, 1987, B2; Eleanor Charles, "Westchester's Airport, Greenwich's Ache," *New York Times*, December 27, 1987, R4; Steven Greenhouse, "French Agree to Buy American Can's Parent," *New York Times*, November 22, 1988, D1, D6; George Judson, "Greenwich Feels Pain of Change," *New York Times*, April 12, 1993, B8; Thomas J. Lueck, "Manhattan Company Is Coaxed Away," *New York Times*, June 16, 1993, B5; Susan Sherreick, "Connecticut Helps to Lure a Business," *New York Times*, November 10, 1993, A1.

5. Tishman Speyer, "Greenwich American Center," http://www.tishmanspeyer.com/properties/Property.aspx?id=20 (accessed January 25, 2010).

6. "Ace to Buy Cigna Unit for $3.45 Billion in Cash," *New York Times*, January 13, 1999, C3; Stacey Stowe, "A Fight Over, of All Things, an Insurance Office," *New York Times*, July 16, 2000, CT10; Milt Freudenheim, "More Suits Filed against Health Insurers," *New York Times*, June 27, 2000, C2; National Trust for Historic Preservation, "Eleven Most Endangered: CIGNA Campus," http://www.

Nationaltrust.org/11most/2001/cigna (accessed June 22, 2005); "Cigna's Self-Inflicted Wounds," *CIO Magazine,* http://www.cio.com/archive/031503/cigna (accessed 22 June 22, 2005).

7. Stowe, "A Fight Over, of All Things, an Insurance Office," CT1.

8. Connecticut Trust for Historic Preservation, "The Most Threatened Historic Places—Updates: Wilde Building, Bloomfield," http://www.cttrust.org/8414?highlight=bloomfield (accessed May 10, 2008); Tyler Smith, "How the Wilde Was Won," *Hartford Courant,* May 21, 2006, http://www.hartfordinfo.org/issues/documents/history/htfd_courant_052106.asp (accessed May 10, 2008).

9. Another example is Union Carbide's corporate estate, discussed in chapter 4. On December 3, 1984, an Indian subsidiary of Union Carbide was responsible for a massive chemical spill disaster in Bhopal, India. In 1986 the corporation sold the building and 100 acres to a real estate investor for $300 million and the rest of the 546 acres to another investor for $40 million. Union Carbide established a twenty-year lease on the building. In 1999, Dow Chemical, Union Carbide's competitor, bought the corporation for $9.3 billion and announced that it would run the consolidated company from Dow's Midland, Michigan, headquarters. By that time Union Carbide's corporate staff stood at 850, and other tenants rented almost half of the building. Eventually Union Carbide paid a settlement of $470 million for the Bhopal disaster. In 2002 the 546 acres sold again to a development firm with plans for a mixed-use project of housing, retail, offices, recreation, and a minor league baseball stadium. Paul Goldberger, "Union Carbide's New Corporate Home: A Metallic Castle Tucked in Woods," *New York Times,* February 20, 1984, B1; David W. Dunlap, "Thawing Corporate Capital Frozen into Real Estate," *New York Times,* August 11, 1991, 340; Mike Allen, "In Danbury, Employees Fear Cutbacks," *New York Times,* August 5, 1999, C6; Eleanor Charles, "Suburban History for Sale, with Architectural Status," *New York Times,* August 14, 2002, C5.

10. I thank Paul Groth for calling my attention to this sequence of change at Hacienda Business Park. "Hacienda 25th Anniversary," *Hacienda Network,* July 25, 2007, special pullout section; Laurie Flynn and Andrew Ross Sorkin, "Despite Ruling PeopleSoft Battles to Stand Alone," *New York Times,* September 11, 2004, C1; Jim Kersetter, "Finally, Oracle Nails PeopleSoft," *BusinessWeek,* December 13, 2004; Benjamin Pimental, "Software Giant to Cut 5,000 Jobs: Ax Falls on Oracle Employees as Well as PeopleSoft Staff," *San Francisco Chronicle,* January 15, 2005, A1; Jeb Bing, "Retail Demand Offsetting Record-High Office Vacancies," *Pleasanton Weekly Online Edition,* March 4, 2005, http://www.pleasantonweekly.com/morgue/2005/2005_03_04.coutlook04.shtml (accessed April 27, 2008).

11. Jim Kersetter, "Finally, Oracle Nails PeopleSoft," *BusinessWeek Online,* December 14, 2004

12. Peter Buchanan, "IBM Flagship," *Architectural Review* 174, no. 1041 (1983): 46.

13. See, for instance, "Portsmouth-UK North Harbor," http://www.portsmouth-uk.com/north_harbour.htm (accessed May 12, 2008), and "Business," http://www.portsmouth.gov.uk/business/index.html (accessed May 12, 2008).

14. Annette LeCuyer, "Roman Villa with Nordic Light," *Architecture* 74, no. 5 (May 1985): 282–287.

15. For instance, Challenger, the headquarters of Bouygues SA, a global construction firm, is the first (and so far the only) corporate estate in France 3 miles from Versailles. Kevin Roche John Dinkeloo Associates, veteran designers of American corporate estates, designed a huge complex on 70 acres. Although

the accomplished British landscape architect Peter Shepheard designed a landscape plan, little of it was carried out, and the palatial building stands out starkly on open lawn. Christophe Girot, "Bouygues," *Landscape Architecture* 80, no. 3 (March 1990): 64–65.

16. William Bredo, *Industrial Estates: Tool for Industrialization* (Glencoe, IL: Free Press, 1960).

17. Meaning a financial, managerial, and technical economy centered on London, still the leading services and financial center in the world.

18. Ken Baker, "Greening Business," *Business Parks: A Building Design Special Report,* no. 944 (July 1989): S5, supplement.

19. Segal Quince Wicksteed, *The Cambridge Phenomenon: The Growth of High Technology Industry in a University Town* (Cambridge, United Kingdom: Segal Quince Wicksteed, 1985): 18.

20. IBM, *IBM at Hursley: Care for the Environment* (Hursley Park, Winchester, U.K.: IBM, 198-?); "Explore Hursley," http://www-05.ibm.com/uk/locations/hursley_explore.html (accessed May 12, 2008).

21. Nevill Mott, T. M.Chalmers, R. W. T. Honeycombe, E. F. Mills, C. W. Oatley, A. J. Watson, and A. D. I. Nicol, "Relationship between the University and Science-Based Industry: Report of the Sub-Committee," *Cambridge University Reporter*, October 22, 1969, 370–376; Segal Quince Wicksteed, *The Cambridge Phenomenon,* 12–23, 40–42, 59–60; "Cambridge Science Park, About, History," http://www.cambridgesciencepark.co.uk/about_history.htm (accessed May 15, 2008).

22. Segal Quince Wicksteed, *The Cambridge Phenomenon,* 40–42.

23. Ibid., 50–65.

24. Exemplary of one of the early developer-built projects, the Warrington New Town Development Corporation built the Birchwood Science Park outside Warrington, Cheshire, on a former World War II ordnance site next to the United Kingdom Atomic Energy Authority, a concentration of government engineers and scientists. A new tack in Britain's postwar, government-sponsored New Town program, Birchwood Science Park initially targeted technology tenants but eventually built out to include a range of enterprises. In the late 1970s, the Thatcher government shut down the entire New Town strategy, but the Birchwood Science Park continues as private development. Baker, "Greening Business."

25. Phil Maybury, "Bristol Fashion," *Business Parks: A Building Design Special Report,* no. 944 (July 1989): S20–23, 25, supplement.

26. Andy King, "Vital Statistics," *Business Parks: A Building Design Special Report,* no. 944 (July 1989): S36–37, supplement. The landscape architects Clouston master-planned a significant number of the parks. In an obvious reference to the eighteenth-century English estate designer Lancelot Brown, nicknamed "Capability," this included Capability Green, built on part of a Brown-designed estate, Luton Hoo, which had been cut off from the main property by a new airport access road. "Industrial Landscape," *Business Parks: A Building Design Special Report,* no. 944 (July 1989): S6–7, supplement; Marcus Binney, "British Architecture Now," *Architectural Design* 59, no. 5–6 (1989): vii.

27. Baker, "Greening Business"; "Industrial Landscape"; Bernard Ede, "The Stockley Park Project," *Landscape Design*, no. 187 (February 1990): 48–51.

28. "Research on the Riviera," *Progressive Architecture* 44, no. 2 (February 1963): 132–137; "IBM, a Laboratory Abroad," *Architectural Forum* 114, no. 3 (March 1961): 98–99; "Dynamic Places—La Gaude," http://www-913.ibm.com/employment/us/extremeblue/location/lagaude.html (accessed May 20, 2008).

29. Manuel Castells and Peter Hall, *Technopoles of the World: The Making of Twenty-First Century Industrial Complexes* (New York: Routledge, 1994), 85–93; Pierre Lafitte, "Birth of a City? Sophia Antipolis," http://www.sophia-antipolis.org/GB/sophia-antipolis/sophia-antipolis/naissance-ville/naissance-ville.htm (accessed May 20, 2008); "Presentation of the Foundation Sophia-Antipolis," http://www.sophia-antipolis.org/GB/fsa/presentation/presentation/presentation.htm (accessed May 20, 2008); "The 'Sophipolitan' model," http://www.sophia-antipolis.org/GB/sophia-antipolis/sophia-antipolis/modele-sophipolitain/modele-sophipolitain.htm (accessed May 20, 2008).

30. "Akeler—Office Development—Paris, Major Office Park," *PropertyMall, Online,* March 4, 2004, http://www.propertymall.com/press/article/11353 (accessed May 20, 2008).

31. For examples in Ireland, see "Park West Business Park," *Irish Architect*, no. 170 (September 2001): 37–42, 44; Citywest Business Campus, http://www.citywest.ie/exec.asp (accessed May 28, 2008). Citywest includes the government-supported National Digital Park. For an example in Australia, see Norwest Business Park, http://www.norwestbusinesspark.com.au/ (accessed May 28, 2008); for South Africa, see "Parc du Cap: An Office Park," *Architect and Builder* 37, no. 5 (April 1986): 2–7; Sarah Singleton, "Crownwood: Landscaping an Office Park at Ormonde, Johannnesburg," *Architect and Builder* 36, no. 9 (September 1985): 2–5; "Woodmead Office Park," *Architect and Builder* 42, no. 7 (July 1992): 2–7; "Ascot Office Park: Port Elizabeth," *Architect and Builder* 46, no. 7 (July 1995): 2–5.

32. Alan Mabin, "Suburbanisation, Segregation, and Government of Territorial Transformations," *Transformation: Critical Perspectives on Southern Africa* 57, no. 1 (2005): 41–63.

33. See Castells and Hall discussion of Japan's Science Cities and Cartuja Science Park outside Seville, Spain, in *Technopoles of the World*, 112–137, 193–206; for Japan Science Parks, "The Scientific Geography of Japan," *Science,* October 23, 1992, 562–563; Dennis Normile, "Bright Science City Dreams Face Sober Realities," *Science* November 18, 1994, 1176–1177; Marco Bontje, "Sustainable New Economic Centres in European Metropolitan Regions: A Stakeholders' Perspective," *European Planning Studies*, 12, no. 5 (July 2004): 703–722. Examples of continental European business parks are Campus M Business Park, Munich, http://www.campus-m.de/bauabschnitt2_en/index.php?n=lage (accessed May 15, 2008), and The Park, Prague, http://www.thepark.cz/ (accessed May 15, 2008); Elena Tomei, "Technolgia Organica: in Prague," *Arca*, no. 217 (September 2006): 54–61.

34. Voula Mega, "Our City, Our Future: Towards Sustainable Development in European Cities," *Environment and Urbanization* 8, no. 1 (1996): 144.

35. Agglomeration literature is extensive, but relevant highlights are: Michael Storpor and Richard Walker, *The Capitalist Imperative: Territory, Technology, and Industrial Growth* (New York: Oxford University Press, 1989); Castells and Hall, *Technopoles of the World*; Annalee Saxenian, *Regional Advantage: Culture and Competition in Silicon Valley and Route 128* (Cambridge, MA: Harvard University Press, 1996). For a useful recent analytical article, see Allen J. Scott and Michael Storper, "Regions, Globalization, Development," *Regional Studies* 37, no. 677 (August–October 2003): 579–593.

36. Su-Ann Mae Phillips and Henry Wai-Chung Yeung, "A Place for R&D: The Singapore Science Park," *Urban Studies*, 40, no. 4 (2003): 707–732; Francis C. C. Koh, Winston T. H. Koh, and Feichin Ted Tschang, "An Analytical Framework for Science Parks and Technology Districts with an Application to Singapore," *Journal of Business Venturing* 20, no. 2 (March 2005): 217–239; Yeuhua Zhang, "Critical Factors for Science Park Development: The Case of the Singapore Science Park," *International Journal of Technology Transfer and Commercialisation* 4, no. 2 (2005): 194–205; Liaw Wy-Cin, "$400m Make-over for Science Park; Move Will Create More Room for R&D Firms and Boost Access to Greenery, Facilities," *Straits Times*, October 22, 2007, http://www.lexisnexis.com:443 (accessed May 10, 2008); Ascendas, "Singapore Science Park Unveils S$400m Redevelopment Masterplan," press release, http://www.ascendas.com/downloads/pr2007/Press_Release_221007 (accessed May 10, 2008).

37. Castells and Hall, *Technopoles of the World*, 57–64, 100–109; Dylan Sutherland, "China Science Parks: Production Bases or a Tool for Institutional Reform," *Asia Pacific Business Review* 11, no. 1 (March 2005): 83–104; Susan M. Walcott, "Chinese Industrial and Science Parks: Bridging the Gap," *Professional Geographer* 54, no. 3 (2002): 349–364; Susan M. Walcott, "High Technology Clusters in India and China: Divergent Paths," *Indian Journal of Economics and Business* 5, special issue (September 2006): 113–130.

38. Dalian Ascendas IT Park, http://www.daitp.com/home.html (accessed May 10, 2008).

39. Keonics, http://www.keonics.com/aboutus.htm (accessed October 20, 2008); STPI, http://www.stpi.in/about.htm (accessed October 20, 2008); Geetha Vaidyanathan, "Technology Parks in a Developing Country: The Case of India," *Journal of Technology Transfer*, June 26, 2007, 285–299; Rolee Aranya, "Location Theory in Reverse? Location for Global Production in the IT Industry of Banglaore," *Environment and Planning A,* 40, no.10 (October 2008) 446–463. Unlike most American pastoral corporate projects that followed earlier suburban residential development, these projects in the developing world foster high-end residential development close by or as part of the same development zone.

40. Quoted in Aranya, "Location Theory," 457.

41. Elizabeth Chacko, "From Brain Drain to Brain Gain: Reverse Migration to Bangalore and Hyderabad, India's Globalizing High Tech Cities," *GeoJournal*, 68, no. 5 (May 2007): 131–140.

42. Jaydip Mehta, "Bangalore Digitally Devided [sic] Global City." Jaydip Mehta Blog, 2007, http://willfindsaway.blogspot.com/2007/10/banglore-digitally-devided-global.html (accessed May 15, 2008).

43. Aranya, "Location Theory"; Vaidyanathan, "Technology Parks"; Walcott, "High Technology Clusters"; Andy Mukherjee, "Commentary: 'Electronics City' Bursting at the Seams," *International Herald Tribune* online, January 21, 2005, http://www.iht.com/articles/2005/01/20/bloomberg/sxmuk.php?page=1 (accessed October 20, 2008).

44. Vaidyanathan, "Technology Parks," 290.

45. International Park, "Park Profile, A World in a Park," http://www.itpbangalore.com/pp_worldinapark.html (accessed May 15, 2008).

46. Michael Storpor and Michel Manville, "Behavior, Preferences and Cities: Urban Theory and Urban Resurgence," *Urban Studies* 43, no. 8 (July 2006): 1257.

47. Robert Fishman, "On Big Beaver Road: Detroit and the Diversity of American Metropolitan Landscapes," *Places* 19, no. 3 (2007): 42–47. Greg Hise, *Magnetic Los Angeles: Planning the Twentieth-Century Metropolis* (Baltimore, MD: Johns Hopkins University Press, 1997); Robert Bruegmann, *Sprawl: A Compact History* (Chicago: University of Chicago Press, 2005); John R. Findlay. *Magic Lands: Western Cityscapes and American Culture after 1940* (Berkeley and Los Angeles: University of California Press, 1992).

48. Bruegmann, *Sprawl*, 220.

49. Richard Harris and Robert Lewis, "The Geography of North American Cities and Suburbs, 1900–1950: A New Synthesis," *Journal of Urban History* 27, no. 3 (March 2001): 262–292; Becky Nicolaides, "How Hell Moved from the City to the Suburbs: Urban Scholars and the Changing Perceptions of Authentic Community," in *The New Suburban History*, ed. Kevin M. Kruse and Thomas Sugrue (Chicago: University of Chicago Press, 2006), 58–79; Andrew Wiese, "'The House I Live In': Race, Class, and African American Suburban Dreams in the Postwar United States," in *The New Suburban History*, ed. Kevin M. Kruse and Thomas Sugrue (Chicago: University of Chicago Press, 2006), 99–119; Findlay, *Magic Lands*, 284–303; Fishman, "On Big Beaver Road"; Tim Davis, "The Miracle Mile Revisited: Recycling, Renovation, and Simulation along the Commercial Strip," in *Exploring Everyday Landscapes: Perspectives on Vernacular Architecture* 7, ed. Annemarie Adams and Sally McMurray (Knoxville: University of Tennessee Press, 1997), 93–114.

50. Findlay, *Magic Lands*, 284–303; Joel Garreau, *Edge City: Life on the New Frontier* (New York: Anchor Books, 1991)*;* Fishman, "On Big Beaver Road."

51. John Brennan and Edward W. Hill, "Where Are the Jobs? Cities, Suburbs, and the Competition for Employment," *Brookings Institution Survey Series*, (Washington, DC: Brookings Institution, November 1999); Robert E. Lang, "Office Sprawl: The Evolving Geography of Business," *Brookings Institution Survey Series* (Washington, DC: Brookings Institution, October 2000) http://www.brookings.edu/~/media/Files/rc/reports/2000/10metropolitanpolicy_lang/lang.pdf (accessed October 2004).

52. Becky M. Nicolaides, *My Blue Heaven: Life and Politics in the Working Class Suburbs of Los Angeles, 1920–1965* (Chicago: University of Chicago Press, 2002); Andrew Wiese, *Places of Their Own: African American Suburbanization in the Twentieth Century* (Chicago: University of Chicago Press, 2004); *The Suburban Reader,* ed. Becky M. Nicolaides and Andrew Wiese (New York: Routledge, 2006) chaps. 7 and 14*;* Timothy P. Fong, *The First Suburban Chinatown: The Remaking of Monterey Park, California* (Philadelphia: Temple University Press, 1994); William H. Frey, *Melting Pot Suburbs* (Washington, DC: Brookings Institution, 2001), http://www.brookings.edu/reports/2001/06demographics_frey.aspx (accessed January 10, 2010).

53. A summary article on ongoing affirmative action efforts in multinational corporations is Gwendolyn Combs, Sucheta Nadkarni, and Michael Coms, "Implementing Affirmative Actions Plans in Multi-National Corporations," *Organizational Dynamics* 34, no. 4 (November 2006): 346–360.

54. Mary Doss, Deere & Company, Manager, News Services reports that Deere & Company has significantly reinvested in Moline's downtown in the past decade and other investors have followed suit, making for a more active downtown environment. Mary Doss, personal communication, Janaury 7, 2010. The efforts in Durham have been led by Greenfire Development, an extraordinarily creative and committed developer group consciously moving against the trend of suburban expansion (I served on a charette

on revitalization of Durham's downtown for Greenfire in the spring of 2006); see their website http://www.greenfiredevelopment.com. For Birmingham's very early and not yet clearly successful efforts, see Michael Tomberlin, "Great Expectation Rising in Downtown Birmingham," *Birmingham News*, May 27, 2010, http://blog.al.com/businessnews/2010/05/great_expectations_rising_in_d_1.html (accessed August 18, 2010). For Hartford, known as America's File Cabinet for its deserted streets, see William Yardley, "Downtown Hartford Stirs from Slumber," *New York Times*, January 4, 2006, http://www.nytimes.com/2006/01/04/nyregion/04hartford.html?pagewanted=1&_r=1 (accessed August 18, 2010). These are indeed exemplary of the encouraging reinvestments in many downtowns, but, as is typical, the revitalization is focused on housing and entertainment, and a committed set of planners and developers drive the reinvestment, often as part of public-private partnerships. While adding economic activity, the results do not match the mix, bustle, and economic scale of these downtowns in the 1950s, and the economic downturn of 2008 has slowed or stopped this process. Even then, many cities cannot muster this level of commitment to redevelopment of disinvested center cities, Detroit being the most heartbreaking example, but by no means the only one.

55. Reid Ewing, Keith Bartholomew, Steve Winkelman, Jerry Walters, and Don Chen, *Growing Cooler: The Evidence on Urban Development and Climate Change* (Washington, DC: Urban Land Institute, 2008); Reid Ewing and Robert Cervero, "Travel and the Built Environment: A Synthesis," *Transportation Research Record: Journal of the Transportation Research Board,* no. 1780 (2001): 87–114; Reid Ewing, Rolf Pendall, and Don Chen, "Measuring Sprawl and Its Transportation Impacts," *Transportation Research Record: Journal of the Transportation Research Board,* no. 1832 (2003): 175–183.

56. Robert A. Beauregard, *When America Became Suburban* (Minneapolis: University of Minnesota Press, 2006); John R. Logan and Harvey L. Molotch, *Urban Fortunes: The Political Economy of Place* (Berkeley and Los Angeles: University of California Press, 2007); Mark Gottdiener, *Planned Sprawl: Private and Public Interests in Suburbia* (Thousand Oaks, CA: Sage, 1977); Marion Clawson, *Suburban Land Conversion in the Unites States* (Baltimore, MD: Johns Hopkins University Press for Resources for the Future, 1971); Robert Self, *American Babylon: Race and Struggle for Postwar Oakland* (Princeton, NJ: Princeton University Press, 2003); David M. P. Freund, "Marketing the Free Market: State Intervention and the Politics of Prosperity in Metropolitan America," in *The New Suburban History*, ed. Kevin M. Kruse and Thomas Sugrue (Chicago: University, ed. Kevin M. Kruse and Thomas Sugrue (Chicago: University of Chicago Press, 2006), 11–32; Arnold Hirsch, "Less Than *Plessy:* The Inner City, Suburbs, and State Sanctioned Residential Segregation in the Age of *Brown,*" in *The New Suburban History*, ed. Kevin M. Kruse and Thomas Sugrue (Chicago: University of Chicago Press, 2006), 32–56; Douglas S. Massey, *American Apartheid: Segregation and the Making of the Underclass* (Cambridge, MA: Harvard University Press, 1993); Thomas Sugrue, *The Origins of the Urban Crisis: Race and Struggle in Postwar Detroit* (Princeton, NJ: Princeton University Press, 1996); See also chapters 8 and 11 in Nicolaides and Wiese, eds., *The Suburban Reader*.

57. Michael A. Stoll, "Job Sprawl and the Spatial Mismatch between Blacks and Jobs," *Brookings Institution Survey Series* (Washington, DC: Brookings Institution, February 2005).

58. Dianne Harris, "Race, Class, and Privacy in the Ordinary Postwar House, 1945–1960," in *Landscape and Race in the United States*, ed. Richard Schein (New York: Routledge, 2006), 127–156.

59. The phrase "carapace of the automobile" was used by Kristina Hill, "Citizen Train: How Direct Democracy, Participatory Design, and Pacific Rim Businesses Are Creating a New Seattle Monorail"

(talk presented at [Re]constructing Communities: Design Participation in the Face of Change, Fifth Pacific Rim Conference on Participatory Community Design, University of Washington, Seattle, September 2–5, 2004).

60. Anne Vernez-Moudon, *Built for Change; Managing Neighborhood Architecture in San Francisco* (Cambridge, MA: MIT Press, 1986); Stephen Wheeler, "The Evolution of Built Landscapes in the Metropolitan Regions," *Journal of Planning and Education Research* 27, no. 4 (2008): 400–416.

61. Bontje, "Sustainable New Economic Centres"; "Shanghai Hopes to Build World's First Truly Sustainable City," http://postcarboncities.net/shanghai (accessed October 20, 2008); "Pujiang Intelligence Valley," http://www.piv-park.com/en/PivShow.asp?SortID=7&ID=8 (accessed October 20, 2008).

BIBLIOGRAPHY

Ackerman, James. *The Villa: The Form and Ideology of Country Houses.* Princeton, NJ: Princeton University Press, 1990.

Albert Kahn Associated Architects and Engineers. "The Design of Factories Today." *Architectural Record* 98, no. 5, (November 1945): 120–138.

Allen, Mike. "In Danbury, Employees Fear Cutbacks." *New York Times,* August 5, 1999, C6.

American Architect—The Architectural Review. "Building for the General Motors Company, Detroit, Mich. Albert Kahn Architect." *American Architect—Architectural Review* 120 (2381), November 21, 1921, 392–394.

American Institute of Architects. "American Can Company." *AIA Journal* 59, no. 5 (May 1973): 128–138.

Anderson, Grace. "A Corporate Villa." *Architectural Record* 175, no. 13 (November 1987): 120–131.

Aranya, Rolee. "Location Theory in Reverse? Location for Global Production in the IT Industry of Bangalore." *Environment and Planning A* 40, no. 10 (2008): 446–463.

Architect and Builder. "Ascot Office Park: Port Elizabeth." *Architect and Builder* 46, no. 7 (July 1995): 2–5.

Architect and Builder. "Parc du Cap: An Office Park." *Architect and Builder* 37, no. 5 (April 1986): 2–7.

Architect and Builder. "Woodmead Office Park." *Architect and Builder* 42, no. 7 (July 1992): 2–7.

Architect and Engineer. "Office Building for the Shuckl Canning Co." *Architect and Engineer* 154, no. 2 (August 1943): 12–17.

Architectural Design. "Bell Telephone Laboratories Holmdel." *Architectural Design* 37, no. 7 (August 1967): 355–6, 339.

Architectural Design. "Deere and Co., USA." *Architectural Design* 35, no. 8 (August 1965): 404–409.

Architectural Forum. "Big Industry Moves to the Country." *Architectural Forum* 95, no. 2 (July 1951): 144–151.

Architectural Forum. "Building in One Package: How the Austin Company Solves Some of Industry's Unique Problems and Applies the Same Approach to Special Buildings of All Kinds." *Architectural Forum* 82, no. 2 (February 1942): 113–117.

Architectural Forum. "Ford Builds a New Automobile City." *Architectural Forum* 93, no. 12 (December 1950): 102–107.

Architectural Forum. "G.M. Technical Center: Industrial Buildings in Large Groupings." *Architectural Forum* 91, no. 1 (July 1949): 70–78.

Architectural Forum. "General Motors Technical Center." *Architectural Forum* 95, no. 5 (November 1951): 111–123.

Architectural Forum. "GM Nears Completion." *Architectural Forum* 101, no. 5 (November 1954): 100–119.

Architectural Forum. "GM's Industrial Versailles." *Architectural Forum* 104, no. 5 (May 1956): 122–129.

Architectural Forum. "Headquarter Offices for American Can Are a Model of Restraint." *Architectural Forum* 134, no. 1 (January/February 1971): 28–34.

Architectural Forum. "Headquarters Building for the Hershey Metals Products Co." *Architectural Forum* 83, no. 2 (August 1945): 108–110.

Architectural Forum. "IBM, a Laboratory Abroad." *Architectural Forum* 114, no. 3 (March 1961): 98–99.

Architectural Forum. "IBM's New Corporate Face." *Architectural Forum* 106, no. 2 (February 1957): 106–115.

Architectural Forum. "IBM's New Industrial Campus." *Architectural Forum* 108, no. 6 (June 1958): 104–107.

Architectural Forum. "Insurance Sets a Pattern." *Architectural Forum* 107, no. 3 (September 1957): 119.

Architectural Forum. "Office Building—North American Life and Casualty." *Architectural Forum* 90, no. 1 (January 1949): 76–81.

Architectural Forum. "Office Buildings." *Architectural Forum* 134, no. 1 (November/February 1971): 27–63.

Architectural Forum. "Research in the Round." *Architectural Forum* 114, no. 6 (June 1961): 80–85.

Architectural Forum. "Small Office Buildings 3. Ranch House Plan." *Architectural Forum* 96, no. 2 (February 1952): 114–116.

Architectural Forum. "The Biggest Mirror Ever." *Architectural Forum* 126, no. 3 (April 1967): 33–41.

Architectural Forum. "The Changing Suburbs." *Architectural Forum* 114, no. 1 (January 1961): 47–106.

Architectural Forum. "Three Small Buildings for Suburban Businesses 1. Sprawling Plan Exposes All Offices to Country Atmosphere." *Architectural Forum* 98, no. 6 (June 1953): 156–158.

Architectural Forum. "Voorhees Walker Foley & Smith." *Architectural Forum* 101, no. 5 (November 1954): 140–147.

Architectural Forum. "Working in the Suburbs: Industry on the Stanford Campus Is Converting Suburb to Satellite, without Jeopardizing Its Opportunity to Be a Garden City." *Architectural Forum* 114, no. 1 (January 1960): 56–62.

Architectural Forum. "Working in the Suburbs." *Architectural Forum* 114, no. 1 (January 1961): 56–69.

Architectural Record. "Restructuring the Corporate Habitat." *Architectural Record* 171, no. 12 (October 1983): 110–117.

Architectural Record. "A Change in Direction for Kevin Roche?" *Architectural Record* 166, no. 2 (August 1979): 93–96.

Architectural Record. "Bell Labs Mirrored Superblock." *Architectural Record* 132, no. 11 (October 1962): 145–152.

Architectural Record. "Big Business Moves to the Country." *Architectural Record* 110, no. 3 (Septemeber 1951): 160–163.

Architectural Record. "Design Elements That Affect Rentability." *Architectural Record* 84, no. 6 (December 1938): 99–102.

Architectural Record. "Designed to Be Functional in Plan, Quiet in Expression: Home Office Building for Phoenix Insurance Co." *Architectural Record* 102, no. 6 (December 1952): 126–135.

Architectural Record. "Electronics Park, Syracuse, New York." *Architectural Record* 105, no. 2 (February 1949): 96–103.

Architectural Record. "Factors Affecting Industrial Building Design." *Architectural Record* 116, no. 1 (July 1954): 151–155.

Architectural Record. "For Electronic Research and Development: Varian Associates, Palo Alto, California." *Architectural Record* 116, no. 1 (July 1954): 156–161.

Architectural Record. "General Electric Research Laboratory." *Architectural Record* 108, no. 1 (July 1950): 124–127.

Architectural Record. "General Motors Technical Center." *Architectural Record* 98, no. 5 (November 1945): 98–103.

Architectural Record. "IBM's Santa Teresa Laboratory." *Architectural Record* 162, no. 2 (August 1977): 91–104.

Architectural Record. "Industrial Group on the Campus Plan." *Architectural Record* 98 no. 5 (November 1945): 116–117.

Architectural Record. "Large Corporation Builds a Research Campus in New Jersey." *Architectural Record* 106, no. 4 (October 1949): 108–114.

Architectural Record. "Office Building near Waltham, Mass." *Architectural Record,* 121, no. (February 1957): 177–183.

Architectural Record. "Office Buildings." *Architectural Record* 130, no. 4 (April 1963): 181–182.

Architectural Record. "Offices for a Manufacturing Plant." *Architectural Record* 88, no. 6 (December 1940): 87.

Architectural Record. "Plant for Manufacture and Assembly of Portable Lamps and Lampshades." *Architectural Record* 85, no. 6 (June 1939): 116–117.

Architectural Record. "Research and Manufacture Combined under One Roof." *Architectural Record,* 98, no. 5 (November 1945): 112–113.

Architectural Record. "Richardson-Merrell Headquarters Wilton, Connecticut." *Architectural Record* 159, no. 2 (February 1976): 82–85.

Architectural Record. "Small Business Buildings, Locations Factors: Decentralization, Zoning, and Parking." *Architectural Record* 107, no. 1 (January 1950): 103–111.

Architectural Record. "Suburban Office Buildings." *Architectural Record* 151, no. 2 (February 1972): 113–129.

Architectural Record. "The Record Reports." *Architectural Record* 108, no. 6 (December 1955): 9.

Architectural Record. "Unique Cross-Curve Plan for IBM Research Center." *Architectural Record* 129, no. 7 (June 1961): 137–146.

Architectural Review. "Pastoral Palazzo." *Architectural Review* 149 (March 1971): 137–146.

Architecture & Building News. "Offices, Moline, Illinois." *Architecture & Building News* 227, no. 21 (May 1965): 979–984.

Architecture & Building News. "Research Center, Yorktown, N.Y." *Architecture & Building News* 221, no. 26 (June 1962): 923–926.

Architecture and Building. "The Durant Building." *Architecture and Building* 52, no. 4 (April 1920): 37–39.

Architettura. "I fasti dell'ellectronica = The Glorious Deeds of Electronics." *Architettura* 36, no. 10 (October 1990): 724–726.

Arts & Architecture. Country Office Building." *Arts & Architecture* 61, no. 6 (June 1944): 19–21.

Arts & Architecture. "Technical Center for General Motors Warren, Michigan." *Arts & Architecture* 74, no. 5 (May 1957): 25.

Ascendas. "Singapore Science Park Unveils S$400m Redevelopment Masterplan." Press release October 22, 2007. http://www.ascendas.com/downloads/pr2007/Press_Release_221007 (accessed May 10, 2008).

Associated Press. "Fire Closes Primerica Office." *New York Times,* October 22, 1987, B2.

AT&T Bell Laboratories. *Welcome to Murray Hill.* Murray Hill, NJ: Bell Laboratories, 1972.

Augur, Tracy B. "Decentralization: Blessing or Tragedy?" In *Planning 1948: Proceedings of the Annual National Planning Conference Held in New York City, October 11–13, 1948,* 27–34. Chicago: American Society of Planning Officials, 1948.

Baker, Ken. "Greening Business." *Business Parks: A Building Design Special Report,* no. 944 (July 1989): S5. supplement.

Balmori, Diana. "Cranbrook: The Invisible Landscape." *Journal of the Society of Architectural Historians* 53, no. 1 (March 1994): 30–60.

Baran, Barbara. "Office Automation and Women's Work: The Technical Transformation of the Insurance Industry." In *High Technology, Space, and Society,* edited by Manuel Castells, 143–171. Thousand Oaks, CA: Sage, 1985.

Barna, Joel W. "Solana in the Sun." *Progressive Architecture* 70, no. 4 (April 1989): 65–74.

Baumeister. "Solana." *Baumeister* 187, no. 4 (April 1990): 32–34.

Beauregard, Robert A. *Voices of Decline: The Postwar Fate of U.S. Cities.* 2nd ed. New York: Routledge, 2003.

Beauregard, Robert A. *When America Became Suburban.* Minneapolis: University of Minnesota Press, 2006.

Beers, David. "Tomorrowland: We Have Seen the Future and It Is Pleasanton." *San Francisco Examiner Image Magazine,* January 18, 1987, 14–20, 38.

Bell, Daniel. *The Cultural Contradictions of Capitalism.* New York: Basic Books, 1976.

Bello, Francis. "The World's Greatest Industrial Laboratory." *Fortune* 58, no. 5 (November 1958): 148–157.

Berry, B., and Y. S. Cohen. "Decentralization of Commerce and Industry: The Restructuring of Metropolitan America." In *The Urbanization of the Suburbs*, edited by Louise H. Masotti and Jeffrey K. Hadden, 431–456. Thousand Oaks, CA: Sage, 1973.

Bing, Jeb. "Retail Demand Offsetting Record-High Office Vacancies." *Pleasanton Weekly Online Edition*, March 4, 2005. http://www.pleasantonweekly.com/morgue/2005/2005_03_04.coutlook04.shtml (accessed April 27, 2008).

Binney, Marcus. "British Architecture Now." *Architectural Design* 59, no. 5–6 (1989): iii–xi.

Birr, Kendall. *Pioneering in Industrial Research*. Washington, DC: Public Affairs Press, 1957.

Bishop, Todd. "Microsoft Reimagines Its Corporate Home." *Seattle Post-Intelligencer,* January 27, 2005. http://seattlepi.nwsource.com/business/209568_msftcampus27.html (accessed May 10, 2008).

Blodgett, Geoffrey. "Frederick Law Olmsted: Landscape Architecture as Conservative Reform." *Journal of American History* 62, no. 4 (March 1976): 869–889.

BOMA International Research Department. *Building Owners and Managers North American Office Market Review: Mid Year 1988*. Washington, DC: BOMA Research International, 1988.

Bontje, Marco. "Sustainable New Economic Centres in European Metropolitan Regions: A Stakeholders' Perspective." *European Planning Studies*, 12, no. 5 (July 2004), 703–722.

Branch, Melville C. "Designing Indoor Environment for Industry, Part I." *Princeton Engineer* 20, no. 1 (October 1959): 16–19, 29–31.

Branch, Melville C. "Planning Environment for Research and Development, Part I: Environment." *Princeton Engineer* 18, no. 1 (October 1957): 23–28, 40–41, 70, 76.

Branch, Melville C. "Planning Environment for Research and Development, Part II: The Planning Process." *Princeton Engineer* 18, no. 2 (November 1957): 23–27, 54–56.

Branch, M. C., and G. Arthur. "Barton. "Research and Development Fitted into a Residential Community." *Landscape Architecture* 50, no. 4 (Summer 1960): 204–211.

Bredo, William. *Industrial Estates: Tool for Industrialization*. Glencoe, IL: Free Press, 1960.

Brennan, John, and Edward W. Hill. "Where Are the Jobs? Cities, Suburbs, and the Competition for Employment." *Brookings Instutution Survey Series*. Washington, DC: Brookings Institution, November 1999.

Brenner, Robert. *The Economics of Global Turbulence: The Advanced Capitalist Economies from the Long Boom to the Long Downturn, 1945–2005*. New York: Verso, 2006.

Bridgewater Courier News"Chronology: Company's Rise and Fall." *Bridgewater Courier News*, May 14, 1995, A-4.

Broehl, Wayne G. *John Deere's Company: The Story of Deere & Company and Its Times*. New York: Doubleday, 1984.

Brownwell, Blaine A. "Birmingham Alabama: New South City in the 1920s." *Journal of Southern History* 38, no. 1 (February 1972): 21–48.

Bruegmann, Robert. "The Corporate Landscape." *Inland Architect* 33, no. 5 (September/October 1989): 33–42.

Bruegmann, Robert. *Sprawl: A Compact History*. Chicago: University of Chicago Press, 2005.

Buchanan, Peter. "IBM Flagship." *Architectural Review* 174, no. 1041 (November 1983): 46–57.

Building Design. "Industrial Landscape." *Business Parks: A Building Design Special Report* no. 944 (July 1989): S6–S7. supplement.

BusinessWeek. "At Bell Labs, Industrial Research Looks Like Bright College Years." *BusinessWeek*, February 6, 1954, 74–75.

BusinessWeek. "Company Flees Maddening Crowd." *BusinessWeek*, March 27, 1954, 53.

BusinessWeek. "GE Gets Small-Business Touch," *BusinessWeek*, April 1952, 118, 120, 122–124.

BusinessWeek. "GM's Showplace for Stepped-Up Research." *BusinessWeek*, May 12, 1956, 103.

BusinessWeek. "Manville Builds New Home for Industrial Research." *BusinessWeek*, November 8, 1947, 44.

BusinessWeek. "Moline's Biggest Bash." *BusinessWeek*, June 20, 1964, 62–64.

BusinessWeek. "New View of Metals." *BusinessWeek*, August 27, 1955, 154–158.

BusinessWeek. "Offices Move to the Suburbs." *BusinessWeek*, March 17, 1951, 79–80.

BusinessWeek. "Wooing White Collars to Suburbia." *BusinessWeek*, July 8, 1967, 96–98.

BusinessWeek. "Research: How Can It Be Controlled." *BusinessWeek*, June 5, 1954, 80–86.

C. M. Guest and Sons. *Conditioned for Research*. Greensboro, NC: C. M. Guest & Sons, 1954.

Cambridge Science Park. "About History." http://www.cambridgesciencepark.co.uk/about_history.htm (accessed May 15, 2008).

Campbell, Robert. "Arts and Crafts Spirit Pervades Corporate Offices." *Architecture: AIA Journal* 77, no. 5 (May 1988): 139–143.

Campbell, Robert. "Intimations of Urbanity in a Bucolic Setting." *Architecture: AIA Journal* 77, no. 1 (January 1988): 72–77.

Campus M Business Park. "Campus M Business Park, Munich." http://www.campus-m.de/bauabschnitt2_en/index.php?n=lage (accessed May 15, 2008).

Capowski, Genevieve Sorter. "Designing a Corporate Identity." *Management Review* 82, no. 6 (June 1993): 37–40.

Carter, Luther J. "Research Triangle Seeks High-Technology Industry." *Science*, November 12, 1965, 867–871.

Carter, Luther J. "Research Triangle Succeeds beyond Its Promoters Expectations." *Science*, June 30, 1978, 1469–1470.

Calhoun, Craig, and Henryk Hiller. "Coping with Insidious Injuries: The Case of Johns-Manville Corporation and Asbestos Exposure." *Social Problems* 35, no. 2 (April 1988): 162–181.

Castells, Manuel, and Peter Hall. *Technopoles of the World: The Making of 21st Century Industrial Complexes*. New York: Routledge, 1994.

Chacko, Elizabeth. "From Brain Drain to Brain Gain: Reverse Migration to Bangalore and Hyderabad, India's Globalizing High Tech Cities." *GeoJournal* 68, no. 5 (May 2007): 131–140.

Chandler, Alfred. *Scale and Scope: The Dynamics of Industrial Capitalism*. Cambridge, MA: Belknap Press of Harvard University Press, 1990.

Chandler, Alfred. *Visible Hand: The Managerial Revolution in American Business*. Cambridge, MA: Harvard University Press, 1977.

Charles, Eleanor. "American Can Selling Its Campus." *New York Times,* August 17, 1986, R6.

Charles, Eleanor. "Suburban History for Sale, with Architectural Status." *New York Times,* August 14, 2002, C5.

Charles, Eleanor. "Westchester's Airport, Greenwich's Ache." *New York Times,* December 27, 1987, R4.

Ciandella, Donald R. "Lagging New Supply, Rising Demand Invigorates Office Sector." *National Real Estate Investor* 38, no. 7 (August 1996): 37–38, 40, 42–45, 91.

"Cigna's Self-Inflicted Wounds." *CIO Magazine*. http://www.cio.com/archive/031503/cigna (accessed June 22, 2005).

City of Portsmouth, United Kingdom. "Business." http://www.portsmouth.gov.uk/business/index.html (accessed May 12, 2008).

City of Southlake. "Incentives History." January 11, 2002. http://www.ci.southlake.tx.us/search/default.aspx?QueryExpr=sabre (accessed May 5, 2008).

City of Southlake. "Sabre Holdings' Headquarters: Project Profile." February 2, 2005, http://www.ci.southlake.tx.us/search/default.aspx?QueryExpr=ontacts (accessed May 5, 2008).

Citywest Business Campus. "Citywest Business Campus." http://www.citywest.ie/exec.asp (accessed May 28, 2008).

Clark, Frederick. "Office Buildings in the Suburbs." *Urban Land* 13, no. 7 (July-August 1954): 3–10.

Clawson, Marion. *Suburban Land Conversion in the United States.* Baltimore, MD: Johns Hopkins University Press for Resources for the Future, 1971.

Combs, Gwendolyn, Sucheta Nadkarni, and Michael Coms. "Implementing Affirmative Actions Plans in Multi-National Corporations." *Organizational Dynamics* 34, no. 4 (November 2006): 346–360.

Connecticut General Life Insurance Corporation. *The New Highways: Challenge to the Metropolitan Region.* Hartford, CT: General Life Insurance Corporation, 1958.

Connecticut Trust for Historic Preservation. "The Most Threatened Historic Places—Updates: Wilde Building, Bloomfield." http://www.cttrust.org/8414?highlight=bloomfield (accessed May 10, 2008).

Corporate Design and Realty. "Hacienda: A Textbook Case in Community Relations." *Corporate Design and Realty* 4, no. 7 (September 1985): 28–32.

Crandell, Gina. "In Capability." *Landscape Architecture* 74, no. 3 (May/June 1984): 49–53.

Crawford, Margaret. *Building the Workingman's Paradise: The Design of American Company Towns.* New York: Verso, 1985.

Creighton, Thomas H. "Pearl Harbor to Nagasaki: A Review of Architectural Programming in the War Years." *Progressive Architecture* 27, no. 1 (January 1946): 42–81.

Curtice, Harlow H. "Accelerating the Pace of Technological Progress." In *The Greatest Frontier: Remarks at the Dedication Program General Motors Technical Center,* 5–12. Detroit, MI: General Motors Corporation, 1956.

Dalian Ascendas. "Dalian Ascendas IT Park." http://www.daitp.com/home.html (accessed May 10, 2008).

Davey, Peter. "Collegiate Corporation." *Architectural Review* 184, no. 1098 (August 1988): 52–57.

Davis, Tim. "The Miracle Mile Revisited: Recycling, Renovation, and Simulation along the Commercial Strip." In *Exploring Everyday Landscapes: Perspectives on Vernacular Architecture 7,* edited by Annemarie Adams and Sally McMurray, 93–114. Knoxville: University of Tennessee Press, 1997.

Dean, Andrea. "Corporate Contrast in the Suburbs." *Architecture: AIA Journal* 74, no. 2 (February 1985): 60–69.

Deere & Company. *Administrative Center.* (video) Moline, IL: Deere & Company, 1990.

Deere & Company. *Challenge to the Architect: Deere & Company Administrative Center.* Moline, IL: Deere & Company, 1964.

DeLong, David G. "Eliel Saarinen and the Cranbrook Tradition in Architecture and Urban Design." In *Design in America: The Cranbrook Vision, 1925–1950,* edited by Robert Judson Clark and Andrea Belloli, 47–90. New York: Harry Abrams, 1983.

Dempsey, Florence. "Nela Park: A Novelty in the Architectural Grouping of Industrial Buildings." *Architectural Record* 35, no. 6 (June 1914): 468–503.

"Design '89: NAIOP Annual Design Development Awards." *Development* 20, no. 60 (November 1989): 42.

Dillon, David. "And Two in the Country." *Landscape Architecture* 80, no. 3 (March 1990): 62–63.

Douglass, Lathrop. "New Departures in Office Building Design." *Architectural Record* 102, no. 40 (October 1947): 119–146.

Downing, A. J. *Landscape Gardening and Rural Architecture*. 1865. Reprint, New York: Dover, 1991.

Doyle, Margaret. "Creating a Corporate Home in the Woods." *Building Design and Construction* 29, no. 6 (June 1988): 128–133.

Dudley, Brian. "Microsoft Expansion to Ripple through the Region." *Seattle Times,* February 10, 2006. http://community.seattletimes.nwsource.com/archive/?date=20060210&slug=microsoft10 (accessed May 10, 2008).

Duménil, Gérard, and Dominique Lévy. *The Economics of the Profit Rate: Competition, Crises, and Historical Tendencies in Capitalism*. Northampton, MA: Edward Elgar, 1993.

Duménil, Gérard, Marc Glick, and Dominique Lévy. "The Rise of the Rate of Profit during World War II." *Review of Economics and Statistics* 75, no. 2 (May 1993): 315–320.

Duncan, James S., and Nancy G. Duncan. *Landscapes of Privilege: Aesthetics and Affluence in an American Suburb*. New York: Routledge, 2004.

Dunlap, David W. "Thawing Corporate Capital Frozen into Real Estate." *New York Times,* August 11, 1991, 340.

Eames, Charles. "General Motors Revisited: A Special Report." *Architectural Forum* 134, no. 5 (June 1971): 21–28.

Ede, Bernard. "The Stockley Park Project." *Landscape Design*, no. 187 (February 1990): 48–51.

Eichstedt, Edward A. "Current Work in Progress: Landscape at the General Motors Technical Center." *Landscape Architecture* 42, no. 4 (July 1952): 166–167.

Eisenhower, Dwight D. "The Rich Reward Ahead." In *The Greatest Frontier: Remarks at the Dedication Program General Motors Technical Center*, 25–29. Detroit: General Motors Corporation, 1956.

Emrich, Ron. "Holmdel Consultant Calls for Bell Labs Demolition, McMansions, Golf Course." *Preserve NJ*, March 4, 2009. http://preservationnj.wordpress.com/2009/03/04/holmdels-consultant-calls-for-demolition-of-bell-labs-mcmansions-golf-course/ (accessed September 13, 2009).

Estall, R. C. "The Electronic Products Industry of New England." *Economic Geography* 39, no. 3 (July 1973): 189–216.

Ewing, Reid, and Robert Cervero. "Travel and the Built Environment: A Synthesis." *Transportation Research Record: Journal of the Transportation Research Board* no.1780 (2001): 87–114.

Ewing, Reid, Keith Bartholomew, Steve Winkelman, Jerry Walters, and Don Chen. *Growing Cooler: The Evidence on Urban Development and Climate Change*. Washington, DC: Urban Land Institute, 2008.

Ewing, Reid, Rolf Pendall, and Don Chen. "Measuring Sprawl and Its Transportation Impacts." *Transportation Research Record: Journal of the Transportation Research Board* no.1832 (2003): 175–183.

Feron, James. "Companies Leave City and Find New Troubles." *New York Times,* October 11, 1983, B4.

Findlay, John M. *Magic Lands*. Berkeley and Los Angeles: University of California Press, 1992.

Fishman, Robert. *Bourgeois Utopias*. New York: Basic Books, 1987.

Fishman, Robert. "On Big Beaver Road: Detroit and the Diversity of American Metropolitan Landscapes." *Places* 19, no. 3 (Spring 2007): 42–47.

Flynn, Laurie, and Andrew Ross Sorkin. "Despite Ruling PeopleSoft Battles to Stand Alone." *New York Times,* September 11, 2004, C1.

Fogelson, Robert M. *Downtown: Its Rise and Fall, 1880–1950*. New Haven, CT: Yale University Press, 2001.

Foley, Donald L. "Factors in the Location of Administrative Offices with Particular Reference to the San Francisco Bay Area." In *Papers and Proceedings: The Regional Science Association Second Annual Meeting, December, 1955, Vol. 2*, edited by Gerald A. P. Carruthers. Cambridge, MA: Regional Science Association, 1956.

Foley, Donald L. *The Suburbanization of Offices in the San Francisco Bay Area*. Berkeley: Regents of the University of California, 1957.

Fong, Tomothy P. *The First Suburban Chinatown: The Remaking of Monterey Park, California*. Philadelphia: Temple University Press, 1994.

Fortune. "A Dramatic New Office Building." *Fortune* 56, no. 3 (September 1957): 164–169.

Fortune. "G.M. Technical Center." *Fortune* 44, no. 6 (December 1951): 82–86.

Fortune. "I.B.M. Banishes Dowdiness." *Fortune* 59, no. 6 (June 1959): 129–135.

Fortune. "Mortimer of General Foods." *Fortune* 50, no. 3 (September 1954): 132–133.

Fortune. "Notes of the Business Landscape, Atlanta 'Really Springing.'" 56, no. 6 (December 1957): 265–266.

Fortune. "Should Management Move to the Country?" *Fortune* 46, no. 6 (December 1952): 142–143, 164, 166, 168, 170.

Fortune. "The Power of a Road." *Fortune* 56, no. 4 (October 1957): 285–288.

Foster, Lawrence G. "Research Row: Rustic Location of Labs along the Lackawanna Aids Industrial Giants in 'Wooing the Muses.'" *Newark Sunday News*, November 13, 1949, 21.

Foundation Sophia Antipolis. "Presentation of the Foundation Sophia-Antipolis." http://www.sophia-antipolis.org/GB/fsa/presentation/presentation/presentation.htm (accessed May 20, 2008).

Foundation Sophia-Antipolis. "The 'Sophipolitan' Model." http://www.sophia-antipolis.org/GB/sophia-antipolis/sophia-antipolis/modele-sophipolitain/modele-sophipolitain.htm (accessed May 20, 2008).

Freudenheim, Milt. "More Suits Filed against Health Insurers." *New York Times,* June 27, 2000, C2.

Freund, David M. P. "Marketing the Free Market: State Intervention and the Politics of Prosperity in Metropolitan America." In *The New Suburban History,* edited by Kevin M. Kruse and Thomas J. Sugrue, 11–32. Chicago: University of Chicago Press, 2006.

Frey, William H. *Melting Pot Suburbs*. Washington, DC: Brookings Institution, 2001. http://www.brookings.edu/reports/2001/06demographics_frey.aspx (accessed January 10, 2010).

GA Document. "IBM Southlake and Village Center, Solana, Westlake and Southlake, Texas." *GA Document*, no. 24 (August 1989): 20–24.

GA Document. "Kevin Roche, John Dinkeloo and Associates, General Foods Corporation Headquarters." *GA Document*, no. 2 (Autumn 1980): 88–91.

Garreau, Joel. *Edge City: Life on the New Frontier*. New York: Anchor Books, 1991.

Geddes, Hugh. "Industrial Parkland: Landscapes of a New Aristocracy." Master's thesis, University of California, Berkeley, 1986.

General Electric. *A Century of Progress: The General Electric Story, 1876–1978*. Schenectady, NY: General Electric, 1981.

General Foods. "'54 in White Plains." *GF News* 13, no. 5 (May 1952): 3.

General Foods. "Follow-Ups: Moving Story." *GF News* 12, no. 7 (July–August 1951): 2.

General Foods. "Goodbye to Subways? GF Takes Option on Site for New General Offices." *GF News Letter* 12, no. 2 (February 1951): 2.

General Foods. "Moving Out." *GF News* 15, no. 4 (April 1954): 3.

General Foods. *General Foods*. White Plains, NY: General Foods, 1954.

General Foods. "We Move Our General Offices to White Plains." In *General Foods Annual Report,* 12–13. White Plains, NY: General Foods, Fall 1954.

General Foods. *GF Moving Day and You*. New York: General Foods, 1952.

General Motors Corporation. "A History of the Development and Construction of General Motors Technical Center, Warren Township, Mocomb County, Michigan." Internal memo. 1956.

General Motors Public Relations. "General Motors Builds Its First 50 Million Cars." Press release. Detroit, MI: General Motors, 1955.

General Motors Public Relations. *Styling: The Look of Things*. Detroit: General Motors, 1956.

General Motors Public Relations. *Where Today Meets Tomorrow: General Motors Technical Center*. Detroit, MI: General Motors Corporation, 1956.

General Motors Engineering Journal 3, no. 2 (1956). Issue devoted to the General Motors Technical Center.

Gibbs, Kenneth Turney. *Business Architectural Imagery in America, 1870–1930*. Ann Arbor: University of Michigan Press, 1984.

Girot, Christophe. "Bouygues." *Landscape Architecture* 80, no. 3 (March 1990): 64–65.

GM Folks 19, no. 6 (June 1956). Issue devoted to the opening of the General Motors Technical Center.

Goldberger, Paul. "Union Carbide's New Corporate Home: A Metallic Castle Tucked in Woods." *New York Times,* February 20, 1984, B1.

Goldstein, Barbara. "Harlequin Plaza." *Landscape Architecture* 73, no. 4 (July/August 1983): 56–59.

Gottdeiner, Mark. *Planned Sprawl: Private and Public Interests in Suburbia*. Thousand Oaks, CA: Sage, 1977.

Gottlieb, Robert. *Forcing the Spring: The Transformation of the American Environmental Movement*. Washington, DC: Island Press, 2005.

Graf, Don. *Convenience for Research*. New York: Voorhees Walker Foley & Smith, 1944.

Graf, Don. "Murray Hill Unit, Bell Telephone Laboratories, Inc." *Pencil Points* 23, no. 8 (August 1942): 34–71.

Granley, David A. and Charles E. Jolitz, "The New General Foods Headquarters: Its Design and Construction—Part Two," *GF Technical Bulletin* 6, no. 2 (June 1952): 2–12.

Granley, David A., and Charles E. Jolitz. "The New General Foods Headquarters: Its Electrical Distribution System." *GF Technical Bulletin* 6, no. 3 (September 1952): 6–8.

Granley, David A., and Charles E. Jolitz. "The New General Foods Headquarters: Its Heating, Ventilating, and Air Conditioning Systems." *GF Technical Bulletin* 6, no. 4 (December 1952): 4–7.

Greenhouse, Steven. "French Agree to Buy American Can's Parent." *New York Times,* November 22, 1988, D1, D6.

Greenwood Village, Colorado. "Honoring Our Heritage, Harlequin Plaza." http://www.greenwoodvillage.com/index.asp?nid=513 (accessed May 5, 2008).

Griefen, R. John. "A Research Park Does Not Live by Research Alone: The Success Story of Technology Square." *Urban Land* 24, no. 3 (March 1965): 3–10.

Gupta, Hinaee. "Microsoft to Add 1,000, Mostly in the Redmond Area." *Seattle Times,* May 21, 1990. http://community.seattletimes.nwsource.com/archive/?date=19900421&slug=1067553 (accessed May 10, 2008).

Hacienda Network. "Hacienda 25th Anniversary." *Hacienda Network,* July 24, 2007.

Hafsted, Lawrence R. "The Future Is Our Assignment." In *The Greatest Frontier: Remarks at the Dedication Program General Motors Technical Center,* 13–20. Detroit, MI: General Motors Corporation, 1956.

Haines, Charles. "Planning the Scientific Laboratory." *Architectural Record* 108, no. 1 (July 1950): 106–123.

Hall, Mildred Reed, and Edward T. Hall. *The Fourth Dimension in Architecture: Impact of Building on Behavior.* Santa Fe, NM: Sunstone Press, 1975.

Hammond, John Winthrop. *Men and Volts: The Story of General Electric.* New York: McGraw-Hill, 1941.

Harris, Dianne. "Race, Class, and Privacy in the Ordinary Postwar House, 1945–1960." In *Landscape and Race in the United States*, edited by Richard Schein, 127–156. New York: Routledge, 2006.

Harris, Richard, and Robert Lewis. "Constructing a Fault(y) Zone: Misrepresentations of American Cities and Suburbs, 1900–1950." *Annals of the American Association of Geographers* 88, no. 4 (1998): 622–639.

Harris, Richard, and Robert Lewis. "The Geography of North American Cities and Suburbs, 1900–1950: A New Synthesis." *Journal of Urban History* 27, no. 3 (March 2001): 262–292.

Hauf, Harold. "City Planning and Civil Defense." *Architectural Record* 108, no. 6 (December 1950): 99.

Havlick, David, and Scott Kirsch. "A Production Utopia? RTP and the North Carolina Research Triangle." *Southeastern Geographer* 44, no. 2 (2004): 263–277.

Hawkins, Lawrence. *Adventure into the Unknown: The First Fifty Years of the General Electric Research Laboratory.* New York: Morrow, 1950.

Hayden, Dolores. "Building the American Way: Public Subsidy, Private Space." In *The Suburban Reader,* edited by Becky M. Nicolaides and Andrew Wiese, 273–281. New York: Routledge, 2006.

Hayden, Dolores. *Building Suburbia: Green Fields and Urban Growth, 1820–2000.* New York: Vintage Books, 2004.

Hayden, Dolores. *A Field Guide to Sprawl.* New York: Norton, 2004.

Herrera, Philip. "That Manhattan Exodus." *Fortune* 76, no. 6 (June 1967), 106–109, 148.

Hewitt, William. "The Genesis of a Great Building—and of an Unusual Friendship." *AIA Journal* 65, no. 19 (August 1977): 36–38.

Hewitt, William A. "Opening Remarks." In *Deere & Company Administrative Center*, 1–4. Moline, IL: Deere & Company, 1964.

Hewitt, William A. "President's Address." In *Deere & Company: Report of the Annual Meeting of Stockholders*, 3–6. Moline, IL: Deere & Company, 1963.

Hewitt, William A. "The President's Letter." In *Deere & Company 1957 Annual Report*, 5–7. Moline, IL: Deere & Company, 1957.

Hewlett-Packard. "HP Timeline—1950s." http://www.hp.com/hpinfo/abouthp/histnfacts/timeline/hist_50s.html (accessed October 13, 2008).

Hill, Kristina. "Citizen Train: How Direct Democracy, Participatory Design, and Pacific Rim Businesses Are Creating a New Seattle Monorail." Paper presented at [Re]constructing Communities: Design Participation in the Face of Change, Fifth Pacific Rim Conference on Participatory Community Design. University of Washington, Seattle, September 2–5, 2004.

Hirsch, Arnold. "Less Than Plessy: The Inner City, Suburbs, and State Sanctioned Residential Segregation in the Age of Brown." In *The New Suburban History,* edited by Kevin M. Kruse and Thomas J. Sugrue, 32–56. Chicago: University of Chicago Press, 2006.

Hise, Greg. *Magnetic Los Angeles: Planning the Twentieth-Century Metropolis.* Baltimore, MD: Johns Hopkins University Press, 1997.

Hise, Greg. "Nature's Workshop: Industry and Urban Expansion in Southern California." In *Manufacturing Suburbs: Building Work and Home on the Metropolitan Fringe*, edited by Robert Lewis. Philadelphia: Temple University Press, 2004, 178–199.

Hoffman, Milton. "Michaelian Was There at the Beginning." *Westchester Commerce & Industry,* January 23, 1977, H4.

Horanic, Joie. "Re-Using Scarce Waters for Suburban Offices." *Landscape Architecture* 70, no. 4 (July 1980): 389–391.

Horn, J. H. *Historic Somerset.* Somerville, NJ: Historic Societies of Somerset County, 1965.

Howett, Catherine. "Pepsico Reconsidered." *Landscape Architecture* 79, no. 3 (April 1989): 82–85.

Hunt, Franklin L. "New Buildings of Bell Telephone Laboratories." *Journal of Applied Physics* 14 (June 1943): 250–251.

Hunt, John Dixon, ed. *The Pastoral Landscape.* Washington, DC: National Gallery of Art, 1992.

Hunt, Mary. "Research Parks: Haven or Hype?" *Corporate Design and Realty* 4, no. 9 (November 1985): 32–35.

Huxtable, Ada Louise. "It's So Peaceful in the Country." *New York Times,* January 17, 1971, D29.

IBM. *IBM at Hursley: Care for the Environment. Hursley Park*. Winchester, England: IBM, 198-?.

IBM Almaden Research Center. "History of the Almaden Research Site." http//:www.almaden.ibm/almaden20/history.shtml (accessed March 13, 2008).

IBM Almaden Research Center. "Quick Facts about the Almaden Site." http//:www.almaden.ibm.com/almaden20/quick.shtml (accessed March 13, 2008).

IBM Hursley Park. "Explore Hursley." http://www-05.ibm.com/uk/locations/hursley_explore.html (accessed May 12, 2008).

IBM LaGaude. "Dynamic Places." http://www-913.ibm.com/employment/us/extremeblue/location/lagaude.html (accessed May 20, 2008).

Industrial Design "Wide Open Spaces." *Industrial Design* 19, no. 2 (March 1972): 37–42.

Industrial Development and Manufacturers Record. "Fourth Annual Survey of Research Parks." *Industrial Development and Manufacturers Record* 134, no. 8 (August 1965): 33–34.

Industrial Development and Manufacturers Record. "ID's Second Annual Report Office Parks for Industry." *Industrial Development and Manufacturers Record* 135, no. 9 (September 1966): 22–23.

Industrial Development and Manufacturers Record. "Office Parks: First Annual Report." *Industrial Development and Manufacturers Record* 134, no. 9 (September 1965): 11–14.

Industrial Development and Manufacturers Record. "The Office Park: A New Concept in Office Space." *Industrial Development and Manufacturers Record* 134, no. 9 (September 1965): 9–10.

International Park. "Park Profile, A World in a Park." http://www.itpbangalore.com/pp_worldinapark.html (accessed May 15, 2008).

Irish Architect. "Park West Business Park." *Irish Architect,* no. 170 (September 2001): 37–42, 44.

Jackson, J. B. "The Popular Yard." *Places* 4, no. 3 (1987): 26–32.

Jackson, Kenneth T. *Crabgrass Frontier: The Suburbanization of the United States*. New York: Oxford University Press, 1985.

Jacobus, John. "John Deere Office Building, Moline, Illinois, USA." *Architectural Review* 137, no. 819 (May 1965): 364–371.

James, Elizabeth. "What Is a Headquarters?" *GF News* 15, no. 5 (May 1954): 1–2.

James, Elizabeth. "Why Move to White Plains?" *GF News* 15, no. 5 (May 1952): 13–15.

Johns, Michael. *Moment of Grace*. Berkeley and Los Angeles: University of California Press, 2003.

Johnson, Jory. "Codex World Headquarters: Regionalism and Invention." *Landscape Architecture* 78, no. 3 (April/May 1988): 58–63.

Johnson, Jory. "Pastures of Plenty: Thirty Years of Corporate Villas in America." *Landscape Architecture* 80, no. 3 (March 1990): 51–52.

Johnson, Jory, and Felice Frankel. *Modern Landscape Architecture*. New York: Abbeville Press, 1991.

Jonca, Richard, David J. Neuman, and Paul Venable Turner. *Stanford University*. New York: Princeton Architectural Press, 2006.

Judson, George. "Greenwich Feels Pain of Change." *New York Times,* April 12, 1993, B8.

Kaiser, David. "The Postwar Suburbanization of American Physics." *American Quarterly* 56, no. 4 (December 2004): 851–888.

Kalvin, Judy. "Hacienda: A Textbook Case in Community Relations." *Corporate Design & Realty* 4, no. 7 (September 1985): 28–32.

Kean, David W. *IBM San Jose: A Quarter Century of Innovation*. San Jose: International Business Machines Corporation, 1977.

Kelly, Mervin J. "The Bell Telephone Laboratories—An Example of an Institute of Creative Technology." *Proceedings of the Royal Society of London. Series A* 203, no. 1074 (October 1950): 287–301.

Kenney, Martin, ed. *Understanding Silicon Valley: The Anatomy of an Entrepreneurial Region*. Palo Alto, CA: Stanford University Press, 2000.

Keonics. "Keonics—About." http://www.keonics.com/aboutus.htm (accessed October 20, 2008).

Kersetter, Jim. "Finally, Oracle Nails PeopleSoft." *BusinessWeek,* December 13, 2004. http://www.businessweek.com/technology/content/dec2004/tc20041213_8884_tc024.htm (accessed May 15, 2008).

Kettering, Charles F. "Let's Turn Around. . . . and Look at the Future." In *The Greatest Frontier: Remarks at the Dedication Program General Motors Technical Center*, 21–24. Detroit, MI: General Motors Corporation, 1956.

King, Andy. "Vital Statistics." *Business Parks: A Building Design Special Report*, no. 944 (July 1989): S36–S37, supplement.

Kliment, Stephen. "Rooms with a View." *Architectural Record* 181, no. 11 (November 1993): 80–85.

Knight, David B., and Tatsuo Ito. "Office Parks: The Oak Brook Example." *Land Economics* 48, no. 1 (1972): 65–69.

Knowles, Scott G., and Stuart W. Leslie. "'Industrial Versailles': Eero Saarinen's Corporate Campuses for GM, IBM, and AT&T." *Isis* 92, no. 1 (March 2001): 1–33.

Koetter, Fred. "The Corporate Villa." *Design Quarterly* no. 135 (1987): 3–32.

Koh, Francis C. C., Winston T. H. Koh, and Feichin Ted Tschang. "An Analytical Framework for Science Parks and Technology Districts with an Application to Singapore." *Journal of Business Venturing* 20, no. 2 (March 2005): 217–239.

Kunstler, James Howard. *Home from Nowhere: Remaking Our World for the Twenty-First Century*. New York: Simon and Shuster, 1996.

Kunstler, James Howard. "Merck: The Corporate Landscape Goes Native." *Landscape Architecture* 83, no. 12 (December 1993): 60–62.

Lafitte, Pierre. "Birth of a City? Sophia Antipolis." http://www.sophia-antipolis.org/GB/sophia-antipolis/sophia-antipolis/naissance-ville/naissance-ville.htm (accessed May 20, 2008).

Laird, Edward H. "Electronics Park: An Industrial Center for the General Electric Company." *Landscape Architecture* 38, no. 1 (October 1946): 14–16.

Landscape Architecture. "Cornell Oaks Corporate Center." *Landscape Architecture* 78, no. 8 (December 1988): 96–99.

Lang, Robert E. "Office Sprawl: The Evolving Geography of Business." *The Brookings Institution Survey Series*. Washington, DC: Brookings Institution, October 2000. http://www.brookings.edu/~/media/Files/rc/reports/2000/10metropolitanpolicy_lang/lang.pdf (accessed October 2004).

Laporte, Dierdre. "Bell Laboratories: The Beginnings of Scientific Research in an Industrial Setting." In *Annals of the New York Academy of Sciences*, edited by Joseph W. Dauben and Virginia Staudt Sexton, 85–100. New York: New York Academy of Sciences, 1983.

Lashinsky, Adam. "Chaos by Design." *Fortune Online*, October 2, 2006. http://money.cnn.com/magazines/fortune/fortune_archive/2006/10/02/8387489/index.htm (accessed May 4, 2008).

Lawyer, Gail. "Largest Office Parks Planned in the Metro Area." *Washington Business Journal*, May 14–20, 1993, 38.

LeCuyer, Anne. "Roman Villa with Nordic Light." *Architecture* 74, no. 5 (May 1985): 282–287.

Leiberman, Henry R. "Technology: Alchemist of Route 128." *New York Times*, January 8, 1968, 139.

Leslie, Stewart W., and Robert H. Kargan. "Selling Silicon Valley: Frederick Terman's Model for Regional Advantage." *Business History Review* 7, no. 7 (1996): 435–473.

Lewis, Barbara. "Hacienda Celebrates Silver Anniversary." *Hacienda Network*, July 24, 2007, 1.

Lewis, Barbara. "Joe Callahan: Visionary with a Penchant for New Projects." *Hacienda Network*, July 24, 2007, 2–3.

Lewis, Pierce. "American Landscape Tastes." In *Modern Landscape Architecture: A Critical Review*, edited by Marc Treib, 2–18. Cambridge, MA: MIT Press, 1993.

Lewis, Robert, ed. *Manufacturing Suburbs: Building Work and Home on the Metropolitan Fringe*. Philadelphia: Temple University Press, 2004.

Life. "Architecture for the Future: GM Constructs a 'Versailles of Industry.'" *Life*, May 21, 1956, 102–107.

Life. "Modern Laboratory." *Life*, September 18, 1944, 79, 81–82.

Life. "Symposium in a Symbolic Setting." *Life,* October 21, 1957, 49–54.

Lincoln, Freeman. "After the Cabots—Jerry Blakeley." *Fortune* 62, no. 5 (November 1960): 171–173.

Link, Albert N., and John T. Scott. "The Growth of Research Triangle Park." *Small Business Economics* 20, no. 2 (November 2003): 167–176.

Logan, John R., and Harvey L. Molotch. *Urban Fortunes: The Political Economy of Place*. Berkeley and Los Angeles: University of California Press, 2007.

Long, George B. "Office Park Development." *Urban Land* 32, no. 1 (February 1973): 10–17.

Longstreth, Richard. *City Center to Regional Mall: Architecture, the Automobile, and Retailing in Los Angeles, 1920–1950*. Cambridge, MA: MIT Press, 1997.

Lotus International. "Dal Parco al Giardino = From Park to the Garden." *Lotus International,* no. 87 (1995): 34–61.

Lowen, Rebecca S. *Creating the Cold War University*. Berkeley and Los Angeles: University of California Press, 1997.

Lueck, Thomas J. "Manhattan Company Is Coaxed Away." *New York Times,* June 16, 1993, B5.

Luger, Michael J., and Harvey A. Goldstein. *Technology in the Garden: Research Parks and Regional Economic Development*. Chapel Hill: University of North Carolina Press, 1991.

Lyall, Sutherland. *Designing the New Landscape*. New York: Van Nostrand Reinhold, 1991.

Lynes, Russell. "After Hours: The Erosion of Detroit." *Harper's* 220, no. 1316 (January 1960): 23–25.

Mabin, Alan. "Suburbanisation, Segregation, and Government of Territorial Transformations." *Transformation: Critical Perspectives on Southern Africa* 57, no. 1 (2005): 41–63.

Manners, Gerald. "The Office in the Metropolis: An Opportunity for Shaping Metropolitan America." *Economic Geography* 50, no. 2 (April 1974): 96–101.

Manville News. "New J-M Expansion Predicted by Brown, Center Is Dedicated." *Manville News*, May 26, 1949, 1.

Marcec, Dan. "Developing a New Landscape: Mixed-Use Projects Are on the Rise in the Dallas Area." *Texas Real Estate Business* (January 6, 2007). http://www.texasrebusiness.com/articles/JAN07/cover1.html (accessed May 6, 2008).

Marchand, Roland. *Advertising the American Dream: Making Way for Modernity, 1920–1940*. Berkeley and Los Angeles: University of California Press, 1985.

Marchand, Roland. *Creating the Corporate Soul*. Berkeley and Los Angeles: University of California Press, 1988.

Marlin, William. "Two Business Buildings." *Architectural Record* 159, no. 2 (February 1976): 81–90.

Martin, Michelle. "An Instant Landmark in Silicon Valley." *World Architecture,* no. 68 (July–August 1998): 67–71.

Marx, Leo. "Does Pastoralism Have a Future?" In *The Pastoral Landscape*, edited by John Dixon Hunt, 209–226. Washington, DC: National Gallery of Art, 1992.

Marx, Leo. *The Machine in the Garden: the Pastoral Ideal in America*. New York: Oxford University Press, 1964.

Massey, Douglas S. *American Apartheid: Segregation and the Making of the Underclass*. Cambridge, MA: Harvard University Press, 1993.

Maybury, Phil. "Bristol Fashion." *Business Parks: A Building Design Special Report*, no. 944 (July 1989): S20–S23, S25. supplement.

McCue, Gerald M. "IBM's Santa Teresa Laboratory: Architectural Design for Program Development." *IBM Systems Journal* 17, no. 1 (1978): 4–25.

McKeever, J. Ross. *Business Parks, Office Parks, Plazas and Centers*. Washington, DC: Urban Land Institute, 1971.

McKeeever, J. Ross. *The Community Builders Handbook*. Washington, DC: Urban Land Institute, 1968.

McQuade, Walter. "John Deere's Sticks of Steel." *Architectural Forum* 71, no. 7 (July 1964): 77.

Meade, Kenneth A. "The Shortage of Scientific and Technical Personnel: What Industry Is Doing About It." *Science*, May 2, 1947, 457–461.

Means, Gardiner. *The Corporate Revolution in America*. New York: Crowell-Collier Press, 1962.

Mega, Voula. "Our City, Our Future: Towards Sustainable Development in European Cities." *Environment and Urbanization* 8, no. 1 (1996): 133–154.

Metha, Jaydip. "Bangalore Digitally Devided [sic] Global City." Jaydip Mehta Blog. 2007. http://willfindsaway.blogspot.com/2007/10/banglore-digitally-devided-global.html (accessed May 15, 2008).

Meyer, Herbert E. "Why Corporations Are on the Move." *Fortune* 93, no. 5 (May 1976): 252–272.

Meyer, Herbert E. "Simmons Likes it Down South." *Fortune* 93, no. 5 (May 1976): 255–258, 266.

Michigan Tradesman"Research Staff Picture History." *Michigan Tradesman* 73 (May 1956): 32–33.

Miller, Nory. "Kevin Roche, John Dinkeloo and Associates: Union Carbide Corporation World Headquarters." *GA Document*, no. 9 (February 1984): 24–27.

Milstein, Mark B., and Stuart Hart. "Weyerhaeuser Company: The Next 100 Years." Washington, DC: World Resources Institute, 1987. http://pdf.wri.org/bell/case_1-56973-233-7_full_version_english.pdf (accessed January 6, 2010).

Mitchell, Cathie. "Black Tie and Terrazzo." *Landscape Architecture* 73, no. 4 (July/August 1983): 58–59.

Moline Dispatch. "'Dying to See Mural' Says Aline Saarinen." *Moline Dispatch,* June 5, 1964, 3.

Moline Dispatch. "Architectural Gem Blends into Countryside." *Moline Dispatch,* August 20, 1989, 3.

Moline Dispatch. "Deere Administrative Center to Open Officially Tomorrow." *Moline Dispatch*, June 4, 1964, 5.

Moline Dispatch. "Deere Deer Comes Down." *Moline Dispatch,* April 9, 1964, n.p.

Moline Dispatch. "The Deere Center: Symbol of Strength." *Moline Dispatch*, June 4, 1964, 24.

Montgomery, Roger. "A Building that Makes Its Own Landscape." *Architectural Forum* 136 no. 2 (March 1972): 22–27.

Montgomery, Roger. "Weyerhaeuser Headquarters." *AIA Journal,* 57, no. 5 (May 1972): 22–27.

Moore, Charles. "Environment and Industry." *Architectural Record* 124, no. 1 (July 1958): 162.

Mortgage and Real Estate Executive Report. "Office and Industrial Vacancies." *Mortgage and Real Estate Executive Report*, April 1, 1995, 6–7.

Mortimer, Charles G. *A Fresh Chapter*. White Plains, NY: General Foods, 1954.

Mott, Nevill, T. M.Chalmers, R. W. T. Honeycombe, E. F. Mills, C. W. Oatley, A. J. Watson, A. D. I. Nicol.. "Relationship between the University and Science-based Industry: Report of the Sub-Committee." *Cambridge University Reporter* 22 (1969): 370–376.

Mozingo, Louise A. "Campus, Estate, and Park: Lawn Culture Comes to the Corporation." In *J. B. Jackson and the American Landscape*, edited by Paul Groth and Chris Wilson, 255–274. Berkeley and Los Angeles: University of California Press, 2003..

Mozingo, Louise A. "The Corporate Estate in the United States, 1954–1964: 'Thoroughly Modern in Concept, But . . . Down to Earth and Rugged.'" *Studies in the History of Gardens and Designed Landscapes* 20 no. 1 (January-March 2000): 25–56.

Mudd, Michael. "William L. Butcher: Three Decades Building Westchester." *Westchester Commerce & Industry, January* 23, 1977, H3.

Mukherjee, Andy. "Commentary: 'Electronics City' Bursting at the Seams." *International Herald Tribune*, January 21, 2005. http://www.iht.com/articles/2005/01/20/bloomberg/sxmuk.php?page=1 (accessed October 20, 2008).

Muller, Peter O. *The Outer City: The Geographical Consequences of the Urbanization of the Suburbs*. Washington, DC: American Association of Geographers, 1976.

National Association of Industrial and Office Parks Educational Foundation. *Creating, Understanding and Enforcing Industrial and Office Park Protective Covenants*. Arlington, VA: National Association of Industrial and Office Parks, 1985.

National Association of Industrial and Office Parks Educational Foundation. *Office Park Development: A Comprehensive Examination of the Elements of Office Park Development.* Arlington, VA: National Association of Industrial and Office Parks, 1984.

National Trust for Historic Preservation. "Eleven Most Endangered: CIGNA Campus." http://www.Nationaltrust.org/11most/2001/cigna (accessed June 22, 2005).

Nelson, Kristin. "Labor Demand, Labor Supply and the Suburbanization of Low-Wage Office Work." In *Production, Work, and Territory*, edited by Allen J. Scott and Michael Storpor, 149–171. Winchester, MA: Allen and Unwin, 1986.

Newark News. "Explains Plans of Laboratory." *Newark News,* August 1, 1930.

Newsweek. "For Corporate Life '57." *Newsweek,* September 16, 1957, 114–115.

New York Times. "$8,000,000 Plant to Spur Research." *New York Times,* June 1, 1945, 13.

New York Times. "Ace to Buy Cigna Unit for $3.45 Billion in Cash." *New York Times,* January 13, 1999, C3.

New York Times. "Curtice Bids U.S. Spur Technology." *New York Times,* May 17, 1956, 1.

New York Times"G.M. to Dedicate Technical Unit," *New York Times,* May 13, 1956, F1.

New York Times. "GE Laboratory to Speed Research in Post-War Use of Electronics." *New York Times,* August 12, 1945, 5.

New York Times. "GE Plans Big Syracuse Output." *New York Times,* September 23, 1945, 32.

New York Times. "General Motors Speeds Research." *New York Times,* July 25, 1945, 23

New York Times. "Johns Manville Starts Expansion." *New York Times,* September 7, 1945, 29.

New York Times. "New Frontier." *New York Times,* May 14, 1945, 16.

Newsweek. "Workshop for Bell Scientists: A $3,000,000 Phone Laboratory." *Newsweek*, August 4, 1941, 44–45.

Nicolaides, Becky M., and Andrew Wiese, eds. *The Suburban Reader.* New York: Routledge, 2006.

Nicolaides, Becky. "How Hell Moved from the City to the Suburbs: Urban Scholars and the Changing Perceptions of Authentic Community." In *The New Suburban History,* edited by Kevin M. Kruse and Thomas J. Sugrue, 80–98. Chicago: University of Chicago Press, 2006.

Nicolaides, Becky M. *My Blue Heaven: Life and Politics in the Working Class Suburbs of Los Angeles, 1920–1965.* Chicago: University of Chicago Press, 2002.

Nimmons, George C. "Modern Industrial Plants, Part I." *Architectural Record* 44, no. 5 (November 1918): 415–421.

Nimmons, George C. "Modern Industrial Plants, Part II." *Architectural Record* 44, no. 6 (December 1918): 532–549.

Nimmons, George C. "Modern Industrial Plants, Part III: Plans and Designs." *Architectural Record* 45, no. 1 (January 1919): 27–43.

Nimmons, George C. "Modern Industrial Plants, Part IV, Discussions of the Various Types of Windows for Industrial Buildings." *Architectural Record* 45, no. 2 (February 1919): 148–168.

Nimmons, George C. "Modern Industrial Plants, Part VIa, The Excessive Turnover of Labor and the Influence of Employee's Welfare Work in Reducing It." *Architectural Record* 45, no. 4 (April 1919): 341–355.

Nimmons, George C. "Modern Industrial Plants, Part VIb, The Excessive Turnover of Labor and the Influence of Employee's Welfare Work in Reducing It." *Architectural Record* 45, no. 5 (May 1919): 451–470.

Nimmons, George C. "Modern Industrial Plants, Part VII, Sears, Roebuck & Co.'s Plant, Chicago." *Architectural Record* 45, no. 6 (June 1919): 506–525.

Noble, David F. *America by Design: Science, Technology and the Rise of Corporate Capitalism.* New York: Knopf, 1977.

Normile, Dennis. "Bright Science City Dreams Face Sober Realities." *Science*, November 18, 1994, 1176–1177.

Norwest Business Park. "Norwest Business Park." http://www.norwestbusinesspark.com.au/ (accessed May 28, 2008).

Nye, David E. *Image Worlds: Corporate Identities at General Electric.* Cambridge, MA: MIT Press, 1985.

O'Mara, Margaret Pugh. *Cities of Knowledge: Cold War Science and the Search for the Next Silicon Valley.* Princeton, NJ: Princeton University Press, 2005.

O'Mara, Margaret Pugh "Uncovering the City in the Suburb: Cold War Politics, Scientific Elites, and High Tech Spaces." In *The New Suburban History*, edited by Kevin M. Kruse and Thomas Sugrue, 57–79. Chicago: University of Chicago Press, 2006.

O'Meara, J. Roger. "Executive Suites in Suburbia." *Conference Board Record* 9, no. 8 (1972): 6–16.

Olin, Laurie. "Regionalism and the Practice of Hanna/Olin, Ltd." In *Regional Garden Design in the United States*, edited by Therese O'Malley and Marc Trieb, 243–269. Washington, DC: Dumbarton Oaks, 1995.

Olmsted, Frederick Law. "The Winning Design by Olmsted and Vaux." In *Forty Years of Landscape Architecture: Central Park*, edited by. Frederick Law Olmsted Jr. and Theodora Kimball, 41–48. Cambridge, MA.: Harvard University Press, 1973.

Olmsted, Frederick Law. *Civilizing American Cities: Writings on City Landscapes*, edited by S. B. Sutton. Cambridge, MA: MIT Press, 1971.

Park, Prague, The. "The Park." http://www.thepark.cz/ (accessed May 15, 2008).

Pegoraro, Rob. "Gawking at Google." http://blog.washingtonpost.com/fasterforward/2008/01/gawking_at_google.html (accessed May 4, 2008).

Pencil Points. "Administration Building by Albert Kahn, Inc., Architects and Engineers." *Pencil Points* 23, no. 3 (March 1942): 126–135.

Pencil Points. "Architects and Defense." *Pencil Points* 22, no. 10 (October 1941): 657–664.

Pencil Points. "Buildings—By John and Donald B. Parkinson, A.I.A." *Pencil Points* 22, no. 5 (May 1941): 330.

Pencil Points. "Insurance Company Home Offices." *Pencil Points* 23, no. 1 (January 1942): 7.

PepsiCo. *The Donald M. Kendall Sculpture Gardens*. New York: PepsiCo, 1997.

Phillips, Alan. *The Best in Science, Office, and Business Park Design*. London: B. T. Batsford, 1993.

Phillips, Su-Ann Mae, and Henry Wai-Chung Yeung. "A Place for R&D The Singapore Science Park." *Urban Studies* 40, no. 4 (2003): 707–732.

Pierce, Bess. *Moline: A Pictorial History*. Virginia Beach, VA: Donning Co, 1981.

Pimental, Benjamin. "Software Giant to Cut 5,000 Jobs: Ax Falls on Oracle Employees as Well as PeopleSoft Staff." *San Francisco Chronicle*, January 14, 2005, A1.

Pivo, Gary. "The Net of Mixed Beads: Suburban Office Development in Six Metropolitan Regions." *APA Journal* 56, no. 1 (Autumn 1990): 457–458.

POD. *Hacienda Business Park*. San Francisco: POD, 1985.

Portsmouth-UK. "North Harbor." http://www.portsmouth-uk.com/north_harbour.htm (accessed May 12, 2008).

Posner, Ellen. "Harmony, Not Uniqueness." *Landscape Architecture* 79, no. 4 (May 1989): 43–49.

Post Carbon Cities. "Shanghai Hopes to Build World's First Truly Sustainable City." http://postcarboncities.net/shanghai (accessed October 20, 2008).

Process Architecture. "IBM West Coast Programming Center." *Process Architecture,* no. 85 (October 1989): 74–77.

Process Architecture. "IBM Westlake/Southlake." *Process Architecture*, no. 85 (October 1989): 106–113.

Process Architecture. "Weyerhaeuser Corporate Headquarters." *Process Architecture*, no. 85 (October 1989): 44–49.

Process Architecture. "Centrum." *Process Architecture*, no. 85 (October 1989): 142–145.

Process Architecture. "Office Complex Development." *Process Architecture*, no. 81 (March 1989): 142–147.

Progressive Architecture. "Changes in the Office Environment: Research Facilities." *Progressive Architecture* 46, no. 7 (July 1965): 154–159.

Progressive Architecture. "Research on the Riviera." *Progressive Architecture* 44, no. 2 (February 1963): 132–137.

Progressive Architecture. "Saarinen's Deere Building Opens." *Progressive Architecture* 45, no. 7 (July 1964): 64.

Progressive Architecture. "Warehouse and Branch Office." *Progressive Architecture* 29, no. 8 (August 1948): 61–66.

PropertyMall. "Akeler—Office Development—Paris, Major Office Park." *PropertyMall*, March 4, 2004. http://www.propertymall.com/press/article/11353 (accessed May 20, 2008).

Ramo, Simon. Interview by Martin Collins, June 27, 1988, Los Angeles. Oral history project of the National Air and Space Museum. http://www.nasm.si.edu.research/dsh/TRANSCPT/RAMO1:HTM (accessed March 4, 2008).

Raskin, A. R. "Key Men of Business—Scientists." *New York Times Magazine*. May 13, 1956, 15, 38, 42, 44, 46.

Rassweiler, Clifford F. "The Johns-Manville Research Center Six Years Later." *Architectural Record* 118, no. 3 (September 1955): 222–224.

Raver, Anne. "Corporate Cottage, Deep in a Forest." *New York Times,* December 22, 1991, 57.

Reed, Philip D. "General Electric's Decentralization Plan." *American City* 63 (October 1948): 7.

Reeves, Richard. "Loss of Major Companies Conceded by City Official." *New York Times,* February 5, 1971, 33.

Reich, Leonard S. "Irving Langmuir and the Pursuit of Science and Technology in the Corporate Environment." *Technology and Culture* 24, no. 2 (1983): 199–221.

Reinhard, L. Andrew, and Henry Hofmeister. "Modern Offices: New Trends in Office Design." *Architectural Record* 97, no. 3 (March 1945): 99–116.

Riess, Susan B. and Bancroft Library, Regional Oral History Office. *Thomas D. Church, Landscape Architect, Volumes I and II*. Berkeley: Regents of the University of California, 1978.

Research and Archeological Management. *Somerset County Cultural Resource Survey, Phase I*. Somerville, NJ: Somerset County Cultural Heritage Commission, 1989.

Rice, Faye. "Environmental Scorecard: The 10 Laggards." *Fortune* 128, no. 2 (July 1993): 122.

Romano, Benjamin J. "Microsoft Campus Expands, Transforms, Inside and Out." *Seattle Times*, November 23, 2007. http://seattletimes.nwsource.com/html/microsoft/2004007121_microsoft11.html (accessed May 10, 2008).

Romano, Benjamin J., Mark Nowlin, and Elise Feigel. "Microsoft's Expansion Over Time." *Seattle Times*, November 23, 2007. http://seattletimes.nwsource.com/news/local/microsoftcampus/microsoftcampus.html (accessed May 10, 2008).

Rosegrant, Susan, and David R. Lampe. *Route 128: Lessons from Boston's High-Tech Community*. New York: Basic Books, 1992.

Rosenzweig, Roy, and Elizabeth Blackmar. *The Park and the People: A History of Central Park*. Ithaca, NY: Cornell University Press, 1992.

Roterus, Victor. *Planned Industrial Parks*. Washington, DC: Housing and Home Finance Agency, 1960.

Rowe, Peter G. *Making a Middle Landscape*. Cambridge, MA: MIT Press, 1991.

Saarinen, Eero. *Eero Saarinen on His Work* edited by Aline Saarinen. New Haven, CT: Yale University Press, 1962.

Saarinen, Eliel. *The City*. Cambridge, MA: MIT Press, 1943.

Saarinen, Eliel. "Detroit Planning Studies." *New Pencil Points* 24, no. 12 (December 1942): 50–52.

Sadovi, Maura Webber. "Tough Times Pressure Maguire to Restructure Debt on Texas Complex." *Wall Street Journal*, April 22, 2009. http://online.wsj.com/article/SB124035983163841451.html (accessed January 13, 2010).

Saxenian, Annalee. *Regional Advantage: Culture and Competition in Silicon Valley and Route 128*. Cambridge, MA: Harvard University Press, 1994.

Schmertz, Mildred F. "Building a Corporate Image." *Architectural Record* 172, no. 10 (September 1984): 103–119.

Schmertz, Mildred. "Recollection and Invention." *Architectural Record* 176, no. 1 (1988): 62–72.

Schuyler, Montgomery. "A New Departure in 'Big Business.'" *Architectural Record* 35, no. 6 (June 1914): 505–507.

Science and Technology Parks of India. "STPI—About." http://www.stpi.in/about.htm (accessed October 20, 2008).

Science. "The Bell Telephone Laboratories at Murray Hill, N.J." *Science*, June 1, 1945, 554–555.

Science. "The Scientific Geography of Japan." *Science*, October 23, 1992, 562–563.

Scott, A. J. *New Industrial Spaces: Flexible Production and Regional Development in North America and Western Europe*. London: Pion Limited, 1988.

Scott, Allen J., and Michael Storper. "Regions, Globalization, Development." *Regional Studies* 37, no. 677 (August-October 2003): 579–593.

Segal Quince Wicksteed. *The Cambridge Phenomenon: The Growth of High Technology Industry in a University Town.* Cambridge, United Kingdom: Segal Quince Wicksteed, 1985.

Self, Robert. *American Babylon: Race and Struggle for Postwar Oakland.* Princeton, NJ: Princeton University Press, 2003.

Self, Robert O. "Prelude to a Tax Revolt: The Politics of the 'Tax Dollar' in Postwar California." In *The New Suburban History*, edited by Kevin M. Kruse and Thomas J. Sugrue, 144–161. Chicago: University of Chicago Press, 2006.

Shanghai Pengchen United Industry Company. "Pujiang Intelligence Valley." http://www.piv-park.com/en/PivShow.asp?SortID=7&ID=8 (accessed October 20, 2008).

Sherreick, Susan. "Connecticut Helps to Lure a Business." *New York Times,* November 10, 1993, A1.

Simo, Melanie. *The Offices of Hideo Sasaki: A Corporate History.* Berkeley, CA: Spacemaker Press, 2001.

Singleton, Sarah. "Crownwood: Landscaping an Office Park at Ormonde, Johannnesburg." *Architect and Builder* 36, no. 9 (September 1985): 2–5.

Skidmore, Owings & Merrill. *Longacres Park Master Plan: The Boeing Company.* San Francisco: Skidmore, Owings & Merrill, 1991.

Sloan, Alfred P. *My Years with General Motors.* New York: Doubleday, 1963.

Smith, Herbert L. "Image Identity and Appeal." *Architectural Record* 174, no. 13 (November 1986): 85–103.

Smith, Tyler. "How the Wilde Was Won." *Hartford Courant,* May 21, 2006. http://www.hartfordinfo.org/issues/documents/history/htfd_courant_052106.asp (accessed May 10, 2008).

Snow, W. Brewster, ed. *The Highway and the Landscape.* New Brunswick, NJ: Rutgers University Press, 1959.

Stanford Research Institute. "SRI Mission and Values." http://www.sri.com/about/card.html (accessed October 13, 2008).

Stanford Research Institute. "SRI's History and Innovations Timeline," http://www.sri.com/about/timeline/ (accessed October 13, 2008).

Steward, Marion. "Hacienda Index." *Hacienda Network*, July 9, 2007, 7, 9.

Stilgoe, John R. *Borderland: Origins of the American Suburb, 1920–1939.* New Haven, CT: Yale University Press, 1988.

Stockwell, Fred F. "Hobbs Brook Park Office Buildings." *Urban Land* 20, no. 4 (April 1961): 3.

Stoll, Michael A. "Job Sprawl and the Spatial Mismatch between Blacks and Jobs." *Brookings Institution Survey Series*. Washington, DC: Brookings Institution, February 2005.

Storpor, Michael, and Michael Manville. "Behavior, Preferences and Cities: Urban Theory and Urban Resurgence." *Urban Studies* 43, no. 8 (July 2006): 1247–1274.

Storpor, Michael, and Richard Walker, eds. *The Capitalist Imperative: Territory, Technology, and Industrial Growth*. New York: Basil Blackwell, 1989.

Story, William. "Advertising the Site through Good Design." *Landscape Architecture* 49, no. 3 (Spring 1959): 144.

Stowe, Stacey. "A Fight over, of All Things, an Insurance Office." *New York Times,* July 16, 2000, 10.

Strickland, Steven. "Whither R&D." *Industrial Development and Manufacturers Record* 134, no. 8 (August 1965): 10–24.

Sugrue, Thomas. *The Origins of the Urban Crisis: Race and Struggle in Postwar Detroit*. Princeton, NJ: Princeton University Press, 1996.

Summit Herald and Summit Record "Zoning Map of the Borough of New Providence." *Summit Herald and Summit Record,* February 24, 1933, insert.

Summit Herald "Big Development in Murray Hill by Bell Telephone Laboratories." *Summit Herald*, August 1, 1930, 1.

Sutherland, Dylan. "China Science Parks: Production Bases or a Tool for Institutional Reform." *Asia Pacific Business Review* 11, no. 1 (March 2005): 83–104.

Taylor, Graham Romeyn. *Satellite Cities: A Study of Industrial Suburbs*. New York: D. Appleton and Company, 1915.

Thomas, Marita. "Superb Teamwork Forges 'Age-Proof' IBM Center." *Facilities and Management* 8, no. 2 (February 1989): 48–55.

Thompson, J. William. "Dulles Corner." *Landscape Architecture* 78, no. 8 (December 1988): 82–87.

Tiller, Kay. "Frito Lay Prairie Campus." *Landscape Architecture* 78, no. 3 (April-May 1988): 41–45.

Time. "Billions in the Pantry." *Time*, June 9, 1958, 86–87.

Time. "Building with a Future." *Time*, September 16, 1957, 91.

Time. "Green, Yellow and Gold." *Time*, May 24, 1963, 93.

Time. "Plowmen's Palace." *Time*, August 7, 1964, 64–65.

Time. "Why Companies Are Fleeing the Cities." *Time*, April 26, 1971, 86–88.

Tishman Speyer. "Greenwich American Center." http://www.tishmanspeyer.com/properties/Property.aspx?id=20 (accessed January 25, 2010).

Tomei, Elena. "Technolgia Organica: in Prague." *Arca* no. 217 (September 2006): 54–61.

Tomberlin, Mike. "Great Expectation Rising in Downtown Birmingham." *Birmingham News*, May 27, 2010, http://blog.al.com/businessnews/2010/05/great_expectations_rising_in_d_1.html (accessed August 18, 2010).

Tunnard, Christopher, and Boris Pushkarev. *Man Made America: Chaos or Control? An Inquiry into Selected Problems of Design in the Urbanized Landscape*. New Haven, CT: Yale University Press, 1963.

Turner, Paul Venable. *Campus: An American Planning Tradition*. Cambridge, MA: MIT Press, 1984.

Tykle, Fredrick G., and Ervine E. Klein. "Unique Architectural Elements of the GM Technical Center." *General Motors Engineering Journal* 3, no. 3 (May-June 1956): 69–77.

Upton, Dell. *Architecture in the United States*. New York: Oxford University Press, 1998.

Urban Land. "Commerce in Menlo Park." *Urban Land* 12, no. 6 (June 1953): 3–4.

Urban Land. "More Payrolls for a Bedroom Community." *Urban Land* 12, no. 5 (May 1953): 3–4.

Vaidyanathan, Geetha. "Technology Parks in a Developing Country: The Case of India." *Journal of Technology Transfer* 33, no. 6 (June 2007): 285–299.

Varian, Russell. "The Founding of Varian Associates." 1958. http://www.varianinc.com/cgi-bin/nav?corp/history/founding&cid=KLJQJIOPFJ (accessed October 13, 2008).

Venable, Tim. "Not Overbuilt Anymore: Industrial Parks Lead Robust Real Estate Recovery." *Site Selection* 40, no. 6 (1995): 902–904, 906, 908–9, 911.

Vernez-Moudon, Anne. *Built for Change: Managing Neighborhood Architecture in San Francisco*. Cambridge, MA: MIT Press, 1986.

Vernon, Raymond. *Metropolis 1985: An Interpretation of the Findings of the New York Metropolitan Regional Study*. Cambridge, MA: Harvard University Press, 1960.

Walcott, Susan M. "Chinese Industrial and Science Parks: Bridging the Gap." *Professional Geographer* 54, no. 3 (2002): 349–364.

Walcott, Susan M., and James Heitzman. "High Technology Clusters in India and China: Divergent Paths." *Indian Journal of Economics and Business* 5, special issue (September 2006): 113–130.

Walker, Peter, and Melanie Simo. *Invisible Gardens: The Search for Modernism in the American Landscape*. Cambridge, MA: MIT Press, 1994.

Walker, Ralph. *Ralph Walker Architect*. New York: Henahan House, 1957.

Walker, Richard. *The Country in the City: Greening the San Francisco Bay Area*. Seattle: University of Washington Press, 2007.

Walker, Richard A. "A Theory of Suburbanization: Capitalism and the Construction of Urban Space in the United States." In *Urbanization and Urban Planning in Capitalist Society*, edited by Michael Dear and A. J. Scott, 383–429. New York: Methuen, 1981.

Walker, Richard, and Robert Lewis. "Beyond the Crabgrass Frontier: Industry and the Spread of North American Cities." In *Manufacturing Suburbs: Building Work and Home on the Metropolitan Fringe*, edited by Robert Lewis, 16–31. Philadelphia: Temple University Press, 2004.

Weiss, Marc. *Rise of the Community Builders: The American Real Estate Industries and Urban Land Planning*. New York: Columbia University Press, 1987.

Westchester Reporter Dispatch. "First Insurance Home Office in City to Open Monday." *Westchester Reporter Dispatch,* April 23, 1953, n.p.

Wheeler, Stephen. "The Evolution of Built Landscapes in the Metropolitan Regions." *Journal of Planning Education and Research* 27, no. 4 (2008): 400–416.

Whyte, William. "End of Exodus: The Logic of the Headquarters City." *New York*, September 20, 1976, 87–94.

Wiese, Andrew. "'The House I Live In': Race, Class, and African American Suburban Dreams in the Postwar United States." In *The New Suburban History*, edited by Kevin M. Krusc and Thomas J. Sugrue, 99–119. Chicago: University of Chicago Press, 2006.

Wiese, Andrew. *Places of Their Own: African American Suburbanization in the Twentieth Century*. Chicago: University of Chicago Press, 2004.

Wilde, Frazar B. *Time Out of Mind*. New York: Newcomen Society of North America, 1959.

Williams, Raymond. *The Country and the City*. New York: Oxford University Press, 1973.

Williams, Scott. "Microsoft Buys Another Building." *Seattle Times,* March 14, 1991. http://community.seattletimes.nwsource.com/archive/?date=19910314&slug=1271531 (accessed May 10, 2008).

Williamson, Tom. *Polite Landscapes: Gardens and Society in Eighteenth-Century England*. Phoenix Mill, Gloucestershire: Sutton Publishing, 1995.

Willis, Carol. *Form Follows Finance: Skyscrapers and Skylines in New York and Chicago*. Princeton, NJ: Princeton Architectural Press, 1995.

Wilson, Louis R. *The Research Triangle of North Carolina: A Notable Achievement in University, Governmental, and Industrial Cooperative Development*. Chapel Hill, NC: Colonial Press, 1967.

Wilson, Richard Guy. *The AIA Medal*. New York: McGraw-Hill, 1984.

Wise, George. *Willis R. Whitney, General Electric, and the Origins of U.S. Industrial Research*. New York: Columbia University Press, 1985.

Wittman, Konrad F. "Planning for Victory: Is Planning the Future?" *Pencil Points* 23, no. 6 (May 1942): 301–302.

Wolffe, Lenard L. *New Zoning Landmarks in Planned Unit Developments*. Washington, DC: Urban Land Institute, 1968.

Wright, Gwendolyn. *Building the Dream: A Social History of Housing in the United States*. New York: Pantheon Books, 1981.

Wright Runstad & Co. "Historical Timeline: Microsoft Corporation Headquarters, 1986–94." http://www.wrightrunstad.com/AboutUs/Timeline/Timeline4_1.htm, (accessed May 20, 2008).

Wy-Cin, Liaw. "$400m Makeover for Science Park, Move Will Create More Room for R&D Firms and Boost Access to Greenery, Facilities." *Straits Times,* October 22, 2007. http://www.lexisnexis.com:443 (accessed May 10, 2008).

Yardley, William. "Downtown Hartford Stirs from Slumber." *New York Times*, January 4, 2006, http://www.nytimes.com/2006/01/04/nyregion/04hartford.html?pagewanted=1&_r=1 (accessed August 18, 2010).

Yamashita, Tsukasa. "Eero Saarinen and His Works—Interview with Paul Kennon." *Architecture + Urbanism,* special issue (April 1984): 209–237.

Zhang, Yeuhua. "Critical Factors for Science Park Development: The Case of the Singapore Science Park." *International Journal of Technology Transfer and Commercialisation* 4, no. 2 (2005): 194–205.

Zukin, Sharon. *Landscapes of Power*. Berkeley and Los Angeles: University of California Press, 1991.

Albert Kahn Associates, Inc., Detroit, Michigan

Archive Department, Kraft Foods, Morton Grove, Illinois

AT&T Archives and History Center, Warren, New Jersey

Cabot, Cabot & Forbes, Boston, Massachusetts

Cambridge Science Park, Cambridge, United Kingdom

Canoga-Owensmith Historical Society, Canoga Park, California

Center for Creative Photography, University of Arizona, Tucson

College of Environmental Design Library, University of California, Berkeley

Digital Collections, Connecticut State Library, Hartford, Connecticut

Deere & Company, Moline, Illinois

Environmental Design Archives, University of California, Berkeley

Environmental Design Library, University of California, Berkeley

Environmental Design Visual Resources Center, University of California, Berkeley

Foundation Sophia Antipolis, Valbonne, France

General Electric Collection, Schenectady Museum, Schenectady, New York

General Motors Media Archive, Detroit, Michigan

Gottscho-Schleisner Collection, Prints & Photographs Division, Library of Congress

Kevin Roche John Dinkeloo and Associates, Hamden, Connecticut

Koetter Kim & Associates, Inc., Boston, Massachusetts

Lucent Technology Archives, Murray Hill, New Jersey

Maul Foster Alongi, Portland, Oregon

National Automotive History Collection, Detroit Main Public Library, Detroit, Michigan

New Providence Historical Society, New Providence, New Jersey

Olmsted Archives, Frederick Law Olmsted National Historic Site, Brookline, Massachusetts

Palo Alto Historical Association, Palo Alto, California

PWP Landscape Architecture, Berkeley, California

Records of the Olmsted Associates, Manuscript Division, Library of Congress, Washington, D.C.

Research Triangle Foundation, Research Triangle Park, North Carolina

Rock Island County Historical Society, Moline, Illinois

San Fernando Valley History Digital Library, Special Collections, Oviatt Library, California State University, Northridge

Sasaki Associates, Boston, Massachusetts

Sears Holdings Archives, Hoffman Estates, Illinois

SWA Group, Sausalito, California

The Spence and Fairchild Collections, Benjamin and Gladys Air Photo Archives, University of California, Los Angeles

United Auto Workers Collection, Walter P. Reuther Library, Wayne State University, Detroit, Michigan

Westchester County Historical Society, Elmsford, New York

Weyerhaeuser Archives, Federal Way, Washington

INDEX

Italicized numbers refer to pages with relevant illustrations.

Office parks (*continued*)

    variations in names, 154

    versus planned industrial districts or
        industrial parks, 151–153

    zoning, 154–155, 179

Offices of Peter Walker and Martha Schwartz,
    187

Office space, center city vs. suburbs, 17

Olin, Laurie, 145

Olmsted Brothers, 33, 55–60 passim

Olmsted, Frederick Law, 1, 9, 108, 222

Page, Russell, 137

Pastoral capitalism

    corporate advantages, 41

    and corporate restructuring 1980s–1990s,
        197–201

    and corporate security, 27

    corporate self-representation through, *16,*
        41–43, 62, 83–85, 99, 115, 122, 123,
        133–136, 137, 140–141,147

    costs, 149

    creating social divide in developing world, 216

    definition, 2

    detrimental effects on metropolitan zones,
        219–220

    disguise of infrastructure, 38–39

    effect on productivity and turnover, 35,
        111, 115–116, 131–132

    facilitating suburban expansion, 34

    fiscal support of residential suburbs, 34,
        107–108, 154

    India, influence of reversing brain drain, 215

    influence of suburban factories, 31

    influence of welfare capitalist factories, 27–28

    innovation diffusion, 14–16

    international proliferation, 202–216

    labor relations with women workers (*see*
        Women's corporate labor and pastoral
        capitalism)

    location in pastoral residential suburbs not
        industrial suburbs, 32

    persistence of ideal, 195, 196

pervasiveness in corporate culture, 216–217

regional distribution, 14

relation to civil defense and Cold War, 24–27

role in evolution of the industrial and
    postindustrial city, 217–219

security measures, 27

as separatist enclave, 220–221

site planning, 20, 38–40

siting along highways, 36–38

and suburban conformity, 35, 40

and suburban taxation, 34

typical site plans, 12–14, *13, 14, 15*

and urban decentralization, 98–99,
    192–193

variations in terminology, 17

vehicle for corporate solipsism, 97–99, 131,
    136, 222

view of and from office buildings, 39–40,
    40, 42, 161

Pastoral landscape ideal

    definition, 10

    expected effects, 11, 28–31, 42–43

    influence on public parks, 10

    origins, 9

    as part of corporate culture, 41–43, 97, 99,
        147, 216

    promotion by Fredrick Law Olmsted and
        followers, 10

Pastoral residential suburbs 10, *11,* 32, *33*

    proliferation, 11

    resistance to commercial incursions, 32–34

Paul, Anthony, 202

Pechiney, S.A., 198

PeopleSoft headquarters, Hacienda Business
    Park, Pleasanton, CA, 201

PepsiCo World Headquarters, Harrison, NY,
    137, 138, 139

    as corporate patronage, 137

    site plan and design, 137–138

Platinum Mile, Westchester County, NY, 34

POD, Inc., 181

Primerica, 198

Prudential Insurance Company, 182

Public parks, 9, 222

URBAN AND INDUSTRIAL ENVIRONMENTS

Series editor: Robert Gottlieb, Henry R. Luce Professor of Urban and Environmental Policy, Occidental College

Maureen Smith, *The U.S. Paper Industry and Sustainable Production: An Argument for Restructuring*

Keith Pezzoli, *Human Settlements and Planning for Ecological Sustainability: The Case of Mexico City*

Sarah Hammond Creighton, *Greening the Ivory Tower: Improving the Environmental Track Record of Universities, Colleges, and Other Institutions*

Jan Mazurek, *Making Microchips: Policy, Globalization, and Economic Restructuring in the Semiconductor Industry*

William A. Shutkin, *The Land That Could Be: Environmentalism and Democracy in the Twenty-First Century*

Richard Hofrichter, ed., *Reclaiming the Environmental Debate: The Politics of Health in a Toxic Culture*

Robert Gottlieb, *Environmentalism Unbound: Exploring New Pathways for Change*

Kenneth Geiser, *Materials Matter: Toward a Sustainable Materials Policy*

Thomas D. Beamish, *Silent Spill: The Organization of an Industrial Crisis*

Matthew Gandy, *Concrete and Clay: Reworking Nature in New York City*

David Naguib Pellow, *Garbage Wars: The Struggle for Environmental Justice in Chicago*

Julian Agyeman, Robert D. Bullard, and Bob Evans, eds., *Just Sustainabilities: Development in an Unequal World*

Barbara L. Allen, *Uneasy Alchemy: Citizens and Experts in Louisiana's Chemical Corridor Disputes*

Dara O'Rourke, *Community-Driven Regulation: Balancing Development and the Environment in Vietnam*

Brian K. Obach, *Labor and the Environmental Movement: The Quest for Common Ground*

Peggy F. Barlett and Geoffrey W. Chase, eds., *Sustainability on Campus: Stories and Strategies for Change*

Steve Lerner, *Diamond: A Struggle for Environmental Justice in Louisiana's Chemical Corridor*

Jason Corburn, *Street Science: Community Knowledge and Environmental Health Justice*

Peggy F. Barlett, ed., *Urban Place: Reconnecting with the Natural World*

David Naguib Pellow and Robert J. Brulle, eds., *Power, Justice, and the Environment: A Critical Appraisal of the Environmental Justice Movement*

Eran Ben-Joseph, *The Code of the City: Standards and the Hidden Language of Place Making*

Nancy J. Myers and Carolyn Raffensperger, eds., *Precautionary Tools for Reshaping Environmental Policy*

Kelly Sims Gallagher, *China Shifts Gears: Automakers, Oil, Pollution, and Development*

Kerry H. Whiteside, *Precautionary Politics: Principle and Practice in Confronting Environmental Risk*

Ronald Sandler and Phaedra C. Pezzullo, eds., *Environmental Justice and Environmentalism: The Social Justice Challenge to the Environmental Movement*

Julie Sze, *Noxious New York: The Racial Politics of Urban Health and Environmental Justice*

Robert D. Bullard, ed., *Growing Smarter: Achieving Livable Communities, Environmental Justice, and Regional Equity*

Ann Rappaport and Sarah Hammond Creighton, *Degrees That Matter: Climate Change and the University*

Michael Egan, *Barry Commoner and the Science of Survival: The Remaking of American Environmentalism*

David J. Hess, *Alternative Pathways in Science and Industry: Activism, Innovation, and the Environment in an Era of Globalization*

Peter F. Cannavò, *The Working Landscape: Founding, Preservation, and the Politics of Place*

Paul Stanton Kibel, ed., *Rivertown: Rethinking Urban Rivers*

Kevin P. Gallagher and Lyuba Zarsky, *The Enclave Economy: Foreign Investment and Sustainable Development in Mexico's Silicon Valley*

David N. Pellow, *Resisting Global Toxics: Transnational Movements for Environmental Justice*

Robert Gottlieb, *Reinventing Los Angeles: Nature and Community in the Global City*

David V. Carruthers, ed., *Environmental Justice in Latin America: Problems, Promise, and Practice*

Tom Angotti, *New York for Sale: Community Planning Confronts Global Real Estate*

Paloma Pavel, ed., *Breakthrough Communities: Sustainability and Justice in the Next American Metropolis*

Anastasia Loukaitou-Sideris and Renia Ehrenfeucht, *Sidewalks: Conflict and Negotiation over Public Space*

David J. Hess, *Localist Movements in a Global Economy: Sustainability, Justice, and Urban Development in the United States*

Julian Agyeman and Yelena Ogneva-Himmelberger, eds., *Environmental Justice and Sustainability in the Former Soviet Union*

Jason Corburn, *Toward the Healthy City: People, Places, and the Politics of Urban Planning*

Louise Mozingo, *Pastoral Capitalism: A History of Suburban Corporate Landscapes*